Praise for Halifu Osumare's
Dancing in Blackness

"Finally someone who knows a dancer's process and a choreographer's vision that has tackled the mystery that is the magic of contemporary African-American dance. In *Dancing in Blackness*, Halifu Osumare has extricated the fundamental influence of Dunham, the choreographic strategies of Rod Rodgers, Eleo Pomare, Chuck Davis, Donald McKayle, and Alvin Ailey, as well as illuminating the paths they created for Jawole Willa Jo Zollar, Bill T. Jones, Garth Fagan, and Diane McIntyre. What a wealth of treasure and scholarly and aesthetic understanding Osumare brings to this often misunderstood and woefully neglected American art. Bravo!"
—Ntozake Shange, author of *for colored girls who have considered suicide / when the rainbow is enuf*

"*Dancing in Blackness* belongs on every dancer's and artist's shelf. It is a wonderful personal telling of the black experience in dance, in art, in life, and of the dance world in Boston, New York, and the whole Bay Area. It is beautifully written—an engaging and fact-filled narrative where you meet the choreographers of the period, their work and visions, trials, successes, and triumphs."
—Donald McKayle, choreographer of *Rainbow Round My Shoulder*

"A must read for insight into a black artist's personal and professional journey."
—Kariamu Welsh Asante, editor of *African Dance: An Artistic, Historical and Philosophical Inquiry*

"Osumare reveals an astonishing ability to evoke and to historicize her lived experience."
—Susan Manning, author of *Modern Dance, Negro Dance: Race in Motion*

"An unapologetic, rapturous travelogue detailing life, love, and an abiding mission to further the place of black dance in global histories."
—Thomas F. DeFrantz, author of *Dancing Revelations: Alvin Ailey's Embodiment of African American Culture*

"Osumare affirms the spiritual and tangible power for dance to teach, energize, heal, and inspire all peoples on this human journey."
—Joselli Audain Deans, consultant, *Black Ballerina*

Dancing in Blackness

UNIVERSITY PRESS OF FLORIDA

Florida A&M University, Tallahassee
Florida Atlantic University, Boca Raton
Florida Gulf Coast University, Ft. Myers
Florida International University, Miami
Florida State University, Tallahassee
New College of Florida, Sarasota
University of Central Florida, Orlando
University of Florida, Gainesville
University of North Florida, Jacksonville
University of South Florida, Tampa
University of West Florida, Pensacola

DANCING
IN BLACKNESS

A Memoir

HALIFU OSUMARE

University Press of Florida

Gainesville · Tallahassee · Tampa · Boca Raton

Pensacola · Orlando · Miami · Jacksonville · Ft. Myers · Sarasota

Library of Congress Cataloging-in-Publication Data
Names: Osumare, Halifu, author.
Title: Dancing in blackness : a memoir / Halifu Osumare.
Description: Gainesville : University Press of Florida, 2018. | Includes
    bibliographical references and index.
Identifiers: LCCN 2017031786 | ISBN 9780813056616 (cloth : alk. paper)
Subjects: LCSH: Osumare, Halifu—Biography. | African American women
    dancers—Biography. | Dance—United States—Biography. | African American
    dance—History.
Classification: LCC GV1624.7.A34 O78 2017 | DDC 792.8092—dc23
LC record available at https://lccn.loc.gov/2017031786

The University Press of Florida is the scholarly publishing agency for the State University
System of Florida, comprising Florida A&M University, Florida Atlantic University, Florida
Gulf Coast University, Florida International University, Florida State University, New College
of Florida, University of Central Florida, University of Florida, University of North Florida,
University of South Florida, and University of West Florida.

University Press of Florida
15 Northwest 15th Street
Gainesville, FL 32611-2079
http://upress.ufl.edu

To my ancestors who paved the way and speak through me
To Tenola and Leroy, my mother and father
To Shango who guided this process and Oya always
And to Gene Howell, my rock

Contents

Illustrations

Foreword

Taking the lead from my longtime colleague and friend Halifu Osumare, I'm going off the beaten track, veering from the usual scholarly introduction to do justice to her personal memoir/social history/biography/commentary. She deserves an in-kind foreword, at least for starters.

I begin with a recollection that Halifu has probably forgotten but that says a lot about her personality, so charmingly revealed in this memoir. Back in 1990 a well-known dance critic and so-called white woman, writing for the *Village Voice* newspaper (*not* Deborah Jowitt, by the way), accused me of being racist for the views I'd expressed at a recent dance conference. This was during the era when I was exploring Africanist (meaning, African and African American) presences and resonances in George Balanchine's Americanization of ballet, in modern dance, and in postmodern dance. I, myself, was surprised by the ubiquity of blackness in my findings: what were supposedly dance forms untouched by Africanist influences were, on careful examination, chock-full of black Diasporan accents. Needless to say, I was shocked and wounded by this critic's accusation. Halifu was the first of a handful of my colleagues to write a letter to the editor contesting this denunciation. Should I even mention that her response wasn't published? In fact, none of the several responses made it to print, except my own, to which the critic was allowed to counterrespond, thus giving her—the accuser—the last word. Well, that's how the system works. But the point here is that Halifu was willing to stand front and center in defending me, putting her own reputation on the line about a highly controversial issue and letting her voice be heard speaking truth to power. This memory is emblematic of the quality of Halifu's friendship with me, which was always about "the work." In turn, the work is and has always been about the friendship, the sisterhood.

The year before, 1989, I'd been invited to participate in a complex project initiated by Halifu, Black Choreographers Moving Toward the 21st Century. What a title! What a concept for the mind to scope out in the late twentieth century! I believe it was through the late gifted scholar/teacher VèVè Clark that Halifu heard about me. Anyway, we hadn't met before, and I was pleased and honored to be invited to join the august convocation of scholars and artists whom you will read about in this book. The 1980s were the decade when the culture wars raged around questions of how, if, and why the "canon" should be revised. (That was, actually, the rub for the *Village Voice* critic: my findings required her to reevaluate her Eurocentric stance.) Taken with the reverberations disseminated by the Brooklyn Academy of Music's 1983 weeklong Dance Black America Festival and Conference and the several iterations of the American Dance Festival's "Black Tradition in American Modern Dance" project, Halifu's brainchild, Black Choreographers Moving, was a significant precursor to the still-evolving acknowledgment and honoring of Africanisms in so-called Europeanist practice. It was a centering force in establishing the credibility of our cultural heritage in the face of establishment pushback from all quarters of "white" academia.

That was the beginning of our collegiality—about a quarter century ago. Even before and certainly since then, Halifu has continued on her unique path in the pursuit and discovery of Africanist excellence in dance practice. This book, then, is a new kind of milestone for her.

What captivates me about *Dancing in Blackness* is that it helps us understand that dance, indeed, is a measure of society and a barometer of culture. Her sociocultural beginnings in the Bay Area of California and her political commitment to African American liberation initiatives were wedded to Halifu's dedication to dance and the power of dance to speak beyond proscenium stages to grassroots communities—and beyond the borders of the United States of America to African and European continental populations. She convinces us of the truth of her path, and so we embark with her on this journey that limns a sometimes intimately detailed self-reflection that is also a historical monograph bursting with unexpected facts and insights. Over and over we see how the personal overlaps with the professional, the private with the public, as she moves back and forth between her history, dance history, and societal developments. Her writing style itself becomes a dance. Some of the information is so colorful that I felt as though I was reading a page-turner novel, unable to stop as I anticipated what was to come next.

Being African American as a "fluid constant"—Halifu's phrase: what a savvy comment! This conundrum is an apt description of the dilemma and the delight of being black. How beautifully Halifu has moved through Diasporan communities on three continents and in five decades, imparting knowledge, making connections, simultaneously learning and teaching. Her discussion of what is black dance is a valuable reassessment, millennial-style, although I am more than ready to lay that discourse to rest and confirm that new questions need to be posed.

Halifu reveals important heretofore undocumented information on the part that dance played in the Black Arts movement of the 1960s and 1970s. Like Amiri Baraka, Larry Neal, and other writers who forged this movement through their particular disciplines, the young Halifu put dance on this map, in the service of social change. She has continued on this path, despite the fact that the United States has failed us, as people of African descent, over and over. She has stuck to her guns! What she said back then, in her Bay Area days, holds true for her today, as she says in chapter 1: "Dance was *my* tool of expression, and I used my growing creative movement style to make my own individual statements about my developing black consciousness." And that consciousness continues to develop, as we see in this work that allows her to retrospectively assess while simultaneously to move forward. She goes on to say that dance became "my platform to explore blackness in its political, racial, cultural, and postcolonial dimensions."

I am writing in flight, on a plane traveling from Berlin, Germany, and returning to Philadelphia, Pennsylvania, where I reside. I'm musing about Halifu's second chapter, "Dancing in Europe." Sadly, her opening reflection remains true today, regarding the phenomenon of African American expatriation to Europe in order "to experience a sense of just being human," but the questionable possibility of attaining that status, since "Europe offers its own racial and ethnic stereotypes that underpin its societies." When asked by Americans why I enjoy being in Berlin (where I visit twice yearly with my husband, a Berliner with family and friends in his hometown), I say that part of the joy is because no one assumes I am a maid or a nanny! And even now, the writer Ta-Nehisi Coates (whom Toni Morrison pegs as the James Baldwin of the current era) recently moved to France because he feels his teenage son cannot grow up normally, safely—free—in the

United States. So the European chapter resonates. There's a freedom, but then there's Europe's own *explicit* racism and *implicit* exotic-erotic syndrome (where we are loved or hated for being black) that makes some of us homesick, despite the drawbacks and the dangers endemic for African Americans at home.

Throughout these chapters, it's lovely the way Halifu spices her narrative with excerpts from her journals. These portions are so clear and on point that I can imagine, somewhere in her heart of hearts, Halifu *knew* she was writing with an eye toward publication. In chapter 4 she discusses her artistic relationship with playwright Ntozake Shange, who changes the author's name from Janis Miller to Halifu Osumare. Our author makes a savvy comparison between herself and Shange: "She was an artistic iconoclast, positioning dance in poetry; I was an artistic iconoclast in dance who wanted to position words and movement in a new relationship. We came together to inspire each other in our quest for a marriage between movement and language." Halifu is positioned in the right place at a timely moment, riding the crest of the Black Arts wave of her era. I shall leave it to the reader to discover the beautiful, expansive meaning of this new name.

And here I conclude, leaving the rich resources contained in this singular book to the avid and careful reader. The roll call of legendary figures whose paths intersected with Halifu's reads like a Who's Who of recent sociocultural history. There is much to learn from this depiction of a life lived in, around, through, and beyond dance. Halifu's multiple actualizations as dancer, choreographer, administrator, community organizer, presenter, scholar, and writer are convincingly chronicled—and it's not over until it's over! I invite you to learn from and experience, firsthand, *Dancing in Blackness.*

Brenda Dixon Gottschild

Acknowledgments

I have been writing this book all my life, and there is no way I could thank all of the people who have gone into making me who I am along the way. Since 1968 I kept personal journals that were vital resources for remembering sequences of events and many generous people. Suffice it to say, if I remembered someone and named him or her in this memoir, then I have implicit gratitude for his or her contribution to the person I have become. The obvious large thank yous go to my mother Tenola, my father Leroy, and my stepfather Herman for my upbringing and the values of love, self-respect, and a dedication to education that they instilled. My husband Gene Howell deserves special thanks for his unconditional love and support, along with knowledgeable advice that was crucial in the remembering and writing process.

Several institutions and individuals were particularly helpful in the various stages over the past four years that brought *Dancing in Blackness* to fruition. I received a small publishing grant from the HArC's Division of the College of Letters and Science of University of California, Davis, from which I recently retired. This allowed me to hire my dear friend, Dr. Linda Goodrich, as my first copy editor in the early draft of the book. She was invaluable and appears in chapter 6 several times as an important dance colleague. I can't thank my friend and colleague Dr. Brenda Dixon Gottschild enough for her insightful foreword to this memoir. Several organizations and people were helpful in the remembering process, such as the Rod Rodgers Dance Company, Bernadine Jennings of *Attitude: The Dancers' Magazine*, Doris Green, Carole Johnson, Ferolyn Angel, Joy Ayo Walker, Terry Ofosu, and the late Nii Yartey and the Department of Dance Studies at the University of Ghana, Legon. Although many of their insights did not make the final edit, I would like to thank several of my Bay Area interviewees, particularly Selimah Nemoy, Denise Pate, Alleluia Panis, and Patricia Bulitt.

I want to particularly acknowledge dancers whom I have met throughout my life and career for the gift of themselves through body and soul. True dancing is a special state of being that requires a particular kind of openness. The joy, pain, and perceptions of life that move through the muscles and skeletal structure to reach the dancer and then the viewer is a special gift that people all of the world have given me in Africa, Europe, Mexico, Jamaica, Trinidad and Tobago, Brazil, Hawai'i, New York, Boston, and the San Francisco–Oakland Bay Area, which allowed me to nurture my own gift of dance and to transfer that gift into words.

DANCING IN BLACKNESS

Introduction

Dance and Blackness

Halifu in Swahili means the independent, rebellious one in the family. My mother tells me I was a headstrong child from the beginning. So, when the playwright/poet Ntozake Shange, a friend I met in Oakland in 1973, gave me my African name as a gift, my destiny caught up with me: my new name revealed my life's path. Also, like my Caribbean cousins in Cuba, Haiti, and Brazil who forged great religions from African belief systems and European Catholicism, I like making connections between things—bringing seemingly disparate elements together—and, of course, doing it my own independent way.

I was born Janis Miller on November 27, 1946, in Galveston, Texas, an island in the Gulf of Mexico near Houston, where they say the "Negroes were always uppity" and too self-reliant. Galveston black folks defied the white authorities by making their social and educational systems the best they could under the circumstances of legal segregation. Still today, after living in the San Francisco Bay Area, the East Coast, and the Midwest, as well as Europe, Africa, and Hawai'i, and traveling to the Caribbean and Brazil, when I go back to Galveston, my people always say, "Oh, you're BOI (Born on the Island); you're one of us." My independent rebellious nature as a black woman, born into a self-reliant black community, forged my approach to my dance career, which is the subject of this book. Along the way, I interacted with some of the artistic, cultural, and political movers and shakers of the 1960s, 1970s, 1980s, and 1990s. As a baby boomer,

I facilitated some of the artistic, cultural, and political projects that defined the radical 1960s and the subsequent decades leading to the twenty-first century.

Dancing in Blackness is a memoir researched from a scholarly perspective about those times through the lens of dance. It is an exploration of the continuing maturation of black dance across time and space—from West Africa to the United States—over three decades (1968–1994) through my personal story. I contextualize my own personal experiences as a key player in the practical and theoretical shaping of the field I call black dance. I view these years through the lens of a dancer, dance teacher, choreographer, researcher, cultural activist, arts administrator, and the beginning of my academic career. I use anthropology, history, political science, and, of course, performance and dance studies to explore my personal experiences, allowing micro and macro levels of my lived experiences to dance in dialogue.

I illuminate my own notable performances, dance classes, choreographies, organizations, national dance initiatives, as well as the seminal artists and scholars with whom I interacted. It will become apparent that these dance events, initiatives, and people all played a part in the development of not only dance performance but also dance pedagogy, analysis, criticism, advocacy, and intersecting humanities discourses. Through my personal relationships you meet Katherine Dunham, Pearl Primus, Talley Beatty, Donald McKayle, Alvin Ailey, Eleo Pomare, Rod Rodgers, George Faison, Albert Mawere Opoku, Kwabena Nketia, Nii Yartey, Kemoko Sano, Bobi Cespedes, Wilfred Marks, Astor Johnson, Brenda Dixon Gottschild, Gerry Meyers, Zita Allen, Jawole Willa Jo Zollar, Cleo Parker Robinson, Joan Meyers Brown, Jeraldyne Blunden, Garth Fagan, Malonga Casquelourd, Mabiba Baegne, Titos Sompa, Zack Diouf, Mor Thiam, Rennie Harris, and so many more.

This is a scholar's memoir because today, as a humanities scholar, I have built a second career as an academic of black popular culture, with dance as only one aspect of my research. I started training for this new life trajectory in the early 1990s (chapter 6) when I went to graduate school, focusing on dance ethnology with an emphasis in the anthropology department of San Francisco State University. Continuing this retraining at the University of Hawai'i, after my first husband and I moved to the fiftieth state, I received my doctorate in American studies in 1999. I wrote my dissertation on the globalization of hip-hop culture as a natural trajectory of the influence of black culture on the world. You will come to see that my two previous books, *The Africanist Aesthetic in Global Hip-Hop: Power Moves* (2007) and *The Hiplife in Ghana: West African Indigenization of Hip-Hop* (2012), follow naturally from my career of "dancing in blackness." Indeed, my second career as popular culture scholar is deeply informed by my experience as a dancer-choreographer with its emphasis on black history through dance.

I may have stopped dance performance physically, but I now embrace Katherine Dunham's concept that one should never stop "dancing" even when incapacitated, as she was in a wheelchair during her last fifteen years. As I have aged, I recognize how I was using the principles of dance—rhythm, shape, space, and dynamics—as I interacted with every aspect of my life in the world. I began to realize how knowing what to say at the right time (rhythm), in the right way (shape and dynamics), and in the correct place (space) create the *choreography* of life itself. As osteoarthritis set in in my knees, based both on heredity and a lifetime of extreme overuse through teaching, rehearsing, and performing dance, I knew I had to find another way to "dance."

Based on what I had learned from dancing and dancemaking, I noticed the way I applied timing and the amount of effort I put into thinking through and then executing social maneuvers. As Susan Leigh Foster has said, in quoting early dance educator Margaret H'Doubler, "Mastery over the body entail[s] an understanding of the 'intelligent appreciation for, and application of, force and effort.'"[1] As I made the transition from dancing to writing dance, I applied the concepts of effort-shape and dynamic force to my tempered rebelliousness, while using the Transcendental Meditation principle—*do less and accomplish more*—that I had learned more than twenty-five years earlier.

As I began to churn out scholarly book chapters and journal articles on hip-hop culture and dance, I realized that I could apply some of the same dance concepts to the writing process itself. Like New Zealand dancer and education scholar Karen Nicole Barbour, I found I could "dance across the page."[2] She found, like I did, that one must be willing to be self-reflexive in one's representations of one's subject matter, not presenting oneself as an objective observer in some positivist etic approach, hiding or being unaware of one's own biases. I learned about this so-called "new" self-reflexivity while studying postmodern anthropology during my master's degree program at San Francisco State University, but I had experienced it before in the writings of Katherine Dunham, particularly in her layered representation of her lifelong research in Haiti woven into a deep personalized story in *Island Possessed*. I realized my own academic writing had to include, in varying degrees, my own story within the context of my research. This approach enabled me to apply the principles learned in the act of dancing itself, as a deeply personal practice. In fact, theory and praxis became intricately interwoven as I began to publish journal articles during my five years at Bowling Green State University, my first academic appointment as a Ph.D. It continued as I got tenure and established my scholarly reputation at University of California Davis, from which I retired in 2016.

This process of writing dancing, for me, becomes a way to represent my multiple experiential roles as dancer, choreographer, producer, cultural activist, and now scholar. Supported by my second marriage to artist-poet Gene Howell, I am able to reflect on the past and assess the connection between artist and scholar. Barbour, as a continuing dancer-practitioner, admits her necessary manifold approaches to accomplish a blending of objective and subjective writing about dance. "So, my embodied subjectivity as a feminist researcher and as a contemporary dance maker must be present in what I write when I write about other dancers too. I need to locate myself in my own particular socio-cultural context, and make my links and relationships to the other women evident in what and how I write."[3] I attempt to do the same.

Of course, self-reflexivity is absolutely essential in memoir. I am mandated to interrogate my own personal motivations and my process of representing dance, my friends and colleagues, and the organizations and projects I have initiated and interacted with throughout my thirty-five-year dance career. It is impossible to be truly objective in one's recollections of people and events. In *Dancing in Blackness: A Memoir*, I attempt to create a confluence between the art form and the sociocultural construct of blackness as "a fluid constant." I explore this rapprochement throughout my career as a practitioner of dance and now as a researcher-writer about dance; hence this is a scholar's memoir about dance.

My own life encompasses much of the celebration, debate, reenvisioning, and artistic explorations of the contentious field called black dance. As anthropologist Clifford Geertz has illuminated, "being there" is an important part of the story. This text is an ethnography of many different places in particular time periods and the actors whom I encountered. As an autobiography it does not portend to be objective in its rendering of those times and actors in those spaces. Geertz accurately captures the trick of ethnography, and, by extrapolation, ethnographic memoir: "'Being There' authorially, palpably on the page, is in any case as difficult a trick to bring off as 'being there' personally which after all demands at the minimum hardly more than a travel booking and permission to land; a willingness to endure a certain amount of loneliness, invasion of privacy, and physical discomfort . . . a capacity to stand still for artistic insults."[4] Geertz goes on to discuss the dilemma of self-reflexive ethnographies, revealing that the entire endeavor becomes "a matter of how to prevent subjective views from coloring objective facts. The clash between the expository conventions of author-saturated texts and those of author evacuated ones that grows out of the particular nature of the ethnographic enterprise is imagined to be a clash between seeing things as one would have them and seeing them as they really are."[5] Which authorial convention dominates is a tricky business, so I do not attempt to resolve the dilemma. I simply treat my own experiences in dance, which intersect with the lives of so many of the great dance personalities of the twentieth century, as a kind of self-reflexive anthropological field study, exposing the reader to those times, places, and people as I unapologetically remember them.

Doing the "Black" Dance

One of the obvious themes of this book is dance itself. Dance, as defined by the great dance anthropologist Katherine Dunham, is a series of "rhythmically patterned movements performed by a sentient being." This is a succinct depiction of a complex process of embodied creative expressions that has many levels and purposes, and I have been on all sides of this art: performer, choreographer, teacher, arts administrator, cultural activist, writer, and scholar.

The reason why I like Dunham's succinct definition of dance is because it encompasses the essential layers of the dance complex that includes the personal, social, cultural, and spiritual—body, mind, and soul—all of which must integrate to produce the true *art* of dance. "Rhythmically patterned movements" connotes creative organization and culture, for rhythmic patterns necessitate learned arrangements evolving from the individual's interaction with his/her culture. Human movement does not evolve in a vacuum; rather, like language, it develops from a distinct relationship between an individual and his/her environment. In fact, as dance anthropologist Judith Lynne Hanna has articulated, dance has many language-like features including syntax and discursive aspects of intrinsic and extrinsic meaning, such as metaphor, metonym, and stylization. In Hanna's intro-duction to *To Dance Is Human: A Theory of Nonverbal Communication,* she treats dance as a social phenomenon in itself and "also as a part of the web of human existence."[6] This necessitates that dance not only has obvious physical attributes but also psychological, social, cultural, political, eco-nomic, and communicative levels as well. The latter realm of communica-tion implicitly suggests that dance can be read as text, a nonverbal language with syntax containing "an expressive form of thinking, sensing, feeling, and moving, which may reflect or influence both the individual and the society."[7]

The idea that these "rhythmically patterned movements" must be per-formed by a "sentient being" is crucial for Dunham and me because it ac-knowledges the importance of human perception and consciousness. The ability to perceive one's individual self in relation to all of the sociocultural realms mentioned above connotes an underlying sensation of conscious-ness and adds a spiritual dimension to the sociocultural realm illuminat-ing the Dance, with a capital *d.* Dunham often talked about the Katherine Dunham Dance Technique as "a way of life" that integrates mind, body, and spirit. Her Afro-Caribbean modern dance codified technique, of which I am a certified instructor, allows all of these levels to be taught as a holistic praxis of dance as central to life itself.

But this interrogation of dance is in conversation with "race," that spuri-ous category of human divisions. In creating a confluence between dance and blackness, the obvious question becomes, "What is *black* dance?" This is a question as old as the Eurocentric descriptions of African dance re-corded in sixteenth- and seventeenth-century travelogues when European explorers first encountered dances and rituals on the West African coast.[8] Hundreds of years later in a fundamentally different sociocultural context, the black dance query continued in the public discourse of "What Shall the Negro Dance About?" that underpinned the 1931 *First Negro Recital in America* by black choreographers Edna Guy and Hemsley Winfield.[9] Guy and Winfield wanted the interpretive dance of black Americans to take its place alongside the celebration and redefinition of the arts—literature, painting, and music—that had been flourishing since the mid-1920s as a part of the Harlem Renaissance's New Negro movement.

From early ethnocentric evaluations of African dance and Africa itself to the 1930s artistic efforts against the looming, grinning minstrel mask as icon of the first indigenous American theater, the dances of Africans and their descendants in the Americas have constituted complex and contentious aesthetic terrain. Dance by blacks has been denigrated yet deliberately appropriated, misrepresented yet serving as an irresistible attraction that helped forge what it eventually meant to be American. As Kemoko Sano (1940–2006), the late choreographer of Les Ballets Africains de la République de Guinée, has said, "All cultures dance, but there is something special about the dance of Africa." This "something special" associated with African-derived dancing, which connects the body, mind, and human spirit in a particular way through infectious rhythms, is as powerful as the human heartbeat.

However, African-derived dancing has also constituted a double-edged sword for its practitioners. The negative side of that historic sword, stereotyping, cut deep. The pigeonholing of the efforts of black choreographers has been rampant ever since black dancers in the 1930s and 1940s had the audacity to consider themselves *artists* contributing to the concert art arena instead of as mere entertainers. For example, dance critic Edward Denby wrote in 1943 about Katherine Dunham's *Rite de Passage*:

> Her handling of dramatic values of abstract form is uncertain. . . . The movement is based on African dance elements but the choreographic plan is that of the American modern school. The latter (like any Western art dancing) gets major effects from many kinds of displacement within the stage area, and out of sharply varied gesture. In African dancing, on the contrary, displacement values are of minor importance, individual variations are permissible, and gesture gets its value by plain reiteration. To reconcile two such different expressive methods is a big problem.[10]

Denby's assessment is Eurocentric, lacking knowledge of the intricacies of the Africanist aesthetic that, to be fair, was not a part of the public discourse of the arts in the 1940s. His appraisal, that "It is a problem that faces all those racially conscious artists who insist on reconstructing a style whose creative impulse is foreign to their daily life,"[11] attempts to limit the exploration that black choreographers of the day were destined to engage. In fact, the investigation of Africanist movement and approaches would become a defining approach of black dance artists for decades to come and, in the process, would enrich the diversity of American concert dance. Early black choreographers had to cope with the growing dance establishment's lack of critical knowledge about black dance artists' cultural and sociopolitical context.

The need for a more enlightened platform for black choreographers' artistic production is why I created Black Choreographers Moving Toward the 21st Century (BCM), a national initiative that lasted from 1989 to 1995 (chapter 6). It became another step in the long journey of black artists creating a counternarrative to the often-uninformed assessment of black choreography. This and other artistic projects were meant to help create what Caribbeanist scholar VèVè A. Clark called "diasporan dance literacy."

Anthropologist and Dunham biographer Joyce Aschenbrenner has written about the power relations at the foundation of dance in America, revealing that "the difference between great traditions and folk art does not lie in the presence or degree of tradition, artistic ability, or ingenuity, rather [in] the potential of imaginative scope, innovation, and ultimately of social and political influence. . . . In a complex society, art involves, and presupposes political and economic power, as well as cultural autonomy—the freedom to pursue alternative expressions."[12] I have felt a strong need to help forge a sense of cultural justice in dance, facilitated at the personal level by my own rebellious, independent nature.

I have been at many of the key historic events of the black dance debate through various initiatives, both proactive and reactive. These significant periods, for me, started in the 1960s San Francisco–Oakland Bay Area, where I came of age, and where I helped forge a West Coast center for African-derived dance. This drive continued with studying dance in places like the University of Ghana, Legon's 1970s School of Music, Dance, and Drama (now the School of Performing Arts), and being a part of the American Dance Festival's "The Black Tradition in American Modern Dance" project to rectify modern dance's long neglect of black dance artists' contributions. This drive in my career culminated with my own statewide Black Choreographers Moving Toward the 21st Century dance initiative that produced black experimental choreographers from all over the nation and positioned them in dialogue with scholars and historians to engage their issues. *Dancing in Blackness* explores many of these historic moments and projects in which I was involved and in the process tells the story of the black struggle for recognition, justice, and self-empowerment through the prism of dance, a discipline only occasionally viewed politically.

The Black Dance Debate

Although the discourses on African and Caribbean dance forms (Hanna 1968, 1976; Thompson 1974, 1988; Dunham 1983; Daniel 1994, 2006, 2011; Castaldi 2006) and the concert fusion dance styles of black Americans (Meyers et al. 1992; Gottschild 1996, 2003; Chatterjea 2004; DeFrantz 2002, 2004, 2014) have often been constructed in different sectors of scholarship, I am making a case in *Dancing in Blackness* for these often discrete dance genres as part of the larger discourse on embodied *blackness*. And exactly what constitutes "black dance" has formed the foundation of both the African-derived and black modern dance discourses. Incessant queries pervade: Is black dance the jazz styles produced by early vaudevillians or the narrative style of Alvin Ailey's Hortonesque modern dance with its often African American themes? Or is it the contemporary fusion styles that utilize black social dance forms like hip-hop? Is a black dancer anyone who dances these aforementioned styles, a dancer of African descent, or a dancer who grew up in a black neighborhood and has naturally taken on the body language and swagger that we often call "black"?

Dance journalist Zita Allen has articulated particularly poignant questions regarding the topic of what is black dance in the American concert arena.

> Is it a black choreographer's work performed by black dancers? A white choreographer's work done by black dancers? Or a black choreographer's work danced by whites? Must it always have a "black" theme? Is it ever abstract? Is it modern, jazz, tap and/or ballet? Is it found only in America or can this label apply to works performed by Senegal's National Dance Company, or Cuba's Conjuncto Folklorico, or any other company consciously trying to preserve its African heritage? Or, is "Black Dance" just an empty label devised by white critics to cover that vast, richly diverse and extremely complex area of dance they know nothing about?[13]

Allen and I raise crucial questions about what we call "black dance" that probably never can be definitively answered. This historical quagmire proceeds from the assumption that race itself has been socially constructed for geopolitical purposes. The race edifice has developed out of the need to rationalize the last five hundred years of the Atlantic slave trade, colonialism, and continued segregation, discrimination, and social and cultural inequalities.

The resulting entrenchment and obsession (particularly in the United States) with race places constructs like "black" and "blackness" at the service of many agendas, including dance. These terms are used by various cultural groups as shortcuts for particular spheres of experience that in fact encompass a wide variety of geopolitical and social spaces (U.S. African Americans, Afro-Cubans, Afro-Brazilian, Haitians, etc.). For better or worse, our racial/cultural terminology has come to have some, if ambiguous, meaning as devices representing particularized experiences. Therefore, in this context, I explore "black dance" to mean the individual and collective dances of any genre performed by black peoples anywhere in the world. This definition allows for what is considered traditional, contemporary, concert, popular, folk, and experimental to all be encompassed within my black dance rubric.

The late Joe Nash, pioneering dancer-turned-archivist of black dance history, designated "The New Negro Dance" of the early 1930s as crucial for the beginning of *modernism* in black concert dance. He contended that the flourishing of interpretive dance, with Katherine Dunham in Chicago, and Winfield, Guy, Randolph Sawyer, Lavinia Williams, Asadata Dafora, and Bernice Brown in New York, put dance on the same exploratory footing as the other arts emerging out of the New Negro movement, like literature and visual arts. Within this new modernism, crucial "new" aesthetic and cultural questions were embedded for these emerging artists to answer:

> And they were confronted with the questions "could the Negro create a vital art form based upon his African and Caribbean heritage?" And if so, "what would the Negro dance about?" The pioneers sought to portray positive images of black culture despite expectations of what they should do or shouldn't do on the concert stage. And what were some of the stirrings in the concert world when Hemsley Winfield and Edna Guy entered the domain of Graham, Humphrey, Weidman and Denishawn, and brought black soul and spirit to the concert stage?[14]

Remember, the black dancer in the United States during the first half of the twentieth century was still suffering from the minstrel image and hence was relegated to chorus-line shake dancers, acrobat-contortionists, or song-and-dance comedian-vaudevillians. By midcentury, many in the latter category were still in blackface, such as the team of Miller and Lyles, who appeared in the 1943 all-black film musical *Stormy Weather*. Miller and Lyles's performance was in stark contrast to Katherine Dunham's quintessential modernist statement in the breakaway dance sequence to Lena Horne's "Stormy Weather" song. Dunham's interpretation of black identity in that sequence was far more internally dignified and reflective than any of the film's other dance and performance sequences, immortalizing her developing Dunham Dance Technique like only the silver screen can.[15]

The social convention of the minstrel mask, looming like a ghostly apparition of the nostalgic slave plantation, has shaped black identity and the larger American identity. Ntozake Shange's exploration of the effects of U.S. theatrical history, with a minstrel mask backdrop in her 1979 play *Spell #7*, attempts to exorcize the demons of that historic image of blackness when seven black artists congregate in an after-hours bar after finishing their stage performance. More than fifty years before, the challenge of the New Negro movement in the mid-1920s and the New Negro Dance in the early 1930s created a crucial juncture—a *group* "breakaway," just like the improvisatory section of the lindy hop, when dance partners are free to improvise, unrestrained by the strictures of couple partnering. Just as Alain Locke's manifesto of the New Negro created the break with racialized interpretations of black culture for literature and art, so too did the modernist movement of black choreographers of the early 1930s for the field of dance. Dance as art has often lagged behind the other art disciplines due to its function in popular vernacular, social, and ballroom forms. I argue that the high art/low art dichotomy was more acute for dance in black culture, particularly since black social dance and its motivating music helped establish American musical theater itself.

The duality of the double-edged sword of black dance, mentioned earlier, is constituted by the recognition of the powerfully expressive and rhythmic bodily vocabulary of the dance of blacks, on one hand, and the relegation of its very practitioners to a naturalized realm of "untrained," "untutored," and "unsophisticated," and therefore as artistically questionable, on the other.[16] Of course, this duality could be argued as well about black music: music critics, for example, called jazz musicians "natural and untrained" at the turn of the twentieth century; and racist white America in the 1950s admonished white teenagers attracted to the R&B-inflected rock-and-roll sound, often called "nigger music." Moreover, dances produced by black Americans to this developing American music, reflecting the questionable black body itself, were the victim of even harsher assessments. When black choreographers had the audacity to enter the modern concert dance world, dance and theater critics historically wrote reviews that stereotyped rather than illuminated black performance.

The field of dance of any cultural persuasion is often viewed as mindless—bodily expression that takes little intellect. Given the Western and Christian denigration of the sensual body and all things associated with it, such as dancing, the linking of African-derived dance forms to a "natural ability," instead of a hard-won skill of artistry, positioned it at a further disadvantage. Although a pervasive black aesthetic was at the foundation of growing American popular performance, white dance critics were trained in assessing the strictures of ballet and creating the criteria for evaluating the developing American modern dance, defined largely by the aesthetic of white dance pioneers, such as Graham, Humphrey, and Weidman. Grasping what black choreographers of the day were attempting by developing the first fusion styles linking ballet, modern, and so-called "ethnic" styles was not yet a priority.

Brenda Dixon Gottschild is arguably the most important scholar on the issue of race and dance. In *Dance Magazine*'s February 2004 issue, on the heels of her 2003 *The Black Dancing Body: A Geography from Coon to Cool*, she wrote a short article called "Is Race Still an Issue in Dance?" She encapsulates what she discovered about many dancers' perceptions about race in her research and the multitudinous interviews she conducted for *The Black Dancing Body*:

> I uncovered a range of perceptions, images, and assumptions, past and present. And this information revealed that there is not a black dancing body—nor a white dancing, or other dancing body—that whatever black or white dance is, it is a complex social and cultural idea based on body image and often body stereotypes. What seemed to define a cultural body, black, white, or brown were not so much physical characteristics as a particular sense of soul and spirit.[17]

Gottschild's "sense of soul and spirit" of the black dancing body leads us back to the "something special," mentioned earlier, about African dance as perceived by Kemoko Sano. A particular kind of physical soul connection in time and space has been identified with the black dancing body. But that connection can also animate anyone who opens up himself/herself to that energy, leading us back to human spirit itself.

Black *popular* dancing styles and their attendant musics, derived from African cultures' intricate body isolations and polyrhythmic complexities, has the whole postmodern world celebrating life with similar social dance moves to a similar beat. Young people in clubs and bars in New York, Paris, London, Buenos Aires, Tokyo, Shanghai, and Lagos are executing (or trying to execute) these African-derived rhythmic isolations of body parts to some form of popular music that has its ultimate origin in African America, and therefore Africa. Yet, I ask: Do many still think of this dancing style as lewd, lascivious, and too sexual as it was described in early European travelogues of African dance, or even the 1920s Jazz Age critiques? Such assessments of African-derived dances continue even in the twenty-first century. One example of this potentially continuing ambivalence about the (black) dancing body can be seen in the controversial worldwide twerking phenomenon that has its origins in New Orleans African American "bounce" culture.

The *performativity* of the body—everyday gestures and body language—is another conceptual way of interrogating race, as well as gender, sexuality, or class. Susan Manning uses the cultural theorists on this subject, such as Judith Butler, Eric Lott, and Michael Rogin, to explore how audiences viewed early modern dance by white and black dancers, while illuminating the predominance of culture in determining who we conceive ourselves to be as Americans: "It is not nature but culture that renders the multiplicity of lived bodies 'feminine' or 'masculine,' 'queer' or 'straight,' 'black' or 'white,' and so on. Performativity is not a monolithic social operation. Rather, differently placed historical subjects conceptualize the relations between physical bodies and social meanings differently."[18] The terms "black dance" or "white dance" might be ambiguous, but one thing is objectively sure: black and white people were/are surely "differently placed historical subjects."[19] African Americans' experience in the United States has been, and continues to be, very different from how most white Americans experience America, creating different meanings associated with the everyday lived experience in the body. As Andrew Hacker told us, the United States is "two nations: black and white, separate, hostile, and unequal."[20] Yet the lingering guiding principle of the United States, "liberty and justice for all," contains the potential for closing the gap between these "two nations," even culturally and artistically.

Dancing in Blackness allows me to explore these various issues around black dance through the many roles I have played as dancer, choreographer, arts administrator, cultural activist, and scholar, and what each role has meant to my personal growth. I naturally survey these intricate black dance issues as I discuss my own artistic and cultural production in the world, as well as how my work has influenced individuals and communities. This book also explores how dance has allowed me interaction with many cultures around the world and, in the process, has given me the tools to access, interrogate, motivate, learn from, and understand principles of life as I grew as a human being.

Doing the (Chapter) Breakdown

From the jigging breakdown style of Master Juba (William Henry Lane) in the 1830s, as the first African American dance celebrity during slavery, to the vernacular breakdown dance of 1980s locking hip-hop style, the idea of "breaking it down" through the body is "a black thing." I use the breakdown metaphor to briefly summarize the following chapters that tell the story of my dance career and personal life throughout various eras and different places.

Chapter 1, "Coming of Age through (Black) Dance in the San Francisco Bay Area," provides a sense of my early dance training, influences, and experiences in dance during the Black Arts movement of the mid- to late 1960s in the San Francisco–Oakland Bay Area, while I explore the personal attributes as a young woman that I brought to the discipline and profession of dance. The early development of West Coast dance—northern California in particular—needs more investigation, and this memoir adds to that knowledge. My coming of age personally and artistically in San Francisco during this seminal period illuminates the West Coast's effect on cultural possibilities and artistic potential in dance. This period becomes a preamble to my eventual European sojourn that allows me to first test myself in the world outside the United States. My international explorations would become increasingly important to my cultural awareness and dance career.

Chapter 2, "Dancing in Europe," primarily explores my developing dance career in Scandinavia: Copenhagen and Stockholm, 1969–70. It investigates the black American expatriate experience in Europe from a black female perspective when U.S. counterculture was globally pervasive. My European experience includes racialized stereotypes and sexuality, as well as the personal choices I make to survive as a black female dancer in Europe. A kind of blackness in relation to "Europeanness" ensues that becomes a part of what I call the "Josephine Baker Syndrome." I reminisce about the beginning of my first European choreographic excursions with my own Copenhagen dance company and the struggle to persist as a dancer in Europe. The chapter also surveys the black male dance teachers in Stockholm—Walter Nicks, Talley Beatty, Vanoye Aikens, and Clifford Fears—promoting what the Scandinavians called "jazz ballet," which was in actuality variations on the Katherine Dunham Technique.

I explore my growing professionalization in the dance field in chapter 3, "Dancing in New York." Coming back to the United States after almost three years in Europe, I first go to Boston to reorient myself to America on the East Coast and to be with the first major love of my life. Teaching, choreographing, and reconnecting with the black community in Boston proves to be a necessary transition to New York City. Becoming a dancer with the Rod Rodgers Dance Company (RRDC) in Manhattan allows me to quickly experience the New York professional dance scene. I explore the RRDC repertoire and my position within the company. I also illuminate the top New York black dance companies in the early 1970s as being in conversation with the continuing 1960s Black Arts movement, which several New York black dance periodicals documented. In doing so, I also examine Eleo Pomare's and George Faison's dance companies and their signature choreography, while contextualizing the place of the Alvin Ailey American Dance Theater in the early 1970s as the growing internationally recognized premier black dance company. I also recollect my own continuing dance-theater explorations, as well as a unique performance opportunity with the New York jazz music scene before I leave that national cultural center.

Chapter 4, "Dancing Back into the San Francisco–Oakland Bay Area, 1973–1976," chronicles my return after five years to my home area, now as a professional dancer-choreographer. I not only get to know my family again, but I also develop the artistic theme central to my developing career, *The Evolution of Black Dance*. I create and produce several evening-length productions during this three-year period and begin to learn arts administration, forming Halifu Productions, which helped catalyze the mid-1970s black dance scene in the Bay Area. I simultaneously finish my undergraduate degree with the help of noted black feminist scholar Barbara Christian. I also meet and artistically collaborate with the poet Ntozake Shange, who gives me my African name, which I begin to use professionally, and am introduced to the musician Kimathi Asante, who would become my first husband and collaborator on many community artistic projects. This chapter establishes my professional reputation in the Bay Area, which will become the foundation of my work over the next seventeen years, but only after my West African sojourn.

Chapter 5, "Dancing in Africa," records my bold move of living alone in Ghana, West Africa, for nine months to study and research the basis of black dance in the Americas. I enroll as an auditor in the School of Music, Dance, and Drama (SMDD) of the University of Ghana, Legon, studying with ethnomusicologist Dr. Kwabena Nketia and dance ethnologist Professor Albert Opoku. I examine the SMDD curriculum as a symbiosis between Western dance pedagogy adapted to traditional methodologies of inculcating the centuries-old dance traditions of Ghana and the development of the internationally touring Ghana Dance Ensemble. I also explore my personal relationships with other African Americans and Ghanaians to further interrogate race and blackness from the new point of view of living in West Africa. I also remember my opportunity to travel throughout five regions of Ghana, as well as an excursion to Togo and Nigeria that broadened my perspective on myself as African American in Africa, as well as West African dance across several countries.

I end this memoir with chapter 6, "Dancing in Oakland and Beyond, 1977–1993," covering sixteen years of my career as dancer, choreographer, dance educator, and arts administrator. During this period I found the nonprofit dance institution Everybody's Creative Arts Center (ECAC), which solidifies my reputation in the San Francisco–Oakland Bay Area as a leader in the growing black dance and multicultural arts movements. I assess my development as a dancer-choreographer, discussing some of my key dance works, as well as the creation of the ECAC's resident dance company, Citi-Centre Dance Theatre, which becomes an important contemporary dance company in the region from 1983 to 1988. My ambitious career agenda is revealed through my simultaneously taking an adjunct dance position at Stanford University and assuming many choreographic and directorial commissions. The chapter articulates how all this artistic and administrative experience culminates in my founding in 1989 a major national initiative in black dance, Black Choreographers Moving Toward the 21st Century.

Because the United States has placed great meaning on "race," it can be called a founding principle and our common ground of lived experience. For better or worse it is also embedded in the way we see dance. Personally, I view my own "blackness" as what I called a "fluid constant." It is a constant because of the way I am perceived racially no matter where I have ventured on the planet, but my blackness is also fluid because of my own personal agency evidenced in the pages of this text. Dance and theater scholar Nadine George-Graves has created a convenient concept she calls "diasporic spidering" that she says, "assumes an individual with agency . . . who creates a life based on experiences. It is a performativity in flux as new information is continually incorporated."[21] Indeed, my individual agency has created a "performativity in flux" in different parts of the United States and across Europe, Africa, the Caribbean, and South America, where I have had to *perform* aspects of my identity as "black" because of my own cultural choices, in addition to living in a racialized world. Dance has been my processual tool to negotiate this contentious fluid constant.

My personal story creates a synergy between the micro level of my career choices and the macro level of race, culture, and dance in the United States and the world. My life's mission has been fearlessly dedicated to what political scientist Melissa Harris-Perry calls the "politics of recognition."[22] Where she reveals the lack of recognition for many black women's efforts, my career in dance has in many ways advocated for my recognition as a "triple minority"—black, a woman, and a dancer.

Coming of Age through (Black) Dance in the San Francisco Bay Area

I entered the world of dance during a crucial period in the United States for black people as a whole: the 1960s. When I graduated from high school in 1965, I had completed three years of modern dance. It was my good fortune to have a high school dance instructor, Mrs. Alice Rocky, who had convinced San Francisco's George Washington High School to offer a modern dance program within physical education. Mrs. Rocky had been a student of Hanya Holm, the German modern dance émigré who had come to New York in 1931 to start the Mary Wigman School of Modern Dance in the United States, and who eventually choreographed several Broadway productions with the new expressive form called modern dance. Mrs. Rocky trained many young girls in the Hanya Holm style of modern dance that used floor work, torso contractions, natural swings giving into gravity, and across-the-floor prances and leaps, much of which I would discover decades later was actually implicit in Africanist dance styles. Brenda Dixon Gottschild has written articulately about the Africanist basis of modern dance and American movement styles in general having their basis in African American vernacular dance. Africanist movement propensities for relaxing into gravity and centralizing movements in the pelvis served as a kinesthetic foundation of the emerging modern dance expressive styles.[1]

High school gave me a sense of dance as an art. I remember Mrs. Rocky occasionally bringing the students to the classroom instead of the studio for dance film days. On one occasion she showed us Martha Graham's *A Dancer's World* on a sixteen-millimeter projector. There was Graham, the diva, sitting in front of the mirror preparing for her role as Jocasta in her *Night Journey*, a dance adaptation of the Oedipus myth, waxing poetic about what it took to become a dancer. *A Dancer's World* was an overview of Graham Technique itself, with many of her famous dancers prancing into the studio space. Bertram Ross (with whom I would later study in New York), David Wood (with whom I would later study in Stockholm, Sweden), and the lilt and elegant Mary Hinkson, one of Graham's two black female dancers, were among the featured dancers. From these exposures to concert dance on film, I got the sense that dance could actually be a profession, not just what we young people did socially at Saturday night parties. This was a concept and prototypical image that would shape the rest of my life.

I took this newfound sense of professional dance with me as I continued to dance as a "hobby" in college, enrolling in the fall of 1965 in what was then called San Francisco (S.F.) State College. I continued my modern dance training with Delores Kirton Cayou (now Nontsizi Cayou), an African American dance professor who was just beginning her exploration of black dance forms, starting the first modern jazz dance course in the S.F. State physical education curriculum. Mrs. Cayou was the next stage in encouraging me to consider dance as a profession. My parents were certainly not impressed with the idea of my majoring in dance ("Everyone knows *we* can dance; why not major in something that can give you a solid job?"). So I minored in dance with a psychology major and set about improving my dance technique. I was challenged to increase my dancing skill when Cayou bluntly told me that I should be better than I was after three years of dance in high school. I set about trying to prove to her that I could improve my balance, leg extensions, and rhythmic sensibilities.

Artistically, during my three years at S.F. State (1965–68), the much-touted revolutionary 1960s found me exploring different dimensions of the developing dance forms that we called "Afro-jazz," "Afro-Haitian," and simply "jazz." In Cayou's dance composition class I experimented with choreography to avant-garde jazz pianist Cecil Taylor's "Unit Structures." I also took dance classes in community studios: Dunham Technique with Madame Ruth Beckford at Peters Wright Studio in San Francisco, and Afro-

Cuban dance with Ed Mock at Gloria Unti's Performing Arts Workshop. Little did I know then that Dunham Technique would serve as the foundation of my future career.

The Bay Area Shapes My Cultural and Artistic Growth

I got my first performing experience dancing an "Afro-jazz" nightclub act with Zack Thompson, a black California dancer who had returned to San Francisco from New York. Zack, originally from New Orleans, had taught and performed in the Bay Area in the 1950s, dancing in the Civic Light Opera and doing television choreography.[2] He then left to perform in Europe and New York, only to return to San Francisco "to show the Bay Area's 'colored children' how to dance professionally," as he always quipped. To establish his name again and make a living, Zack wanted to choreograph a commercially viable Afro-jazz revue with live drummers that could be booked in nightclubs, as well as for the concert stage. He asked Nontsizi Cayou to recommend two female dancers from the S.F. State dance program, and she advocated for my friend drama student Judith Holten and me. Zack taught us his combination of modern, ballet, jazz, and Afro-type movements, choreographing a production that was commercial enough to entertain drinking patrons in clubs but had enough dance integrity for the concert stage.

I was excited to put all of my training to work for an audience, and dancing with Zack Thompson became my first paid performing job. He dressed Judith and me in African-style costumes, and our Afro-jazz revue became a regular act at the Half Note, a majority-black neighborhood bar on Divisadero and Grove Streets. During the mid-1960s, after the Civil Rights and Voting Rights Acts, when "black" was beginning to be "in," a superficial allusion to Africa was considered "hip" and "cool." It took at least another decade for knowledgeable and researched African-derived performance to become the norm. Zack would go on to help found a multidisciplinary performing company in 1969 called Black Light Explosion and eventually, in the early 1970s, his own Zack Thompson Dancers, Inc. (chapter 4).

This was not the only professional experience for which Nontsizi Cayou recommended me. When the 1967 touring *Show Boat* by Jerome Kern and Oscar Hammerstein came to San Francisco's Curran Theatre for the last two weeks of its national run, one of its black female dancers had literally "jumped ship." Cayou recommended that I audition for the show's black choreographer, the Los Angeles–based Claude Thompson. The day I went to the theater on Geary Street to audition, I was scared to death. But whatever I did, Mr. Thompson liked me, and I was hired for two weeks to dance in my first big Broadway touring production, with this version of *Show Boat* starring famed actor Carroll O'Connor. The original 1927 musical had actually taken the developing Broadway musical genre to a new level, featuring the celebrated black actor-singer Paul Robeson, who made the "colored" dockworker song "Ol' Man River" famous.

The script also called for a group of black dancers as a part of the cast; black dancers, therefore, were always assured work whenever *Show Boat*, as a theatrical musical staple, was revived. Being in such a famous commercial production while I was still a dance student in college was a chance for me to examine the life of a professional commercial dancer—in this case Broadway "gypsies" who earned a good living going from one commercial show to the next. As this was the end of a long tour, the *Show Boat* dancers were simply trying to get to the tour's end, and teaching me about the life of a Broadway dancer was the last thing on their minds. The main thing I observed about their career was that their dancing became a rote routine. They had their stage appearances timed to the second, knowing exactly how much time they had to be dressed for their next entrance, which would grudgingly interrupt the card game that they had going on backstage. They went onstage and "sold" the dance number to the audience and then rushed back to where the card game had been interrupted. Observing this routine was enough for me to get the picture of the Broadway commercial dance world.

I asked myself, "What about the *art* of dance?" Where was the intensity of dramatic and spiritual involvement with their work that Martha Graham talked about in *A Dancer's World*? I was not putting in all these years of training to only come offstage and play cards before my next entrance. I decided then and there that I would never sell my art simply for money. Dance had to be something more than a mere job. My place and era— San Francisco in the late 1960s—was drawing me into the world of black dance with all of its inchoate 1960s dimensions, from Caribbean-styled jazz to Afro-Haitian and U.S. modern jazz dance. *My* dance approach would have to interrogate personal and cultural identity and provide an inroad to self-knowledge.

Thankfully, Mrs. Cayou's modern dance classes were rigorous and supplemented with master classes from some of the greats who were her friends. We had master classes with the nimble Mary Hinkson of the Martha Graham Company, whom I had seen on film in high school. We even had a master class from the dance pioneer himself, Alvin Ailey. I still remember a jazz combination he taught us that I have used in my own classes. My undergraduate S.F. State training with Nontsizi Cayou was foundational to my early dance training, allowing me the courage to venture out into the Bay Area dance community.

Nontsizi Cayou eventually became a seminal figure in the development of the black dance movement in the Bay Area. In fact, over time, she helped Bay Area black dance add its voice to the revolutionary artistic mix with her dance company Wajumbe Performance Ensemble that included African-based dance forms. Expanding beyond classical modern dance, Cayou started this dance company out of S.F. State University (formerly S.F. State College) to reflect an increasing black consciousness that was about reclaiming African culture as a part of a critical "new" self-perception. Dancers such as Blanche Brown, who went on to form the Bay Area Haitian dance company Group Petit la Croix in the 1980s, started with Wajumbe, as well as the late Katherine Dunham Technique instructor and dancer Alicia Pierce. Cayou was able to negotiate a slot for Wajumbe at the 1977 FESTAC (Second World Festival of Black Arts) in Lagos, Nigeria, testifying to the company's hard work to become a dance representative of the Bay Area. San Francisco State University became a primary site of a new black consciousness, not only through student political activism but also through dance and cultural activism.

Yet this was not the region's first experience of African-based dance. Oakland's Ruth Beckford, the first black graduate of the dance department at UC Berkeley, who had danced with the famous Katherine Dunham Dance Company, brought Dunham Technique as Afro-Haitian dance to Oakland and San Francisco as early as the 1950s with her dance company. She also made Afro-Haitian dance and Dunham Technique the basis of the first dance program in the Oakland Department of Parks and Recreation. This elegant, dark-skinned black woman, with her thin waist blossoming out into full African hips, and sporting one of the first short-cropped natural coiffures, was considered the "Mother of Black Dance in the Bay Area." Her primary goal was to create productive, self-respecting young women through dance in social context, following one of Katherine Dunham's primary philosophical concepts, "Socialization through the Arts." Here was a community dance teacher who had strict, graduated levels of technique with "dance exams" that had to be passed in order to go from one level to the next. In the late 1960s Ruth Beckford was the hub for the serious black dancer and those white dancers who felt the call of "a different drummer." Miss Beckford (Miss B) became a teacher-mentor to Drs. Naima Gwen Lewis, Yvonne Daniel, and Albirda Rose, as well as Nontsizi Cayou, Deborah Vaughan, and myself, all of whom helped establish variations on the Dunham Technique legacy in the Bay Area and across the country.

Every one of Miss B's classes was strenuous, with a meticulous approach to learning the Dunham Technique and Haitian dance, all leading to nothing short of self-mastery. The Dunham barre, from the beginning "press-ins" and "flat-backs" to the "up and overs" that left one's thighs screaming, required exact body placement, endurance, flexibility, and musicality. I discovered my butt and my thighs in a way that I had never experienced them in traditional modern and ballet, and I moved to polyrhythmic drums that inspired the soul as well as the body. Here was a black woman's technique that was based on her observations as an anthropologist viewing the dances of the West Indies, and creatively incorporating her interpretation and extrapolations of those dances into the genres of modern and ballet that she had studied as a young dancer in Chicago. Dunham Technique felt different, it felt holistic, and it felt well-conceived.

The most revolutionary aspect of Miss B's classes, for me, was that drummers accompanied them, not a pianist playing Bach, Beethoven, and Mozart. The 6/8 and 4/4 rhythms of Afro-Haitian music were riveting, with the battery of drummers often led by Bay Area drummer Butch Haynes. These rhythms began to open an inner cultural ear that I didn't even know existed. After the dance barre warm-up, we had center-floor isolations—learning to separate the head, shoulders, rib cage, and hips from each other in order to "play" the drums' polyrhythms in the body. Never before had I been expected to be so masterful with my center torso. Sure, I had learned to lock my spine in exact placement for ballet, contract it from the pelvis for Graham Technique, and relax it from the waist for Limón Technique swings. But to carry two or three rhythms in the torso at once was definitely a different cultural experience.

Moving across the floor was divided into two parts: (1) what Miss B called "sight-reading" and (2) execution of a specific Haitian dance. Sight-reading trained our eyes to become aware of subtle nuances of movement without being verbally instructed. We simply had to observe a repetitive movement that progressed across the floor and then repeat it ourselves moving across in lines. It was hilarious to see all the versions of what the dancers thought they saw, like the old adage of a story changing as it passes from ear to ear, or the concept of the relativity of perception of the individual mind, which I was learning as a psychology major at S.F. State. Yet over a semester of classes, it was also amazing to observe the change in the keenness of our observations that "sight-reading" developed in Miss B's students. It was, in fact, an ingenious method of developing our ability to learn choreography quickly. These were the elements of dance I was acquiring from a completely new cultural perspective in Ruth Beckford's Afro-Haitian dance classes.[3]

The Bay Area's growing African dance consciousness was not coincidental to the evolving touring national dance companies from Africa itself. Established as postcolonial redress to attempted cultural obliteration, a part of European colonialization of Africa, world-class dance theater companies, such as Les Ballets Africains de la République de Guinée, the National Dance Company of Senegal, and the Ghana Dance Ensemble, all toured in the Bay Area in the late 1960s and 1970s. They performed in top venues like San Francisco's Curran Theatre and Oakland's Paramount Theatre. Experiencing professional African dance directly from the Motherland was indeed a boost to the growing African cultural consciousness in the Bay Area.

Locally, this African-based dance culture had been thoroughly established with Miss B, and continued with the Wajumbe Performance Ensemble at S.F. State, Naima Gwen Lewis's dance company in the East Bay, Deborah Vaughan's Dimensions Dance Theater in Oakland, and eventually Blanche Brown's Group Petit la Croix in San Francisco. The Bay Area's strong foundation in African-Caribbean dance soon became the platform for the many 1970s and 1980s prodigious African and Caribbean dancer-musicians who are now associated with the San Francisco–Oakland Bay Area: Malonga Casquelourd's Fua Dia Congo (Republic of the Congo), Zak & Naomi Diouf's Diamano Coura (Senegal and Liberia), C. K. Ladzekpo's African Music & Dance Ensemble (Ghana), Jose Lorenzo's Batucaje (Brazil), Luis, Bobi, and Guillermo Céspedes's Conjunto Céspedes (Cuba), Wilfred Marks's Dance Kaiso (Trinidad & Tobago), and many others. These artists and companies were the reason for San Francisco and Oakland becoming a center for African and African-based dance classes and professional dance companies, particularly at Everybody's Creative

Arts Center/CitiCentre Dance Theatre that I founded in 1977 (chapter 6). This African-derived dance tradition continues today with Oakland's current Malonga Casquelourd Center for the Arts. The San Francisco–Oakland Bay Area was rife with a strong statement of the resistive, but celebratory, African-based dance scene as a part of the region's reputation as a site of revolutionary multiculturalism.

San Francisco–Oakland Bay Area's Revolutionary Culture

I grew up in San Francisco, with my mother, stepfather, and three sisters, having moved there from Texas in 1957 for "better opportunities for Negroes," as I was told. As a child, I only infrequently went across the Bay Bridge to Oakland in the East Bay with my family to visit our cousins. But as a nineteen-year-old, a year after graduating high school, moving away from home, and living in San Francisco apartments with student roommates, I began to explore Oakland and Berkeley. As I continued my community dance classes, I eventually moved to Berkeley, while carpooling with other S.F. State students across the bay to the campus. Although Oakland and San Francisco are only about twelve miles apart, Oakland, which then had a majority black population, is very different from San Francisco.

Bay Area culture fit very well with my iconoclastic personality and helped shape its contours. California in general, and the Bay Area in particular, has achieved a reputation for being the bastion of American counterculture, from politics to sexuality, and from the black consciousness movement to general collective social activism. In fact, the seminal events, personalities, and social movements in the region during the 1960s were ground zero for the shift to a new cultural *zeitgeist* that was occurring throughout the entire world, and I partook in this cultural change in my own way. The brewing revolutionary black cultural and political consciousness, as a part of the 1960s sociocultural shift, became the Black Power and the Black Arts movements. Cultural theorist Amy Ongiri rightfully notes: "The historical moment of both the Black Power and the Black Arts Movements was the formative movement, not only for contemporary understanding of African American identity, but also for ideas of blackness in African American cultural production, characterized by artists and intellectuals of the era as 'the new thing' but naturalized into contemporary African American culture as 'authentic' Blackness."[4] Indeed, "the new thing" pervaded my undergraduate years at San Francisco State University and shaped my personal and artistic consciousness as a black female and as a dancer-choreographer.

San Francisco and Oakland (as well as Berkeley) had a symbiotic relationship in the development of "the new thing." Literary historian James Edward Smethurst captures the 1960s relationship between the two sides of the Bay:

> The campuses of Merritt College and the University of California Berkeley nurtured the early Black Power and Black Arts Movements in the East Bay that did ultimately reach across the bay to San Francisco. What were initially the ad hoc efforts of a handful of students grew to have an enormous impact on the movements and their public image across the United States. These early efforts figured prominently in the genesis of the journals *Soulbook* and *Black Dialogue* (and ultimately the *Journal of Black Poetry*) as well as in the formation of Revolutionary Action Movement, the Black Panther Party and Us [Organization].[5]

The literary journals Smethurst mentions were crucial to the revolutionary black consciousness developing in the region. Merritt College (then on Grove Street—now Martin Luther King, Jr. Blvd.) in North Oakland become a hotbed of activism, because of the Afro-American Association initiated by Khalid Monsour (Donald Warden), which was a study group in African and African American history at Merritt College. This group developed *Soulbook*, which in turn, influenced key figures like Huey Newton and Bobby Seale, future founders of the Black Panther Party for Self-Defense.

Although the literary arts are usually emphasized when examining Bay Area activist history, I emphasize the often overlooked place of dance in this 1960s revolutionary mix. This rich culturally alternative environment allowed me, at age nineteen, to explore my growing infatuation with African-based dance to live drumming, and to investigate the underlying cultures behind these dance forms, as well as their history in relation to black identity. My undergraduate years would become my introduction to *blackness* through dance that was not limited to the United States, but indeed worldwide. My growing international perspective fit very well within the Bay Area's brand of black consciousness as a part of a multiethnic Third World perception of global oppression.

The Spanish-speaking Mission District in San Francisco, for example, was evolving the long-standing radical theater group the San Francisco

Mime Troupe, as well as other institutions that were linked to the black arts movement. "So it is not surprising that a vital poetry and performance community arose in the Mission District that included," according to Smethurst, "African Americans Ntozake Shange and David Henderson, Asian American Jessica Hagedorn, Chicano Juan Felipe Herrera and Nuyorican Victor Hernandez Cruz."[6] These artists would become, in fact, the artists of color movement with whom I would eventually interact from 1973 to the mid-1980s. In the Bay Area, black, Chicano, and Asian studies grew in parallel, and this growing cadre of multicultural artists produced work about the discrete cultures, as well as their common oppression.

Armed with this new revolutionary cultural curiosity, I explored my own artistic approach through choreography at several venues, including the Sunday showcases at the Black Panthers headquarters (the Oakland Learning Center) in East Oakland. Since the growing *political* militancy regarding black liberation that the Black Panther Party (BPP) represented was not my *personal* approach, in 1967 and 1968 I struggled with exactly how I could contribute to the movement. My answer was to take my solo choreography to the Panthers' Sunday showcases and offer it as my *creative* contribution to the "revolution." My dance solos were welcomed at the Panther's Sunday community gatherings, and this became my personal involvement in the Black Power political movement and the new revolutionary consciousness in the Bay Area. Dance has always been central to African American culture; therefore dance in service of social change, I thought, was a valid and effective means of communicating the shifting black political consciousness. I don't remember the exact dance pieces that I performed, but they had to be an amalgam of what I was learning from Zack Thompson, Ed Mock, and Ruth Beckford, as well as my own developing choreographic voice from my S.F. State dance classes.

In late 1967, I decided to teach my own dance class as a cultural political statement. This was the period when student demonstrations on the S.F. State campus were heating up, before the conservative S. I. Hayakawa was hired as president of the university. This was also the time when the Black Panthers in Oakland were beginning to create an armed resistance to police brutality. By this time, I was living in Bernal Heights above the Mission District in San Francisco and was able to get a recreation room donated at the Good Samaritan Community Center on Potrero Street. It was a big, hulking room with tables and arts-and-crafts supplies, and not really set up for dance. But it had the most important thing: a sprung hardwood floor. I created thirty *handmade* flyers with crayons and put them up in strategic spots throughout San Francisco's North Beach and Haight-Ashbury districts, as well as at the university and in the Mission. To my amazement thirty-five people showed up for my first dance class, which consisted of Dunham Technique from Ruth Beckford, Afro-Cuban learned from Ed Mock, and modern dance and the little jazz I had learned from Nontsizi Cayou.

I was about to teach my first community dance class, and I was nervous as hell. Could I really teach what others had so painstakingly taught me? Could I make the dance material my own and let my own personality reveal itself through the warm-up exercises and dance routines? Could I actually create a flow from beginning to end and let people also have a good time in the process? These were the questions spinning though my head as I walked up the stone steps of Good Samaritan for my first, in retrospect, overly prepared dance class. I did everything: registered the students, collected the money for what was to be a one-month workshop, and set up my own record player to accompany my movements (audiocassettes were not on the market yet, let alone iPods). From the first plié through the across-the-floor progressions to the cool-down and the final "thank you for coming," my class did indeed flow. I could teach dance! No one had actually *taught* me how; dance pedagogy was not a part of the dance curriculum at that point. But something innate in me had emerged clearly that day during my first dance teaching experience. The smiles and hugs from my students afterward were validation enough that I could lead people though a movement experience with their bodies and make magic happen. My life's path was beginning to reveal itself. Although I was still not willing to say I would major in dance at S.F. State, I knew at that point that I wanted to be a professional dancer.

Meanwhile, on the heels of the Civil Rights (1964) and Voting Rights (1965) Acts, and the late 1960s Black Power movement (Stokely Carmichael had given his famous Black Power speech in October 1966 at UC Berkeley), we forged a Bay Area version of the Black Arts movement that helped redefine, for my baby-boomer generation, who black people were becoming. In 1966 a short-lived cultural venue, the Black House, was established in San Francisco with several Bay Area playwrights and poets like Ed Bullins, Marvin X, and Jimmy Garrett. East Coast nationally recognized artists Amiri Baraka (then known as LeRoi Jones), Sonia Sanchez, and saxophonist Joseph Jarman (later to become a member of the Art Ensemble of Chicago) arrived to connect with the West Coast artists. The Black House featured a revolutionary new black music and staged plays of the new militant persuasion. LeRoi Jones held community meetings to inculcate the new manifesto of the Black Arts movement that he and writer-theorist Larry Neal had developed on the East Coast. The basis of this manifesto, Neal said, was "radically opposed to any concept of the artist that alienates him from his community." He also proclaimed that the Black Arts movement "is the aesthetic and spiritual sister of the Black Power concept."[7]

To link the artistic and political wings of the movement, Jones also created a written "Communications Project," which was ostensibly an outline for how to implement the Black Arts movement within the larger project of what he called *building* black consciousness in the black community. The basic mandate of the document was to "clarify or agitate, reinterpret, or retell" the issues pertaining to the black community, including "What to do in case of riots." Jones's "Communications Project" was published in a special "Black Theatre" issue of the *Drama Review* in the summer of 1968. It is a comprehensive outline of all the areas that should be addressed to get the message out to the people, including newsletters, newspapers, comic books, and posters. Politically, it clearly stated the agenda should be "anti-Vietnam, anti-genocide, and economically starting neighborhood block associations, welfare recipients' organizations, and rent strikes." The cultural component is most important to me, and it included reeducation about black history, philosophy, and traditions that would be inculcated through drama, poetry, mixed media, music, and *dance*. Therefore, dance was viewed as a legitimate medium of *propaganda* to help change the consciousness of the black community. Most importantly, the Black House in San Francisco is mentioned and linked to the S.F. State Black Student Union.[8]

Hence, the cultural and aesthetic connection through the Black Arts movement of some of the major black artists and theorists on both coasts was an important occurrence, furthering the development of the aesthetic arm of the Black Power movement in the Bay Area. Ongiri notes the seminal importance of these black intellectuals of this time period:

Jones, Neal and other Black Arts practitioners and critics positioned social change and identity struggle at the center of an aesthetic agenda for an entire emergent African American literary tradition and intellectual class. Their demand to clarify the aesthetic dimensions of "Black Art" in relation to the political demand for the creation of discrete spaces in which to articulate that aesthetic shaped the way in which an entire generation of critics and practitioners would define their role within culture and society.[9]

My emphasis on dance and the arts as a valid vehicle for social change was being validated with the articulated philosophy of the Black Arts movement.

The Black House in San Francisco was one such "discrete space" to which Ongiri alludes, articulating the new black aesthetic. It featured protest theater with Ed Bullins's plays, such as *Dialect Determinism (or The Rally)* and *Clara's Ole Man*. There was also Marvin X's poetry often accompanied by avant-garde jazz music, a genre already established by recognized musicians like John Coltrane, Archie Shepp, Ornette Coleman, and Pharoah Sanders. A few times I performed dance improvisations, which had become my specialty in those days, to the revolutionary new music at the Black House. With my personal independence, free-spirited dance improvisation came easy to me. My spirit would give over to the music, and my body would establish a visual dialogue that carried me to new inner dimensions and inspired many of the musicians at the Black House with whom I collaborated.

But due to disunity in Bay Area black activism, the Black House was not destined for a long life. Ultimately a split between the so-called "revolutionary nationalists" and the "cultural nationalists" resulted in "Eldridge Cleaver and BPP [evicting] Marvin X, Bullins, and most of the other artists from the Black House in 1967, essentially eliminating it as an important Black Arts site."[10] The demise of the seminal, but short-lived, Black House in San Francisco was indicative of the revolutionary nationalists' belief that *culture* was not going to save black people, and Cleaver lead this camp in the Bay Area. Ironically enough, it was the cultural nationalists who were the most adamant about separation from whites and the need to focus on the African cultural past; the revolutionary nationalists were amenable to integration with whites and class-based arguments concerning world revolution. Obviously, there were many contradictions overlapping these categories; for example, Amiri Baraka, who was perceived to be in the cultural nationalist camp, was originally attached to his New York North Village bohemian community that was multiracial. In the Bay Area, the two community activist camps—black cultural enclaves versus crossracial coalitions—were equally potent and plagued by disunity.

Today, I am most interested in the social *performance* of these various cultural and political camps during the seminally transformative 1960s, and how the public *presentation* of these ideologies actually helped form the political camps. Scholars like art historian Craig Peariso emphasize the theatrics of the dramatized public displays of political character and divisional politics. He argues that groups and individuals like Eldridge Cleaver, the Youth International Party (Yippie), and the Gay Activists Alliance (GAA) "may in fact mark the emergence of a different approach to political dissent." He rightfully points out that their social and political activism was "understood as efforts to negotiate the challenges of present radical politics at a time when . . . the possibility of opposition appeared to have been historically foreclosed."[11] Indeed, one must remember that these late-1960s counterculture efforts, on the heels of the Civil Rights Act, were uncharted territory, and like actors in a drama, members were trying on different possible "roles" in newly developed organizations for resistive change. But, despite the inevitable in-fighting within 1960s revolutionary activities, the black political and cultural movement continued at various sites such as my S.F. State campus.

Dance Becomes My Revolutionary Expression

Dance was *my* tool of expression, and I used my growing creative movement style to make my own individual statements about my developing black consciousness. When I first entered S.F. State in 1965, I joined the Negro Student Association; within one year and before the infamous 1968 S.F. State Strike, that organization had morphed into the militant Black Student Union (BSU). The eventual student protests with the BSU at the center precipitated the academic field of ethnic studies when S.F. State started the country's first black studies department and eventually the School of Ethnic Studies (in which I would eventually go on to get my master's degree in the early 1990s).

Moreover, another component of the S.F. State revolutionary movement prompted the continuing honing of my abilities as a dance teacher: the Experimental College. As an appeasement to students' growing demand for a voice in their education, particularly for nontraditional classes, the Experimental College was created. This was an actual student-led bureaucracy funded by the Associated Students that accepted or rejected courses taught by students for other students and community members using university facilities. Many S.F. State students who were exploring the new hippie lifestyle, centered in San Francisco's Haight-Ashbury district (where I lived for part of my undergraduate years), could gain experience through experimental courses from macramé weaving to astrology. Even though they were noncredit courses, many students got their first experience teaching through the Experimental College, with class titles reflecting the times: "Witchcraft of the Middle Ages Made Practical," "Alchemy for the Whole Family," "Expanding Your Consciousness with Ken Kesey's Bus Rides," "Mao Tse-Tung's Red Book Interpreted for the D Student," "Protecting Yourself During Civil Disobedience," and *my* course, which I called "Primitive Jazz Dance."

"Primitive Jazz Dance" was an obviously naive appellation that alluded to my accumulated study in modern, jazz, and Afro-based dance forms available at the time.[12] In the late 1960s we were not yet sophisticated about the nuances of our own colonized language, and my 1967 dance class title illuminates my own complicity in belittling African-based dance forms in those early years even while I attempted to elevate the stature of black dance. This is the insidious nature of cultural hegemony: it is embedded in the deep structure of the language, representing the unconscious thought patterns that can often be more oppressive than overt racism. Like the searchlight gaze of Foucault's "panopticon," the "master's" assessment of the "slave" becomes internalized, remaining long after the master has physically been extricated.[13]

I wrote my course syllabus for "Primitive Jazz Dance" with class descriptions, goals, and objectives, and it was accepted. The class was held in the dance studio where I studied in my accredited dance classes in physical education. It was also the same room where the famous Alvin Ailey had taught after coming from New York the previous summer for a one-week residency to teach his Horton modern dance technique. I felt like I was teaching on hallowed ground, and I got Kenneth Nash, who was to become an internationally famous percussionist,[14] to be my drumming accompanist. By the time the semester started, I had forty students registered, two-thirds of whom were white.

The racial makeup of my class disturbed the leadership of the militant Black Student Union, to which I belonged. I was asked to meet with Jimmy Garrett, the BSU president, in the organization's office. When I arrived I naively thought he was going to tell me he wanted to take the class. Instead, the wispy chocolate-brown brother smiled and motioned for me to come closer to his corner of the large, open office. He started with, "I hear your dance class has a lot of students and is going really well." I knew it! He really wanted to make a connection between the BSU and my class; I knew I could bridge the gap between politics and the arts. He continued with, "I also understand you have over half 'honkies' in the class." Uh-oh, could there be a hitch to my enthusiasm? I didn't see "honkies"; I saw enthusiastic white folks who really wanted to learn dance from me. Then he lowered the hatchet: "Sister, as a member of the BSU, you should know that is counterrevolutionary. We need to teach our dance to our own kind, in order to wake up their sleeping consciousness." Then he finished, looking at me gravely: "I had a meeting with some of the leadership and we want you to eliminate this situation and we will help you recruit some more brothers and sisters, so you can teach a proper class. We want you to be successful."

I was so taken aback that at first I didn't know how to respond. I certainly was for the "good cause": I had stopped straightening my hair and gotten a short Afro, paid my BSU dues, and read Frantz Fanon's *The Wretched of the Earth*. But I'd be damned if I was going to be dictated to about who could and couldn't take my dance classes. My stubborn individualism came through loud and strong as I blurted out my rejoinder: *"Well, I really was wondering why more of the BSU members were not already taking my dance class. If you and other members were there it would change the percentage of blacks in the class, and the whites wouldn't dominate. That's another way of looking at it. And furthermore, there is no way I'm going to put supportive and enthusiastic students out of my class, whatever color they are. I want to stay a part of the BSU, but not if you think you can dictate to me the makeup of my class."*

Garrett had been trying to get a word in edgewise but couldn't, as I continued my defensive litany. After my tirade, the only thing he could say was, "Well, if you gonna play like that you go ahead, but you need to get your head together, Sister." I retorted: "My head is more together than you can imagine. I know what I'm doing and why I'm doing it. I would love to have more black students in my class; so if you want to help with that, I'd welcome it. You know when the classes are, and maybe I'll even see you there." With that, I walked out of the BSU office.

This encounter with Garrett became my first indication that dance, in its cultural and racial context, was not a benign art-for-art's-sake creative endeavor but was politically charged in the context of a radically changing American culture, where what was "black" and who defined it, and, more importantly, who was to be the consumers of this newly developing "black" culture, were going to be much-debated issues. At a 2016 screening of *Agents of Change* in San Francisco, a poignant film documentary on 1960s student activism and the S.F. State Strike,[15] Jimmy Garrett and I met again. I mentioned our 1967 encounter around my dance class, and he simply said, "Well, that's the way it was back then."

The Bay Area, in the late 1960s and early 1970s, became ground zero for social, political, and cultural activism for the country and, as I would realize later, the world. The Black Panther Party, the Black Arts movement, the San Francisco State Student Strike, the UC Berkeley Free Speech movement, the anti–Vietnam War movement, the Free Huey and Free Angela Davis protests, and the hippie drop-out-and-tune-in counterculture all converged into the tumultuous times that shaped my consciousness and the trajectory of my life.

On the black cultural front, an important local KQED public television series by Maya Angelou (1928–2014) emerged called *Blacks, Blues, Black!* This was a ten-part series of one-hour shows written and hosted by Dr. Angelou that examined the influence of African American culture on modern American society. It included Bay Area black dancers and actors, such as Danny Duncan and Blondell Breed (Mwanza Furaha) who were important to creating the local black arts scene. It also included African scholars and musicians, linking Africa with African America in poignant and entertainingly cultural ways. As Dr. Angelou was a practitioner of several performing arts, theater skits, children's games, singing, drumming, and dance were used to tell the story of the black American journey. This mainstream televised show was an example of the late 1960s representing a crucial shift in the consciousness and representation of black people in American society.

This was the sociopolitical context in which I developed my first sense of a black dance consciousness that has driven my career, first as a dancer-choreographer (1968–99), and arts producer and cultural activist (1977–94), which this memoir covers, and now a dance and popular culture scholar (1993–present), which will be the subject of a future memoir. Little did I know in the 1960s that my choice of dance (or did it choose me?) would become my platform to explore blackness in its political, racial, cultural, and postcolonial dimensions. Dance was also to serve as an international language, connecting me to future students, artists, and scholars in Spain, France, Holland, Denmark, Sweden, Mexico, Ghana, Nigeria, Togo,

Kenya, Malawi, Trinidad & Tobago, Jamaica, and, more recently, Brazil, in ways that I could never have imagined. The universality of dance and music allows a bridging of cultures in dynamic people-to-people ways far beyond the spoken language, physically and spiritually reaching out and connecting across all kinds of borders.

Leaving the San Francisco Bay Area

My international travels started in that fateful year of 1968, when it seemed like the United States was falling apart. After the assassinations of John F. Kennedy in 1963, Malcolm X in 1965, and Martin Luther King Jr. and Robert Kennedy in 1968, violence seemed to be the social (dis)order. The urban revolts of the "Long Hot Summer" of 1968 across the nation were the final dramatic political occurrences signaling me to leave the country. I wanted to experience who I was becoming in another social, political, and cultural context. After three years studying at S.F. State, dancing with Zack Thompson, and taking many college and community dance classes, I felt it was time to dance in another country. After all, the S.F. State Strike had actually started in the spring semester, becoming the precursor to the complete shutdown of the university in the fall 1968 semester, with no classes being held. Completing my fourth year and earning my bachelor's degree seemed an impossible task for the times. The combination of the national black call for "Burn, Baby, Burn," and the local chaos of the student campus rebellions, presaging a national crisis in higher education, triggered my acting upon a long-held desire to travel internationally. I wanted to get outside of the racially charged climate of the country. Like dancer Josephine Baker and writers Richard Wright and James Baldwin before me, I left the country to find out who I was as a human being outside of the definitions of race according to the United States of America.

At age twenty-one, in August 1968, I left San Francisco with my friend Deidre Montague and traveled by car across country to the East Coast, where we were to leave for Europe. My mother, Tenola, was fearful of my traveling abroad and urged me not to go. My biological father, Leroy, now living in Oakland, simply told me that I should do what I felt I needed to do. Arriving on the East Coast, Deidre and I first stopped in her hometown of Washington, D.C., to see her mother before going on to New York. The only thing that I remember about that first time in D.C. was that one day while I was walking down the street, a black man yelled out of his car, "Girl, why don't you straighten your hair?" Wearing a short natural Afro hairdo in 1968 was not the norm, and I was already getting a sense of the difference between the "progressive" West Coast and the older "conservative" East Coast, particularly Washington, D.C., which bordered the southern states of Maryland and Virginia. From there we went to New York City for what we first thought would be an immediate flight to Spain. But as this was my first time in New York, I could not pass up the chance to study with some of the icons of dance in the cultural capital of my art form.

I spent September dancing in New York with Haitian dance legend Jean-León Destiné (1918–2013) and Nigerian drummer/teacher Babatunde Olatunji (1927–2003). Destiné taught at the famous New Dance Group Studio, which was founded in 1932 by leftist artists with the philosophical motto, "Dance is a Weapon of the Class Struggle."[16] With their Depression-era political awareness, the New Dance Group always included black dancers among their teachers and students like dancers Pearl Primus and Donald McKayle; therefore, it was not a surprise to find Destiné teaching at this particular studio. I took several Haitian dance classes with him, excited to have my first "authentic" class directly with a Haitian who had also performed in the Katherine Dunham Dance Company. Mr. Destiné could detect my seriousness and was kind enough to take me to dinner after class one evening to encourage me to pursue dance as a career. At dinner that evening, he advised me to get the most out of my European trip and gave me some of his European dance contacts. We maintained our mentor-student relationship over the years, and I took his classes every time I went to New York.

The experience with Baba Olatunji was my initiation into the *spiritual* dimensions of dance for the first time. Olatunji had migrated to the United States in 1950, enrolling as an undergraduate at the historically black Morehouse College in Atlanta. He became the first African drummer to garner a major recording contract with Columbia Records in 1959 with his *Drums of Passion* album, and therefore the first to popularize West African drumming in the United States. In 1968 he had his own dance and music school in Harlem, and I went there to take an African class. I don't remember the name of the dance teacher; but I do remember that halfway through the class Baba Olatunji himself came in to drum. As the ending crescendo of class each student was called in front of his drum to improvise. I found myself responding to Olatunji's drums in a way that I had never done before. I wrote in my newly started personal journal:

The sound reached out like a cool breeze and blew me along with it to other dimensions—into a beautiful garden where it was just the drums and me—to where it was just the music and dance; it was warm, it was glowing; it was everything.

Babatunde Olatunji allowed me to experience the spirit embedded in the dance, not just the bodily execution and the mental associations, but the *soul* of dance. I would have these spirit experiences at other points in my love affair with dance, but that this was my *first* time seemed destined to happen before I left my place of birth for places yet unknown.

Our plan to take a plane to Spain was abandoned when we found out we could take a Yugoslavian freighter, accommodating fifty passengers, to any Mediterranean destination from Algeciras to Barcelona for two hundred dollars, leaving October 10. Having only about one thousand dollars (remember, this is 1968), this price fit within the budget, leaving enough for a few months of travel before I had to figure out exactly what I was going to do to survive financially. One must remember this was a period when the free hippie spirit within U.S. culture, the center of which I had just left in San Francisco's Haight-Ashbury district, was influencing the entire world. Onboard the ship we immediately met young Americans striking out for a travel adventure like Deidre and I were, and we quickly found out that there was a "hippie network" between Morocco and Spain that followed a hashish drug and "love" trail. As long as we met like-minded people on this trail, we would be able to survive. This was the "turn on, tune in, and drop out" era when 1960s youth culture was on the ascendancy, and we recognized each other. I wore short, above-the-knee African wraps, had read all of the Eastern-oriented Hermann Hesse books, and smoked hash and keif, if marijuana was not available—I was a black hippie.

Deidre and I met two young women on board the ship, one of whom was going to visit her sister, who was the girlfriend of a wealthy trader in Tangier, Morocco, the first Mediterranean stop for the ship. Landing in Tangier on October 20, we decided to accept our new friend's invitation to stay at trader Bashir's home for a few days. For me, this was a chance to actually set foot on African soil, to get a sense of the continent; it was the northern part above the Sahara, but it was still Africa. We would stay for a few days and then take a local ferry across the Bay of Gibraltar from Tangier to Algeciras, Spain. The sight of all the brown-skinned people in turbans and robes in the bustling commercial tourist port city of Tangier was fascinating as our first cultural experience outside the United States. The sound of the *muezzin* from the mosques calling the Muslim faithful to prayer several times a day, and the brown women in their body-covering *djellabas* peering through the open slits in their veils romantically felt like the call of Africa. At age twenty-one, this place was too hard to resist for young adventurous African American women testing our wings for the first time.

We ended up staying in Tangier, exploring the intricate cobblestone streets of the Medina (Old Town), for ten days before moving on to the interior of Morocco, to the city of Marrakech, and then even farther south to Goulimine, the first oasis on the Sahara. The Moroccans were fascinated to see brown-skinned women with wooly hair who were Americans; this was incongruent to them in the late 1960s. In Marrakech we stayed at a four-dirham-per-day pension where we met other hippies and explored the famous large Djemaa el-Fna marketplace, where snake charmers, storytellers, fire-eaters, exotic-spice sellers, and the Ganowan dancers (Senegalese people who had migrated up to Francophone North Africa) all performed and attracted huge crowds.

The all-male Ganowan Senegalese dancers were permanently integrated into Moroccan culture and were expert dancers and drummers. The dancers used large metal castanet-like hand instruments to accent their rhythmic movements with the drums. At the peak of the dance they performed many leg kicks while in a squatting position, similar to Ukrainian Cossack Hopak dancing. At one point in the Ganowan performance, a very dark elder dressed in red who had been playing a string instrument got up and danced in front of Deidre and me, ending in a slight bow to us. This was my first recognition of sub-Saharan black Africa, and I realized why we were meant to start our journey on the continent. The next day, when we ventured into the marketplace again, I went to the dancing elder and shook his hand; he said a few words that I could not understand, but we had a moment of recognition beyond language that is still with me; Africa was calling.

By November 8 we arrived in Goulimine, a small oasis town at the southern tip of Morocco before Mauritania. Goulimine, one of the last Moroccan towns with a weekly camel market, was known as the gateway to the desert—the great Sahara. In 1968 Goulimine was not catering to tourism and therefore had few native hustlers, limiting the hassles we usually received as Americans. The Moroccan people of this region are very different because they are a part of the Tuareg "blue people," so called because of the indigo blue dye in their draped cloth that actually penetrates into their skin, giving it a bluish tint. I was drawn to this small town because of the famous Dance of Guedra, a well-publicized women's ritual. Today the dance is done only for tourists because of dwindling camel herds that used to be the center of the weekly festival where the dance was performed.

I enjoyed the slower pace of Goulimine and was able to participate in another women's ritual: the painting of the hands with henna. Henna hand painting is a traditional beautifying craft that transforms the hands or feet into intricate jewelry-like artwork. Goulimine women were less guarded with their faces uncovered, and along with the more relaxed pace of both sexes, the town was a pleasant experience. Deidre and I ended up spending ten days in Goulimine.

After almost one month in Morocco, I began to experience myself differently regarding race. I recorded this new self-perception in my journal:

> Here in Morocco, and especially in Goulimine, I am aware of my brown color in the sense that I am the same color as most of the people and they recognize this too. Yet, I don't feel any of the same "racial" vibrations when I go out. Here I am a human being first, and everyone treats me as such. The only time the old feeling of being guarded as a black person comes is when white American or European tourists come in droves, like unwanted locusts into my new environment.

I began to feel myself relaxing into my own skin in a new way. This is the experience of most black people outside the United States, particularly in a nonwhite country. This is a feeling we can rarely have in the United States.

On one of our last days in Goulimine, we got the thrill of the Moroccan trip: the Dance of Guedra was enacted at an evening festival. I had already done some research on the dance and had bought tourist postcards of the women performing the dance. The dancing women that night looked just like the postcard image: they wore the indigo cloth that draped the entire body but the face, and were adorned with their intricate headdresses and lots of jewelry. Guedra is done as a ritualistic trance dance to the Guedra drum, with handclapping and chants by the participating community that surround the dancers in a circle. A soloist or group of women in the kneeling position, with rhythmically undulating torsos and intricate hennaed-hand and finger gestures, dances Guedra. As the dancers move in this kneeling position, they can perform back bends with shoulders touching the ground behind them as they continue the uninterrupted rhythmic undulation and swaying movements. The women often close their eyes as they move to the trance of the drums and chants, invoking a very esoteric atmosphere among the entire community. I was witnessing dance in its spiritual dimensions that seemed to transform not only the dancers but also the entire community.

The Dance of Guedra created the sense of an ancient ritual that narrates a story of the four directions and their universal principles. I also got the feeling that it might be the precursor of what we know as Middle Eastern belly dance today. It was an honor to witness this special dance in its cultural context in the late 1960s before many tourists had "invaded" Goulimine. I found out later that Katherine Dunham brought the Royal Troupe of Morocco to New York to perform in one of her last Broadway concerts, *Bambooche!,* at New York's 54th Street Theater in 1962, and I wondered whether the Dance of Guedra was included in the performance. Always looking for cultural connections in the African diaspora, little had I known that four years before my trip to Morocco, Dunham had included Moroccan dance in one of her last shows before her company disbanded. Morocco became my introduction to Africa long before I would actually journey south of the Sahara.

I spent my twenty-second birthday on a rainy day back in Tangier, on the eve of finally crossing from Africa to Europe. My state of mind was reflective, examining exactly what I was doing. I might have been bold as a young black woman buying a one-way international ticket to see the world, but I also had my doubts. I mentally explored my uncertainties and eventually arrived at trusting my personal choices and the journey that I had carved out for myself. The next day Deidre and I finally crossed over into Spain and the beginning of my circuitous route to a dance career in Europe that would last two years.

2

Dancing in Europe

Intangible dreams of people have a tangible effect
on the world.

JAMES BALDWIN

There has been a long historical trajectory of African American expatriates in Europe who leave not only to escape U.S. racial codes but also to escape the psychological aspects of racialization itself—to experience a sense of just being human. They may have been able to achieve the former, but the latter is questionable, as Europe offers its own racial and ethnic stereotypes that underpin its societies. In the nineteenth century, Frederick Douglass had to go to Europe to become completely free from his slave status, by having British friends buy his legal freedom after living in the North as a runaway. It was on his 1846 trip to England that "British supporters led by Ellen Richardson of Newcastle upon Tyne raised funds to buy his freedom from his American owner Thomas Auld."[1] Painter Henry O. Tanner was another nineteenth-century expatriate who went to Paris and died there, and whose works of art in 1896 were accepted into the Salon of the Académie des Beaux-Arts. In the twentieth century, artists Augusta Savage and Lois Mailou Jones; authors Chester Himes, Claude McKay, Langston Hughes, and Richard Wright; musicians Charlie Parker, Dexter Gordon, Nina Simone, and Paul Robeson; dancers Katherine Dunham, Talley Beatty, Vanoye Aikens, and Eartha Kitt all had European expatriate artistic periods in which they sought to escape from the strictures of American racism.

France in particular attracted several expatriate black Americans, such as Josephine Baker, James Baldwin, Nina Simone, and others. The French had been able to negotiate between its image as an open society for its African and Caribbean colonial subjects and the reality of its implicit racism. But, as Bennetta Jules-Rosette illuminates, France's projected image was enough for beleaguered African Americans:

> The image of a colorblind France of liberty and equality had intrigued African American artists and expatriates who settled in France between the 1920s and the 1950s. Ignoring the plight of the Senegalese soldiers and the rising North African and Antillean populations migrating to France during the interwar years, African Americans sought new freedom in a society that was not, in their terms, overtly segregated.[2]

James Baldwin's expatriate story is particularly famous. He published his first novel, *Go Tell It on the Mountain*, in 1953 in Europe, which explored black urban life from a black perspective, a work he could write only from the distance of Europe. But in his essay "Discovery of What It Means to Be an American" (1961), he admits that "Europe itself is not the ultimate utopia for black American writers seeking out their identity, but states that this power was always his to manage." Baldwin "does manage to reinvent himself in Europe and emerge unconstrained from the view of his native country; yet the irony in his essay concludes with the continent that gave him freedom, was [also] the continent [where] the slave trade and the initial concepts of race originated."[3] James Baldwin, after many celebrated books, essays, and plays, as well as becoming an important participant in the U.S. Civil Rights movement, eventually settled in Saint-Paul de Vence in the south of France, where he died in 1987.

I, too, found this European paradox during my two-year Scandinavian sojourn, where I was allowed a certain amount of individuality, which could turn just as quickly into a stereotypical representation of blackness. Yet Europeans' mythic gaze toward me was more controllable because of their obvious recognition of my particular personal distinctiveness. Europe is able to distance itself from the inhumanity of the racialization process because its colonial subjects were contained within their own wretched national circumstances and not enslaved on European soil. Yet, as the actual originators of racial difference and the idea of the Global South, they are forever implicated in historic colonial injustice, sociopolitically and psychologically.

The other famous African American expatriate story is that of Josephine Baker, who became so synonymous with Paris that she has a street named after her. She found an acceptance and celebrity in France when she arrived with La Revue Négre in 1925 that she never could have achieved in the segregated United States. Broadway had "discovered" the profitable venture of black musicals that went beyond the minstrel image, first with *Shuffle Along* in 1921 with music by the famous Eubie Blake, lyrics by Noble Sissle, and book by Flournoy Miller and Aubrey Lyles. The Jazz Age ushered in a series of all-black Broadway musicals, with the vitality of black dance and music previously relegated to black communities and the growing "Chitlin' Circuit." The American mainstream and Europeans were being exposed to black culture that had more group agency. Josephine Baker, a young performer from a poor community in East St. Louis (where Katherine Dunham would bring professional dance sixty years later), had worked her way into the chorus line of *Shuffle Along*, which became her entry into international fame.

Despite her perceived skinny physique, Baker's theatricality was responsible for her popularity and eventual chance to travel to Paris with an assembled new show known as La Revue Négre: "Baker's ticket to Paris came from Caroline Dudley Reagan, a young society woman who wanted to stage a black revue, such as *Shuffle Along*, *Runnin' Wild*, or *Chocolate Dandies*, in Paris. Reagan wanted to show Parisians 'real' Negro music and dance."[4] As Baker grew in fame during her early years as an exotic dancer and later into a black French icon, her performances "were based on appropriating and manipulating racialized gender stereotypes in her *danse sauvage* and glamour images."[5] This was the reality even as she utilized improvisations on real African American social dances like the Charleston, and the French became avid consumers of this exotic Africanist female lure. As I have said elsewhere:

French fascination with African and African American cultures is evidenced by the inspiration that French Cubist painters [like Matisse and Picasso] found in colonial France's stolen African art, as well as the Josephine Baker phenomenon in Paris of the twenties and thirties. Viewing French culture from this perspective, by the end of the 20th century [and now the twenty-first century] hip-hop becomes a part of a historic continuum of France's involvement with black cultural production.[6]

Therefore, before French appropriation of hip-hop culture today, Josephine Baker, as a real human being with aspirations for her life and career, played into European perceptions of so-called African "primitivism" through her performance. Baker's black female body came to symbolize France's racial imaginary, even as the country embraced her unique individual contributions to their country. The perception of me as a black woman in Europe, forty years later, was mitigated by my choice of a different route than commercial dance and theater, but not enough to escape European historic perception of blackness. Because of the racialized and gendered aspects of Baker's and my own European experiences, a brief exploration of these aspects of European engagement with the black female body is warranted.

Europe, the Baartman Phenomenon, and the Black Female Dancing Body

The contested terrain of the black female body and the ambivalent European gaze was brought into sharp relief in the early nineteenth century with the case of Saartjie (Sarah) Baartman, dubbed the Hottentot Venus. At twenty-one years old, the young Khoisan South African woman from the Cape Town region, tricked into going to England for lucrative employment in 1810, was put on circus-like exhibition in London and Paris as the exotic Other. Europeans' preoccupation with Saartjie Baartman's ample buttocks, as she was displayed for a fee on a pedestal for all to view from different angles, served as a particularly blatant example of white ambivalence toward the black female body. She became the object of horrendous scientific and medical research that formed the foundation of European conceptualization of African female sexuality.

It was Baartman's buttocks, in fact, that influenced the fashionable mid-nineteenth-century European female bustle. This racialized fashion embodied a "highly idealized representation of female sexual identity, at once exaggerated and concealed by the structures of adornment."[7] As evidenced by the personal exploitation and abusive popular-culture references to her body, as well as her adoption as a muse by several "serious" artists, Saartjie Baartman—the Hottentot Venus—became the symbol of European neurosis about the black female body.

How has the nineteenth-century approach-avoidance Baartman phenomenon translated into the twentieth and twenty-first centuries' dance
and everyday life? Gottschild writes, "In this savage-versus-cultivated dia-
lectic the buttocks symbolize the historical dichotomy between Africanist
and Europeanist aesthetic principles."[8] Africanist dance aesthetics privilege
a democracy of body parts, with the divisions of the torso—head, shoulders, rib cage, pelvis, and buttocks—having their own individual sphere
to reflect and interact with musical rhythm. Antithetically, the Europeanist approach to the body and dance privileges a "straight, uninflected torso"
that "indicates elegance or royalty and acts as the absolute monarch, domi-
nating the dancing body."[9] African dancing was seen by early Europeans on
the continent as obscene and unruly, and therefore it had to be controlled.
Yet, this attempted cultural management lasted only through the Victorian
Age in the United States, becoming utterly defeated by the 1920s Jazz Age,
when young white Charleston dancers relaxed their torso, bent their backs,
protruded their behinds, and danced intoxicating polyrhythmic movements to the new ragtime sound that was evolving out of New Orleans and
other southern cities and invading the whole country. It is at this moment
in the historical trajectory of black dance that Josephine Baker entered the
European scene.

As African Americans of the 1950s and 1960s began entering the studios of modern dance and ballet en masse, a new ambivalence developed.
We had to oscillate between the particularized black dance classes and the
white modern dance and ballet studios. New York choreographer Jawole
Willa Jo Zollar, artistic director of the all-black female Urban Bush Women
company, choreographed a 1995 dance about the black female butt called
Batty Moves and captured the often schizophrenic nature of black dancers entering the larger dance world. Before her dancers take the stage with
their ample behinds, she begins the piece standing downstage at a micro-
phone, heuristically telling her personal story about studying dance in a bi-
furcated world of black and white dance styles:

I wanted to create *Batty Moves* because I had started to get con-
fused. I started out dancing as a young child, having fun, and then I
went to college and started studying modern dance and ballet and
I started kinda holdin' and pushin' and tuckin'. Then I'd go over to
the African dance class and party and be all loose an' movin', and I'd
go to my classes over here and I'd be holding, pushin' and tuckin'

[demonstrating tucking the buttock under] and apologizing and everything, and I'd go back over here and be movin' it, and I just decided I needed to find a way to bring both traditions together.[10]

As Zollar paints this vivid verbal picture, she dramatizes by establishing a part of the stage for the African dance experience and another for the European ballet classes, and as she moves back and forth between the two spaces, one physically, mentally, and emotionally sympathizes with her exhaustion.

This opening scene of *Batty Moves* not only personalizes the ambivalence within which many black dancers have been caught but also simultaneously illustrates the hierarchy of the dance world that a young black dancer, even today, is often forced to endure in order to become a concert performer. Zollar's *Batty Moves* proceeds to celebrate the black behind ("batty" is Jamaican Patois for butt) through choreography that blends African, modern, and Brazilian capoeira to live drumming. One section of the piece has the six-member ensemble standing in a line with their backs to the audience dancing to various rhythms of the drums, with sweaters tied around their waists and hanging over their butts to accent that body part. It becomes an audacious celebration of the black behind through dance. Dance scholar Ananya Chatterjea rightly notes: "However, *Batty Moves* is much more than a comment of sensuality and sexuality. It is also a strong statement about the politics of aesthetic preference."[11] The political choice that Zollar has made is clear: she represents *all* of her dance training to celebrate the black aesthetic in a world that denigrates, while being attracted to, those same movement values, as well as the bodies that continue to produce them.

Although I could not articulate this history or its sociocultural implication for my black dancing body as I entered the European dance scene in 1968, I did intuit much of it. When I crossed over into Spain from Morocco, I would experience some of these dynamics from southern Spain up to Scandinavia over the next two years.

Traveling through Spain to Barcelona

After spending a day in Algeciras, Deidre and I took a train to Málaga (the birthplace of Pablo Picasso) in the Andalusia region of southern Spain, which shares a strong history with North Africa via the Moors. The train excursion revealed beautiful, changing winter scenery, which I was unused to, having grown up in the Bay Area with evergreens and the lack of real seasons. The last of the bright yellow and red leaves were falling, and the winter landscape was captivating. The Mediterranean coast was breathtaking with aqua-blue beaches, but even back then it was dotted with new seaside *nouveau riche* communities being erected along the coast.

After only a couple of days in Málaga, we went to the mountain city of Grenada, with its whitewashed houses built right into the side of the mountains. It was fascinating to see majestic cliffs with carved-out entrances to homes and businesses. Granada had even more Arabic influences with majestic architecture, such as the famous Alhambra citadel and palace built by the Moors.

One night we went to the Sacramonte area of the city in the hills with the cliff dwellings. Instead of a tourist group excursion, we took a city bus up to Sacramonte because Deidre and I wanted to see some flamenco dance on our own. When we got there, it was fairly dark with few streetlights; the nightclubs hadn't yet opened for the tourist business that came to Sacramonte every night with busloads of international travelers to experience Spain's gypsy culture. As we strolled down a dark cobblestone street, a slim man in a hat pulled down over one eye approached us and simply gestured for us to come with him. Although we thought twice about the invitation, we decided to trust him because, after all, we had come for an adventure.

He led us to a nightclub that was carved into the mountain with a whitewashed entrance, electricity, and a bar set up like any nightclub. A gathering of about twenty people, who were obviously friends, were casually drinking and chatting. Deidre and I sat down and tried to be as inconspicuous as possible. Then a guitarist started a haunting rhythmic melody, and the seated people started clapping a syncopated beat and rhythmically stomping their feet to keep time. The man who had led us to the location got up and started dancing in an intense rhythmic, proud manner, hesitating occasionally in one spot to join the intricate hand clapping of the community, while a song from the guitarist entered the musical mix. Then a sturdily built woman in her forties took the floor, with her protruding hips, fast-paced feet, and elegant arm gestures. She took us to another realm where rhythm, movement, and song blended into a great crescendo. The gathered Spanish gypsies sang, whistled, and clapped, developing an atmosphere of community just as we had experienced with the kneeling Dance of Guedra in Morocco (chapter 1). We later found out that the dance of the man and woman is a particular brand of flamenco in Andalusia called the Zambra Gitana, which has strong Middle Eastern origins. That night our gypsy friends dubbed us the *Gitana Morenas* (Brown Gypsies). From Morocco to Spain, dance was allowing us to witness the overlapping of ancient cultures between Muslim Arabs and Christian Spanish.

Later, when the tourist bus arrived and the people started pouring into the cave bar, we witnessed the difference between indigenous culture and tourist performance. The show that emerged for the tourists by the same dancers and musicians was simply a rote execution of the dance and music that we had just witnessed before the visitors arrived. The same dance, rhythm, and song were performed, but the passion, intensity, and commitment were definitely absent. What evolved before our eyes was the collective agency in which indigenous people, all over world, engage when their culture becomes spectacle for outsiders. The Grenada gypsies gave just enough of themselves to please the tourists but withheld the heart of their culture for themselves, which we had just intensely felt in the preshow gathering. Indigenous peoples enact collective agency when their culture is cultivated for display, and resistance becomes the *withholding* of the soul behind the dance and music.

From Grenada, Deidre and I headed to Alicante, where we got a boat to the Spanish island of Ibiza. This island was a part of the hippie circuit that young Americans were following in 1968, and we went along for the ride. We arrived on December 4 in time to spend Christmas on the island. Deidre had a New York friend on Ibiza named Ira, a tall black man with a patch over one eye who had become "king" among the hippies on the island. When he told everyone that we were his "sisters," we garnered a particular prestige among the pot-smoking hippie community living on Ibiza. These young and mostly white people, with their rebellious Western behavior, lived side by side with the conservative indigenous Ibisicans, with their strict Catholic religion and women who wore mostly black dresses, complete with their famous black wool blankets. They always seemed as if they were in mourning for the crucifixion of Christ.

Ibiza is a part of the Balearic Islands that also include the islands of Minorca, Formentera, and Majorca, the largest of the islands. These islands actually became an autonomous region of Spain in 1983 and have increasingly become big tourist destinations for the rest of Europe and the United States. When I was there in 1968, hippies from all over the world had invaded Ibiza in particular, and I spent a month and a half there, traveling to Majorca once. Dance was not a part of that experience, but much weed smoking and hanging out with my freewheeling newfound "friends" rebelling against their parents' culture was. Deidre hooked up with Ira and decided to go off traveling with him to parts unknown, leaving me to fend for myself. As my money was fast running out and I was now alone, I took a ship from Ibiza to Barcelona to continue my dance quest and to try to find a job with my artistic skills.

I arrived in Barcelona on January 16, 1969, and immediately settled into my first experience of a vibrant, fast-paced Spanish city that offered a lot of urban stimuli. I found a small room in a pension near the famous Plaça Reial (Royal Plaza), a famous square in Barcelona with Gothic architecture that has become a big attraction. As a tourist, I became enthralled with the Spanish churches, apartment buildings, parks, and other structures of Catalonian architect Antonio Gaudí, who had a strong sense of nature in his architectural design.

But my main task was to find a dance job as quickly as possible. In many ways I felt like I was back in the States because black music pervaded the radio airwaves and public spaces. I wrote in my journal:

Urban Spanish people seem to love black people—our looks, spirit, soul, and vibrations. They're all trying to imitate soul music. That's all you hear on the radio, television, and discotheques—sounds by James Brown, Otis Redding, Aretha Franklin. It's amazing! I walk down the streets receiving all these stares, thrown kisses from the men, and general comments about me, and I take it all in!

I knew I could use this Spanish fascination with blackness in my pursuit of a dance job, and I did. I found out which was the largest and most lavish Barcelona "discotheque," the name for a dance club in the 1960s. I wore my best miniskirt, boots, and a tight-fitting top over my skinny 125-pound frame and went to the club one day to talk to the club manager. At that time "go-go girls" were hired to dance on platforms in discotheques to inspire the patrons to dance and, of course, to buy drinks. I knew that my calling card was my blackness—what I call the Josephine Baker Syndrome—and that alone could get me a meeting with someone with the authority to hire me as a dancer.

As soon as I walked into the club, all eyes were on me, and I asked for the manager in the "Spanglish" that I was developing to communicate in

Spain. The front doorman fell all over himself summoning a person who could take me to a back office for the meeting. I told the discotheque manager: "I'm a black American professional dancer who is living in Barcelona, and I want to dance for you with my own music. I will give you a show three times a night for a fee." I had brought a cassette tape of music— Earth, Wind & Fire, Stevie Wonder, Aretha Franklin, The 5th Dimension, etc.—with me from the United States just for this purpose. The Barcelona discotheque manager looked at me incredulously, but I knew I represented dollar signs to him because through me he had in the flesh the "authentic" pop culture he was selling. He immediately asked me what I would charge. I gave him what I knew was a high salary, and he quickly said "Yes" with one stipulation: I could not tell the Spanish go-go dancers in the club what he would pay me because my salary would be twice as much as they were receiving. I agreed, accepting my first European job, with blackness as my selling point.

My Barcelona discotheque job quickly became a routine with my three dance shows a night. On most days, I would arrive back at my pension room at 4:30 a.m. and sleep until 2:00 p.m. Although dancing in a commercial setting, I imagined I was on a concert stage doing what I did best: improvising to music that I love. The deejay would put on the tape that I provided (all the other girls danced to whatever he decided to play), and I would go into my own world on my dance platform. I noticed that the discotheque patrons all stopped talking and drinking when I danced, fascinated that they were being treated to a black American female dancer who obviously was dancing to her own music in her own cultural style. I was experiencing what I call the Josephine Baker Syndrome in Spain. The respect that I engendered among the Spanish patrons in this context of an alcohol-centered commercial environment was an experience that I am sure Josephine Baker must have felt some forty years earlier in France. Racialized and gendered perceptions of blackness and femaleness were at the core of both of our lived experiences, separated only by time and era. Although it felt positive in this particular experience, I was aware that there was a range of possible audience reactions within this commercial entertainment arena, and I would certainly go on to experience that range in various dance experiences during my expatriate European sojourn.

Moving through Paris and Amsterdam to Copenhagen

Four months in Barcelona allowed me to save enough money to move farther northward, looking for where I could actually settle and build my *concert* dance career. The train system in Europe allows for easy access between countries, like Amtrak in the United States moving between states. By late May 1969 I left Barcelona and decided to check out Paris, the supposed capital of "black Europe." However, I found the French to be extremely arrogant and not nearly as warm as the people I had encountered in Morocco or Spain. Although I had studied French during my three years at S.F. State, my French was not fluent, and Parisians were extremely impatient with my slow, stumbling attempts at their language. My only positive experience was taking a dance class at the American Center France in Paris, known today on its website as "The Hub of Franco-American Exchange." In 1969 a French West African female dancer was giving an African dance class, to which I rushed: I ended up taking three of her classes. Although I cannot remember the teacher's name and style, I do recall finding her classes to be like a "home" that I could not find anywhere else in Paris. I stayed in the city for two weeks and then moved on to Amsterdam, where the hippie circuit was alive and well.

Arriving in Amsterdam in June 1969 was a completely different story. I loved the seventeenth-century architecture facing the canals and bridges running throughout the city and found the Dutch to be much friendlier than the French. The name of the most populous of the Netherland cities is derived from a Dutch word meaning "a dam for the Amstel River." Historically, the Dutch were known for harboring Jews fleeing Nazi Germany, and the house on Prinsengracht Street where Anne Frank and her family hid is now a national museum that I visited. There was much to see, including Amsterdam's famous red-light district, the Rossebuurt, where prostitution is legal, and female sex workers sit in the red-fringed windows of small houses like moving mannequins for all to see and buy. This street and the government-regulated sex work has become a tourist industry with organized bus tours that come with Amsterdam hotel rentals, representing the Netherlands' cultural attitude about regulating controversial, but inevitable, cultural practices like prostitution.

In the late 1960s, another cultural inevitability was the international hippie movement with its rock and pop music and drugs. The government of

Holland recognized the 1960s cultural *zeitgeist*, and instead of banning pot like the United States and other European countries like Germany, decided to regulate soft drug use by sanctioning specific public sites where it could legally take place. I had recently left San Francisco, a center of "hippiedom" with venues like the Fillmore Auditorium ("The Fillmore") that held rock concerts with Jimi Hendrix, Janis Joplin, and Big Brother and the Holding Company. Young people openly smoked pot and stared wide-eyed at performers after dropping LSD pills. Therefore, it became a déjà vu experience finding an entire city that was participating in this American youth culture to the extent that Amsterdam was.

My favorite activity was sitting in outdoor cafés in Leidseplein Square near Amsterdam's canal ring by day, and finding out about what hippie music group was performing that night at one of the drug-sanctioned clubs. I heard that three months earlier, in March 1969, the newlyweds John Lennon and Yoko Ono had come to Amsterdam to stage a "Bed-in for Peace." Instead of taking a usual honeymoon, they had invited the global press into their room at the Amsterdam Hilton to discuss world peace for twelve hours every day.[12] I witnessed that the youth culture in which I had participated back home had become a world phenomenon. This alternative youth culture was partially the reason why I was able to survive for more than six months in Morocco, Ibiza, Spain, and now Amsterdam.

Connecting to my hippie youth culture yielded several new personal relationships. I met black Surinamese artists living in Holland (their colonial mother country), white Dutch hippies, and other Europeans enjoying the freer Netherlandish lifestyle. Sonja, a very sensitive Dutch girl, became one of my best friends and took me into the inner circle of much of Dutch culture. Peter Lundstrøm, from Denmark, became a friend and lover, a very down-to-earth guy in his late twenties who was sensitive and respectful. He would later become my contact when I moved on to Copenhagen, which would figure prominently in my European dance career. I met an American photographer who became interested in me as a fashion model, and I did several paid fashion photo sessions that helped me to survive financially.

However, even in this freer cultural environment, I was ever-aware of my blackness, which set me apart and engendered many different reactions to me as an individual. Mostly I was aware that Europeans, as well as blacks living in Europe, were not used to black women who had a sense of individual public freedom as I did. I wrote in my journal:

Being a black woman is a complex thing because we have such a difficult position in the grand scheme of things. People are not used to seeing a "free" black woman. If they're white maybe they never even noticed that black women really existed. If they're black themselves, they're amazed and astounded, and expect to automatically "get into something" with you. Neither group realizes that you are an individual with your own inner self and experiences that don't necessarily make you compatible with them. But, in some way they're looking to drain you—fuck you—physically or mentally. Rather than simply flow with you, they want to conquer you somehow. Each person puts a different mask on me, or tries to make me into his/her own image. This I can't use; this I must be careful of; this I must guard against.

In the late 1960s, crime was not as it is today, and I was relatively safe as a lone woman traveling in foreign countries. But having this sense of how I was being perceived as a *black* woman by the majority of people with whom I was coming in contact in Europe saved me many times from compromising positions at best, and abuse at worse. The Amsterdam sojourn lasted only six weeks, and I began making preparations to move on to Copenhagen, Denmark, where I intended to really begin a creative dance career by any means necessary.

I arrived in Denmark on July 14, 1969, ten months after leaving San Francisco. Although I enjoyed the taking-it-one-day-at-a-time adventure I had been on until that point, I began to feel the need to be settled again and to restart my career in Europe. Peter Lundstrøm had given me the address and phone number of his mother to contact in Copenhagen, and I did. I had very little money, as usual, and desperately needed the kindness of strangers. I found Mrs. Lundstrøm to be very kind and generous; she offered me a place to stay for a few weeks, as a friend to her son, until I could find my own place and establish myself. Her daughter Ulla and Ulla's boyfriend, Bjørn, quickly became my friends, showing me the sights of Copenhagen.

One night Ulla, Bjørn, and I went to see Odetta (1930–2008), the noted African American folk singer, at one of Copenhagen's premier venues, Tivoli Gardens. She was a godsend, allowing me to reconnect to black culture in a way that I needed by that point. Odetta put on a two-and-a-half-hour show, filling the audience with warmth and intimacy that transported me back to the United States, allowing me to hear and feel the joy and pain of my people again. After her performance, the three of us went backstage to her dressing room, and I got a chance to meet her. I wrote in my journal: *We looked at each other and our eyes danced. We kissed, and we both felt like we knew each other.* One line from a song she sang that night was, "If anybody asks you, we're the Children of God." That is the feeling with which Odetta left me that night in Copenhagen, propelling me onward.

Another black artist's concert in Copenhagen that I enjoyed was South African jazz pianist Abdullah Ibrahim (then called Dollar Brand).[13] I went to see him at the famous Montmartre Jazzhus on Store Regnegade Street, which booked world-class jazz artists.[14] As I was already schooled on different genres of jazz music during my college years by different men I had dated, I was ready for Ibrahim's particular style of jazz piano that reflected not only Thelonious Monk and Duke Ellington but his own South African influences from Cape Town. I heard gospel, as well as occasional East Indian sounds that had become prominent in the San Francisco hippie movement but also were a part of the cultural mix of South Africa. Ibrahim's jazz music reminded me of my focus in dance improvisation and the inner places that it took me. His music also reminded me of being technically grounded while having the inner freedom to trust where the movement/music takes one. Hearing Abdullah Ibrahim that night in Copenhagen reminded me of what I came to Europe for: to really dance my own dance. Interestingly enough, in a few years I would do just that with Ibrahim in New York (chapter 3).

As I had decided to make Copenhagen my home for a while, I needed money quickly and found out about an entertainment agency that contracted and placed go-go dancers in clubs throughout Denmark for short periods. After only a week and half in the city, I went to the agency's office, and again my blackness was the selling point. The manager told me that the only job he had immediately was in a small town called Middelfart on Denmark's Jutland Peninsula in the country's archipelago of islands. Copenhagen, as the metropolitan capital of the country, is on the island of Zealand, and the small town of Middelfart is located on the island of Funen. I had no idea where I was going; I just knew that I needed quick money, so I took the job. The only hitch was they told me I would have to be the deejay as well as dancer and that I had to wear what was called "the nude look." I said, "I don't dance topless, if that's what you mean." The manager assured me that "the nude look" simply meant wearing something a bit sheer on the top. I figured I could dance around this "sheer top" thing and would make it work.

Middelfart was indeed a small town (even today its population is only 37,000 people), and I am absolutely sure I was the only black woman, or black person for that matter, in the town during the two weeks I was hired as the only entertainment in the only club in town. My apartment and the bar were both on Østergade, the main street of the town, and when I walked down the street during the day it was like being in the Twilight Zone: everyone would freeze whatever action in which they were engaged and stare at me with mouths wide open. The first time it happened, I became extremely self-conscious, but the ability to freeze the town's actions soon became a power game that amused me to no end.

In the club each night, smug smiles or perplexed brows met my gaze as I literally danced in a cage, with the record player. My cage actually became my protection because it meant that the gawking half-drunk Danish men could not touch me. The image of a caged bird (à la Maya Angelou) or a caged animal often came to mind. But I fought the image and simply lost myself in my dancing, which became my immediate escape. Interestingly enough, the name of the bar in which I danced in 1969 was Pappegøn (Parrot), so my caged bird metaphor actually fit the name. When I came out of the dancing cage, some men would often try to reach out and touch my butt, which I would never allow. I would slap their hands away and quickly walk by, holding my head proudly high as I passed through the patrons' tables.

The rather rural Middelfart dance experience was quite different from my urban Barcelona discotheque job; this was small-town Denmark, and the people had never seen a black woman up close and personal. I had come to Europe to pursue a professional concert dance career, and here I was dancing in a little bar in nowhere Denmark, with drunken white men ogling me. Is this what Josephine Baker felt when she first got to France, dancing in her banana skirt costume, with all the Frenchmen eyeing her up and down? But she was in a large revue patronized by rich theatergoers. Did class really matter? Was I somehow "prostituting" my art form? I wrote in my journal:

I feel the machine-like nature of people, programmed by their culture and responding unthinkingly like robots. I watch the young boys in the club looking like 60s longhair hippies, but acting just like their pot-bellied middle-aged fathers next to them. All are trying to have a "good time." The people play games on all levels as I sit in a roped cage. I am a bird in a cage; but when I dance, I fly, I soar. Then even the cage cannot bind me, for the physical surroundings no longer exist. But soon the music stops and I must change the record, and there I sit in my cage again, looking out at the faces and the empty eyes, looking through the cage at me. I sit there like an object that calls for reactions; each reaction really telling more about the person himself than me. Is this what the Venus Hottentot felt as an African woman in white Europe a century and half ago?

I asked myself, "Is this what my ancestors felt when they danced 'freely' on Sundays in front of the plantation Big House and lost themselves in their revelry, only to return to their slave quarters for Monday's fieldwork?"

The only ameliorating experience of this job was a friendship I developed with a young man in the town, Vagn Styr Rasmussen, who showed me the beautiful nature reserves surrounding Middelfart by day. Several times Vagn took me out on the beautiful archipelago waters in his boat. But mostly I had to focus on my ultimate purpose: make the money and get back to Copenhagen so I could focus on finding a place to teach dance. My ultimate goal was to find other dancers who wanted to create modern dance choreography and begin my artistic career in Europe.

European Dance Career Begins in Copenhagen

By August 2 I was thankfully back in Copenhagen at Mrs. Lundstrøm's home, now with some earned funds to find my own apartment, as well as to jump-start my European dance career. According to dance ethnologist Lena Hammergren, black dance was beginning to have a pervasive influence in many forms in Scandinavia by the 1960s:

> America had had a corporeal impact on cultures in the Nordic Region. . . . Some of the most interesting theatrical dance genres to migrate to the Nordic countries during the twentieth century were various styles of African-American and Caribbean jazz dance. Starting in the 1960s, these movement vocabularies became codified as jazz techniques that were tried out by young and old, by amateurs and professionals, by people living in cities and in small towns. Arriving in Northern Europe, "jazz" was afforded many socio-cultural func-

tions and was used for pleasure, fitness, therapy, education and aesthetic expression.[15]

Given the increasing popularity of the dance style I wanted to teach, I did some research to find out if there was already an expatriate black dancer in Denmark from whom I might get advice and with whom I might even collaborate. I knew that there had to be an inchoate creative dance scene in Copenhagen with a few African Americans.

The name that emerged through my inquiries was Doug Crutchfield, a Cincinnati, Ohio, native who had come to Denmark in the early 1960s to dance. Cincinnati had produced many great black musicians such as the pop musicians the Isley Brothers, Bootsy Collins, and Randy Crawford, but most had to leave the city to find fame and fortune. Of course, dance is a completely different business than music; the road to fame in the dance world is much harder and narrower. According to a 1970 *Ebony Magazine* article on Crutchfield, he was the son of a Baptist minister who did not approve of his profession or his homosexuality, and therefore Crutchfield left home as a teenager for New York and eventually to Denmark.[16]

One must remember that in the early 1960s, when Crutchfield arrived in Denmark, the Civil Rights movement had not yet produced the 1964 Civil Rights Act that made it unlawful to discriminate on the basis of race. Hammergren emphasized this point in her discussion of why several African American dancers migrated to Scandinavia:

> It may seem strange that so many talented African-American dancers settled, for shorter or long periods, in what was at the time the quite marginal artistic geography of the Nordic region. But during the 1950s and 1960s it was still difficult for African-American dance artists to find employment. In the US European Americans held the majority of college teaching positions, and only 4 percent of the dance programmes employed teachers in jazz dance. In this situation, the Nordic region offered good working conditions, at least to start with, when jazz dance became the new dance craze and the demand for experienced jazz dancers and teachers was high.[17]

By the time I arrived in the country in 1969, Doug Crutchfield was fairly well known in Denmark, specializing in dance classes for the elderly at De Gamles By (The Old Person's Place), a senior citizens' facility.[18] He also commuted to Stockholm, Sweden, where he performed with a local ballet company and taught jazz and ballet at Lund University. Hammergren notes that Crutchfield had first taught at George Mills's dance school, the George Mills Moderne Ballet Skole. Mills was an African American dancer who was established before Crutchfield, but by 1965, Crutchfield had opened his own school.

I was able to meet Doug Crutchfield once, but he was not very friendly or helpful, and therefore I tried other avenues to get my dance career started. My impression of black dancers who had migrated permanently or seasonally to Europe at that time was that they had claimed their particular country and their status there as "Mr. Jazz Ballet" (there were no women whom I knew of). They attracted their Scandinavian students and patrons of the arts interested in black dance forms, and anyone encroaching upon their turf was perceived as a potential threat who could siphon off their students and audience.

One crucial difference between Denmark and Sweden regarding American expatriate dancers was that Denmark had a much less developed dance scene with fewer established dance institutions for immediate employment. Therefore, the American pioneering spirit came in handy, and establishing one's own school and institutional infrastructure in Copenhagen was fairly easy. Hammergren concurs: "The pedagogues in Denmark often founded their own schools whereas the dance infrastructure in Sweden offered the possibility of being hired at established or emerging schools, for example the Ballet Academy in Stockholm."[19] I knew that media attention would help me start my own dance classes in Copenhagen, and luckily I met an American journalist who knew a writer for one of the main Copenhagen newspapers. In mid-August 1969, I landed an interview with the arts editor, Helle Hellman, of the major Danish newspaper *Politiken*. She was able to capture my particular enthusiasm for dance in a major artist profile, complete with a large headshot that appeared in that newspaper. The timing of this article in the mainstream media could not have been better, as I had arranged with the small American Center on the outskirts of Copenhagen, in a district called Christianshavn, to teach a "jazz ballet" class once a week.

The term "jazz ballet" was particular to Scandinavia, developing from positioning black dance forms within the European ballet tradition. Hammergren suggests that the term in the Nordic region stemmed from "a sensitivity to how jazz ballet had moved to the forefront as a commonly recognized concept and how conceptual borders between modern ballet and modern jazz were flexible."[20] With wide regional Danish public interest in this relatively new American dance form, the newspaper story piqued the interest of Danish dance enthusiasts in me as an artist and, more importantly, in my dance workshop, which was to begin the following week. This ostensibly became the beginning of my artistic dance career in Europe.

On September 1, 1969, I enrolled thirty-five students in my jazz ballet class. Using my cassette tape of music that had accompanied my Barcelona dance gig, I was able to successfully inaugurate my teaching career. I wrote in my journal: *I had my first class today. It ran smoothly—it flowed so that most of the time it required no thought of what I was saying; it just came out. It's exciting watching my life unfold. This is the best move I've made so far. It feels good to be really dancing again.* The students were so excited that they kept telling more and more friends about the class. The venue of the American Center was not that large, so the students had to be limited to forty, but I did expand to two classes per week, and my career was quickly launched.

What I *culturally* took for granted as the capabilities of the human body through dance was completely new and liberating for my Danish students in the late 1960s. "In several of my sources it has been articulated how mesmerizing the practice of the jazz technique was when people encountered it for the first time in a dance studio," as Hammergren notes, "and this experience forms a significant part of the arrival narratives [of black dancers to Denmark]." She goes on to give dance gymnast and author Lis Engel's impression of her first class: "She explains how fantastic it felt to suddenly realize how you could isolate your hips while walking and move them from side to side."[21] This was also my observation in my own classes at the American Center: whatever movements I taught them, my Danish students were so grateful for the seemingly liberating experience. To move their bodies with torso isolations, central to black dance forms, allowed them to feel a level of "democracy" of the human body, a kind of corporeal liberation.

Hammergren suggests, from a twenty-first-century theoretical perspective, that there were many motivations for the Danish interest in my "Primitive Jazz Dance" classes in Copenhagen at the time:

With today's critical vocabulary at hand, it is possible to query the willingness [of Danish dance students] to open up to unknown dance forms, and to perceive it as a desire that stresses self-enrichment and appropriation rather than as a means to develop a more nuanced understanding of culturally significant movement practices. At the same time, these critical perspectives also help us appreciate how important different African-American dancers and dances were in mobilizing new modes for people of relating to their bodies. In this way the migrating pedagogues and dancers have also been integral to Nordic dance history and have helped redefine the national "borders" of this particular geography.[22]

Human motivations are always multidimensional. I'm sure my students in 1969 Copenhagen were inspired by their own self-improvement through my new liberating black dance classes, although some were perpetrators of cultural appropriation at the same time. Whatever their individual motivations for taking my dance classes might have been, for me, having interested people willing to pay for my knowledge was enough.

Once I had established myself as a legitimate professional dance teacher in Copenhagen, I desperately wanted to connect with other dance artists to choreograph and perform. I cannot remember exactly how I met Diane Black, who became my creative colleague and friend, but expatriate Americans establish community beyond race and class in foreign countries, and Jewish New York dancer Diane Black and I recognized that we had mutual artistic goals and were definitely dealing with the same underdeveloped Copenhagen dance scene. These two practical facts alone made us artistic comrades. Diane and her husband, Mardav (Martin David), a graphic artist, had joined a small artistic collective that had a playhouse with a stage, the Ry Teatre on 7 North Fælledvej Street. This band of theater artists and musicians had established this performance space for experimental theater and dance. Diane was working with the actors who had already premiered a successful dramatic play. Our dance potential and the availability of this performance venue were all the right ingredients for Diane and I to form a choreographic collaboration and eventually a Danish dance company.

Diane Black was a former dancer with the Alwin Nikolais Dance Company in New York who had gone to Paris in 1966, where she started a small dance company before moving to Copenhagen. Her artistic background in Nikolais's company meant that her artistic focus was abstract and experimental, incorporating props and light in innovative ways. In the dance world, Nikolais (1912–1993) was one of the first successful New York choreographer/designers to combine motion with various technical effects, eschewing overemphasis on dance technique and established choreographic patterns. He became assistant to Hanya Holm (see chapter 1) after World War II, and when he started his own company in the 1950s, his own choreographic focus became total theater. Nikolais often deemphasized the human body itself, using it like another stage prop in his stated goal of relieving the dancer from the human form.[23]

Therefore, Diane and I came from completely different dance backgrounds—hers in an abstraction of the human form and movement, and mine in total submersion in the humanizing spiritual embodiment of an African-based modern dance. However, what we found we had in common was a belief in improvisation as a means to choreography and a trust in the spontaneous aspects of dance. Our openness to movement experimentation—albeit from different cultural perspectives—was our binding aesthetic that was to serve as our foundation for our first small dance concert we called *Upspring*.

Upspring premiered on November 7, 1969, at the Ry Teatre with Diane and I as artistic codirectors, along with three Danish dancers we had recruited and trained: Ingrid Dal, Charlotte Frederiksen, and Pia Heinonen. The opening of *Upspring* was marketed as a "Dance Revolution" in Denmark. We received a decent-sized article in the *Politiken* and a short notice with a photo in the smaller Copenhagen paper *Information*. Helle Hellman again wrote the more extensive article in *Politiken*, calling our premiere "a revolutionary innovation in contemporary choreography" (figure 1). We viewed our own artistic efforts as the introduction of a new level of dance experimentation that we perceived was not happening in Copenhagen at that time. Hellmann reinforced that vision, writing, "The two American dancers hope that the show will mean the beginning of new advanced Copenhagen dance environment."[24]

From the beginning we emphasized that improvisation was going to be a central part of advancing the local dance scene: "'*Upspring* has a piece of music with a fixed frame, but within it we all improvise,' tells Diane Black. 'Each performance we provide is so different from the previous one.'"[25] This first dance performance at the Ry Teatre realized the multidisciplinary vision of the venue's collective, which consisted of Niels Anderson's theater group Labyrinth, and musicians Robert Leievre and Arne Würgler, and Mardav as visual designer. So our newly formed dance group was situated in an experimental theatrical collective of young American and Danish artists exploring new frontiers of the performing arts. Diane and I were

envisioning dance, not as classical ballet, entertainment dance, or the simple dance gymnastics popular in Scandinavia at the time, but as an art form
on the level of theater and music that could be explored in its many dimensions to awaken the human spirit. Moreover, we were doing that exploratory work in Denmark at a time when the theatergoing public was ripe for
cultural exploration and existential expansion.

Personally I was moving from one friend's house to the next and really
needed my own place, and now that I had a steady income from teaching,
I looked for my own apartment. In December 1969, after the premiere of
Upspring, and in the dead of Danish winter, I moved to the small suburban
coastal town of Vedbæk, north of Copenhagen. It was about a thirty-min-
ute train ride from the city to my small basement apartment, with its own
entrance, within a suburban home. I never felt any racial discrimination in
my pursuit of a place to live, as I had in San Francisco, reminding me of
why, besides my general curiosity, I had decided to become a black American expatriate in Europe. I might be subject to the overarching stereotype
of the loose female black "Jezebel" who can be easily sexually approached,
but I was never discriminated against regarding basic human needs, like
housing, medical care, or employment opportunities. The distance of
time eclipses the exact reason I chose to move outside the city where I was
working, but I'm sure cost and finances were involved. All I remember is
that the apartment was nice and cozy, well-appointed with good heating
that was an absolute necessity in the subzero temperatures of Danish win-
ters. I was now established as a Danish resident with a profession, working
with artistic colleagues, and with a nice residence of my own. It had taken
one and a half years since I left San Francisco, but I had made Copenha-
gen/Vedbæk my first home outside the United States.

Magic Lotus Dance Theatre

Diane Black and I continued working toward a professional modern dance
scene in Copenhagen, and within three months of the premiere of our
first concert *Upspring*, we had formally established a dance company that
we called Magic Lotus Dance Theatre. The influence of 1960s exploration
of Eastern religions and cultures with concepts like meditation obviously
influenced our naming of the company. The general Danish public was
comfortable with the name, even in English, because it fit the times. Re-

member, by 1970 mainstream culture was beginning to incorporate hippie counterculture. *Hair: The American Tribal Love-Rock Musical* had already had its Off-Broadway premiere in 1967 at Joseph Papp's Public Theater, and in that same year the Robert Joffrey Ballet had premiered its psychedelic ballet *Astarte* at New York's City Center Theater. *Astarte* made the cover of *Time Magazine* in March 1968 as a kind of sign of the times, so the name of our small Danish dance company fit perfectly into the cultural *zeitgeist* of the beginning of the 1970s.

On February 21, 1970, Magic Lotus Dance Theatre premiered at the Kunstindustrimuseet (Museum of Art and Design) in Copenhagen in their showroom, in collaboration with the museum's light show called *Solvognena*. Being American with a vision of internationalizing and positioning the Danish dance scene in the hip new counterculture paid off. A major Copenhagen museum sponsored the premiere of our new dance company that had expanded to eight dancers, including the two codirectors. Joining Ingrid, Charlotte, and Pia were three new dancers: Charlotte Eskildsen, Ida Koch, and Elizabeth Madsen (figure 2). An eight-member all-female dance company directed by two Americans and performing experimental modern dance at the Kunstindustrimuseet was a significant achievement at the beginning of the 1970s. I was on my way to realizing my artistic dreams.

The media helped build the premiere of Magic Lotus Dance Theatre with a full-page article in the *B. T. Frokosten* newspaper that captured our views of dancing and choreographing in Copenhagen: "To USA-danserinder i København: Her er provinsielt, men godt" (Two U.S. dancers in Copenhagen: Here it is provincial, but good). The article by Lars Blicher-Hansen situated Diane and me as representing the two U.S. coasts, New York and San Francisco, as well as the European countries where we had been before Denmark. In the section of the article on me, Blicher-Hansen emphasized my having been a "go-go danserinde" as a means of making money to survive, as well as the fact that I taught "Primitive Jazz Dance" in Copenhagen, although Diane's style of dance was never mentioned. There was never any written mention of our races, but I always felt those two particular points about my career choices had racial undertones. The Josephine Baker Syndrome of the exotic black Jezebel, rather than a strong self-directed black woman, was definitely connoted.

The title of the article said much about our two different perspectives on Denmark. Diane emphasized the European openness to the arts: "It is difficult to earn money, but in this country we have the opportunity to choose a way of life so it is possible to continue working as an artist. There is always an audience who appreciate the fact you create something." We were both grateful to be unknown foreigners but garnering attention from the dance community, media, and general public for our art. In this sense Denmark was "godt" (good). But I offered criticism of Denmark in my perceptions recorded in the article. Blicher-Hansen had this to say about my critique, quoting me verbatim:

> Both she [Diane] and Janis Miller are quite happy to stay here, but Janis Miller, who is unmarried and unengaged, does not hide her opinion about us. "Denmark is terribly provincial, you know. It lacks full diversity of people that one finds everywhere else, at least in those countries that have or have had colonies. I can, for example, see it when I sit on the train. If there is a group of foreigners talking in their own language, the Danish passengers nearest become nervous. There seems to be an intolerance of strangers, and I would like to see [Denmark] discontinue being so provincial."[26]

Denmark had been a part of the worldwide European colonial regime but had relinquished its holdings long before the anticolonial independence movements starting in the 1940s and 1950s. Yet, unlike France, England, the Netherlands, and Germany, it did not have any of its former colonial subjects living within its borders.[27]

Even given these historic facts, when I read my 1970 sentiments on Denmark, I realized how much my independent nature was in full force that my future name (Halifu) would encompass. I was never one to hold my tongue and took advantage of the media attention to voice my ambivalence about Danish culture during the premiere of my new dance company. My recorded sentiments were indicative of my boldness, which would only grow stronger in the future. Diane and I were both grateful for the opportunity that Copenhagen offered to continue our dance careers, but I, in particular, was very aware that Danes, as liberal as they are, were not totally comfortable with the foreign Other in 1969.

Publicity for the Magic Lotus Dance Theatre, with me as a black dancer, was a chance for Denmark to show its cultural open-mindedness, yet several news photos revealed the more complex social subtext. A casual photo with Diane and me walking down the street dressed in our winter coats and scarfs, which appeared in the *B.T.* article, included a middle-aged Danish man walking behind us. The man was clearly eyeing me in the photo. This was the kind of visible attention I had become accustomed to as a black woman in Denmark. Another side to my marked (black) visibility was in a notice for the show at the Kunstindustrimuseet in the *Berlingske* newspaper, which featured a solo dance photo of me in wrapped African cloth and with the short natural hairdo I wore at the time. Printed publicity photos in other news sources, which included both Diane and me, showed us in typical dancer tights and leotards. Although I appreciated the newspaper using my "African look," the *Berlingske* photo placed an obvious emphasis on my Africanist aesthetic as a selling point for this experimental dance and light show at the museum. The positioning of my blackness was a part of the new cultural *zeitgeist* that had swept through Europe in the past five years that appropriated the counterculture in the United States and became a part of the particular imaging of the Magic Lotus Dance Theatre. And the fact that I was from San Francisco, the epicenter of New Age social experimentalism, was important.

The successful premiere of the Magic Lotus Dance Theatre emboldened me to further explore my personal dance philosophy. My journal became my best friend, in which I confided my deepest thoughts about my growing artistic aesthetic and beliefs. I viewed modern dance as the saving grace of Western dance because of its focus on the creative *investigation* of movement, where the exploration of motion itself was infinite. My view was that classical ballet was finite, with sixty-four movements all having a codified name, and that jazz dance, with its own set of standardized named steps, such as kick-ball-change and hitch-kick, was in the same vein. One journal entry was written before the premiere of the dance company:

> *Ballet and jazz are not growing, organic, creative dance forms. Modern dance saves Western dance because it is the product of rebellion away from this stagnation. From this position Duncan and Graham approached dance from a spiritual philosophical point of view. With this approach they introduced the vital element of authenticity—the thread linking the outer physical to the inner spiritual, the source of every physical movement that represents truth. Africans do it by being completely free and letting the inner become the outer for all to see (trance state). The East Indians do it by following a precise strict code of movement corresponding to their*

religion. Some kind of link—mental, sensual, or metaphysical—is necessary in dance to create the road to the inner source, in order to create truthful dance.

The above journal passage shows clearly how we are a product of our era. My 1960s consciousness, which dictated my focus on an inner process of creativity as the only "authentic" way to create art, is clear. However, it is important to emphasize that at this point in my development I linked Western modern dance with other dance traditions in Africa and India, noting that what links them is a conscious connection to an inner creative source that must be tapped by the individual dancer or the tradition itself. That I did not include Katherine Dunham in the pantheon of the mothers of modern dance, who also created a rebellious movement investigation, is a testament to the biased dance history that one is taught even today in most college dance departments, invisibilizing the great black contributions. Although my perception was pretentious, I record it here because it represents a strain in my conceptualization of dance that determined my work with Diane Black and the Magic Lotus Dance Theatre, as well as some of my future choices for my dance career.

Moreover, I began to conceptualize my sense of the body and its centers of natural movement that drove this stage of my choreography. My journal read: *Each part of the body has its own center of gravity. The movement from those individual centers emanates and receives their strength from the physical center of the whole body from the neck to the navel (the torso).* For me, my aesthetic philosophy was not theory but a way of life. bell hooks examines this same sense of aesthetic awareness in growing up black and rural: "Aesthetics then is more than a philosophy or theory of art and beauty; it is a way of inhabiting space, a particular location, a way of looking and becoming." Then she goes on to concretize aesthetics in relation to one of the houses she grew up in: "In one house I learned the place of aesthetics in the lives of agrarian poor black folks. There the lesson was that one had to understand beauty as a force to be made and imagined."[28] This is exactly the mode in which I entered upon my quest to articulate my conception of aesthetics in dance. My developing perceptions directed my choreography with the Magic Lotus Dance Theatre and my work with Diane Black. I was truly a child of the 1960s and a product of the San Francisco Bay Area, a kind of amalgamation between the Black Arts movement and hippiedom.

I would get marijuana high and write about how I saw dance particularly in relation to music. One such poem was "And Music Makes Me Dance":

And Music Makes Me Dance

. . . and Music makes me Dance
Sweet vibrations of tastes divine
Movement spiraling thru space
to touch my spirit
Music of the spheres
Music of my Soul
Echoing sounds of bitter-sweetness of yesterdays
and the cool release of tomorrow

. . . and Music makes me Dance
The Eternal Dance
Of Yes I Am
The always Dance
Of rhythms multiplied
Blending in and out of each other in harmony
Chords that pluck the strings of my Soul
Drums that stir the beat of my Heart
Sheets of sound
That you can almost reach out and touch
Notes of vibrations that tenderly strike the subtlety of my spine
Fullness of stillness that you can almost become

. . . and Music makes me Dance
My Spirit wants to sing
My Body knows its own movement
My feet feel the rhythms of the Earth
Yes, Music makes me Dance
For is there really any other way To Be?

This was young Janis Miller in Copenhagen, starting her professional dance career—exploring, stretching out, finding her unique individual voice, and exploring *blackness* from my own dance viewpoint.

However, something in me knew even with my strong individual philosophical dance perspective, my actual training was still not finished, and

I needed to continue to study *technically* as I developed my career. But there really weren't strong technique teachers in Copenhagen in the *kind* of dance I wanted. My journal read: *My goal now is to become a real dancer, master my technique, and go deeper into the essence of movement through developing a firm basis of teaching my movement style and translating this essence into choreography.* Therefore, I took a break from the company and traveled to Stockholm, Sweden, where several professional dance schools flourished, and where I had heard that important American New York dance instructors taught, including Talley Beatty, a former dancer with the Katherine Dunham Dance Company. In April 1970 I traveled by train from Copenhagen to Stockholm, a five-and-a-half-hour train ride (654 kilometers, or a little over 400 miles), and went to study at Stockholm's famous Balettakademien (Ballet Academy).

Teaching and Studying Dance in Stockholm

Stockholm is the largest city in Scandinavia, with 1.4 million people in the urban area and 2.2 million in the larger metropolitan region. As such, it has always had a larger economy than Copenhagen and is among the top ten regions in Europe by GDP. Located in southeast Sweden, the city is actually spread across fourteen islands on Lake Mälaren in the Stockholm archipelago overlooking the Baltic Sea. The city is known for its emphasis on urban aesthetics, with the Stockholm Metro used as an art gallery for famous murals extending the length of the transportation system.

Dance in Sweden, until the late 1950s, was dominated by the Royal Opera's ballet program, which was the only dance training available. Then the Balettakademien opened its doors in central Stockholm in 1957 with the mission "to give the opportunity for a comprehensive education that besides classical ballet also included contemporary dance and jazz."[29] This became necessary because major international choreographers in concert dance were beginning to use more fusion styles—blending ballet, modern, and jazz—than ever before, creating a demand for comprehensively trained dancers. Well-known ballet choreographers like Glen Tetley and Antony Tudor, for examples, were using modern dance with classical ballet, and Gerald Arpino, Jerome Robbins, and Peter Gennaro were including jazz dance in their dance fusions. Jerome Robbins's *West Side Story* had toured to Stockholm after its 1957 Broadway premiere and was later revived by Swedish choreographers. Of course, no one recognized that Katherine

Dunham had pioneered a seminal fusion style since the late 1930s that included Afro-Caribbean dance, influencing several of these more recognized white male choreographers.[30] Stockholm's Balettakademien got on the bandwagon and hired many American dancers to introduce professional modern and jazz dance training into the Swedish dance scene, and this was the reason I wanted to go to Stockholm to continue my own training while living in Scandinavia.

The Balettakademien, from its inception, had an egalitarian and populist mission regarding styles offered and its perceived student base, which included both professionally oriented and recreational students. Their stated mission even today is to "offer a broad variety of dance classes for adults, young people and children in a diverse range of dance disciplines, from beginners to professionals." The focus on diversity in curriculum and a range of student types was the main motivation of the founder, Lia Schubert, an Austrian Jew who moved to Stockholm in 1950. Her family had moved to Paris to escape the persecution of Jews in the late 1930s, but as Nazism swept into France she found herself discriminated against at the Conservatory of Music in Paris, from which she was ousted in 1942, and spent time in a concentration camp in France. When she arrived in Stockholm with her past training in dance and theater, as well as her personal history with anti-Semitism, she was determined to build a school of inclusiveness. Lia Schubert's personal experience of marginalization and oppression drove her desire to build a dance school that could help heal those social ills through dance, and the Balettakademien continues until today under that mission.

When I arrived to study there in 1970, Ms. Schubert had already left the directorship, and the ballet choreographer Ivo Cramér had taken over the helm of the school. There were many top American teachers, including David Wood of the Graham Company and, surprisingly, Vanoye Aikens, one of Katherine Dunham's main company members, who had just left her company in 1963, when she disbanded after twenty-seven years. At the Balettakademien I could begin to formally study Graham Technique with one of her main dancers and continue my Dunham training with Vanoye Aikens's jazz focus, as well as continue classical ballet at a higher level. I threw myself into consuming as many technique classes as I could, all the while being scrutinized as the only black American female on the scene.

After one week of classes at the Balettakademien, the American ballet teacher, who comanaged the school, asked me who I was, and after realizing I was a dancer-choreographer in Copenhagen, he asked me if I would be interested in teaching at the Balettakademien. I expressed enthusiasm for teaching at the school, and he immediately set up a trial jazz class for me to teach that a few of the teaching staff observed. After my audition class I was offered a contract that I couldn't pass up: a large monthly salary and a free apartment in Gamla Stan (The Old Town). This became my first *professional* dance instructor position within an established school, replete with a respectable salary, all the free classes I wanted, and free accommodations. I went back to Copenhagen, broke the news to Diane, and began packing.

By early May 1970 I was living and working in Stockholm. Each week I taught two jazz dance classes to the professional students in the certificate program that the school offered, and two jazz classes to the recreational students in the evening. I was now reaping the benefits of being a black female artist in Europe in the professional dance world. Living in Old Town, with its cobblestone streets and quaint old shops run by older Swedish people who spoke little English, allowed me to get to know several sides of Stockholm. The city still had its unique cultural traditions while aspiring to become the New York of Scandinavia.

Jazz Ballet and Dunham Technique in Sweden

Like in Denmark, I wanted to know the historical background of black dance forms in Sweden, as well as who were the pioneers. I quickly found out that Walter Nicks (1925–2007), former Katherine Dunham dancer, was one of the first to introduce what Scandinavians began to call "jazz ballet." According to Hammergren, Lia Schubert brought Walter Nicks, with whom I would later dance in New York in the 1980s and at the Dunham seminars in the 1990s, to Stockholm within a few years after founding the Balettakademien:

> According to the narrative, Lia Schubert . . . met African-American dancer Walter Nicks at an international summer school in Krefeld, Germany, in 1959 and invited him to Stockholm to give a course in jazz dance the following year. It was a summer course designed mainly for professionals and advanced students, and it was an immediate success. Among the students, were not only well-known actors,

but also ballet dancers from the Royal Swedish Opera in Stockholm and from the Finnish Opera in Helsinki.[31]

Here we see the importance of key women in dance who were responsible for the proliferation of black dance forms in Europe: not only Katherine Dunham but also Lia Schubert.

Walter Nicks's dance classes were Dunham Technique filtered through his own movement sensibilities. In fact, most of Dunham's company members who toured with her in Europe between 1940 and 1963 became culturally comfortable in those countries from the Mediterranean to the Nordic regions. It was no coincidence that the majority of the black dancers introducing jazz ballet to Scandinavia were former Dunham dancers; therefore the form of modern jazz dance spread in Sweden was actually variations on Dunham Technique. Lia Schubert, who became the populist dance leader in Sweden, recognized these highly professionally trained black dancers and knew they were the ones to aid her mission to create a *different* kind of dance school in Stockholm: "In Sweden, under the auspices of Lia Schubert, Nicks became a consultant at the University of Stockholm (1960–67), a guest instructor at the Swedish Ballet Academy (1960), and performed there with his small company (1961–65). He appeared several times on Swedish television in the 1960s, and of particular importance was the series 'Introduction to Jazz Ballet' with Schubert (1966)."[32]

It is important to note that in order for Nicks to become "Mr. Jazz Ballet" in Sweden, he had to establish himself in several key institutions besides the Balettakademien, including Stockholm's Staten Dansskola (State Dance School), where he taught between 1967 and 1971. He also choreographed the Swedish production of *West Side Story* in 1968, as well as a 1969 live telecast concert of Duke Ellington's sacred music with the Duke Ellington Orchestra that was performed at the Gustav Vasa Church in Stockholm. In this manner, Walter Nicks had established professional dance by black Americans in Sweden before I arrived in Stockholm in 1970. I heard his name as the primary representative of jazz ballet everywhere, even though he was not physically there during the year I spent dancing and teaching at the Balettakademien.

The names and categories of African American dance are not coincidental, reflecting the politics of race and naming outside of the control of its practitioners. Again, the term "jazz ballet" represented a particular choice in Scandinavia for a conglomeration of dance styles by expatriate black dance artists. Hammergren gives an overview perspective on the politics of Europe's naming of dance styles by blacks:

> It has been argued that it was Europe that labeled the professionally performed African-American jazz dance as a specific genre. African-American choreographer and pedagogue Donald McKayle has explained the arrival of different jazz-related movement practices to Europe, recounting how he and his colleagues often talked about themselves as modern dance artists in the late 1950s, but when they were invited to Europe the branding of jazz dance took place. . . . In 1965 the [Alvin Ailey] company visited some of the Nordic countries for the first time. Although Ailey worked with a mix of dance techniques, his company became an integral part, together with pedagogues, in establishing jazz dance in this new Nordic context.[33]

Therefore, by the time I got to Scandinavia, if one was a black dancer, no matter what style one taught, one was designated as performing and teaching "jazz ballet." In this way, race got etched into the Scandinavian dance field, particularly because black dance styles were new to this region of the world.

The "jazz ballet" term became expedient for marketing purposes, but at the same time it became a double bind for the black dancer in Scandinavia. Just as Katherine Dunham in the United States was actually developing a new style of modern contemporary dance, racial codes of the mid-twentieth century dictated that what she was doing be called "Negro dance." It would not be until the post–Black Arts movement of the late 1960s and 1970s in America that black dancers themselves began to redefine their own aesthetic and situate themselves in the continually developing modern dance scene of the United States (chapter 3). Jazz dance is a legitimate form with its own aesthetic and history, but that was not necessarily what all black dancers were exploring in Scandinavia. For me, in Copenhagen *my* dance style had skirted the broad categorical stroke of jazz ballet because I was paired with a *white* dancer, even though I continued to use my own defiant "Primitive Jazz Dance" term when I *taught* dance.

Besides the decade-long primacy of Walter Nicks and his establishment of jazz ballet in Sweden, other former Dunham dancer/choreographers were also a part of the Stockholm dance scene. Talley Beatty (1918–1995) was an occasional teacher at the Balettakademien, whom I viewed then as almost a dance "god," but I never got a chance to take his classes. Along with Walter Nicks, Talley Beatty was one of the main black dancers responsible for promulgating their brand of contemporary dance throughout Scandinavia. Beatty was born in Louisiana but grew up in Chicago, as did Dunham. After leaving Dunham's company in 1946, he garnered a reputation as an important choreographer, with such works as his solo *Mourner's Bench* about grief in the southern black church over lynching, which was a part of his *Southern Landscape 1865* suite. Beatty also created many ballets for the Alvin Ailey American Dance Theater such as *Come and Get the Beauty of It Hot*, which is an extraordinary fusion of ballet, jazz, and modern. I wouldn't actually *meet* Talley until I hired him to choreograph for a dance company collective I helped to start in my home area of Oakland in the late 1980s (chapter 6), as well as studying with him in the early 1990s at the annual Dunham Technique Seminar in East St. Louis.

One of Talley Beatty's dancers with whom I did study was Herman Howell, who was originally from Brooklyn and became Talley's dance captain in several ballets. By 1970 Herman Howell was a jolly, overweight middle-aged man who made us laugh as well as sweat in his rigorous jazz classes at the Balettakademien. Herman, like many black dancers, had worked in both concert and commercial dance. He had taught at the June Taylor ballroom school in New York, where Randi Frønsdal, one of Finland's teachers of jazz ballet, studied. He also danced with "Donald Mc-Kayle in his *District Storyville*, and in Alvin Ailey's television taping of *Revelations* for the show *Lamp unto My Feet* in 1961."[34] Herman taught *real* jazz dance rather than a modern derivative, and through him I was able to further develop my jazz technique, mastering his intricately syncopated rhythmic phrasings. All serious students of jazz dance studied with Herman Howell at the Balettakademien in the early 1970s.

Another important black dance artist in Sweden was Clifford Fears (1936–1988), who was originally from Detroit. He had left Sweden after many years, just before I arrived, but his teaching legacy was felt everywhere and discussed by students at the Balettakademien. He was also a former Dunham company member, as well as a former dancer with Alvin Ailey. Like Dunham, Fears was very independent and had started his own dance school in Stockholm:

In Sweden Clifford Fears was one of a few African-American teachers to start his own school. He had started teaching at the Ballet

Academy in 1962, but in 1964 he founded a school with courses in jazz, ballet and modern dance for children and adults, amateurs and professionals. The School was supported by Dunham and also named after her, the Katherine Dunham School. Fears returned to the US in 1970, with the intention of starting a school in his hometown of Detroit, and the Swedish school closed down.[35]

Upon returning to Detroit, Fears did start his own company, called Clifford Fears Dance Theatre, but he had a hard time getting the financial support he needed. Penny Godboldo, codirector of the Institute for Dunham Technique Certification (IDTC), studied with him and continues his legacy through the teaching of Dunham Technique in Detroit. But before Fears left Stockholm, he had securely establish the Dunham legacy in Sweden through his Katherine Dunham School as a part of Swedish dance history.

Another Dunham dancer with whom I studied, Vanoye Aikens (1917–2013), also secured the Dunham legacy in Sweden. Hailing from Georgia, Aikens attended a few years at Morehouse College and went into the U.S. Navy for a year and half. Upon his discharge he went to New York to study dance and met Lenwood Morris, the Dunham company's ballet master. Morris led Aikens to the company in 1943, and Aikens became Miss Dunham's primary dance partner, performing in all of her major ballets until the disbanding of the company in 1963. Like other former Dunham dancers, Aikens was very comfortable in Europe after years of international touring, and he did several subsequent dance projects in France and Italy, finally ending up in Stockholm at the Balettakademien. When I first saw Vanoye Aikens's name on the teaching schedule, I did not know he had been a Dunham dancer, but upon reading his bio, I realized I had come "home" and could continue my Dunham Technique training with him. His teaching had a strong jazz distinction, along with typical Dunham flatback, fall and recovery, and hinges. Vanoye Aikens became an important dance mentor during my time in Stockholm, always sharing dance advice with me.

The sum total of all these important African American dancer-teachers was nothing short of astounding when one contemplates the aggregate of knowledge, creativity, and movement expertise that had migrated to Stockholm in the 1960s and 1970s. Hammergren coined the term "movementscape" to capture the amassed black dance talent that had migrated to

Sweden and "had transmitted their expertise between places and groups of people and how it intertwine[d] 'local human experiences and social divisions and global social structures of power.'"[36] Indeed, I too was amazed at the level of cumulative black dance talent to which ironically I had access in Europe. Being both a teacher and student put me in a peculiar position, but I was always humble in the classes of my dance elders, giving them all due respect from a student's perspective.

Besides Vanoye, I also studied with the former Graham dancer David Wood (1925–2002), who would go on to be the founder of the dance department at the University of California, Berkeley, along with his wife, Marni Wood. He had distinguished himself as a soloist with Martha Graham for fifteen years, starting with Hanya Holm and also dancing with Alwin Nikolais, José Limón, Doris Humphrey, and Charles Weidman, the primary pioneers of modern dance in the United States. When I took Graham Technique classes with David Wood, the atmosphere was like sacred dance space. When he entered the room, students immediately stood at attention, he would then bow to the class, the piano accompanist would strike the first musical chord, and students began the Graham floor exercises as a prechoreographed sequence. The floor work was rigorous with body swings, torso spirals, and pelvis contractions and releases. Ultimately, the Balettakademien provided me with some of the top teachers in concert dance of all styles, offering a unique opportunity to hone my dance technique and performance artistry.

As a teacher-student I was very aware of how I was being observed as the only black American female, as well as how I had entered a highly professional dance scene that I had not known in the more *community* atmosphere of the dance scene in the Bay Area. I wrote in my journal:

In this beginning period at the Balettakademien I am being carefully scrutinized. All the dance world is here with its different types: the prissy, young, snobbish ballet boys, the young ego-ridden girls who think because they can lift their legs high they know all about dance, the gay, hands-on-the-hip ballet and jazz teachers with all their clichés, the serious young graduating professional students, who really want to create with dance, and the recreational students who just want to have a little fun—all melting into what is called the dance world in Stockholm. Settling in, taking it all in, using the opportunities to develop my craft, and as always working on myself.

Besides teaching the professionally enrolled certificate students and the evening recreational ones, I also did some choreography. The school had concerts that I took advantage of to continue my own creative dance-making, and in those studio performances I received recognition. One piece that I choreographed, *March of the Created*, would become a theme in several larger works that I was to choreograph when I got back to the States. In my journal I continually wrote about how I was cognizing how the roles human beings assumed in life seemed to be either predestined or socialized into them through their life experiences—the nature-or-nurture debate: the pot-smoking hippie, the alpha male, the manipulating sensual female, the arrogant colonizer, and the slave-mentality victim. In this choreographic work, I created character movement phrases that each iconic character repeated on a stage diagonal to give the impression of an incessant "march" of characters who were *trapped* in their characteristic movements representing their social roles. *March of the Created* generated a lot of discussion at the Balettakademien, which was my goal.

I was also a dancer in a television dance special. I was cast to perform in a jazz piece choreographed for Swedish television by Jewish American choreographer Joel Schnee. Being the only black American female professional dancer in Stockholm at the time, I was bound to get the gig. I remember it as a neurotic scene, with the choreographer and his assistants chain-smoking and barking out orders to us dancers. But this was one of the first times that I experienced dance for the camera, and the experience allowed me to conceptualize dance cinematically, where the camera shots and the editing process were the final choreographer. This television dance experience became a part of my continuing European learning process before I would go back home to begin my professional dance career in the United States. Stockholm ultimately provided the training and professional dance contacts that I needed to continue a new level of dance professionalism.

At the end of May 1971 I flew back to the United States, having spent a little over a year in Stockholm, nine months in Copenhagen, and a total of two years and seven months outside the United States between North Africa and Europe. I had tested my wings as an individual in the world, got a small taste of the African homeland in Morocco, proved myself as a black woman artist in Europe, began to find my own choreographic voice through my first dance company in Copenhagen, and improved my dance technique and performing in Stockholm. I now needed to return to the land of my birth and begin to make my own professional statement as a dancer-choreographer. Before leaving Stockholm, I had a meeting with Ivo Cramér, the Balettakademien director, and he gave me a short, succinct letter of recommendation that read:

> This is to testify that Janis Miller has been engaged for one year as a teacher of Jazz Dance at the Ballet Academy of Stockholm. Miss Miller is a very good teacher and has shown especially interesting results with jazz improvisation classes. She has done some impressive choreography for our ballet workshop. It is a pleasure for me to give her my best recommendation.
>
> Stockholm, May 28, 1971
> Ivo Cramér

I took this recommendation not only as proof of my newfound international dance career but also as validation to myself that I was ready to try my hand at a professional dance career now in the United States.

3

٭٠٠٠٠٠٠

Dancing in New York

We seek balance! We are not of this insanity;
it's the cultural expression that allows us
to manifest ourselves as a different people.

BERNICE JOHNSON REAGON,
FOUNDER OF SWEET HONEY IN THE ROCK

After almost three years in Europe, I was ready to take on the United States again with all of what Bernice Reagon calls its "insanity." American complexity is based on contradictions, ironies, cultural juxtapositions, the profit motive often as first consideration, and, most importantly, its black culture at the center of its national identity. This latter characteristic is taken for granted while being its saving grace. In Europe I was able to experience my individuality, as well as my blackness, in a way that only being outside of the peculiar U.S. "insanity" affords. But I was more than ready to jump back into my culture with a fierceness that I had never known. I was ready to teach, organize, and choreograph to tell my vision of the American insanity through dance. I wrote in my journal:

> *Being back in the States, I am viewing the complexity of this society from a more mature head; more understanding, or at least a new willingness and openness to bite into this thing called life in the United States, much more than before my flight away from the madness. This country forces one to examine and "dig" oneself because of all the chaos and contradictions of a frustrated and continually exploring so-called melting pot society.*

But before I was willing to take on New York, the center of the dance world, I went to Boston.

Boston held not only the first test case for my new dance professionalism and reentry into black culture, but personally it held my first major love. I had met Donna Maynard on Ibiza, and as two of only a handful of black women on the island in 1968, we immediately tuned into each other, and, as the lingo goes today, "we hooked up." I had had a few affairs with women during my S.F. State undergraduate years, but I considered those relationships as part of the hippie "free-love" exploration of the times; I was definitely into men. So this "thing" with Donna definitely took me by surprise, as it got deeper, moving me into uncharted territory since I had convinced myself that I could never really be with a woman. We had traveled through Spain together and left each other in Paris when she came back to the United States. Because our feelings for one another were definitely not abating with distance, she returned to Europe to visit me for a month in Denmark when I lived in Vedbæk. Of course, my distant relationship with her was happening in between affairs with men in Scandinavia, but nothing was as serious as what Donna and I had. Therefore, coming back to the States to live with her in her hometown of Boston, I had to finally admit that I was definitely bisexual.

Getting to Know Boston before New York

Boston, as the largest city in New England and the capital of Massachusetts, is etched in the American historical memory with its seventeenth-century European Puritan beginnings as the center of one of the earliest colonies, as well as its eighteenth-century prominence in the American Revolution. Coming from the West Coast, I had a stereotypic image of Boston as the center of proper New England Puritan culture, where people said "cah" for "car" and "cahn't" instead of "can't." But in reality, particularly in the early 1970s, it was a predominantly Irish Catholic and very segregated city of about a half million people. In Boston, I was definitely back in racist America with its blatant intentions to continue Jim Crow segregation. I remember having to threaten a downtown Boston hotel with a NAACP lawsuit because it conveniently had no rooms on the arrival of my younger sister, Brenda, who came to visit me; the hotel had taken my legitimate reservation by phone a week earlier. Needless to say, she and her friend got the room.

I lived with Donna in the South End on West Springfield Street, still one of the poorest areas of the city, even with gentrification. We lived on the third floor of a three-story brownstone walk-up. The population of the South End has always been diverse, with Irish, Lebanese, Jews, African Americans, and Greeks. I remember our neighborhood as a diverse group of poor and lower-middle-class folks, bordering the predominantly black Roxbury District, where the Elma Lewis School of Fine Arts taught dance to young black children, and where I would occasionally teach dance.[1]

Donna was a black woman two years older than I, who was trying to find her life's purpose. She was a good organizational administrator and had entered into a business relationship with an arts impresario, Henry Atlas, and together they had formed the Institute for Contemporary Dance (ICD). This was a non-profit organization established to provide more diverse professional dance styles and teachers to the Boston area. Henry and Donna entered into an arrangement with nearby Harvard University, across the Charles River in Cambridge, to use campus facilities to hold their weekly dance classes. Henry was a graduate student at Harvard and had registered ICD as a student organization. Hence, I had a new dance platform, with dance classes held in the center of East Coast academia. I was able to begin teaching, making money, and training local dancers in my style of modern jazz dance, which always had an Afro-Haitian and Dunham focus from my early training with Ruth Beckford, and reinforced by Vanoye Aikens in Stockholm.

Teaching for ICD was my inroad to both Boston's dance and black communities. ICD and I were both new to Boston, and I helped establish its community profile for quality dance classes. Since ICD was a graduate student organization, Harvard loaned the group its gymnasium, not dance studios, so my instruction spaces were huge, hardwood sprung-floor venues without mirrors. Almost immediately the dance community responded by filling my dance classes in large numbers. Young, eager black and white dance students supported ICD because of their thirst for "modern" dance that was still developing, the style of which depended on who was teaching it. Coming out of my early training in the San Francisco Bay Area, my dance style was modern-based with a strong influence of Dunham and Afro-Caribbean dance, with live drumming as opposed to taped piano music. Young black people, exploring their newfound blackness on the heels of the Black Power and Black Arts movements, flocked to my classes.

Ever-shifting labels for the evolving black dance styles by Boston's African American teachers were abundant. Dance instructor Bill Mackey, a former New York dancer with Eleo Pomare and Rod Rodgers, taught "Afro-American Dance," while Danny Sloane, a teacher on loan from the Elma Lewis School of Fine Arts, taught "Jazz Dance." Gus Solomons Jr., formerly with Merce Cunningham and now directing his own company, came from New York to occasionally teach his modern dance styles for ICD. Consuelo Atlas, a solo dancer with the Alvin Ailey American Dance Theater who occasionally came back to Boston, taught Horton modern dance, and the white teachers Becky Arnold, Martha Gray, and Beth Soll taught various forms of modern dance. At this point, I dropped the "Primitive Jazz Dance" title of my class and began teaching more delineated dance styles; for ICD I taught "Modern Jazz," "African," and "Haitian Folkloric."

The 190-mile distance between New York and Boston created a dance corridor for recognized dance artists to come to teach dance in New England. Although New York had studios with a diversity of dance styles under one aegis, such as the Clark Center and the New Dance Group, where I studied with Jean-León Destiné (chapter 1), the dance scenes in other eastern seaboard cities, like Boston, were not as progressive. It was a time when African American styles of modern dance were being positioned within the accepted forms of concert dance for the first time, and ICD was on that cutting edge in Boston.

The black press supported ICD's efforts to particularly augment the black dance classes in the Greater Boston area. The *Bay State Banner*, a daily newspaper serving the African American community, published a September 1971 story in the entertainment section called "New Dance Classes Offered." ICD's roster of black teachers and dance styles were emphasized, targeting me as one of the local anchor teachers who had recently returned from Europe. My European sojourn was becoming a marketing asset for me, but the creative black dance styles that I and other black dance instructors taught were augmenting a new cultural awareness in black communities nationwide. The article ended with, "Because these dance forms are a part of our culture as black people, classes will be designed to bring out cultural awareness and togetherness through emphasis on group dance, as well as individual awareness of one's creative self-expression through movement."[2] The black press "got it" and supported the collective efforts of the black dance teachers of ICD.

Early 1970s Dance Classes and the New Black Consciousness

Dance classes accompanied by conga drumming became a primary tool for inculcating and developing black awareness. The drums played for certain African-derived movements awakened cultural memory in black communities in the United States. The *Bay State Banner*'s recognition of the "cultural awareness and togetherness through emphasis on group dance" highlighted the collective approach of several black dance classes in Boston, particularly during the end of classes, when community dance circles were encouraged, where individuals took turns in the center, creating a traditional African dance circle. Privileging *community* creativity over individual competitive skills was a new cultural method introduced in the late 1960s into professional black dance training. It was prompted by the Black Arts movement initiating a creative new black consciousness that swept across black communities in the 1970s. This new focus on the communal learning experience, advanced in the black dance movement of the late 1960s and early 1970s, provided a particular group dynamic through dance.

There was also a kinesthetic collective experience prompted by improvisational modern dance during the same period, such as the work of Anna Halprin in San Francisco and Steve Paxton in New York. Dance theorist Susan Leigh Foster engages the term "kinesthesia," which she says psychologists envisioned as "a perceptual system that synthesized information about joint positioning, muscular exertion, and orientation within space and with respect to gravity." She also notes that neurobiologists more recently have utilized the concept of kinesthesia to "explore how the brain senses bodily movement." Importantly to my dance explorations, she also rightfully asserts that dance pedagogy has "consistently cultivated understanding of the existence and importance of kinesthetic awareness."[3]

It is the kinesthetic experience embedded in various forms of dance that triggers individual and group resonances with particular movements and also links them to cultural memory and awareness. This is what I experienced in the Bay Area during my transition from (white) modern dance to (black) modern dance accompanied by drumming: an "inner ear" opened, allowing me to *hear* the drum and feel my body responding in a way that I had not physically and psychically experienced before. Yet this embodied experience was something I already *knew* within my own spirit and only had to be awakened *mentally*; in the 1970s we only intuited this inner awareness that African-derived dance invoked. It would be thirty years before black dance scholarship would evolve to the point of researched conceptual links between the body, mind, and spirit. Yvonne Daniel, for example, has revealed that, "Embodied Knowledge—that is, knowledge found within the body, within the dance and drumming body—is rich and viable and should be referenced among other kinds of knowledge."[4] However, much fieldwork, research, and collaborative experiences by African and diasporan artists within their dance/drumming traditions would have to happen before we would have a researched knowledge base about what we were experiencing in those early days. But eventually an embodied understanding of the links between Africa, the Caribbean, and the United States would emerge and become common wisdom.

What I am exploring is not *essentializing* black dancers in the least. The black dance artists teaching for ICD in Boston taught a wide variety of classes that cannot be stereotyped only as "black dance." Gus Solomons Jr., for example, taught Cunningham Technique with little or no emotion; Cunningham dance is about motion itself rather than movement narratives with emotional meaning. Solomons assembled his dance phrases in a very linear architectural mode, as Solomons had been trained at MIT as an architect before moving to New York. Consuelo Atlas taught the Ailey style of Lester Horton Technique, a dance technique inspired by groundedness in Native American dance, which Ailey had learned as a member of Horton's Los Angeles company in the early 1950s. The technique remains the technical base of the Ailey Company until this day. As we were discovering our African dance roots and defining a new stage dance by U.S. black dance artists, we allowed all honest creative expression. We never limited what a black dance artist could and should do; everyone was free to create *within* and *without* black cultural traditions. Essentialism is confining and limiting; we were about broadening our embodied knowledge, moving past what I call the "slave mentality" that rendered Africa and its dances as primitive, while exploring the body and motion in all forms.

Foster highlights the late dance theorist Randy Martin's (1957–2015) concept of a social kinesthetic that encompasses the cultural *zeitgeist* among black artists, and dancer-choreographers in particular, in the 1970s. She concludes that "Randy Martin posits the existence of a social kinesthetic, a set of movement attributes or traits that make evident the deeper affinities between movement and culture."[5] Indeed, the idea of a kinesthesia that evolves from a social group dynamic was exactly what was happening among black dance artists and their students, as well as within dance companies directed by black choreographers, in the 1970s.

Kinesthesia refers to the "sensation" of movement. The African-derived dances that we were exploring in classes and in performance were based on impressions in our cultural memory as a diasporic people. Even if we did not have a repertoire of African dances, such as mandiani, kuku, lamba, dundunba, and the sabar cycle that has become commonplace in the twenty-first century, we had the collective phenomenon of exploring a communal memory that we had been taught to *hate*, even though that kinesthetic memory had remained in our social dances throughout the centuries. In the 1970s, black dancers were beginning to decolonize not only our minds but also our bodies. Foster reveals Martin's understanding of this trend contained in African diaspora cultural forms: "Martin emphasizes the politics implicit in a given kinesthesis. He posits a connection between a decolonized worldview and a preference for decentered movement, and points to the range of contemporary practices including capoeira, contact improvisation and hip-hop that celebrate an off-balance and risk-oriented investigation of the body's capacities for movement."[6]

Indeed, my cultural exploration through dance and drumming was celebrating "off-balance" risk-taking and was, both kinesthetically and socio-politically, bringing me in balance with myself. We were embodying risk through democratizing the body in my classes, and putting the center of different movements into different zones—shoulders, hips, head, and feet—rather than an autocratic center only in an uplifted core in the solar plexus. Looking back at my community-based dance classes, I realize this decentering process implicit in African-derived movements helped open some to a decolonized worldview. In the process we began to shed the socialized politics of black middle-class respectability and engaged African-centered approaches to the body and our community. This collective exploration among artistic black communities in the early 1970s was diverse, but it simultaneously expressed common cultural preferences that shifted what it meant to be "black," allowing us to end the twentieth century in a much better, self-empowered place than when we entered it.

Dancing and Choreographing in Boston

Boston became my point of reentry into black American culture after such a long time living in Europe. Another inroad, besides dance, was through an organization headed by a Ghanaian Paramount Chief, Nana Kobina Nketsia IV. He had founded a black cultural organization that I joined. This was an informal community group in Boston to teach African Americans about traditional African societies. An Oxford-educated anthropologist, Nana Nketsia was a Fante from the Sekondi-Takoradi area of Ghana. As an adjunct professor at the University of Massachusetts, Amherst, he came to Boston once a month to "hold court." I don't remember exactly how the group was formed, but somehow I heard of a real African chief who wanted to teach American blacks about African culture, and I eagerly joined. He taught us about traditional African social structure, such as eldership, chieftaincy, and democratic organizational structures within traditional African villages. Nana Nketsia's group of twenty black Americans formed into a mock African social structure, including bestowing the oldest female with the title of Queen Mother. Twenty-five years old at the time, I made up my mind that I would have to go to West Africa, not only to learn traditional dance but also witness this social structure directly for myself. Little did I know that within five years I would travel to Ghana and stay in Nana Nketsia's family compound.

Our informal cultural group of African Americans became an excellent way for us to explore traditional African society within our own group dynamics. This allowed us to comprehend, as much as possible in an urban American city, the way traditional Fante village structure worked. Looking back, I'm sure Nana Nketsia was also conducting his own experimental anthropological fieldwork to see how a group of African Americans who claimed interest in traditional African cultures would behave when organized in such a manner. But he conducted his experiment with personal warmth and a genuine connection to each one of us, and in the process created a real family among the participants, with him as the benevolent patriarch.

I remember feeling a sense of how much our community group's dynamics felt socially balanced, with women's voices structured into the decision-making power relations. The Fante are a matrilineal group, which accounts, in part, for a seemingly gender-equitable traditional social structure. Our organization experienced normal conflicts, but we also experienced traditional commonsense methods for resolving those disagreements. In this way, Africans living in the United States in the early 1970s interacted with African Americans, often in informal private settings that were not about media publicity or fanfare but about real cultural exchange in a time when blacks were searching for roots beyond the United States and hungry for all things African.

Besides my personal relationship with Donna and my exploration of African culture, dance continued to be my primary reason for being in Boston. I continued to study with some of the New York master teachers coming to Boston to teach for ICD; I never had a professional ego regarding taking classes with other dance teachers. Martha Graham's statement that I first heard in high school in the film *A Dancer's World* (chapter 1), "It takes ten years to make a good dancer," always rang in my ears, and I knew that my training had not been consistent but sporadic. Therefore, every opportunity I got to study with a good teacher, I did.

As I mentioned, ICD brought in many New York dancers like Gus Solomons, Consuelo Atlas, and Anna Sokolow. One weekend the dance organization brought Rod Rodgers for a three-day workshop. I was excited because I knew he was one of the big-time black choreographers in New York, and I could learn from his modern style in the Eric Hawkins tradition. Staying in the back of the studio, I took all three classes and enjoyed Rod's emphasis on flexibility, rhythmic complexity, and connecting one's movements into a melodic flow. To my surprise, after the third class he called me to the front to have a talk. Although he knew that I also taught dance for ICD, he asked me what my career plans were. I said I wanted to continue teaching and start choreographing in Boston. Then he made a life-changing statement: "Well, if you ever want to move to New York, come and see me because I think you could work in my company." This was a dramatic invitation to join a professional New York dance company, and although I was not ready to move to New York then, I mentally filed the invitation away for the future.

Then, choreographing was on my mind and in my body. I had things to say onstage, and many of the dance students in my classes were ready for a major black theatrical statement to express our collective sense of our changing cultural and spiritual consciousness. At twenty-five I was feeling empowered, having survived three years in Europe essentially by myself, while codirecting the Magic Lotus Dance Theatre in Copenhagen and creating *March of the Created* for the Balettakademien in Stockholm (chapter 2). I wanted to develop that choreographic work about my growing existential sense of how individuals were trapped as actors in their perceived social roles, and to couple that with my increased sense of how central black culture was to American identity. The result became an evening-length work called *Changes, Or How Do You Get to Heaven When You're Already in Hell?* that premiered March 11 and 12, 1972, at Wheelock College Auditorium in Boston and was produced by the Institute for Contemporary Dance.

Donna and I created a dynamic working relationship, with her serving as producer of the weekend performances and with me as the choreographer-artist, making our personal relationship mutually beneficial on a professional level as well. Gail Phillipo (now Nuru Dafina), who eventually became one of the most accomplished African drummers in the country, designed an effective advertising flyer and program art. Her drawing for *Changes* showed a human figure with a rope constraining its body from neck to feet, depicting human enslavement on several levels. Looking back, *Changes* was my first real attempt at a historical look at the black experience that would become a signature of my dance career for decades. I would later go on to develop this underlying theme into *The Evolution of Black Dance*, which would tell my version of *Roots*—the journey from Africa to the Americas through dance.

Changes was truly ambitious, with a forty-member cast of dancers and musicians performing two acts that included three different scenes each. Part 1, "The Big Conquest," consisted of "The Big Conquest," "Ropes and Chains—Who Is the Victim?" and "The Streets, Jim? Nothin' Happenin', Baby!" The titles themselves give a sense of my inchoate attempt to capture our roots in Africa, the Middle Passage, and the postslavery social and economic marginalization that would create the underground economy of urban street characters, today called the 'hood. For the African scene, "The Big Conquest," I hired African drummer Yusef Crowder, who had his own African dance company, along with percussionists Mpelelezi Kasimu and Nathan Spivey, with Obalijeg Durr on percussion (who would later become Consuelo Atlas's second husband when she moved back to Boston). In the "Ropes and Chains" scene, I danced a duet called "The Rape," with one of my white male dance students, Frank Colardo, playing the slaver who rapes a captured African woman, revealing the female plight in the slave trade.

In the South End, I had plenty of chances to observe black/Latino street culture on busy Tremont Street near West Springfield, where I lived. Many of the scenes I created in "The Streets, Jim?" were from characters I observed on that main thoroughfare running through the South End of Boston. It was definitely the *other* side of Boston, not what was predicted in John Winthrop's 1630 "City Upon a Hill" sermon that established the ideal of Massachusetts Bay Colony. Twentieth-century politicians like Ronald Reagan and John F. Kennedy invoked this same vision of Boston as the original American beacon of hope. But *Changes* portrayed the underbelly of Boston through the choreographic characters I saw in the South End.

Changes, Or How Do You Get to Heaven When You're Already in Hell? continued after intermission into part 2, "Comin' on Down," with three more scenes: "Hip Party, USA," "Spirits Descending," and "March of the Created." The recorded music for "Hip Party, USA" was eclectic, representing my varied musical taste from psychedelic R&B, soul, and Eastern music: Janis Joplin, Sly & the Family Stone, James Brown, and Buddhist Temple Bells. The opening of part 2 attempted to hold a mirror to youth culture in urban America regarding all that we considered cool and hip in the early 1970s: numbing drugs, counterculture fashion, and rebellious pop music. This scene exposed the actual underlying cultural excesses and crass materialism through choreographed archetypes from the previous scene's street characters intermingling with New Age hippies. It was like my version of *Hair the Musical*, with an emphasis on black characters. "Spirits Descending" was an attempt to bring my growing spiritual perceptions into the sociocultural picture I was painting. Black cloth–covered figures appeared and moved through the stage space to Arabic chants of the Koran and Japanese Noh music. The message was that the spiritual sphere, even though we cannot see or touch it, intermingles with our social world and has an influence.

The finale, "March of the Created," was an elaboration of the original choreography that I had created in Stockholm, with characters of each of the previous sections reappearing on a strong stage diagonal with repetitive movement phrases representing their distinct social roles. This was an effective ending for *Changes* because it made the ultimate statement of the entire evening: we are all playing social, cultural, political, and historical roles, often unreflectively. Can we change that historic programming and do something different with our lives? Can we become *conscious* players on the stage of life and save ourselves from the hell we have created for ourselves? Ambitious, precocious, and youthfully empowered, *Changes, Or How Do You Get to Heaven When You're Already in Hell?* was indeed my first major choreographic statement that was more theatrical philosophy than choreography. It made a major social statement and was definitely noticed in Boston.

But there was a personal layer to my choreographic message, which I attempted to disguise because it was too painful to become the centerpiece of the "changes" I was addressing. My relationship with Donna was not as idyllic as I had anticipated; after all the years we had waited to be together, our time in Boston was marred by infidelities and conflict. I spent many nights waiting for her to come home while drinking myself to sleep. In retrospect, this experience of unrequited love was important for me to experience to understand the dark side of life that had heretofore eluded me. This was so mainly because I had never allowed myself to be that emotionally vulnerable before. I began to understand what blues singers were talking about, and it was certainly no double-entendre party. Every bit of my personal pain went into my choreography and story, supposedly hidden behind history and social commentary.

While I was an unknown artist receiving little coverage from the mainstream media like the *Boston Globe*, the black press again was important in bringing attention to my work with a major review of *Changes*. Kay Bourne of the *Bay State Banner* wrote an accurate and revealing review called "'Changes' Stirs Old Memories." After she recounted the audience response to my evening-length production with their thunderous applause and a standing ovation, she proceeded to tell the story of her "first unrequited love affair," and how she took a short story she had written about the affair and turned it into a play for her college theater class. Ouch! My personal "changes" were not as disguised as I had thought. Bourne went on to say: "In a disguised autobiography every voice is the author's. Oh there are shadows of scenery or the sweep of history and shapes of people not really ourselves. But basically everybody says and everything does what is necessary to feed the single psychic venturer."[7]

As a good theater critic, Bourne saw through my elaborate social history journey to what the piece was: a disguised diatribe about my love relationship and my experience of dishonesty and emotional pain. Bourne hit the nail on the head when she observed: "Because it's 'disguised' to the writer at least the story never gets personal in any way that would teach us something about how to rise or fall in life. It only remains intense." Revisiting this review of *Changes*, Bourne made an important point for all artistic endeavors: it must be truthful. If I had somehow opened up my hidden meaning and exposed myself within my elaborate libretto for *Changes*, I might have been able to touch my audience even more deeply. Bourne continued:

> Really all there is to learn from all [the scenes] is that it must be something Janis Miller feels intensely about. But what is it she feels? The story not told in *Changes* was that of a particular black woman. There was the praise of black women overall that was very present in the dances, and very stimulating to the audience. But Janis Miller's story has yet to be written by her if that's what she wants to do.[8]

Although she did praise my choreography and my "striking talent and ability to hold together a company," while noting several good performances by Bill Mackey, Danny Sloane, and my good friend singer-dancer Arnold Scott (now known as Illanga), Bourne gave me something to contemplate for my next choreographic endeavor, while letting me know I still had more personal and artistic growing to do.

After my evening-length forty-member cast choreographic work, I felt like I had done the job I had come to Boston to do. I had become a successful teacher in one of the growing non-profit dance centers of Boston—the Institute for Contemporary Dance—continued my dance study with some of the best New York choreographers, and reentered black culture through my work with Nana Nketsia. Moreover, my major artistic work with *Changes* had galvanized the black community of Boston. I had also been through the emotional grind with Donna Maynard and felt that we needed physical distance again to see if we really wanted to be together.

As fate would have it, Consuelo Atlas was ready to leave her prominent dancer status (second only to Judith Jamison) in the Alvin Ailey American Dance Theater and move back to her hometown of Boston to start her own dance company. She had grown up near Donna in Cambridge, and they stayed in close contact. Consuelo let her know that she was ready to give up New York's dance limelight and come back to Boston to be with her husband, Henry Atlas. I remembered Rod Rodgers's invitation to join his company, and when I heard that Consuelo would be giving up her apartment in Manhattan's Lower East Side, I asked her if I could sublease her apartment. The fates were opening up for me again, showing me my next "dance move," and I took it. Consuelo moved out of the major U.S. dance center and back to where she could do her own artistic work. In Boston, she started her own company—Impulse Dance Company—that became the resident company of the Joy of Movement Center,[9] both of which are still going strong today, even though Consuelo died tragically in 1979 at age thirty-five. Simultaneously I was moving to the Big Apple to begin what I considered to be the ultimate test—dancing in a professional dance company in New York City.

Dancing in New York with Rod Rodgers

I landed right in the center of the reality of Manhattan in the Lower East Side, just south of Union Square in Consuelo Atlas's apartment on the corner of Third Avenue and East Thirteenth Street. It was a recently renovated building, with the apartments containing newly laid hardwood floors and new appliances, but to get into the front door, I would often have to solicit help moving nodded-out junkies out of the way. In May 1972, this was not the gentrified area of Lower East Side it is today with chic cafés, antique dealers, flower shops, and the Classic Stage Company, one of the most prestigious contemporary Off-Broadway theaters. Growing up in the so-called ghetto of the lower Fillmore in San Francisco in no way prepared me for the reality of the poor, drug-ridden, downtrodden life of street people in my neighborhood. Allan Tannenbaum paints the sociopolitical picture in his *New York in the 70s*:

> Dirty, dangerous, and destitute. This was New York City in the 1970s. War still raged in Vietnam, fueling resentment against the federal government. Nixon and the Watergate scandal created even more cynicism and skepticism. Economic stagnation coupled with inflation to create a sense of malaise. The Arab oil embargo brought the misery of long lines to buy gasoline. Conditions in neighborhoods like Harlem and Bedford-Stuyvesant were horrendous, with abandoned buildings and abject poverty. The subways, covered everywhere with ugly graffiti, were unreliable. The parks were in decay, home to muggers and rapists. Crime was rampant, and the authorities were powerless to stop it.[10]

I felt many of these social dynamics when I arrived in New York City, and I cried every day for the first week. It was impossible for me to ignore the misery that surrounded me daily. I called Donna and my mother several times that first week, just trying to process the reality of my new life. This former San Francisco hippie/expatriate-in-Europe/black dancer could not stomach the reality of New York. Both Donna's and my mother's advice was: "You went there to do dance! Try to ignore the street people; you have to put on blinders to get through the streets and into the dance studio." I slowly had to become insensitive and ignore the blight and misery in order to survive, but it never came easy. I grew even more aware of how each of us has to deal with the multiple layers of life from the psychological personal to the social and political realities, from the inner self to the collective social. I wrote in my journal that first week:

> In New York now; the rain pours down in buckets; in solitude, living alone again. Survival is struggling to overcome, to get beyond what I see and experience here. Life is demanding its due that must be understood, or perish. Hypnotizing rain, splashing against the windows, like my tears. Testing new wings and confidence. Fear of the future, but strength to see it through—a little clarity with a lot of apprehension. Donna's love? Missing her warmth already, but beginning to feel peace, and purpose. Having a direction, work ahead, all there is to learn. Looking out at the streets—a vicious circle that strangles. New York: naked, raw, human nature. New York's oppression is its differences between people that separate and become barriers for each other.

I eventually overcame my depression, using the incredible artistic and theatrical life of New York as an antidote for the devastating street realities.

Black dance companies in the 1970s existed within a larger New York dance and experimental theater world that was the most sophisticated in the country. La MaMa, the experimental theater company, was founded in 1961 by a black woman, Ellen Stewart (1919–2011). As Stewart said from the beginning, "La MaMa is the place where emerging artists learn from established artists and where artists from around the globe share work and ideas."[11] Richard Schechner's theater company, the Performance Group, was beginning in SoHo with a psychoanalytical approach to performance art. Rudolph Nureyev, who had defected from Russia's Kirov Ballet in 1961 and danced with several European companies, was then making appearances with the Martha Graham Dance Company in New York, continuing to break down the long-term barrier between ballet and modern dance. Twyla Tharp started working at Greenwich Village's Judson Church, beginning to mainstream avant-garde dance that had been developing the so-called postmodern dance scene since the early 1960s, with dancer-choreographers like Steve Paxton, David Gordon, Deborah Hay, and Yvonne Rainer.

Rod Rodgers's dance studio, then at Twelfth Street and Fifth Avenue, not too far from Washington Square Park, was my solace where I found like spirits serving the dance "gods." We all experienced the joy of movement alone and together, striving to bring forth the aesthetic and social dance messages of our artistic director. The day I met Rod in his office to let him know I was there to take him up on his Boston offer, he immediately welcomed me and let me know that he was glad to have me in his company, while having his secretary set me up on the company roster for the payroll. He immediately told me about the technical work I needed to improve, particularly my port de bras (arm carriage), as I was known for my special use of my hands that made angles like wings, rather than extending the length of the arms. I told him I was his canvas, and I wanted to improve technically and artistically to become a New York professional dancer, as I set about learning the company repertoire.

Rod Rodgers was born in Cleveland, Ohio, but raised in Detroit, growing up in a dancing, performing family with his father and mother as post-vaudevillian dancer-singers who also ran a talent agency. In a 2000 television interview called "African American Legends" with Dr. Roscoe C. Brown for CUNY-TV, Rod said, "Coming out of Detroit as a music town, and being encouraged to be in the arts because that is like what my family did, I came to New York looking for a better way to do it, really."[12] As a second-generation African American dancer, he also talked about the tenor of the times when he started the Rod Rodgers Dance Company in New York in 1966, when "artists of the minority became part of the struggle to speak for people who are not speaking for themselves." Inaugurating his dance company on the heels of the assassination of Malcolm X, Rod wanted not only to further his interest in experimental modern dance, having studied with Eric Hawkins, José Limón, and Martha Graham, but also to use his dance platform to make social statements about the plight of black America.

Rod's repertoire represented an eclectic platform of dances that ranged from abstract percussion dances to modern jazz performed to popular music, as well as strong social commentary works about American society.

Rod was known as an articulate, intelligent choreographer who gave many lectures at universities and wrote essays about dance and the social times. When he was asked what his dance message was, he said the following in that CUNY-TV interview:

> There were two parts [to my repertoire]. First, I came up in a family of entertainers, and I always felt the programs we did had to have a certain element of entertainment; people just had to be able to enjoy themselves. And secondly, I had a cousin named Molly Moon, and her husband was a guy named Henry Lee Moon, who was the Editor of Crisis Magazine [for the NAACP], and through my involvement with them, they were constantly encouraging me as an artist to include in my art something that addressed serious issues. So we developed a series that we're best known for called "Poets and Peacemakers" that has within it the writings of Langston Hughes and images of Martin Luther King, Jr.'s struggle. We did a wonderful piece on Duke Ellington, and a piece on heroic women of color dedicated to Harriet Tubman.

This statement reveals Rod Rodgers's artistic motivations, including a sense of a social responsibility that most black artists felt in the late 1960s and 1970s. He wanted to use his creative platform to educate and make a difference in America's racial and social justice movements prominent during those times.

The Rod Rodgers Dance Company (RRDC) continues today under the artistic directorship of Kim Grier-Martinez, with his classic repertoire that can be broken into three major categories: (1) Signature Works, (2) Rhythm Dances, and (3) Poets & Peacemakers Series.[13] When I danced with RRDC in 1972, Rod was working on the first two, and the third category came after I left the company in 1973. The only current Signature Work in the repertoire, which was performed during my tenure, is Box '71, a Rodgers choreographic work that made a major sociopolitical statement, receiving wide critical acclaim. In Rod's words, Box '71 is "a study in confinement, dedicated to Soledad Brother George Jackson and the men who were massacred at Attica." George Jackson, a member of the Black Panther Party, was given a prison sentence of one year to life for an alleged theft of seventy dollars from a Los Angeles gas station in 1960. While serving his sentence, he was charged with the murder of a white prison guard at

California's Soledad Prison along with two other inmates, and hence was thereafter called one of the Soledad Brothers. He was killed at San Quentin Prison during a daring prison escape on August 21, 1971. During his ten years in prison George Jackson became an avid Marxist, prison reform activist, and writer, with his *Soledad Brother: The Prison Letters of George Jackson* published first in 1970 and later reissued in 1994.

Rod's second motivation for *Box* was the Attica Prison riot in Attica Correctional Facility in Upstate New York just two weeks after Jackson's death at San Quentin. These two prison revolts made international news and strongly affected black people in the United States. In the turbulent late 1960s and early 1970s, artists like Rod Rodgers were becoming aware of what Michelle Alexander describes in her book *The New Jim Crow: Mass Incarceration in the Age of Colorblindness* (2012). However, in the early 1970s, there was no pretension of a postracial discourse, with the unthinkable election of a black president being thirty-five years away; we were still fighting for basic civil rights and processing the meaning of "black power" in all arenas, including dance.

Rod's *Box* became a major timely dance statement by a black male choreographer. Two black males, one dressed in tattered clothes on a platform behind bars and the other on the stage in a suit and tie and carrying a briefcase, danced the piece. As a study in confinement, the work juxtaposes the traditional incarceration behind prison walls with the prison often created by the American Dream driven by capitalism. As black Americans worked hard to gain access to basic rights of citizenship in the 1970s, they also pushed for economic access to the middle class in larger numbers, and Rod thought it important to also critique the class aspirations of black Americans, which in his assessment were just as potentially confining as being imprisoned. In *Box*, the man behind bars knows he is contained and continually grabs the bars while peering out to "freedom." The businessman outside the box is first preoccupied with time and his social status, continually checking his wristwatch. Slowly the two characters' gestures and movement phrases begin to coincide, even though the man outside the box does not see the jailed one. As their movements become more and more similar, the businessman begins to intuit his own imprisoned and mental social space, and ultimately his life. When he *finally* notices his jailed counterpart, he begins to trace the prison bars and realizes that they are in the same situation. Turning back to his own confined social space, he begins to trace an invisible box like a mime and enacts being thrown down and handcuffed by invisible authorities. In the end they become the same, both imprisoned by their two social realities.

Box became an important signature work of RRDC because it was an unabashed conceptual dance exploration that spoke to the disproportionate incarceration rate of black men, as well as the often stultifying U.S. social conformity that still exists today. In 1972, Rod Rodgers himself performed the businessman, while one of his main male soloists, Ron Pratt, danced the imprisoned man. The accompanying music was a score of experimental abstract sounds and avant-garde jazz. Noted *New York Times* dance critic Don McDonagh reviewed a July 31, 1972, performance of the RRDC at Alice Tully Hall in Lincoln Center and said this about *Box*: "The forcefulness of the pairing was underscored by the restricted square of space that each paced and restlessly occupied. In its tiny allotted area, the work said more with economy of means than others manage with larger scaled works."[14] Rod's aesthetic approach was always based on investigating the basic elements of movement—space, rhythm, design, and dynamics—and in *Box* he astutely used space and dynamics in particular to make a major sociopolitical statement. Although McDonagh did not engage the obvious real-life social motivation behind the piece regarding the tragedy of George Jackson and the Attica prisoners, which was explicitly stated in the audience program, the message to the audience was crystal clear. Rod's message remains relevant into the twenty-first century, making *Box* a timeless sociopolitical work in the field of modern dance.

The part of Rod Rogers's repertoire called Rhythm Dances was particularly unique and always appreciated by the (white) modern dance world. These dances represented a direct influence of his tenure with Eric Hawkins, who, after dancing with Martha Graham's company (and marrying her), started the Eric Hawkins Dance Company in 1951. Hawkins was known for his interdisciplinary approach to dance with props, sets, original music, and Eastern philosophy. Therefore, the artistic lineage of Rod had several branches, including black vaudeville entertainment via his parents and classic modern dance via his New York training from some of the original founders of the genre. The Rhythm Dances section of the company repertoire reflected his merger of these two very disparate theatrical traditions. I performed in *Percussion Suite* (1967), *Tangents* (1968), and *Rhythm Ritual* (1972), the latter of which was created on the company while I was a member.

Dancers in the Rhythm Dances repertoire performed with percussion sticks, playing composed rhythms along with the percussive, yet melodic, musical accompaniment. I remember the rehearsals for *Rhythm Ritual*, where half the day was spent musically, sitting on the studio floor and learning the different rhythmic parts that each dancer would have to play in unison and individually. Then during the rest of the rehearsal day these percussive stick rhythms were inserted into choreographed energetic modern dance phrases, blending Rod's theatrical strands. For *Rhythm Ritual* the music accompaniment was conga drumming that he himself would often play visibly onstage. A kind of Afro-modern choreography emerged that was riveting, and not easy to perform. But once we mastered the art of being dancers and musicians at the same time, it was exciting and exhilarating to turn, extend, plié, and contract, all while playing the percussion sticks, in pairs, trios, and unison ensemble sections.

I also danced *Tangents* set to a musical score by Henry Cowell and Lou Harrison. This work was more classical modern–oriented and was taught to me by Barbara Roan, one of Rod's early white dancers who knew his repertoire backward and forward, and who had also danced with Eric Hawkins. In *Tangents* we had to dance with long, thin rods that made a swishing wind sound when swung through the air with our fast-paced athletic choreography. The thin rods became extensions of our arms, elongating the bodylines far into the performing space. Rod was both a modern dance choreographer in the classic sense as well as a modern jazz dancemaker with a complex Africanist rhythmic sensibility.

The part of his repertoire under the Signature Works umbrella in 1972 was an exploration of various black themes that utilized contemporary R&B music. Rod performed a love duet with the late dancer Shirley Rushing in *To Say Goodbye* to a ballad by Roberta Flack, and set a full company work, *Don't Need No Help*, to music by Ashford and Simpson. But the signature work in the black dance tradition that everyone loved was his *Shout*, performed to Donny Hathaway's "To Be Young, Gifted, and Black." This was a solo dance to Hathaway's cover of the Nina Simone's civil rights anthem that was first recorded on her 1970 *Black Gold* album; Hathaway had quickly covered the hit single on his 1970 album *Everything Is Everything*. Rod first set the work on Thomas Pinnock, a Jamaican dancer-choreographer who occasionally danced with the company, so everyone considered *Shout* a male solo in the RRDC repertoire. However, Rod felt that I had the energy, strength, and conviction to perform this solo dance representing the tenor of the times, and he taught me the dance as a new female dancer in the company.

Shout could not help but be a literal interpretation of the early 1970s statement of black self-empowerment engendered by the Civil Rights and Black Power movements. The dance, following the song, attacked the underutilized, latent talent waiting to be expressed in the black community while simultaneously celebrating unique black individualism and collective gifts. I was totally surprised that Rod chose me, as a woman, to dance the work, and I dove into learning and performing it with a vengeance. I wanted to prove that it was not a *male* solo but rather a black *dancer's* solo that could be performed effectively by either sex. All that I felt about being young, gifted, and black myself went into my performance, and my *Shout* solo became a featured part of the repertoire everywhere RRDC performed.

One performance at the Statue of Liberty Park, as part of Rod's 1972 summer Parks and Recreation contract, was especially intense. When I performed a pitch-attitude turn that ended with me staring right at the iconic statue, I seized the moment to focus my performance attention on this symbol of so-called "liberty and freedom." That turning moment in the dance was filled with my attitude about the rights so often denied my people as the only "unwilling immigrants" brought and enslaved in the United States of America (figure 3). *Shout* was the RRDC piece that allowed my unique qualities to be noticed, garnering me a mention in that same *New York Times* review by Don McDonagh: "'Shout' an expressionistic portrait danced by Janis Miller was far from the enclosed world of *Box* and moved easily and sensuously around with a beautiful flow of movement."[15] Though short and succinct, my part of the review was positive. I had come to New York to dance, and within five months I had a favorable *New York Times* dance review, which was no small feat.

In six short years the Rod Rodgers Dance Company had built a strong reputation in New York, and the year I danced with him we performed at a wide variety of venues, allowing me to experience a range of the New York dance scene. Besides the New York City parks that summer, we also performed for a unique program called the Dancemobile. This groundbreaking organization, which took professional dance companies directly into neighborhoods of New York's five boroughs, was a performance experience that allowed me to see more of New York outside of Manhattan and to share my art with an audience that may never come to a theater. Inaugurated by the Harlem Cultural Council (HCC) and funded by the NYC Department of Cultural Affairs and the New York State Council on the Arts, it was a mobile stage unit on the back of a big truck that parked on a designated street in a residential neighborhood. A stage unfolded, complete with danceable marley flooring, as well as theatrical lights and curtain wings for stage entrances and exits. After sundown, the performance would begin, and people came out of their brownstone apartments to the streets, sat on the front stoops, or simply watched hanging out of their front windows. Rod told me that each community had a committee that worked along with the Dancemobile administration to aid in preperformance neighborhood publicity. Many of the families would bring sandwiches and soft drinks to share with us to show their appreciation. The Dancemobile was a rewarding community connection, allowing the dancers to give the dance back to the people who generated many of the cultural and movement nuances that the RRDC choreography captured.

The origin of the Dancemobile was actually the result of the hard work of black dancer Carole Y. Johnson, a soloist with the Eleo Pomare Dance Company. She started the Dancemobile in 1967 as the primary organizer. It is significant that a *dancer* learned the administrative duties of fund raising, publicity, finances, and negotiations with stakeholders from the city, the state, corporate sponsor Hoffman Beverages, and the neighborhood representatives. As Carole states, "A spiritual force had empowered me to pull the many threads together and make the Harlem Cultural Council's dream a reality."[16] The HCC had successfully run a Jazzmobile, founded by well-known pianist Billy Taylor, for three years prior to the Dancemobile. It was only natural that dance would be included in a model that took the arts directly to poor black and Latino communities, becoming an important art form presented by the HCC. But there was a sociopolitical motivation as well: Carole states the real purpose of the Dancemobile was to "establish activities that might help to prevent the riots that had happened in other cities from happening in New York. . . . With the threat of summer riots, everyone seemed anxious to help this novice in every area of producing to get the project accomplished."[17] Black despair and rage have motivated many new economic, social, and, in this case, cultural projects to make a difference in the communities' attitudes, especially during the summer months. I kept marveling at the fact that a dancer organized the first two years of the Dancemobile. I now realize that Carole's example became a model that I was eventually destined to follow back in my home in the Bay Area (chapter 6).

As Carole Johnson notes, the primary *artistic* mandate of the Dancemobile was to create works that would play well to a black and Latino neighborhood audience. The Dancemobile was truly established for an audience who rarely came to formal theater but could appreciate good art. By 1972, most of the black dance companies participated in the summer Dancemobile, and RRDC was one of the primary companies. The neighborhood people loved the fact that we came to perform just for them, and my performance of *Shout*, with its musical anthem of "To Be Young, Gifted, and Black," was always a big hit. It was personally fulfilling dancing that piece in Harlem or the Bronx, where the people really *needed* that kind of cultural and personal reinforcement, and I could feel the bond that I was forging with them as I performed. I had heard that the larger New York dance scene eschewed the Dancemobile for pandering to the people and not presenting "substantive" challenging dance works. But I viewed this criticism as the typical elitism of the white modern dance world and felt proud of the black dance companies of New York for bringing the art of dance directly to the people—giving it back from whence it came.

Another of my important performances with RRDC was "Soul at the Center," a series of black theatrical performances at Lincoln Center for the Performing Arts produced by noted black theater and television producer Elis B. Haizlip (ca. 1930–1991). The RRDC performed on July 31, 1972, at Alice Tully Hall, and it was reviewed by *The New York Times*. I was unaware at the time of the real significance of this Lincoln Center series that had been organized by key black New York movers and shakers like Haizlip and Clarence Jones, publisher of the *New York Amsterdam News*. "Soul at the Center" ran from July 24 to August 3 and featured dance, music, and literary artists such as poet/author Nikki Giovanni; R&B singers Bobby Womack, Ashford and Simpson, Donny Hathaway, and Labelle; gospel singers Sister Rosetta Tharpe and Shirley Caesar; Latin Jazz pianist Eddie Palmieri; avant-garde jazz pianist Cecil Taylor; jazz vocalists Betty Carter and Novella Nelson; and blues singer Taj Mahal, among others. The other New York dance company in the series, besides RRDC, was the George Faison Universal Dance Experience.

The artists were organized into various configurations for each "Soul at the Center" performance. RRDC was paired with none other than the late great Cuban master drummer Mongo Santamaría (1922–2003). I was very aware of the great honor of performing on the same show with Santamaría, a rumba *quinto* conga master and a Latin jazz percussionist who had recorded a top-ten hit, "Watermelon Man," with Herbie Hancock and composed the jazz standard "Afro-Blue." RRDC got great audience exposure among the Cuban and jazz music fans with that strategic pairing with Mongo Santamaría (figure 4).

Haizlip, as producer of the entire series, saw this project at Lincoln Center as an inroad into a mainstream New York venue developing out of his public TV-13 WNET show called *Soul*. He had this to say about the series in the audience program: "Presently 'soul' is in vogue. I do hope that this time we are able to fill some of these dignified and solemn buildings we are being offered with vibrations so strong, so mean, that never will another enter without acknowledging our presence here. Throughout this series of 'Soul at the Center' please remember that." Today, we can substitute his colloquial term "mean" for "black," because that's what he actually meant. We were *integrating* the hallowed halls of one of New York's major theater venues for the first time, and black dance was an essential part of that cultural assimilation process. Today, Haizlip would be proud that "Jazz at Lincoln Center" has become a major part of the venue's programming, directed by the virtuosic and multitalented Wynton Marsalis.

The RRDC performance at "Soul at the Center" was a major production in a prestigious black context, and therefore Rod featured six of his best black dancers from his multiracial company: Ronald Pratt, Aramide Smci, Shirley Rushing, Ellis Frazier, Noel Hall, and me. Rod usually sought the best black stage technicians that he could find; hence, behind the scenes reflected what one saw onstage. Our lighting designer for this performance and many others was Shirley Prendergast, the Obie Award–winning lighting designer for the Alvin Ailey Dance Theater, the Negro Ensemble Company, and many other top black performing companies. For "Soul at the Center," Rod put forth his strongest "black" work, including, *Box, Shout, To Say Goodbye, Don't Need No Help, Eidolons* (from a larger work, *The Conjuring*), and a new ensemble piece in which Rod himself performed, *Harambee!* (Forward with Unity). The latter work's program notes read: "A ritual of the inspiration, martyrdom and a spiritual resurrection of Black leaders. This dance-drama is dedicated to martyred black leaders and to the nameless thousands who have been brutalized or murdered because they were Black." Rod's roles in this choreographic work were as Onri-tele, a visionary or seer, and as Oluko, a teacher.

The early 1970s was a serious time for making overt black statements in theater and dance. In New York, the Black Arts movement was in full gear—Barbara Ann Teer's National Black Theater was going strong in Harlem—and black choreographers had an obligation to contribute to the developing black cultural discourse of the times. Rod Rodgers was a major voice in that narrative in New York dance in the 1970s.

Before the "Soul at the Center" performance, RRDC toured to Detroit, where Rod had booked museum, theater, and school performances for the company over the course of one week. As his hometown, Detroit offered Rod a large network of presenters and a dedicated audience base; he was viewed as local boy who made good in big-time New York City. The company stayed at his family's inn and restaurant called the Rapa House. Rod's mother, LaJune Rodgers, was a strong and beautiful woman who ran the Rapa House as a motel that doubled as a Creole cuisine restaurant, and also served as an after-hours jazz club. While the company stayed at the Rapa House, we had a chance to experience Rod's roots in the black entertainment and arts community that his family nurtured. The sign outside the three-story brownstone building at 96 E. Vernor Highway, between Woodward and John R. Vernor, said, "Rapa House Concert Café," and that's exactly what it was. I stayed up many nights to hear good after–2:00 a.m. jazz when Detroit musicians stopped in after finishing their regular gigs.

As mentioned before, Rod's parents were dancers on the vaudeville circuit, and he and his brother, Ernie Rodgers, noted jazz saxophonist and music professor at Wayne State University, grew up in a touring performing arts environment. Ernie revealed the lifestyle he and Rod were raised in during an interview:

> My parents were adagio dancers, ballroom stuff. We [the family] were all dancing; we were always on the show. My bed was in the dressing room. I can remember being in the dressing room with Duke Ellington in the late 30s. I remember he didn't put his pants on [because] he didn't want to wrinkle them. Walked around in his shirttails! I was always on the bandstand trying to listen to musicians. Cootie Williams' horn was the first horn I played.[18]

From Ernie Rodgers's colorful description of their childhood, it's obvious that he and Rod grew up in one of the seminal Detroit black venues—ostensibly one of the stops along the Chitlin Circuit—that helped develop black entertainment in Detroit. When the family stopped touring, they settled in Detroit, and that's when they started an artist-booking agency. LaJune Rodgers took charge of the agency and moved it into the Rapa House when her husband died.

Before the RRDC tour to the Midwest, I was not aware of the depth of Rod's entrenchment in this early form of black performance, but in staying at the Rapa House I became fascinated with Rod's roots in black entertainment culture. It allowed me to understand the depth of his commitment to black dance forms and audiences while simultaneously being steeped in the concert modern dance world. Like most black choreographers, he saw no conflict between these seemingly disparate parts of his artistic life and easily slipped in and out of these different performance cultures.

The RRDC tour to Detroit was an artistic success, with many sold-out performances and a chance for me to see the Midwest for the first time. It would not be my last, as twenty-eight years later I would live one hour south in Toledo, Ohio, married and with my first tenure-track academic position at Bowling Green State University. Detroit would then become my frequent soulful black culture getaway, and I always remembered my 1972 Rapa House experience.

After such an intense summer performing schedule, the company was given a short break, and I went back to Boston to see Donna. We went for a respite on Martha's Vineyard, where her parents had a home in Oaks Bluffs, the black district on the island. When I returned to New York, one of my last performances with RRDC was the opening of the fall 1972 dance season on Broadway. Yes, in those days, the major dance companies started the new performance season with appearances in Broadway venues. An indication of the status of RRDC in the broader New York dance scene is that Rod was invited to be on the Broadway roster for that year. This was again an optimal opportunity for me in my quest to consume the New York dance scene as much as possible.

The RRDC performed at the ANTA (American National Theatre and Academy), one of the few non-profit theater organizations in the for-profit Broadway theater district.[19] The dance season that year also included the Martha Graham Dance Company, American Ballet Theatre, the Anna Sokolow Dance Company, and others. Dancing with Rod Rodgers had proven to be an extremely rewarding experience because it allowed me to test my dance skills and artistry within the context of *the* standard for concert dance in the United States. It also allowed me to be thoroughly involved with the developing dance discourse within the Black Arts movement that had started in the 1960s and continued in the 1970s as a part of the reeducation and empowerment of black people in the United States. Dance, though often overlooked in the historical record of the times, was an integral part of the public discourse that was being articulated in the Black Arts movement. The RRDC was at the center of establishing the *professional* dance statement within this seminal political and sociocultural movement of the times.

New York City's Black Dance Scene in the 1970s

The Rod Rodgers Dance Company (RRDC) existed within a prolific black dance scene in New York City in the 1970s and was considered a part of the second-tier dance companies by choreographic recognition, technical level of dancers, and size of budget and administrative structure. At the top, of course, was the internationally recognized Alvin Ailey American Dance Theater. The second tier was right above a myriad of smaller dance companies directed by black choreographers such as Ron Pratt (when he wasn't dancing with Rod), Fred Benjamin, Otis Sallid, Chuck Davis, and others, who mainly had "pickup" dancers. Rod's main competitors in the second tier of black dance companies were the Eleo Pomare Dance Company and the George Faison Universal Dance Experience, neither of which is still in existence. As it was highly competitive to be accepted into Ailey's company, the majority of black dancers in New York in the 1970s went back and forth between the three dance companies occupying this second tier, as well as the smaller, third-tier companies.

Each of the three second-tier choreographers was known for his distinct choreographic aesthetic. Eleo was considered the "bad boy" of the scene, with his 1960s signature work *Blues for the Jungle* (1966) about the street life of New York, and his solo piece *Narcissus Rising* (1968), where he played the role of a motorcycle biker wearing only leather dance trunks, boots, and a cap. George Faison, a former Ailey dancer, was known for his modern jazz choreography represented by his signature *Suite Otis* (1971), a soulful and often humorous interpretation of Otis Red-

ding's classic R&B and blues songs. I visited both of these two choreographers' studios when I first arrived in New York and chose the RRDC because of the eclectic mix of Rod's repertoire that allowed one to perform
both classic modern dance and soulful jazz-inspired choreography. But
the Alvin Ailey American Dance Theater was always, and still is, considered the undisputed pinnacle of the black concert dance scene of New
York City and, indeed, the world.

But how did this black dance hierarchy come about? What preceded
this New York black dance scene that I found in 1972, regarding opportunities and venues available to black concert dancers and choreographers?
The answers are important to examine in terms of the larger sociopolitical
U.S. revolution going on at the time. An extensive quote from Zita Allen on
the website for the documentary film *Free to Dance: The African American
Presence in Modern Dance* assesses the times:

> During the 1950s and '60s, the story of blacks in American modern
> dance was part of the most dramatic political and social upheaval
> since the Civil War, and this would be reflected both onstage and
> off. The NAACP launched an attack on the segregated public school
> system in five states. Rosa Parks, a middle-aged African American
> woman, defied custom by refusing to give up her seat on a Montgom-
> ery, Alabama bus to a white man. A 14-year-old black boy named Em-
> mett Till was brutally disfigured and murdered for allegedly whistling
> at a white woman in Mississippi. These and other events triggered
> two decades of turbulence that ended with the dismantling of a sig-
> nificant part of a system of institutionalized racism. At the same time,
> there was an explosion of creativity among black dancers and chore-
> ographers that heightened both their impact and their image. Art imi-
> tated life and life imitated art with ricocheting reciprocity.[20]

Understanding this social and political shift caused by African Americans standing up for their rights of citizenship as human beings also allows one to comprehend the shifting dance world. My performance of
Rod Rodgers's *Shout* in the RRDC, Faison's *Suite Otis*, Pomare's *Blues for
the Jungle*, and, without a doubt, Ailey's *Revelations* created a canon in the
professional dance world that explored the great contributions of black
culture and people despite the tragedies and indignities of black life in
America.

Allen's seminal online essay places dance right in the midst of this socio-political upheaval rather than as a peripheral, inconsequential art form:

> There were no blacks in America's modern dance companies, which were still predominantly white, at the beginning of the 1960s. But as black dancers and choreographers stormed the barricades, demanding schools to nurture their talent and outlets to express it, the names of this new ever-growing phalanx of talent became legion: Judith Jamison, Loretta Abbott, . . . Alvin Ailey, Consuelo Atlas, . . . Talley Beatty, Ruth Beckford, Delores Brown, Janet Collins, Carmen de Lavallade, Judy Dearing, . . . George Faison, . . . Dyanne Harvey, Thelma Hill, Mary Hinkson, Louis Johnson, . . . Dianne McIntyre, Donald McKayle, . . . Joe Nash, John Parks, Al Perryman, Joan Peters, Eleo Pomare, . . . Rod Rodgers, Kelvin Rotardier, . . . Sylvia Waters, Dudley Williams, Billy Wilson, Lavinia Williams, Sarah Yarborough, and on and on.[21]

Although some modern dance companies had a few token blacks, the opportunities were extremely limited for people of African descent in the concert dance fields of modern and ballet. Allen's invoking key names of black dancers of the 1970s era creates a challenging litany of invisibilized dance history that allows one to comprehend what the racial and political shift in the United States meant for the dance world, with New York as the center of that change.

The racial shift in dance did not go unnoticed by New York's dance critical establishment. For example, Allen assesses how the *New York Times* dance critic John Martin, who helped establish modern dance philosophy and criticism, viewed the emergence of blacks in modern concert dance even during the World War II era:

> Even *New York Times* dance critic John Martin felt compelled to take note of this phenomenon, declaring in his book, *The Dance* [1945]: "A development that is destined to have great significance in the postwar world is the emergence of a number of highly gifted negro artists." Acknowledging the hurdles blocking black artists' progress since the era of blackface minstrelsy, Martin admitted that until now African-American performers had been "confined almost exclusively to the inertias of the entertainment field." He also acknowledged that in modern dance the black dancer "found a medium for

expressing himself in forms of his own devising," and was able to "find his rightful place in the creative arts and to do so with impressive results."[22]

Martin, as the *New York Times* dance critic from 1927 to 1962, had unchallenged power to critically establish the entire modern dance field, and for him to acknowledge the racial shift in dance, even before the Civil Rights movement, was crucial. In the 1940s he recognized the prolific dance oeuvre of Katherine Dunham, who trained and/or influenced many of the early black dancers, as did Pearl Primus, who was beginning to make important social dance statements in the 1940s like her *The Negro Speaks of Rivers* (1944) and *Hard Time Blues* (1945).

This dance history literally set the social stage for the Alvin Ailey American Dance Theater to emerge on the New York scene in 1958. Alvin Ailey (1931–1989), having been the artistic director of the Lester Horton Dance Theater in Los Angeles after Horton's death in 1953, came to New York with Carmen de Lavallade to dance in Broadway's *House of Flowers* in late 1954. The Truman Capote–Harold Arlen production had a Caribbean theme and needed a strong black cast, which provided work for two reigning black New York performers, Pearl Bailey and Diahann Carroll. It also provided work for newcomers who were to become some of New York's next-generation black creative artists: Carmen de Lavallade, Geoffrey Holder, and Alvin Ailey. The fact that de Lavallade and Ailey were enticed to New York from Los Angeles by the promise of work in a commercial Broadway production is indicative of the life of black modern dancers: they had to take work where they could get it, which, in turn, developed a nonelitist attitude about the different venues for dance. As Donald McKayle is famous for saying, "There's only two kinds of dance: good dance and bad dance." Broadway, Las Vegas, nightclubs, or the concert stage all became opportunities to present dance artistry, a model set by Katherine Dunham a generation earlier.

But Alvin Ailey was not really satisfied with dancing on Broadway or in any one else's concert dance company, yearning to have his own vehicle for his unique choreographic voice. In his autobiography he recorded his frustrations with the lack of opportunities for black dancers in New York in the late 1950s:

In 1958, there were many terrific black dancers in New York City, and yet, except for an occasional concert or art show, there was no place for them to dance. True, Martha Graham used black dancers in marvelously creative ways, but aside from that the New York City concert dance scene was basically closed to black dancers. There was practically no way for us to fulfill our compelling desire to participate fully in the dance world. There was no Lester Horton on the East Coast dance scene. Even against those long odds, I very much wanted to be a choreographer.[23]

The dance world has benefited from Ailey's choreographic ambitions and organizational acumen in establishing his own company that has lasted sixty years at this writing.

He assembled dancers from his work in subsequent Broadway shows, as well as from his dancing with Donald McKayle, and started a small group, first with a codirector, Ernest Parham, a former Katherine Dunham dancer, with whom he could share expenses. Some of his original dancers were Claude Thompson (the choreographer for *Show Boat* for whom I had danced in San Francisco [chapter 1]); Charles Moore, who would go on to form his own company; Jacqueline Walcott; Clarence Cooper; Lavinia Hamilton; Crystine Lawson; and Talley Beatty. His first work they rehearsed was *Blues Suite* (1958), "a dance about the Dew Drop Inn of my Texas childhood," with costumes by Geoffrey Holder, revealing the secular side of rural Texas life: "We didn't have a penny to spend on anything, so the costumes were made out of women's slips and feathers from the Salvation Army."[24] The picture that emerges of the beginning of the most popular internationally touring modern dance company is one that many dance companies across the globe know all too well: a shoestring budget and a prayer, bolstered by courageous creativity and a thirst to say something of importance.

Back then Ailey could not have imagined the current multimillion-dollar-budget thirty-member company, with a second apprentice company, a full-fledged accredited dance school, and national youth outreach programs. But even in 1972 the company had become fairly established with many accolades. Ailey was given an honorary doctorate of fine arts from Princeton University, and Japanese dancer Masazumi Chaya joined the company, eventually becoming associate artistic director. By then Judith Jamison had become his premier female soloist and received the distinguished *Dance Magazine* Award that year, and Ailey was commissioned to choreograph *Carmen* for the Metropolitan Opera. The Ailey company had already received its second State Department–sponsored European and North African tour and a prestigious six-week tour to the USSR, the first for an American modern dance company. The New York performing arts establishment recognized these significant accomplishments of the Alvin Ailey American Dance Theater, even though, in the early 1970s, the company was nowhere near financially stable. However, when I danced in New York, it was undisputed that the Alvin Ailey American Dance Theater was one of the top modern dance companies in New York.

What exactly did Ailey give to the world of modern dance and the ongoing development of black concert dance? How were the priorities of black dance furthered through his choreography? What is the aesthetic legacy that he started in New York? According to dance theorist Thomas F. DeFrantz: "Ailey encoded aspects of African American life and culture in concert dance. These 'aspects'—aesthetic imperatives termed 'Africanisms' by cultural theorists—flourish in the movements of dancers Ailey worked with; they are also embedded within the very choreography Ailey made. They emerge in compositional strategies, choices of music, structuring of performance, casting, and approach to company operations."[25] DeFrantz's taxonomy of black cultural priorities encrypted into Ailey's approach includes the movements themselves. It is at the level of the kinesthetic that the Africanist aesthetic is most potently apparent as the center of ontology (social relations among a group), epistemology (mode of cultural transmission), and metaphysics (spiritual connection with the ancestors) of African peoples. In American black dance—concert or vernacular—the Africanist aesthetic, founded in African performance principles, became transformed for a different social context, yet recognizable in body language, social attitudes, and relationship of dance with music. This aesthetic surfaced in African American choreographers like Alvin Ailey as a powerful theatrical force.

Ailey's *Blues Suite* and *Revelations* (1960), as well as Faison's, Pomare's, or Rodgers's dance classics, are quintessential records of this aesthetic that was rarely understood by the early New York dance establishment. For example, Ailey's characters in *Blues Suites*, such as the coping mechanism of the black male "pimp walk," and Pomare's junkie giving himself a drug "fix" onstage in *Blues for the Jungle*, were elevated to prototypical American characters on the concert stage, echoing exactly what I was experiencing in the

New York City streets. Faison's choreographic use of Otis Redding's music allowed the audience to embody the joy and pain of blackness woven into every one of Redding's screams and hollers, along with the rhythmic punch of the music. When I danced Rodgers's *Shout*, the audience rode the waves of black aspirations in every attitude turn, defiant hip thrust, and raised "right on" fist.

The actual *movements* of Ailey's *Revelations* had the same impact then as they do today. In *Revelations* the audience experiences beleaguered hope with upwardly stretched screaming arms in the "Pilgrims of Sorrow" opening section that transcends race and reaches deep in the human soul that had been "(re)buked," a sentiment with which many social groups around the globe can identify. The audience also feels the joyous celebration of spiritual triumph in the finale "Move, Member, Move" with the devout hand-on-the hip attitude of the church women in yellow dresses and large hats telling the congregation to keep their "eyes on the prize." In these staged black characters and choreographic scenes, the Africanist aesthetic becomes illuminated in the inseparability of the dance and music. In the process, black concert dance fulfills its mission of giving back to the people their own aesthetic and historical survival mechanisms.

As the Alvin Ailey American Dance Theater became the symbolic black dance company of the 1960s and 1970s, it was in the right place at the right time, where the era of racial integration and the center of American dance came together. In the initial founding of his company, Ailey's mission to present his early "blood memories" represented in *Blues Suite* and *Revelations*—the secular and sacred sides of black life—was in lockstep with the needs of the country, and he provided an accessible inroad into the African American experience that was nonthreatening for the American concert stage of high art. DeFrantz offers more insights into the social positionality of Ailey in these early days:

In large part, his carefully groomed, nonconfrontational troupe presented work that represented black experience to cultural outsiders. Without the benefit of wealthy patrons who might have funded his early explorations of dance form, Ailey built his company's success from the committed labor of his dancing collaborators, a "devoted band of friends, men and women whose professional lives were, in effect, a work of hopeful activism," from his own affable, articulate persona, which normalized American race relations for an international audience, and from a repertory chosen to showcase an accessible and glamorous vision of dancing black bodies in several theatrical milieux.[26]

Indeed, Ailey's early choreographic choices allowed him to be accepted within the concert dance world obligated to partially open its racial doors, as other social arenas were doing in the 1960s and 1970s on the heels of hard-won civil rights legislation.

Ailey's aesthetic and choreography were more acceptable to the dance establishment than were other black choreographers in New York. Rodgers's *Box*, for example, was appreciated for its experimental conjunction of dance and pedestrian gesture, and it served its purpose of making the audience uneasy. Pomare's confrontational in-your-face character in *Junkie* leaves the stage and enters the audience to directly challange startled viewers. Unlike supporters of the postmodern dance aesthetic of Jawole Willa Jo Zollar and Ishmael Houston-Jones in the late 1980s and beyond, dance audiences in the 1960s were not used to Pomare's breaking of the theatrical fourth wall. Neither was Katherine Dunham's earlier 1950 *Southland* ballet about southern lynchings tolerable to assimilationist America in the pre–Civil Rights era.[27] Ailey offered themes and a choreographic approach that revealed the heart of historic black culture without offending, thereby furthering his popularity.

The black middle class was looking for a legitimate black concert dance company with propriety, with which they could identify the long-suffering black experience, as well as celebratory black dances as an antidote to that historic pain. DeFrantz justifiably adds: "Ailey's organizational gambit followed the lead of integration-minded black visionaries invested in 'race progress,' leaders who believed that 'the improvement of African Americans' material and moral condition through self-help would diminish white racism.'"[28] The international dance world and the American black middle class were both poised to allow the Alvin Ailey American Dance Theater through the sacrosanct doors of the concert dance world, at the highest level.

But there were other smaller black modern dance companies that were more in tune with New York's 1960s Black Arts movement and Pan-Africanist initiatives that had emerged while Ailey was establishing his black concert dance reputation. One such company was Movements Black, which would eventually have a direct connection to Alvin Ailey. John Parks joined the Ailey company in 1970, becoming one of Ailey's lead dancers and advisors, as well as one of Judith Jamison's main dance partners. But before joining Ailey, he had established Movements Black in 1966 to make a major statement in dance regarding black culture and politics. I interviewed John Parks in 2015, now dance professor in the School of Theatre and Dance at the University of South Florida. He emphasized the interdisciplinary nature of Movements Black, as the dancers worked with other black artists who were exploring the same kind of 1960s revolutionary black statement:

> My dancers were my wife at the time, Judi Dearing, Ron Pratt, who would go on to dance with Rod Rodgers, and Miriam Greaves who also danced with Olatunji and Chuck Davis, whom I encouraged to focus on his love of African dance. We worked with the best [avantgarde] jazz musicians, like Archie Shepp, Sun Ra, and Cecil Taylor, who were also about breaking down barriers. We also collaborated directly with [Black Arts poet] LeRoi Jones and painter Romare Bearden, as well as his dancer wife, Nanette Bearden.[29]

Although Movements Black, as a dance company, was short-lived, it represented young New York black artists addressing the times and the shifting voice of blacks in all arenas of society, ensuring that dance was also making a black *revolutionary* statement loudly and clearly.

For John Parks, Movements Black was not just about *art* but instead about how they viewed their *lives* from the perspective of liberating the black world:

> We were Pan Africanists and mainly dancers; but we included musicians and artists as a part of our collective. We would raise money from our performances to get people out of prison. We wanted to expand the consciousness of people of color, and to introduce black dance [as a concept]. To show you how Pan Africanist we really were, Judy's and my first daughter, Aissatou, was baptized in Guinea by the newly elected president Sékou Touré, when Black Power spokesman Stokely Carmichael was just becoming involved with Guinea; and Judy toured as a performer with [South African singer] Miriam Makeba [who eventually married Stokely].[30]

John was serious about Pan-Africanist political affairs, with his dance company members taking part in far-reaching international black radical events that would shape the times on several continents. The following was Movements Black's mission statement:

> Dance is a barometer of the times and presently there is a revolt going on in the realm of the young Black choreographers. There has been little space available and even less enthusiasm shown by the present dance establishment for these choreographers to be able to present their works to the public. As a result there are fewer and fewer works being done by Black choreographers. . . . Because of the present state of our society and the rejection of the status quo where the Black man is concerned, Black choreographers are gaining some recognition of their own. These black choreographers, especially the younger ones, having studied all the previous forms of contemporary dance, are combining those forms with the ethnic and social dance forms that are part of their great heritage, to give a dance theatre for which the main purpose is to communicate with Blacks, about their Black identity. . . . Movements Black's main theme is to give a total Black experience through dance.[31]

John Parks's political background in dance, in some ways, was an anomaly in the Ailey company, but because of John's organizational and political experience, Ailey respected him as a trusted advisor. John remembers joining the company at a tenuous time when Ailey was considering disbanding it. "But then he got the State Department–sponsored Russian tour that helped save the company financially," Parks said. But John had the guts to tell Ailey that he was selling himself short by only receiving salaries from the government for the length of the tour: "I told him that given the times, the U.S. government would not let his black dance company fold, and he should ask for more, including a building and more financial support." But Ailey did not listen to him and settled for the terms of the State Department's contract. Hence, John refused to go on the Russian tour with the company. Now, in retrospect, John says: "I was young, arrogant, and immature. But I've learned since." However, this political confrontation between Ailey and Parks shows the different artistic and political camps among black artists during the revolutionary times of the early 1970s, which I encountered during my brief dance stint in New York City.

There was also a burgeoning *African* dance community that was a part of the black dance scene in New York in the early 1970s, the foundation of which had been laid as early as the 1930s. Asadata Dafora (1890–1965), a middle-class Sierra Leonean trained in opera, came to New York in 1929 and by 1934 produced his first African musical drama, *Kykunkor* (The Witch Woman), which introduced New York and African American dancers to West African dance and music. Dance historian Lynne Fauley Emery summarized *Kykunkor*'s significance:

> It was the first performance by black dancers on the concert stage which was entirely successful. It revealed the potential of ethnic material to black dancers, and herein lay Dafora's value as a great influence on black concert dance. It was Dafora who first experimented with African heritage thematic material, and his success caused other dancers to do the same. [John] Martin stated that *Kykunkor* was "a revelation of the possibilities of the field" and it proved to be just that. *Kykunkor* proved that black dancers working with material from their own heritage could be successful on the American concert stage.[32]

In the 1930s Dafora's stage work also helped prove to the white literati of New York that Africa was not their stereotypic "savage" image, just as the New Negro movement was making that statement through literature and performing arts in a revolutionary new way. Dafora's solo work *Ostrich Dance*, with its minute isolation movements of the torso, head, and arms, in symbolic imitation of the bird has become a classic work in several companies' repertoires.

Two other important black dancer-choreographers followed in the 1940s. Pearl Primus (1919–1994), originally from Trinidad, built upon Dafora's inroads, positioning African theatrical material after her Rosenwald Fellowship research in West Africa and her presentation of the Liberian welcome dance, Fanga, in performance. Of course, Katherine Dunham started her first New York school in 1944 in Caravan Hall, Isadora Duncan's old studio, and then moved to West Forty-Third Street in 1945. In 1952 the Dunham School expanded to Katherine Dunham School of Cultural Arts, where everything from dance, drama, ethnological fieldwork techniques, languages, and music for dancers was taught. The student population was racially integrated, with many future dance and film stars coming to study at the Dunham school, such as Eartha Kitt, James Dean, Marlon Brando, and Peter Gennaro.

Many African American dancers interested in furthering African and Caribbean dance forms studied in New York with these early pioneers, furthering the dance traditions of Asadata Dafora, Pearl Primus, and Katherine Dunham. Some of these were Joe Commodore, Alice Dinizulu, Merle (Afida) and Joan Derby, Chief Bey, and Montego Joe. Nigerian Babatunde Olatunji had established his dance and music school in Harlem by the beginning of the 1960s (chapter 1), coming on the heels of the success of his *Drums of Passion* album with Columbia Records.

The Dinizulu family is a perfect example of the cross-fertilization of African American and African performers in New York. New Yorkers Gus and Alice Dinizulu formed the Dinizulu Drummers and Dancers that continues today. Nana Yao Opare Dinizulu (Gus) was one of the first African Americans to begin drumming in New York and became an initiated Akan religious priest and chief during a 1965 trip to Ghana. His wife, Alice, was a former dancer with Asadata Dafora and taught his dance style until Ghanaian traditional dance and drumming became the signature of the dance company. Direct contact with traditional African cultures, as well as the influence of some of the early West African performers immigrating to the city, became the hallmark of the African dance scene in New York. The Dinizulu legacy continued through their son Nana Kimati Dinizulu (1956–2013), who also became a recognized African drummer in his own right through several trips to Ghana, where he studied with master drummers such C. K. Ganyo, with whom I also studied in Ghana in the late 1970s, and at the annual Dunham Seminars in the 1980s.

As New York has always been a mecca for Caribbean and South American immigrants and artists, these dance forms were added to the African diasporic forms in the city. Haitian dancer Jean-León Destiné, whom I met in 1968 (chapter 1), arrived in New York as early as 1949, dancing on Broadway and teaching Haitian dance in New York and becoming associated with Jacob's Pillow as a teacher. Brazilian capoeira master Jelon Vieira added his Brazilian dance mastery to the mix of New York City in the 1970s. He is recognized for being one of the first masters, along with Loremil Machado, to introduce the Brazilian danced martial art of capoeira to the United States.

This New York lineage of African and African diaspora dance and music grew from African Americans' need to discover their root heritage before slavery, which could only come through learning and sharing the dance and music traditions of their African ancestors. What they received were the dances' meanings, purposes, and functions within traditional societies, which in turn furthered their knowledge base of the philosophical aspects of the Africanist aesthetic itself. These dance companies and drum ensembles that emerged in New York started from this general cultural need and became the basis for the cultural nationalist movement within the United States in the late 1960s and early 1970s.

When I was in New York in 1972, the late Chuck Davis (1937–2017) was establishing himself with a dance model that bridged African dance and modern dance. The Chuck Davis Dance Company, formed in New York in 1968, performed what he called "traditional African and African American dance" with the repertoire split between these two distinct styles. I remember going to his studio to watch one of his rehearsals, which were always lively and humorous, like Chuck's personality. Now his African American Dance Ensemble is associated with the American Dance Festival at Duke University. (He was born in Raleigh, North Carolina.) Chuck Davis has been known as the convener and host of the largest annual African dance festival in the United States, DanceAfrica, sponsored by the Brooklyn Academy of Music for forty years; today DanceAfrica is under the artistic directorship of well-known New York choreographer Abdel R. Salaam. Chuck Davis represented the African dance legacy that came out of the 1960s and 1970s—a period of reclaiming African American history that necessitated the inclusion of dance on both sides of the Black Atlantic.

Doris Green is another important artist in this African dance story in New York, as a scholar of ethnomusicology and music notation, as well as a professional African drummer and dancer. She has been a Fulbright scholar in West Africa studying and notating many of the rhythms in relation to the dances. As a graduate of Brooklyn College, she was the first to teach an African dance course at that institution in 1969 and later became a faculty member at NYU, teaching African dance. Doris Green was instrumental in getting the first Ghanaian, Godwin Agbeli, to teach dance and music at NYU in 1972, the same year that I danced with Rod Rodgers.

The first major West African touring company—Les Ballets Africains de la République de Guinée—performed in New York in 1960, which established a regular U.S. touring schedule. Green notes that the big controversy around the New York performance of Les Ballets Africains was whether the women would be allowed to be topless for some of their dances, as a part of their traditional costuming. Then in 1971 the National Dance Company of Senegal performed at the Brooklyn Academy of Music. Ten years had made a huge difference in the receptivity to traditional African dance and music in New York, and this performance advanced the stature of the efforts of the New York African dance community.[33]

The fundamental difference between the role of dance and music in African and Euro-American cultures has been a central issue with which black Americans have had to grapple historically. Dance and music for African peoples, as I have said before, is absolutely "inextricable from worldview and personal and group identity,"[34] making it unnecessary to craft terms such as "art" for concepts that are central to the daily lives of the people. Restoring African cultural integrity, which includes the dance and music, after African cultures had been so denigrated over time, was a Herculean task assumed by the New Negro movement of the 1920s and 1930s and the Black Arts movement of the 1960s and 1970s. The New York African dance community was a pioneer in wrestling with this cultural dilemma and struggled to forge one of the first "authentic" African dance and music sites in the country. This cultural project was strongly under way when I arrived in 1972 and had joined the general New York black dance community.

Rod Rodgers was very conscious of the African American cultural link to Africa and the African diaspora. Besides positioning the company to be a part of the seminal FESTAC '77 event in Lagos, Nigeria, he often used African drummers as a part of our New York performances, as well as always including African-based dance classes on the public schedule at his studio. Chief Bey (James Hawthorne Bey, 1913–2004) was one such drummer with whom Rod liked to work. Rod always had an evening dance class series for the general public at the studio where we rehearsed during the day, and the evening dance classes featured the late Pearl Reynolds, former member of the Katherine Dunham Dance Company, teaching Haitian dance and Dunham Technique. He saw Miss Pearl's classes as foundational to his studio's dance offerings, and I continued my Dunham Technique and Haitian training by taking her classes at Rod's studio. For the majority of the black modern dance community, African-derived dance was an integral part of our training. The two wings of the black dance community—modern and African—were linked, and most choreographers and dancers studied and performed a variety of fusion dance styles that encompassed versions of both. As I was developing my own sense of who I was as a black dance artist in the early 1970s, performing with a choreographer who was also intellectually at the forefront of the black dance discourse was important to me.

Black Dance Periodicals Become the Voice of the Art

The need for a black dance periodical that could offer a knowledgeable insider perspective to the developing black dance scene in New York in the late 1960s and early 1970s was answered by *Feet*, founded and edited by Carole Johnson from 1970 to 1973. It was becoming increasingly important to publish a discursive platform for the black wing of the New York dance world, and *Feet* provided this. The purpose of the periodical was to give a voice to the evolving black dance choreographers and dancers to address their issues and publicize their performances and community outreach activities. Rod Rodgers was one of the occasional contributors to *Feet*. According to dance historian Susan Manning, "The inaugural issue established an ambitious list of goals, including creating more employment for black companies, taking dance performances into black communities, developing an archive on black dancers and choreographers, and helping black colleges find teachers." Manning also quotes Johnson's definition of black dance as

> any form of dance and any style that a black person chooses to work within. . . . Since the expression "Black Dance" must be all inclusive, it includes dancers that work in (1) the very traditional forms (the more nearly authentic African styles), (2) the social dance forms that are indigenous to this country which include tap and jazz dance, (3) the various contemporary and or abstract forms that are seen on the concert stage, and (4) the ballet (which must not be considered solely European).[35]

After founding the Dancemobile, Carole Johnson again became an important link between the practitioners of black dance and their audience, dance presenters and the media. Her magazine, *Feet*, facilitated the articulation of the evolving black dance platform, from its practical needs of employment to discursive areas of revisionist meanings and dance classifications by the black wing of the New York dance field.

The mantle of regularly published black dance periodicals was taken up next by dance critic William Moore (1933–1992) and black dance historian Joe Nash (1920–2005) with *Dance Herald: A Journal of Black Dance* from 1975 to 1979. This journal was actually named after a leftist journal published in 1937 that had included writings by prominent choreographers like Katherine Dunham and Edna Guy. Joe Nash was a former dancer with

Pearl Primus who took an interest in archiving the growing memorabilia of black dance from the 1930s, and William Moore had been a lecturer of dance history and criticism at Lehman College and the Alvin Ailey School. I would later work with both of them as a panelist with the American Dance Festival's Black Tradition in American Modern Dance project, as well as hiring them to participate as panelists in the humanities component of my own Black Choreographers Moving Toward the 21st Century dance initiative in 1989 in the S.F. Bay Area (chapter 6).

The current publication that partially fills this need for a black dance periodical is *Attitude: The Dancers' Magazine*, founded by Bernadine Jennings in 1982, which she continues until today. *Attitude* situates black dance as a part of the larger representation of New York dance because, as Jennings articulates, "it was created as a result of *Feet* and *Soho Weekly News*." Her mandate, as a black dancer herself, is to illuminate the black choreographers and the efforts of the New York black dance scene within the larger context of New York dance. In the past the magazine has covered what she calls "the regulars: Alvin, Talley, Donnie, Louis Johnson, Alma Lewis, Jones/Hayward, Judimar [School of Dance] in Philly, Arthur Hall and Tubby (Morton Winston), the Broadway scene, Fred Benjamin, Glenn Brooks, all the Clark Center alumni, and Rod Rodgers and Eleo the Pope, who we were all affiliated with."[36] Although Carole Johnson, Joe Nash, and Bill Moore had carried the mantle of black dance criticism earlier, Jennings continues this ongoing effort while illuminating *all* areas of New York dance.

Thomas DeFrantz has written about what he calls the "cultural divide" of white dance critics and the African American dance aesthetic. Using Zita Allen, he asserts:

In 1980 Zita Allen described the severity of this cultural divide in "which critics seem so totally unfamiliar with Afro-American cultural heritage and history and ignorant of the processes of their interaction with, and influence on, their own." That they were "ill-equipped to either identify those roots or determine when they are being demeaned and denied or drawn from for inspiration." Two decades later, this cultural divide persists.[37]

Therefore, periodicals by black dancers such as *Feet, Dance Herald,* and the current *Attitude* are important in the continuing need for black dance criticism from an informed perspective by those involved in the genre.

I would eventually illuminate this problem and add my voice to the issues of proper contextual black dance criticism later in my career as a producer and cultural activist back in the San Francisco–Oakland Bay Area. But looking back, I was definitely stimulated early in my career by the sheer amount of black dance activity, as well as the dancers' and choreographers' level of participation in the exploration of black consciousness, from performance and audience development to the advancement of poignant rhetoric, in early 1970s New York.

Doing My Own Thing in New York

Always having a strong drive to choreograph and to make my own artistic statements, I pursued some of my own projects while dancing with the RRDC in New York. After the Boston success of the evening-length *Changes, Or How Do You Get to Heaven When You're Already in Hell?*, I fancied myself a theatrical writer as well as a choreographer. I had been experimenting with writing narratives for several of the archetypical characters from my dance *March of the Created*. These narratives first appeared in my personal journal as poems, but slowly I began to produce fleshed-out monologues for the female characters. Eventually, what emerged was a script called "Four Women: Images of the Black Woman in Monologue, Song, and Dance," which I tried to stage.

By this time I had moved from the Lower East Side into midtown New York on Fifty-Fifth Street near Lincoln Center. This was a completely different world, reflecting another side of New York for me to explore. I loved the restaurants in that area, and when I could afford it, I went to Lincoln Center's music, theater, and dance performances, thoroughly immersing myself in the vibrant New York performing arts scene. During this period, I met several black women in New York's jazz music circles with whom I became friends. Vikki McLaughlin was a young woman who was trying to find her own voice and purpose while being a partner to the famous jazz pianist Stanley Cowell. He had studied with Rahsaan Roland Kirk at Oberlin College and had become well established in the New York jazz scene. Vikki eagerly joined my effort to perform *Four Women*, because it gave her a chance to potentially find her own artistic niche.

Another female artist with whom I worked on *Four Women* was the jazz singer Dee Dee Bridgewater. I met Dee Dee through Vikki, and she was also on board with my theatrical project, as her singing career had not yet gotten strongly established. My *perception* of Dee Dee at that time was that, like Vikki, she was being "buried" in the shadow of her then husband, trumpeter Cecil Bridgewater. Of course she would eventually go on to become a celebrated jazz singer, winning a 1998 Grammy for her album *Dear Ella*. But in 1972, she too wanted a vehicle in which she could show her talents in New York.

The three of us spent many hours in Vikki and Stanley's loft apartment working on scenes of *Four Women*. Here were multitalented twenty-something black women working with my theatrical script that had music and dance woven into its structure. But it was not a traditional musical; it was a whole new genre. It was similar to the "choreopoem" genre that Ntozake Shange would make famous just four years later on Broadway with *for colored girls who have considered suicide/when the rainbow is enuf*. The three of us pooled our resources to find a venue and a producer, but our efforts never bore fruition; none of us had enough time to give to the project, and it eventually dissipated. But in the process I forged some New York friendships and developed *Four Women*, which would eventually be staged after returning to California (chapter 4).

Another part of my own artistic interests—dance improvisation—flourished in a seminal weekend at the Artist House owned by the late famous jazz musician Ornette Coleman (1930–2015). Being friends with wives of two prominent jazz musicians—Stanley Cowell and Cecil Bridgewater—was an inroad into the highest levels of New York jazz in the early 1970s. Ornette Coleman's Artist House was an important venue where the most internationally recognized jazz musicians performed. This was one of the advantages of living in New York City as the cultural capital of the United States. During a weekend of three performances in the fall of 1972, I was privileged to perform with a convocation of key jazz musicians at the Artist House: alto saxophonist Ornette Coleman, trumpeter Don Cherry (1936–1995), bassist Jimmy Garrison (1934–1976), drummer Ed Blackwell (1929–1992), and pianist Dollar Brand (Abdullah Ibrahim), whom I had first heard in Copenhagen (chapter 2).

Coleman was an iconoclastic jazz musician who helped usher in a new music genre called "Free Jazz" that emphasized even more improvisation and harmonics than the previous bebop era. He developed his Artist House as "a studio performance and living space for artists of all kinds,"[38] located at 131 Prince Street in New York's West Village. Each night of my Friday, Saturday, and Sunday performances with the band, I arrived at this small venue with folding-chair seating to warm up and talk with the musicians. Ornette Coleman, also born in Texas, had already been recognized as a jazz innovator in Los Angeles, where he first met Don Cherry and Ed Blackwell. By the time he arrived in Manhattan in November 1959, he had already recorded the seminal *The Shape of Jazz to Come* for Atlantic Records, announcing his revolutionary jazz style to the music world. His appearance at the Five Spot Café in the East Village, originally planned as a two-week engagement, lasted two and a half months, and his unorthodox sound caused a major stir among music critics.

Coleman's free musical structure was exactly what inspired me to dance, as with my first explorations of Cecil Taylor's music as a dance undergraduate at S.F. State. I always wanted to explore the synapsis between sound and motion in my jazz improvisation classes. It was a testament to Ornette's artistic exploration to have invited me to perform with this distinguished group of musicians. When I performed with him, he had already received the first Guggenheim Fellowship ever given for jazz composition and had recorded his orchestral work *Skies of America* with the London Symphony earlier in that year of 1972. My weekend dance engagement at the Artist House was a true honor.

Each night of our performances at the Artist House was packed with music lovers; after all, with a Coleman-Cherry-Brand-Blackwell-Garrison collaboration, jazz history was being made. I knew enough about jazz music that I was fully aware of how unique this opportunity was: I was invited to add my dance improvisation to their groundbreaking music. I had already fallen in love with one of Coleman's most famous musical pieces, "Lonely Woman," which I had used in my choreographic work *Changes* in Boston. Ornette and I got along really well and met before the performance each night to talk about the intersections of music and dance, and I cherished those talks. As a result, my dance performances were completely *free*, without any preplanned choreography.

I gave myself permission to use all that I knew about dance, driven by all that I had personally become at that point. I loved exploring the rhythmic piano style of Dollar Brand and would dance in close proximity to his piano. Of course, Ed Blackwell's drums were a driving force, while the melodic riffs of Coleman and Cherry were my impetus to find spontaneous repetitive phrases that I added to their musical phrasings. I agree with dance scholar Jonathan Jackson's appraisal of the place of improvisation in black vernacular dance, which can also be applied to African American modern dance improvisations: "The central principle on which my analysis is based is that in African-American vernacular dancing improvisation *is* choreography."[39] Rather than preparatory antecedent, *improvisation*, with its riffing, repeating, layering, and ritualization, according to Jackson, is choreographic creation in the *moment*, predicated on the summoning of individual and collective energies in the moment-by-moment act of dancing.

What Jackson calls dance "vamping," so prevalent in the music to which I was dancing, is the antecedent to choreographic inspiration that can lead to the innovative improvised dance solo. To rest, I would often vamp a repetitive rhythmic movement on the periphery of my dance area, often with my eyes closed; this would allow me to just listen for a new musical inspiration. As Jackson analyzes, vamping establishes the "groove, or a sense of repetitive on-goingness."[40] The music evolving from these great musicians each night at the Artist House was the communal groove from which newly inspired improvised choreography would emerge in my spirit, flowing into my dancing body.

My instantaneous choreography wove in and out of the space surrounding the musicians, as well as a small open area carved out for me on the side of the bandstand. "In such an environment, sources of meaning cannot be limited exclusively to sonic morphologies such as the order of notes, orchestration, timbre, and the like," as musician and music scholar Dana Reason says about the multidimensions of the improvisational music environment: "Meaning is also located in the ways in which improvisers situate their bodies, change their facial expressions, and use their voice to accompany notes, gesture, silences, or phrases."[41] In my dance improvisation experiences with musicians, I found that the *multidimensionality* of meaning is even more heightened when a dancer interacts with musicians; my music colleagues at the Artist House were stimulated in fresh new ways by my dance interacting with their music, and their own bodily gestures while doing their art became even more enlivened in dialogue with my art.

Ultimately, "improvisation restages a vital component of what it means to be human and to have to adapt to social, environmental, and cultural imperatives as a function of being in the world,"[42] and this revitalizing humanity is exactly what everyone at the Artist House that weekend—musicians, dancer, and audience—experienced. My weekend of performances with these great jazz musicians was something that I will never forget, and the experience became a highlight in my early dance career, letting me know that I had something unique to offer the world of dance and music.

My Artist House dance experience in the jazz music world enhanced my awareness that I really needed to develop my own choreographic voice; I really wanted to do my own thing. But I also realized New York was too big and too competitive for me to develop my own work fast enough for me. They say New York is the "Big Apple" that must be bitten into if one wants to test the waters of a professional career in the arts. I had done that! I had proven to myself that I had skills enough to dance in one of best modern dance companies in New York and perform at some of the most prestigious venues, such as Lincoln Center and the ANTA Broadway theater. I had gotten a favorable *New York Times* review and performed with some of the most respected jazz musicians in New York. I had proven I could make it in the dance world in the Big Apple, and by the fall of 1972, I knew that in order to do my *own* choreography I would have to go back to the San Francisco Bay Area, known for cultural experimentation and a strong black consciousness.

I told Rod that I was leaving to return home, where I had not lived since leaving in 1968 for Europe. He was taken aback and said: "But the dance world is just now beginning to notice you. Why leave now, when you are really just starting to achieve a new level of recognition in New York?" I told him that I really had to do my own dance thing, and knew that New York was *not* the place for me to develop my dance aesthetic; plus, I really didn't like living in New York. My sensibilities were in the San Francisco Bay Area, where I knew I could manage the social and cultural environment. Rod gave me his blessings, told me that he knew I would make it, and wished me well.

Transition Back to the San Francisco Bay Area

That November 1972, I went back to Boston to see Donna again. We had mended our relationship, and she told me that she needed a change and would be willing to move to California with me to start fresh. She needed a few months to get her life in order to make such a move, so we took three months as a transition period. During that time, we made one trip at the end of December to Provincetown on Cape Cod, one of her favorite New England sites. We viewed the pending transition from the East Coast to the West Coast as a new chance for us to really be a strong couple after all of our emotional changes and long periods of living apart. We were ready to really live together now, and California represented that opportunity, as well as my transition back home to continue developing my own dance-theater career. Leaving Boston on February 17, 1973, we loaded up Donna's old refurbished car and drove cross country. I insisted we take the southern route because I wanted to stop in Galveston, my birthplace, on the way back to California. I wrote in my journal:

> *Left Boston; on the road again. Donna and I going to meet our destiny head-on—a little tattered and torn, but not completely worn from the years of tears and pain that are so necessary to shed skin and move along the road of rebirth. I have the time for my crops to grow and be shed at harvest time, because the beat of dreamless days will be exposed and the glory of the Creator will shine through. Going into my past, ready to view from whence I came in Galveston, before plunging into my future and learning to be more in the every-present now.*

In Galveston we stayed with my stepmother, Esther, my father Leroy's second wife. Esther and I were very close, and I considered her my second mother even then. She was totally accepting of Donna, but we never presented ourselves as lovers. In the 1970s many black gay couples simply did not make a public display of "being together." In black communities, the unspoken edict regarding homosexuality was (is): "Do what you do, just don't make a public display of it, and everything will be cool." Donna and I followed the cultural code around my relatives, and everything *was* cool. Relatives like my grand-aunts and -uncles, sisters and brothers of maternal grandmother Alberta, received us with typical southern hospitality and told me stories of my childhood that I had forgotten. On Galveston Island in the Gulf of Mexico, I was traveling back to the days of my early childhood, and it served as a perfect transition on my way back to San Francisco, the city that raised me.

While in Galveston, I intuited both the joy and pain of being black in America through the lives of my relatives while hearing about the social indignities they endured in the South. Being in Galveston with Donna, I saw myself in relation to my people who were from the World War I and II generations. Their stories made my own developing black consciousness more rooted in a personal lineage. I began to view myself as a part of a black transition generation, born in the mid-twentieth century as a part of the postwar baby boomers, and the first inheritors of the benefits of civil rights. We were the first to speak out and say, "Black Power!," "I'm Black and I'm Proud," "No more war, the Viet Cong never called me a nigger!," and "To hell with middle-class values; we will set our own standards." I was going back to San Francisco to make my mark, to make my artistic cultural statement that spoke to my generation. Europe had allowed me to see myself as an individual artist, and New York had professionalized me, but the San Francisco–Oakland Bay Area would provide the theatrical and social stage tailor-made for me to find my unique artistic voice.

Diana Black og Janis Miller.

De danser revolution

— Vi laver noget, som folk aldrig har set mage til i København, siger *Janis Miller* og *Diana Black*, som i denne uge danser forestillingen *Upspring* i Ry Teater.

Diana Black kommer fra New York, hvor hun optrådte med The Alwin Nikolais Dance Company. I to år havde hun sit eget balletensemble i Paris. Nu bor hun i København, hvor hun underviser i dans samt arbejder med teatergrupper. Hun har optrådt i *Romon* på Det Lille Teater og medvirker i *Narren*, som har premiere i slutningen af denne måned på Ry Teater på Vester Fælledvej 7. Samtidig med premieren på dette stykke indledes en ny æra for Ry Teater, idet hele huset bliver kollektiv bopæl for Niels Andersens teatergruppe, Labyrinten, Diana Blacks dansetrup samt musikerne Robert Lelievre og Arne Würgler.

Men først Upspring.

I København mødte Diana en anden amerikansk danser, Janis Miller, som vor læser tidligere har stiftet bekendtskab med. Janis kommer fra San Francisco via Spanien og Frankrig og har siden vi skrev om hende sidst fået over 30 elever i primitiv jazz (en blanding af moderne og afrikansk dans) — men kun et midlertidigt lokale på Christianshavn, desværre.

Upspring, som danses af Janis, Diana og tre af deres elever, betegnes som en revolutionerende nyskabelse inden for nutidig koreografi. De to amerikanske dansere håber, at forestillingen vil betyde begyndelsen til et nyt avanceret københavnsk dansemiljø.

— Upspring har som et stykke musik en fast ramme, men inden for den improviserer vi alle, fortæller Diana Black.

— Hver forestilling vi giver, er således forskellig fra de foregående.

Upspring kan ses på Ry Teater fredag den 7. november kl. 19, lørdag kl. 19 og 21 og søndag kl. 19 og 21. Billetter kan købes ved indgangen.
helle

Figure 1. Danish news article from *Politiken,* November 1969, Copenhagen, Denmark. Courtesy of author.

Above: Figure 2.
Magic Lotus
Dance Theatre,
Copenhagen, 1969.
Author and Diane
Black (*center*).
Courtesy of author.

Right: Figure 3.
Author performing
Rod Rodgers's *Shout*
at Statue of Liberty
Park, 1972. Courtesy
of author.

LINCOLN CENTER FOR THE PERFORMING ARTS

Alice Tully Hall

LINCOLN CENTER PRESENTS

SOUL AT THE CENTER

Monday Evening, July 31, 1972, at 8:00

Rod Rodgers Dance Company

RONALD PRATT   SHIRLEY RUSHING

ARAMIDE SMCI   JANIS MILLER

ELLIS FRAZIER   NOEL HALL

Mongo Santamaria
Atlantic Records

All dance works on this program choreographed by ROD RODGERS
Lighting Design for Rod Rogers Dance Company by SHIRLEY PRENDERGAST

"Soul at the Center" is grateful to Clarence Jones, publisher of the NEW YORK AMSTER-
DAM NEWS, for special participation in the support and promotion of these concerts.

The taking of photographs and the use of recording equipment are not allowed in this auditorium. Members of the audience who must leave the auditorium before the end of the concert
are earnestly requested to do so between numbers, not during the performance.

FIGURE 4. "Soul at the Center" program (Rod Rodgers Dance Company). Courtesy of author.

ENTERTAINMENT

HALIFU: BLACK HISTORY THROUGH DANCE

The internationally acclaimed dancer and choreographer Halifu with guest artists Raymond Sawyer, Jose Lorenzo and Raymond Johnson, is presenting her exciting "I Believe," an extension of "The Evolution of Black Dance" on May 9, 10 and 25 in the Bay Area. In anticipation of this major cultural event, THE BLACK PANTHER talked with Halifu last week.

The Evolution of Black Dance is a "lecture demonstration of the way the dance of Black people has coincided with the moods of each historical period — from Africa until today." With dance, music and narration, the audience is carried from the ritual harvest dances of Africa, to the joyous festival dances of Brazil, to slavery court dances, to the latest "soul dances" of today using the music of the popular Black soul-rock group, "Earth, Wind and Fire."

For the past year Halifu and her group have taken her program into grammar, elementary, high schools and colleges throughout the Bay Area, presenting half-hour or hour demonstration-lectures to enraptured audiences in every case.

Asked why she decided to take her program into the schools, Halifu replied: "Today we see our young people, especially in the lower school levels, less and less connected to their history and to current social movements —the dynamics of happenings

now. When I was in school (during the 60s) protest was part of everyday, on many levels. There was no way to escape involvement.

"Now with Black people reaping on the surface some of the benefits of our struggles, there is nothing pulling the attention of our kids onto themselves. As a result clothes and styles become the primary concerns of our kids, making them more susceptible to all the worst influences in this society.

AWARENESS

"I wanted to use my art to turn awareness around, so youngsters could reconnect themselves with struggle and where they really are today. I wanted to provide education about Blackness combined with entertainment they could respond to."

Asked about the response the group received in the schools, Halifu answered: "Everywhere there was overwhelming enthusiasm. We'd walk into the schools and the atmosphere was like death was happening; students, teachers and administrators tolerating each other, hostile, angry — a kind of stand-off nothing happeningness.

"Under those circumstances, the result of a sterile educational system that will not provide adequate funds, lacks initiative and innovation and breeds mediocrity of both students and teachers, it did not take much to produce a response.

Worldwide acclaimed dancer and choreographer, HALIFU.

"The children, at all ages, would be held by the performance, related to it and would throng backstage after the program to compliment us, ask us intelligent questions and generally express themselves in a very 'adult' manner about how much they enjoyed the show.

"At first some teachers and administrators would be up-tight about us coming, convinced that nothing could interest their kids in learning. Afterwards, they would invariably be enthusiastic and grateful that we were able to both entertain their kids and educate them at the same time.

"THE PROBLEM"

"We took this opportunity to point out to both teachers and administrators that the problem was not the kids, but an educational system devoid of creative teaching methods that denies kids the respect and the facilities for proper education."

"I Believe" consists of 12 dances utilizing the popular Bay Area dancers Raymond Sawyer, Jose Lorenzo and Raymond Johnson, and featuring also Benji Dunn, Aisha Kahlil, Evia Marta, Brenda Miller, Paula Moss and Jamal Hamilton.

The May 9 performance will be held at Martin Luther King, Jr. High at 1781 Rose Street, in Berkeley. The May 10 performance will be held at Roosevelt Jr. High School, at 460 Arguello Blvd., San Francisco. On May 25, "I Believe" will be presented at the Son of Man Temple Community Forum, at the Community

Figure 5. *Black Panther* newspaper review of *The Evolution of Black Dance,* May 1975. Courtesy of author.

Figure 6. Rehearsal for *The Evolution of Black Dance*, 1974. *Front to back:* Aisha Kahlil, Ntozake Shange, and author. Courtesy of Kimathi Asante.

FIGURE 7. Going to Kaasi funeral near Kumasi with drummer; Ghana, 1976. Courtesy of author.

FIGURE 8.
Author dancing
gonje in Tamale
with young girl
at petol bar.
Courtesy of
author.

Figure 9. Finale of first ECAC Multicultural Festival of Dance & Music, Berkeley
Community Theater, 1977. Kimathi Asante (*front row, second from left*), Naima Gwen
Lewis, Jose Lorenzo, author (*center*); Fania Davis (*fourth from right*). Courtesy of author.

Figure 10. Flyer for performance of *The Evolution of Black Dance* at ECAC, 1980. Caligraphy by Selimah Nemoy. Courtesy of author.

FIGURE 11. Author and Linda Goodrich dance at ECAC Twenty-First and Webster studio, 1979. Courtesy of Harry Wade.

Figure 12. Publicity photo of CitiCentre Dance Theatre members. *Standing, left to right:* Leon Jackson, Debra Floyd, Linda Goodrich, Daniel Giray; *seated, left to right:* Author, Roger Dillahunty. Courtesy of Harry Wade.

Figure 13. Talley Beatty with CitiCentre Dance Theatre. *Standing, left to right:* Roger Dillahunty, author, Talley Beatty, Linda Goodrich, Debra Floyd; *seated, left to right:* Robert Henry Johnson, Soyinka Rahim. Courtesy of Daniel Giray.

FIGURE 14. Leon Jackson and author perform as a part of CitiCentre Dance Theatre. Courtesy of Harry Wade.

The Stanford Committee on Black Performing Arts presents

CITICENTRE DANCE THEATRE

The Eastbay's Modern/Jazz Dance Company

"moments of real eloquence"
—*S.F. Chronicle*

including
Halifu Osumare
*of the Stanford
Dance Division*

Saturday,
October 25, 1986
8:00 p.m.

Dinkelspiel
Auditorium
Stanford University

$8 general
$6 students/senior
Advance Tickets at Tresidder Box Office, Stanford
Charge by phone 723-4317
For Information call: 723-4402

The Committee on Black Perfoming Arts

Harmony House • 561 Lomita Drive • Stanford University • Stanford • California 94305

FIGURE 15. Poster of CitiCentre Dance Theatre performing at Stanford University, 1986. Courtesy of author.

A R E S I D E N C Y I N T R I B U T E T O

KATHERINE
DUNHAM

CHOREOGRAPHER, ANTHROPOLOGIST, EDUCATOR

MAY 1–27, 1989
STANFORD UNIVERSITY

Photo: ©1968 Dwight Carter

C O O R D I N A T E D B Y COMMITTEE O N B L A C K P E R F O R M I N G A R T S

Public Lecture Demonstration

A WALK THROUGH KATHERINE DUNHAM'S LIFE
FREE. Sunday, May 7
3:30 pm, Memorial Auditorium
Presented by The Lively Arts
Call: 723-2551

A Stanford Centennial Symposium

KATHERINE DUNHAM AND HER CONTRIBUTIONS TO AMERICAN DANCE
Friday, May 12, 8:00–6:00 pm
All Day Fee: $20; with lunch: $25
Presented by Committee on Black Performing Arts
Co-ordinator: Yvonne Daniel
Call: 723-4402 for location

Public Community Classes

Saturdays, May 6, 13, 20, & 27
Ravenswood Recreation Center
Donohoe St. (at Cooley St.)
East Palo Alto
1:00-2:30 pm - Dunham Dance Technique (Dunham)
3:00-4:30 pm - Dance Anthropology Seminar (Dunham/Stroud)
3:00-4:30 pm - Senegalese Drum Workshop (Thiam)
Presented by City of East Palo Alto & S.U. African & Afro-American Studies
For fees call: 853-3140 or 723-3781

Academic Courses
(For Stanford Students Only)

All Classes Taught by Dunham in May
Anthropology 109:
TA/Th 1:15-3:15 pm
Dances of the African Diaspora
(Taught from beginning of Spring by Goldstone)
Dance 159: M&W 2:15-3:45 pm
Afro-Caribbean Dance Techniques
(Taught from beginning of Spring by Chatman)

Exhibit

DUNHAM IN COSTUME & PRINT
Photos, Memorabilia, & Books by and about Katherine Dunham
April 14 - May 31
S.U. Meyer Library
Opening Reception, April 14, 4:00 pm
with guest lecturer, Dr. Albirda Rose
Presented by Committee on Black Performing Arts
Call: 723-4402

Dunham Residency Choir, Halifu Osumare

FIGURE 16. Poster of the 1989 Stanford Dunham Residency. Courtesy of author.

FIGURE 17. Author with members of Kwacha Cultural Troupe, Malawi, July 1990. Courtesy of author.

FIGURE 18. Author meets Dr. H. Kamuzu Banda, then president of Malawi, July 1990. Courtesy of author.

Figure 19. BCM panel of scholars and artists, Theater Artaud, 1989. *Right to left:* Brenda Dixon Gottschild, Joe Nash, Julinda Lewis-Ferguson, Jawole Willa Jo Zollar, Cleo Parker Robinson, and Donald Byrd. Courtesy of Kathy Sloane.

Figure 20. Author with Ghanaian scholars after Fulbright Fellowship talk, Institute of African Studies, University of Ghana, Legon, October 2008. *Left to right:* Patience Kwakwa, Nii Yartey, author, Dr. Esi Sutherland-Addy, Dr. Kwabena Nketia. Courtesy of Terry Ofosu.

4

Dancing Back into the San Francisco–Oakland Bay Area, 1973–1976

Dance is Life, and Life is a Dance.

HALIFU OSUMARE

After being away for five years, I arrived back in the San Francisco–Oakland Bay Area in early March 1973. Returning was about refamiliarizing myself with my home area and establishing a reputation as a dance and theater professional. But before I could focus on career building, I had to reunite with my family. This proved to be checkered because five years was a long time. I was overwhelmed seeing my mother, Tenola, again; she was always loving and supportive, even if she didn't understand my roving independence. My reunion with my stepfather, Herman, was interesting because I had defied him so much growing up in his household that he still didn't know how to fully situate me in his scheme of the world. My father, Leroy, who lived in Oakland, was cool as usual because he always had a live-and-let-live philosophy. My younger sisters' reactions to my return were dependent upon their age. Brenda, the second daughter, three and a half years younger, was welcoming; my younger sisters, Pat and Baby Tenola, were more reticent because I had missed so much of their growing-up years. The youngest, Tracey, almost twenty years my junior, didn't know me at all because she was only a baby when I left. I immediately asked Mama if I could take her on little excursions in San Francisco so we could establish our sisterly relationship, although then she felt more like my daughter. I was a twenty-six-year-old black woman who had already lived in Morocco, Spain, Amsterdam, Copenhagen, Stockholm, Boston, and New York, and now I was finally back home. Little did I know then that I would only be back for three years before going overseas again.

Donna and I moved to Oakland, which was always less expensive than San Francisco, even before the city's complete gentrification and "yuppifi-cation" as the Mecca for counterculture misfits and gay freedom. We found a flat on the corner of Telegraph Avenue and Twenty-Seventh Street, near the Sutter Medical Center in the "Pill Hill" district, just blocks away from downtown Oakland. Our second-story flat was spacious with hardwood floors and a large living room for entertaining, becoming a great party space for our black community that we quickly formed.

Joining the Black Meditators

Almost immediately after we moved to Oakland, we connected with the Transcendental Meditation Centers, an organization established to pro-mote Maharishi Mahesh Yogi's very popular Transcendental Meditation (TM) in the black community. The Indian guru who had initiated the Beatles into TM came to the United States to teach the art of meditation in a non-Eastern cultural context: there was no need to change one's life-style; just meditate twenty minutes twice daily and receive all the benefits of an illuminated life. Given the black cultural and political revolution of the early 1970s, black folks were more likely to be recruited into meditation by other black folks; hence the mission of the TM Centers organization. We met black TM teachers Don Coles and Vishwa (Jamie Scott), and they invited us to an introductory TM lecture held on the UC Berkeley cam-pus. Their organization of black meditators got together once a month for group meditation followed by a potluck party, with dancing to the latest R&B music. Our living room was destined to become a perfect place for some of those monthly meditation gatherings.

Donna and I felt TM was an intriguing way of getting to know progres-sive black folks in the East Bay, but we weren't immediately sold on the benefits of TM. I had become a smoke-every-day weedhead and truthfully did not think that anything else could make me feel as mellow, relaxed, and centered. But the initiation fee was reasonable for the first day of instruction plus three days of follow-up "checkings" to ensure the correct meditation procedure. When the April 1973 day came for us to be initiated into TM, we were met by Alice Gilliam, a female TM teacher who later became our good friend. Transcendental Meditation from that day onward was a life-altering experience, becoming a foundation for the lives we were establishing.

After receiving my mantra in the initial candle-lit ceremony and then closing my eyes and using it for the first time, I immediately felt its power. I got in touch with my own inner spirit in a way that I had never felt before. Smoking marijuana might have made me feel mellow, but it never took me beyond my myriad thoughts. I have always been a spiritual person, but after leaving the Catholic Church at age eighteen, organized religion never felt right for me again. I was too independent in my thinking and character to conform to religious tenets that I felt were mostly tainted by man-made interpretations of universal spiritual principles. TM, for me, was a spiritual *methodology*, not a religion, which allowed me to experience God within. I had never felt my own spirit, separate from my identification with my body, and meditation provided that. I remain a TM meditator even today, and its foundational tenet—"Do Less and Accomplish More"—has become my way of life, focusing on my goals from a centered perspective and strategizing to realize them.

Although I went on Transcendental Meditation retreats in beautiful Marin County settings and slowly began to lessen my dependence on marijuana, Donna actually found her life's path in TM by going on a teacher training course in Ethiopia that started that July 1973. Transcendental Meditation Centers had convinced Maharishi and his top administrators to increase the number of its black teachers by offering a special course on the African continent just for their organization. Several of our monthly black TM meditators decided that they wanted to kill two birds with one stone: become TM teachers and see the African continent for the first time. The course was held at the Haile Selassie College of Agriculture in Harar, Ethiopia. Donna didn't have the money for the course, but she set her mind to it, and to my amazement she put together several thousand dollars and was able to join the historic TM Teacher Training Course in Ethiopia that produced many new black TM teachers. Even my best friend, Sandra McGee, whom I had known since I was nine years old when my family first arrived in San Francisco in 1957, had become a meditator and went on the Ethiopia teacher training course. Today Donna Maynard (now Sananda Ananda-Maynard) remains a prominent TM teacher in Los Angeles, having found her life's calling during this time.

Ntozake Shange Gives Me My African Name

As for me, I was on a mission to continue my dance career by choreographing and producing my own evening-length works. I was dedicated to establishing myself in the black artistic enclave of the Bay Area, where I could find dancers and artists of like spirit who wanted to give voice to our new-found black consciousness. One of these artists, who would go on to international fame, was Ntozake Shange (Paulette Williams), whom I met in July 1973, when Donna was on the TM Teacher Training Course. Ntozake had already changed her name and was known in the Bay Area as a black feminist poet. Ntozake had both a black and feminist consciousness, and she positioned those two subjectivities in a way that caught the attention of the black creative community that she promoted on her own radio show on San Francisco's community radio station, KPOO.

Two years younger than I, Ntozake came to the Bay Area from Los Angeles after finishing her master's degree in American studies at University of Southern California. She was a restless, very intense chain-smoker who thought deeply about the sociopolitical state of black America, as well as the often-marginalized place of black women. I was a peaceful meditator, naturally a feminist without publicly claiming it, and focused on the socio-cultural state of black America through dance. Our personalities were different, but we came together in our artistic work. I was a dancer-choreographer-writer in search of a way to marry those genres to illuminate the black experience; Ntozake was a writer and dance student who innately felt the relationship between movement and the word. She was an avid student in my and others' dance classes and wrote intensely about her love life with black men. Her writing explored a unique way of bringing those experiences together in her own language that the literary critic Alice H. G. Phillips called "verbal runs and trills, [mixing] in syncopations, [spinning] out evocative hanging phrases, variations on themes and refrains."[1] She was an artistic iconoclast, positioning dance in poetry; I was an artistic iconoclast in dance who wanted to position words and movement in a new relationship. We came together to inspire each other in our quest for a marriage between movement and language.

Ntozake and I both began to realize our quests at the same time, but her work would revolutionize theater. Her poems that would eventually be assembled into *for colored girls who have considered suicide/when the rainbow is enuf* were written over the two years she lived in the Bay Area before she returned to her native New York region. Between 1973 and 1975 Ntozake gave poetry readings in which I performed dance improvs, and she performed in my Bay Area production of *Four Women: Images of the Black Woman in Monologue, Poetry, Song, and Dance*. *For colored girls* developed from the mind of a sensitive and brilliant writer who wanted to dance, and many times she woke me up at 3:00 a.m., calling to read me one of her latest poems. She would then have to get up by 8:00 a.m. to drive to Sonoma State University fifty miles north of San Francisco, where she taught in the women studies department to make a living.

In her introduction to the *for colored girls* book, Ntozake wrote brilliantly about her dual love of poetry and dance during this Bay Area training-experimentation period:

> Such joy and excitement I knew in Sonoma, then I would commute back the sixty miles to San Francisco to study dance with Raymond Sawyer, Ed Mock, & Halifu. Knowing a woman's mind and spirit had been allowed me, [but] with dance I discovered my body more intimately than I had imagined possible. With the acceptance of the ethnicity of my thighs & backside, came a clearer understanding of my voice as a woman & as a poet. The freedom to move in space, to demand of my own sweat, a perfection that could continually be approached, though never known, was poem to me, my body & mind ellipsing, probably for the first time in my life. Just as Women's Studies had rooted me to an articulated female heritage & imperative, so dance as explicated by Raymond Sawyer & Ed Mock insisted that everything African, everything halfway colloquial, a grimace, a strut, and arched back over a yawn, was mine. I moved what was my unconscious knowledge of being in a colored woman's body to my known everydayness.[2]

I named the dancer Ed Mock in chapter 1 as one of my dance influences also, and he had remained a popular force in Bay Area dance into the 1970s. He and I would dance together in one of Ntozake's productions in New York in 1981 after she became famous (chapter 6). Raymond Sawyer was a former New York dancer-choreographer who had moved to the Bay Area in the early 1970s and became another influential teacher and performer in the black dance movement there during the mid-1970s. He would perform in several of my productions during this period in my own growing career.

I joined Ed Mock and Raymond Sawyer as a recognized dance figure in the 1970s as the Bay Area black dance scene was exploding into a vital part of the rising black arts consciousness. Ntozake Shange, who had been born into an upper-middle-class black family, would become a close friend and major artistic force throughout my life. Besides her working in my *The Evolution of Black Dance* in the public schools and performing in the Bay Area production of *Four Women*, I would end up choreographing several of her plays that eventually became theater staples.

But nothing would be as life-changing as Ntozake giving me my African name, "Halifu Osumare," because up until 1973 I had been "Janis Miller." My African name would seal the destiny to which I was born. Ntozake never mentioned in print that she had given me my name; she simply started calling me by the name she bestowed on me in August 1973. While Donna was still on the Ethiopian TM Teacher Training Course, Ntozake arrived at our Telegraph Avenue home one summer afternoon with a sealed envelope. I made us tea, and we sat crossed-legged on the floor pillows, chatting about her latest poem and about my ambitious plans to produce *Four Women*, in which I asked her to participate as an actor. At an appropriate moment, she revealed the envelope and simply said: "I have a gift for you. I know we have known each other for only about a month and a half, but I was compelled to research an African name for you. After I leave, please pronounce it and read its meaning; and if you want to keep it, then it is yours. If you don't feel it is you, then please don't feel bad about discarding it. How you want to use this gift is up to you."

I was totally surprised and honored, having often contemplated an African name for myself. Having come of age in the late 1960s black consciousness movement, many young African Americans felt that our names were *slave* names, inherited from our ancestral families' slave masters. But Ntozake actually took the time to research a name for me based on how she saw my personality. The paper she gave me read:

Halifu–Swahili–"The Shooting Arrow"
Osumare–Yoruba–"The Deity of the Rainbow"

Ntozake left me in a very contemplative mood. I knew a new name was potentially life-changing, and I didn't take it lightly. For one month I never told anyone else about the name but instead thought about it deeply each time I came out of my daily meditation. I also researched the name further. With no Internet for instant research, I simply went to the library and found several African naming books. The meaning of "Osumare" was clear: the deity of the rainbow among the Yoruba of Nigeria, similar to the serpent deity, Damballa, of the Fon people of Benin. "Osumare" connotes the wisdom of the cyclical cosmos from which all things emanate.

But the naming book had given an interpretation for "Halifu" different from Ntozake's meaning. Consulting several other African naming books, I found out that "Halifu" was Swahili spoken in East Africa and was a *verb* that meant to oppose, contradict, rebel against, or disobey. Furthermore, it gave examples of how the word is used within particular terms: *halifu mfalme* (to rebel against the king) or *halifu sheria* (to rebel against the law). I immediately identified with this definition. My independent spirit was definitely rebellious, making it imperative for me to find my own way. My family's opinions mattered to an extent, but I always followed my own spirit telling me what to do. I, therefore, combined my two new names thusly:

Halifu Osumare–"The Rebellious, Independent One in the Rainbow"

After one month of contemplating this new name and its meaning, I knew it was me. I never changed it legally but assumed it professionally. When I would later enter graduate school, the university administration made me choose one rather than using both names with one as an a.k.a. I chose "Halifu Osumare," and that is what I have remained throughout my professional career. When I eventually went to Nigeria during my first trip to West Africa, the Yoruba people asked me, "Where did you get the name Osumare," and "Do you know what it means?" When I answered correctly, they always said, "You are welcome," and I appreciated the approval. Yet, as a dancer I did not take my surname "Osumare" right away; for over a year I performed professionally simply as "Halifu" and occasionally as "Halifu (Janis Miller)" during the name transition period. But eventually I began using both names and have never second-guessed my choice.

After Donna got back from the TM Teacher Training Course in Ethiopia, she told me she too had been feeling a name change; she returned as NaNa Maynard. "Nana" is a Ghanaian title that connotes chieftaincy and can be bestowed on male or female royal leaders among the Akan people. The first and only "Nana" that we had known was Nana Nketsia, the Ghanaian chief with whom we had studied in Boston (chapter 3). Her connotation for her new name of "NaNa" was "she whose breast was full of milk" to nourish the people. Becoming an initiated teacher of Transcendental Meditation had given her a new level of confidence as a spiritual guide to which her new name referred. So Halifu and NaNa, formerly Janis and Donna, decided to renew our relationship and newfound individual identities by taking a one-month trip south to discover Mexico. Our relationship was not based on being "lesbians" but on being spiritual beings on a quest together. Although I had explored the lesbian community in Boston, I had decided early on that, for me, lesbianism was another entrapping social "box." My perception of our relationship was that I simply loved NaNa, who happened to be a woman.

We drove out of Oakland on August 11, 1973, and headed southward first to the Big Sur coastal region. After hiking in the Los Padres Mountains, we drove along the beautiful California coastal highway to Encinitas and camped out on the beach. We then drove to Baja California and stayed in Mexicali on the U.S.–Mexico border. After crossing into Mexico to the state of Nayarit, we stayed in the town of Tepic and then San Blas, where we had an introduction to Mexican culture with a beautiful wedding fiesta that we attended.

Later in August we took an all-day bus trip to Mexico City, where I was able to pursue my lay interest in the black heritage of Mexico. Even then, without a college degree, I was pursuing my research interest in world black culture, with each international excursion presenting a possibility of discovering another part of the African diaspora. In Mexico's capital I met Dr. Gonzalo Aguirre Beltrán (1908–1996), an anthropologist who was assistant secretary for popular culture and extracurricular education. He was one of the few Mexican anthropologists who had trained with Africanist anthropologist Melville Herskovits and researched the African influence in Mexico, particularly in the state of Vera Cruz. NaNa and I were planning to visit Vera Cruz, a major port city on the Gulf of Mexico, where during the colonial period African slaves were imported to work in the fields and shipyards. My meeting with Dr. Beltrán was immensely helpful and gave me a sense of the African diaspora in Mexico, which was little considered at that time. He gave me one of his published articles on the African presence in Mexican society and discussed his interest in facilitating the integration of marginal populations like Afro-Mexicans into national society.

But before moving on to Vera Cruz, we had to see the famous Ballet Folklórico de México at the beautiful Palacio de Bellas Artes (Palace of Fine Arts), next to Alameda Central Park. Ballet Folklórico de México, founded by Amalia Hernández (1917–2000) in 1952, has become a cultural ambassador for Mexico with their international touring and impeccable representation of the many cultural regions of Mexico through dance. The Palacio de Bellas Artes had become their home, where they performed several times weekly. That afternoon NaNa and I went to see them, and the ranges of dances, from indigenous Indian to the Spanish *zapateo* footwork dances, were absolutely mesmerizing. Amalia Hernández was a pioneer in developing Mexican *ballet folklórico,* which transposed indigenous folk dances to the concert stage. Her staged dances also influenced the *ballet folklórico* movement in California that paralleled the La Raza identity movement, just as the Black Power and Black Arts movements paralleled each other. Both cultural movements spurred a significant Third World cross-fertilization in the Bay Area among communities of color (chapter 1).

Seeing the premier Mexican dance company reinforced my belief that dance is central to regaining cultural integrity and that Amalia Hernández was like the Katherine Dunham of Mexico. In fact, the Katherine Dunham Dance Company had toured to Mexico in 1947, and they were so popular that the company remained there performing for two months. It has been said that Hernández's approach to Mexican dance presentations was in the grand style of the Ballet Russe of early twentieth-century Europe, with elaborate costumes, scenery, and lighting, just as Dunham's was. Although there is no proof, it is not inconceivable that Hernández was also influenced by seeing the Dunham Company in the 1940s; it's possible that she could have been inspired by Dunham's performance spectacle for her own Ballet Folklórico de México. I know that Dunham, always the anthropologist, researched the black influences in Mexico and choreographed her 1948 *Veracruzana* ballet just a year after returning from the company's Mexican tour, premiering it at Ciro's nightclub in Hollywood.

At the beginning of September, NaNa and I took a grueling twelve-hour second-class train ride to Vera Cruz. At the train station a very dark-skinned train porter helped us with our bags, and I knew immediately that Vera Cruz was the home of Afro-Mexicans. We thankfully found the affordable seaside Hotel Royal right on the Gulf of Mexico, and we often started our mornings meditating on an isolated part of the harbor. Once, when I came out of meditation and opened my eyes, I contemplated the history of the port of Vera Cruz and its relationship to the African slave trade. In my later research I found out that "during the colonial period, it was the most important port in New Spain, the connection to ports and the Atlantic trade creating a large wealthy merchant class, which was more prosperous than that of Mexico City."[3]

I would later learn that given the fact that Vera Cruz and Galveston, my birthplace, were both important ports on the Gulf of Mexico during the slave trade, many Africans were brought to New Spain (Mexico) through Vera Cruz to work the gold and silver mines, and runaways would either head north across the Rio Grande or escape by ship to Galveston, "becoming some of the first black Texans."[4] Something in me was voraciously interested in this history, which is why we were in Vera Cruz, but it would be decades later before I would understand the full implications of these historical connections in the African diaspora.

The next day we went to Mocambo Beach on the outskirts of Vera Cruz near the town of Boca Del Rio. At a restaurant on the beach we were able to listen to some good mariachi music, complete with marimba and harp musicians. But the highlight for me was to see the bamba dance, performed by small girls, to "La Bamba" music. This dance of Vera Cruz shows the cross-cultural fertilization of Mexico with Cuba and Puerto Rico, as witnessed in the hip movements and female costumes of the dance. The music "La Bamba," made famous in the United States by Rickie Valens's 1959 rock-and-roll hit, is actually *son jarocho*, which blends Spanish seguidillas, fandangos, and Cuban zapateados and Guajiras.[5] Viewing the bamba dance was the highlight of the Mexican trip.

As our funds were quickly depleting, we had to leave Mexico. I felt grateful to have viewed dance in both a proscenium setting in Mexico City and a folk setting in Vera Cruz. We arrived back in Oakland two weeks later on September 10, tired but renewed and ready to work together again on my dance-theater projects.

Restarting My Bay Area Dance-Theater Career

It had now been six months since returning to the Bay Area, and I had become acquainted with the key artists and the general black cultural community. It was time to position my own artistic voice in the creative scene. To establish a regular income I got an adjunct dance instructor position in the fall of 1973 in the Department of Physical Education at San Francisco (S.F.) State, teaching jazz and improvisation classes. It was interesting returning to that campus after leaving in 1968, when so much chaos was beginning to brew and eventually became the seminal S.F. State Strike. The battle had been fought and won with the establishment of the first College of Ethnic Studies in the country. My being a former student in the university's dance program meant the faculty members, including Nontsizi Cayou, were familiar with my dance skills, and I parlayed that status into a temporary lecturer position. Having a steady income from teaching dance afforded me the time to finally work on producing my play *Four Women*; it was now ready for the stage. After the thwarted attempt to stage it in New York, I knew that the East Bay was the place to find the right actress-dancers and finally mount the production for my home area to experience not only my choreography but also *my* form of theater.

Like in Boston, NaNa and I again proved to be an excellent creative team, as we proceeded to produce *Four Women: Images of the Black Woman in Monologue, Poetry, Song, and Dance.* NaNa's official title was business manager and producer, and she began to look for venues and construct a marketing plan, and I set about finding the artists to make *Four Women* come alive. The play was based on the concept of the song that Nina Simone had made famous on her 1966 *Wild Is the Wind* album, vividly portraying four images of black women: Aunt Sarah's matronly resiliency during slavery, Safronia as the tragic mulatto, the enticing prostitute Sweet Thing, and the strength and rage of Peaches, who represents the collective reaction to the historic oppression of African Americans. My *Four Women* was a kind of riff on the song's concept, using four actresses to portray many more black female characters as either archetypes or stereotypes, depending on one's perspective. My job was to find four female artists who could play multiple roles, often diametrically opposed to each other. I wanted to offer a range of black female characters who could reveal the pathos and triumphs of black life in America through a woman's lens.

My half year getting to know contemporary Bay Area black artists, including musicians, singers, and actors, as well as dancers, paid off. I found four multitalented female actors, allowing the two Bay Area stagings of *Four Women* to be great successes. I had already asked Ntozake Shange to be one of my performers, and she had agreed. Then, she was known as a writer-poet who had already published in a new anthology, *Third World Women*, and was a member of Third World Communications, an organization that brought together many revolutionary people of color. Being in *Four Women* was an opportunity for people to see her as a stage performer. At that time she was a shy, introspective writer, and I had to work hard as director to reveal her theatrical qualities and make her dramatic roles come alive. I like to think my *Four Women* production prepared her theatrically for *for colored girls*, in which she herself performed on Broadway. The three other women were equally talented: Stephanie Jack was a writer and at the time was finishing her undergraduate degree at S.F. State. Nashira Mzuri Ntosha was a dynamic community activist actor who was also into music. Ota (Delores Pierce) was a singer with the Tom McElroy Trio. These were my four women; as the director of the production, I had only one stage appearance in a cameo dance solo.

Four Women consisted of twelve scripted characters over three scenes that explored large areas of black history through its many iconic roles. The female characters were essentially representations of reactions to black victimization but also included ones that represented proactive agency at the center of black historic survival. It started with a prerecorded overture of Billie Holiday's "Some Other Spring" fading into Bessie Smith's "He's Got Me Going," leading into the first character as "Little Mable" played by Ota, whose main line was, "I loves to party!" Other characters included "Sweet Thang," "The Junkie," and "The Mod Jet-Setter," who says, "Style is the most important way to make it in this world," turning out to be prescient of twenty-first-century consumerism. The drama continued with "The [homeless] Rag Woman," "Young African Girl," and "Juju Woman," all played by Ntozake. Scene 3 contained the "Slave Woman," played by Nashira, while Ota sang "Sometimes I Feel Like a Motherless Child," accompanied by my passionate dance solo that I choreographed and danced. The final characters were two proactive roles, one from the past and one from the 1970s present: "Church Woman" performed by Ota ("Hallelujah! When I lay my burdens down"), and "Revolutionary Woman," played by Stephanie ("If we all link hands together, we can stand up").

The drama ended musically with the John Coltrane classic "A Love Supreme," performed by live musicians, along with the whole cast onstage singing a song led by Ota. The music included piano, saxophone, flute, bass, congas, and percussion, the latter of which was played by my old high school boyfriend Damon Choice. *Four Women* was a family affair, and it received thunderous applause and critical acclaim. The play was timely for 1973, when the black community was still processing what the Civil Rights and Black Power movements meant, while continuing to deal with the same old community problems of drugs, poverty, the shifting place of the church, as well as the sweeping social and cultural transformations happening everywhere in the Bay Area.

The two venues that NaNa found for us to perform *Four Women* were a community center in Berkeley called the Rainbow Sign and the Mills College Concert Hall in Oakland. The Rainbow Sign was a small, professionally run cultural center owned by Mary Ann Pollar, who was a friend to the famed folk singer Odetta (chapter 2). Mary Ann and her husband created the Rainbow Sign as an intimate theater space with a seating capacity of one hundred and produced many quality performances. I also taught occasional dance classes at the Rainbow Sign, creating a mutually beneficial relationship between Mary Ann and me. Mills College, as a nationally recognized women's university with strong dance and music departments, was on another scale that provided us a larger and more diverse audience. NaNa got a student club, the Black Women of Mills College, to sponsor the performance, and part of the proceeds went to the Mills Black Student Union (BSU).

In the early 1970s, black artists, the new BSUs on college campuses, and politically oriented organizations collaborated to create positive, consciousness-raising events. In fact, the Mills College performance of *Four Women* was reviewed by the *Black Panther* newspaper. The October 27, 1973, review assessed the production: "There is no shallow sentimentality or debasing moralizing as these victims of a loveless, racist, male-dominated society pour out their hearts. There is no bitterness either." My European dance sojourn and dancing with the Rod Rodgers Dance Company of New York were used as my main publicity credits. With this positive local review, *Four Women* announced to the Bay Area that I was an artist of note, and the community was now expecting more.

I was definitely on a mission, choreographing and directing several theatrical productions after *Four Women*, as well as increasing my community dance-teaching schedule on both sides of the Bay. I wrote and choreographed another production called *Body 'N Soul*, and also created a large production as a fund-raiser for the Transcendental Meditation Centers called *Ours in Spirit*. This latter production was an evening-length show that included dance, live music, and acting skits that spoke to the black experience but also to the need to elevate our spiritual consciousness. This was a major "coming out" for the black Transcendental Meditation community, with *Ours in Spirit* performing to a sold-out house and produced by NaNa. My sister Brenda had also become a dancer and actress, having earned her undergraduate degree in dance from S.F. State, and I cast her to act and dance in the production. Dr. Phillip McGee (1942–1999), who later became the dean of the S.F. State College of Ethnic Studies, was also an actor in the production in a scene that I wrote for Brenda and him.

After these community productions, I received a major choreographic commission in February 1974, when well-known black TV journalist Belva Davis asked me to choreograph Nina Simone's "Four Women" for her *All Together Now* show on KPIX-TV, a local CBS affiliate. She had seen my *Four Women* play at the Rainbow Sign and wanted to showcase my choreography to the famous Simone song on her weekly television show. My choreographic work being on Belva Davis's television show, as a result, promoted my developing talents to a broader Bay Area audience.

I had become a major artistic catalyst in the Bay Area within a year of returning from the East Coast, and NaNa and I together became a dynamic duo in the black cultural community. I wanted my growing community popularity in teaching dance to match my fast-developing reputation as a choreographer-performer. I decided I should teach more *community* dance classes, not just within academia at S.F. State. So I scheduled classes in San Francisco and Oakland at various studios: Anna Halpern's Dancer's Workshop on Divisadero Street in San Francisco and Dimensions Dance Theater, a black dance company and school that started in the late 1960s, in Oakland. At that time, my professional image (what today would be called my "brand") was marketed as a one-name artist that was still tied to my birth name: "Halifu (Janis Miller)."

Yet even with these increasingly successful community artistic projects, I had never been the "starving artist" type: I always sought employment within stable educational institutions. Therefore, in January 1974 I accepted a position as a dance lecturer at Stanford University, thirty-five miles south of San Francisco on the peninsula in Palo Alto. John Cochran, a respected actor who was hired to teach drama in the Stanford drama department, had also been appointed the director of the Committee on Black Performing Arts (CBPA), part of that university's answer to 1960s students' activism for black studies. He hired me to teach dance in the Stanford Dance Division, with which he had a "faculty diversity" agreement, as well as to choreograph the black theater productions that he produced under CBPA.

Stanford University would offer me stable employment until I decided to leave the Bay Area again.

Cochran's first Stanford play that I choreographed was the Ossie Davis musical *Purlie*. One of the cast dancers for that production was none other than the first black woman astronaut in space, Dr. Mae Jemison. Stanford attracted the best and brightest, and Mae was a Stanford undergraduate chemical engineering student who loved to dance. She took all of my dance classes, which she claimed helped her in many educational areas like self-presentation, critical thinking, and problem solving. She was an excellent *Purlie* cast member who gave it the vibrant humor that the musical demanded.

When Mae Jemison became a medical doctor and eventually a famous astronaut, she always mentioned my name as one of her most inspiring teachers during her undergraduate years at Stanford. Decades later in the early 2000s she was invited to Bowling Green State University, where I had my first tenure-track position, as a keynote speaker for a university-wide education conference. She again reiterated the importance of dance to a comprehensive liberal arts education and the role of inspirational teachers, like myself, to her undergraduate success. This, of course, raised my stature while I was at that particular institution, and Mae and I remain friends today.

The Bay Area Black Dance and Theater Movement in the Early 1970s

I was able to grow my artistic career so quickly upon returning to the Bay Area because of the region's cultural development after the onset of the West Coast Black Arts movement in the late 1960s. Sandra Richards, noted theater and African American studies scholar at Northwestern University, was then a graduate student in the Stanford theater department, and she wrote an overview of the Bay Area black performing arts scene for the April 1974 "Black Theater" issue of *Black World/Negro Digest*. Her assessment provided a comprehensive account of the Bay Area's major artistic players and institutions in black theater and dance during the period when I returned home. The magazine's cover and opening articles were about Ed Bullins, a noted Black Arts movement playwright who figured prominently in the 1960s in both the East and West Coast movements. But the majority of the magazine's issue was spent on "Reports on Black Theater" in key black cities: New York, Cleveland, Chicago, Detroit, Washington,

D.C., Atlanta, Los Angeles, and the San Francisco Bay Area, the latter of which was contributed by Richards. She divided her Bay Area report into theater groups in San Francisco and those in the East Bay, and in the process recorded the prolific black theatrical activity in the Bay Area. Although Richards's report is primarily about drama companies, dance was situated within the survey as well.

Richards lists six major black theater companies in San Francisco in the early 1970s. One of these was Grassroots Experience directed by John Doyle, which she notes is the only one "to consistently introduce Ed Bullins' work to the area."[6] Grassroots Experience produced drama at the Potrero Hill Neighborhood House, one of the few San Francisco districts where blacks who emigrated from the South could rent housing. She also mentioned John Cochran, who ran the Black Repertory Theater while teaching at Stanford. This company was in the Fillmore or Western Addition, the other S.F. black district where I was raised as a child when we first arrived from Texas.

Richards's assessment of one of Black Repertory Theater's productions is telling about how race played into audience perception of Bay Area black theater in the early 1970s. Cochran produced Richard Wesley's play *The Black Terror,* and, as Richards writes, "Predictably, reactions to the Wesley play were strong and divided." She goes on to say that this audience division was along racial lines, "with whites tending to see the revolutionaries as folks 'running through the jungles' (no kiddin'; that's what one 'critic' wrote!) and Blacks reacting very positively."[7] Black theatrical productions could be polarizing during the sociopolitical times of the early 1970s. Blacks wanted plays and images that reflected them and their contemporary political struggles, which Wesley's play accomplished. But white audiences, and particularly white critics, were not used to black rage, even after the riots and nationwide conflagrations after Dr. Martin Luther King's assassination in 1968. Whites, during these times, were still asking, "What does the Negro want?"

Richards continues with other San Francisco theatrical companies that had *interdisciplinary* approaches. One was United Projects/Black Light Explosion Company, which was also housed in the Western Addition. Jim Larkin and Michael Catlett headed it, and Richards notes that this group had a "permanent paid staff and a building" on Grove Street. As the Western Addition had been going through major gentrification since 1963, the fact that Black Light Explosion Company had a "permanent" facility was unique. Black Light Explosion, the artistic arm of United Projects, presented drama and dance concerts, with regularly scheduled dance and martial arts classes. Richards notes that a Guadeloupe dancer, Rama, also taught and performed Caribbean dance at Black Light Explosion. Significantly, one of its other dance teachers was Zack Thompson, with whom I had danced as a teenager before leaving for Europe (chapter 1).

Richards recognizes other San Francisco theater companies in the early 1970s. Buriel Clay was an important artistic figure in the black theater scene during this period, providing one of the only programs in playwriting with his Black Writers' Workshop and producing some of the first emerging regional Bay Area playwrights. Tragically, he died in a car accident in May 1978, just as he was about to produce three local plays at the then Western Addition Cultural Center. Today this venue is known as the African American Art & Culture Complex, with a small theater dedicated to him called the Buriel Clay Theater. The Hunter's Point district, near the San Francisco naval shipyards, which also attracted many southern black workers migrating northward, gave rise to the B&D Experimental Theater Company run by Mary Booker. She produced Bea Richards's *A Black Woman Speaks*, which I also would later produce in Oakland in the 1980s (chapter 6).

Richards finishes the San Francisco report with Earl Anthony's African People's Repertory Theater in Daly City, just south of San Francisco: "It functions basically as a producing company, jobbing in different directors and assembling new casts for each show."[8] Anthony did produce a well-known Peabody Award–winning writer-director-educator, Glenda Dickerson (1945–2012). Her *Unfinished Song* for the African People's Repertory Theater company showcased African and Afro-American folktales and songs. Richards takes time to note Dickerson's influence on updating the Bay Area's knowledge and potential of black theater, commenting on the difference between the West and East Coast theater scenes at the time:

> Dickerson was brought in from Howard University to introduce ritual theater to the Bay Area. Yes, we are that far behind the happnin's in the East, but this time-lag in ideas is intimately related to the temperament of the area: nationalistic and Pan-African concepts have a harder time taking root, given the seemingly open racial atmosphere and generally more leisurely style of living.[9]

Richards recognizes an odd ambiguity about the Bay Area black community. It is both radical in its advancement of new and revolutionary sociopolitical ideas but less cohesive in terms of a black body politic. This contradiction lies in the *levels* of black social change. In many ways, the Bay Area black intelligentsia was far ahead of the masses of black people, who were less politically unified, particularly in San Francisco, than in other black enclaves nationally, such as Chicago, Detroit, and Harlem; however, Oakland had a larger percentage of blacks than San Francisco in its population and was less contradictory in its black-identified politics. As a member of the black artistic vanguard, I always had to push past this contradiction, and I like to think that my work in dance helped to create more cultural cohesion, but I did it primarily in Oakland, and not San Francisco, as will become clear in subsequent chapters.

The East Bay had fewer institutionalized theater companies; instead, Oakland and Berkeley developed small groups that worked on college campuses. Nora Vaughn's Black Repertory Group was an exception, with a small but viable facility and a company that focused on many of the classics in black theater, such as James Weldon Johnson's *God's Trombones* and Lonne Elder III's *Ceremonies in Dark Old Men*. Black Rep, as it is still called today, has always maintained its facility in Berkeley, starting out of Downs Memorial Church on Boise Street, then moving to a fifty-seat Alcatraz Street space. Today, supported by the City of Berkeley, the theater company resides in a 250-seat theater facility on Adeline and is directed by Dr. Mona Vaughn-Scott, the daughter of the founder. The Oakland Ensemble Theater, which would eventually become the most established black theater company in Oakland, had just been founded under the direction of Ron Stacker Thompson on Thirteenth Street with a 160-seat facility, opening in January 1974 with *No Place to Be Somebody*. The Oakland Ensemble Theater would eventually go on to produce musicals that included dance, as Thompson was a choreographer as well as a theater director.

One of the primary points Sandra Richards makes in her article about the early 1970s Bay Area black theater scene, particularly in the East Bay, was its close connection to the newly established black studies departments in higher education:

> On the college scene, Black theater seems to be flourishing. Characteristic of these groups are their origins in Black or Ethnic Studies Programs and the easy interchange between college campus and community. On the one hand, the Black Studies Programs provide a very necessary nourishing atmosphere for the groups, but on the

other, placement here rather than in Drama or Theatre Arts Departments means that they have difficulty in getting access to facilities and to technical skills and experience. The close relationship between campus and community is fostered in almost all cases by the fact that most of the college directors also have their own community-based theater companies, and there is a constant flow of personnel from one to the other.[10]

Examples of this "close relationship between campus and community" were Richard Gant at Laney College and Ron Stacker Thompson at Merritt College, two of the community colleges that had become hotbeds of black consciousness-raising.

Merritt was the home of the Afro-American Association (see chapter 1) that would become the breeding ground for the Black Panther Party for Self-Defense. Before establishing his own community facility, Ron Stacker Thompson had benefited from Merritt's black-consciousness focus; he directed *Amen Corner* and Hansberry's *To Be Young, Gifted, and Black* on campus. As historian Donna Murch proclaims: "Study groups, black student unions, and protests for a Black studies curriculum became important means of consciousness-raising. As a result, many of the radical groups that emerged later in the decade stemmed from this early period of black student activism."[11] By the early 1970s, after many of the college departments had been established, they continued, especially Merritt, to engage community activism, using theater and dance as catalysts for nurturing black consciousness. My *Four Women* being produced by the black student organization at Mills College in Oakland is my own example of the symbiotic relationship between college black studies and the West Coast Black Arts movement. John Cochran's Committee on Black Performing Arts at Stanford, for which I started teaching dance, was a rare exception, with black theater lodged in the drama department as opposed to black studies.

Despite the lack of actual established black theater facilities, the East Bay had more annual festivals and ad hoc groups producing black cultural events in the early 1970s. One such group was the African People's Performing Arts Company directed by Adhaimbo, a black male community leader. He produced a festival in conjunction with the newly established African American Kwanzaa holiday period celebrated between Christmas and New Year's. The inaugural festival in 1973 included Black Dimensions

Dance Theater (to become Dimensions Dance Theater), my *Four Women* play, and a group called the Family Nitoto. This entire production benefited the black studies program at Berkeley High School, one of the only black studies departments at the public secondary school level in the country. This again points to the close relationship between the establishment of the black studies movement in education and black community theater and dance in the activist Bay Area.

These black educational institutions understood that the way to establish a relationship with the black masses was through the arts, which could be used, in turn, to raise sociopolitical issues and educate audiences about black history. For example, I would eventually write and choreograph *The Evolution of Black Dance*, focused on the African retentions within black American history through the lens of the body and specific historical dances. Richards notes that these theatrical productions and large community festivals in relation to educational institutions helped provide shared scarce resources, as well as develop a sense of unity that was crucial for the early 1970s black political and cultural movement in general.

One last black theater company, which would figure into my choreographic career in the 1980s, should be noted: San Francisco's Lorraine Hansberry Theater (LHT). Artistic director Stanley Williams (1950–2010) and executive director Quentin Easter (1953–2010) founded LHT in 1981, and it still thrives today as the city's primary black theater. Williams and Easter established the theater company under the namesake of the first black female to have a serious award-winning drama, *A Raisin in the Sun*, on Broadway in 1959. LHT became known as a professional black theater in the Bay Area, producing quality works by an eclectic array of black playwrights: Nobel laureates Wole Soyinka, Derek Walcott, and Toni Morrison, and Pulitzer Prize–winning writers Charles Fuller, Alice Walker, and August Wilson. They also had a strong focus on the plays of Ntozake Shange, several of which I choreographed in the 1980s (chapter 6). Until recently, the artistic director of LHT was Steven Anthony Jones, a veteran core actor at San Francisco's American Conservatory Theater, with which I also worked as a choreographer in the 1980s and 1990s. Indeed, the early 1970s was the launching pad for serious black theater and dance, serving as the foundational platform for dedicated theater and dance companies, such as LHT and Dimensions Dance Theater, as well as my own CitiCentre Dance Theatre for a period in the 1980s.

Because the social and cultural activism of the continuing West Coast Black Arts movement created a definitive social *zeitgeist*, the early 1970s laid the foundation for subsequent decades of Bay Area black arts. This dynamic spirit of the times resulted from a symbiosis between the general increased education of blacks and people of color, spurred on by the advent of black and ethnic studies, and the developing community black theater and dance movement. This reciprocal relationship was an extension of the late 1960s Black Arts movement, which did not dissipate in the Bay Area. As English literature scholar Mike Sell notes: "The relationship among institutions, communities, and the peculiar ontologies and epistemologies of performance are foundational dynamics of both the Black Power and Black Arts movements. Both movements devised Black Nationalist strategies to effectively respond to the complications of race politics of the American political scene in the 1960s."[12] Nowhere was this made clearer than the San Francisco–Oakland Bay Area.

My artistic focus within the Bay Area's social *zeitgeist* was on culture and not necessarily politics. I perceived that cultural education through dance-theater would awaken the community's cultural memory and continue the link to our African heritage. I argued that this embodied cultural memory had become an unconscious strategy of surviving the politics in each American historical era. Ongiri, using Black Arts movement theorist Larry Neal, discusses this very idea of "memory" in the artistic productions of the 1970s as a bridge between culture and politics:

> The notion of African American cultural production as "race memory . . . art consciously committed, art addressed primarily to Black and Third World people," as Larry Neal declared in "Reflections on a Black Aesthetic," as well as the notion that African American identity is born out of a struggle with racism, urbanity, and the consequences of slavery, are both a direct legacy of the Black Arts Movement's struggle to redefine African American cultural production.[13]

However, in the early 1970s we were just beginning to learn revisionist world and American history that included blacks in any substantive way. Traditional history texts definitely did not promote a positive view of American blacks in relation to Africa. In 1974, I must admit my approach was more an *essentialist* cultural approach; I simply didn't know enough about the realities of Africa and African diasporic cultural connections. But

I realized I needed to conduct dance research on the African continent it-self, and my next two years in the Bay Area would be in preparation for that necessary journey to Africa.

Finishing My Undergraduate Degree and Preparing for Africa

The year 1974 was an important one for me. I had been back in the Bay Area from the East Coast for a year and had established myself as a dancer-choreographer-dramatist by teaching dance and producing my dance-theater performances with NaNa's help. But I had not finished the bachelor's degree that I started at S.F. State in 1965, leaving for Europe after the spring 1968 semester. In three years I had accrued 86 units with a psychology major and dance minor. By now I realized that I was fooling no one but myself by attempting to major in anything but dance and theater arts. Also, after all of my performance and life experiences over the past six years, I had no inclination to go back to finish my last year at a formal college. I don't know exactly how I heard about the University Without Walls in Berkeley (UWW-B), but I found my way to their office just across the street from the University of California, Berkeley, in spring 1974. I was just the kind of student they were looking for, having completed a significant number of units from an accredited institution with substantial career experience in my field. They laid out a plan of action for me to earn my remaining units needed to graduate with a degree in dance and theater arts, which included documenting all of my artistic experience in a formal portfolio, writing a thesis, and choreographing a culminating production. That performance piece became *The Evolution of Black Dance*, which turned out to be a defining work of my career, morphing into many theatrical incarnations.

The University Without Walls (UWW) was (is) a national movement steeped in just the kind of educational mission that encompassed my educational goals as a dance professional. The UWW movement started in the early 1970s primarily for working adults with families and community responsibilities, with an educational mission based on a theory of qualitative life change. The Berkeley branch was under the auspices of the Western Institute for Social Change that still exists today. My desire to finish my undergraduate degree in a nontraditional institution was definitely motivated by "strong inner imperatives arising from the developmental tasks of [my life],"[14] and UWW became an important next step for me. If I could finish my degree under these circumstances and get credit for my artistic experiences, I was all in.

The Berkeley office of UWW had key artists and scholars on its board of directors, who formed a pool of faculty supervisors. David Henderson, a Black Arts movement poet and writer who was teaching English and African American literature at UC Berkeley's African American studies department was one such member of the UWW board. We became colleagues and friends, but I would choose his then wife, scholar Barbara Christian (1943–2000), noted black feminist literature scholar, as my formal advisor. Christian had earned her doctorate in English literature from Columbia University in 1970 and the next year had become assistant professor at UC Berkeley.[15] She helped establish the African American studies department there, and in 1978 she became the first black woman to receive tenure at UC Berkeley, a major accomplishment indeed. She sought community involvement early in her academic career and joined the board of directors of UWW while she was working on tenure. It was my good fortune to have her as my advisor, because when she heard about my career experience and what I was doing artistically in the Bay Area, she fully got behind my educational endeavors, assuring me that with my experience, past credits from S.F. State, and current thesis plans, I would have no problem. I spent personal time at her Berkeley home, going over my résumé and having her guide me on how to represent my European and East Coast dance experiences for my portfolio. She also guided me in writing my thesis, a written version of the history of black dance based on my culminating production.

The Evolution of Black Dance had been building within me since the Boston production of *Changes*. That earlier production had delved into black history through dance, but now I wanted to solely focus on how dance played a significant role in black historical survival. Re-creating what I considered to be African principles of dance and music became my raison d'être. I began my research by considering different periods of history from West African dance, slavery and plantation dances, the 1920s Jazz Age and the Charleston, and the 1930s lindy hop from the Big Band swing era, and so on. *The Evolution of Black Dance* was not just a performance but rather a researched lecture-demonstration that utilized my developing writing skills. I conceived of the script as allowing the performers and me to educate the audience about the various performed historic dance scenes through narration. It was tailor-made for public school performances, as well as stage concerts. This was the first time it dawned on me that I was as interested in research and writing as I was in dance performance. *The Evolution of Black Dance* became the first linking of my twin passions: dance performance and academic scholarship.

By the fall of 1974 I officially enrolled at UWW, and I used the rest of the year to develop the script and the dance scenes. My research, artistry, and spirituality came together in a unified manner, and I began booking performances of *The Evolution of Black Dance* with a stellar cast of performers. I premiered *The Evolution of Black Dance* through Richard Navies's African American Studies Department for school administrators and teachers at Berkeley High School on October 30, 1974, and subsequently in many schools from elementary to high schools throughout the Bay Area. I formed an administrative organization I called "Halifu Productions," and I learned how to contact schools, book performances, and invoice the schools for my performance fee. I sometimes used the subtitle "From African Dance to Soul Dance," starting each performance with my narrated lines, "Dance is life, and it is in everything we see around us."

I used three multitalented female dancer-performers for the school version of *The Evolution of Black Dance*: Ntozake Shange; Elvia Marta, an excellent dancer originally from Panama who was working on her dance degree at S.F. State; and the dancer-singer Aisha Kahlil, who would later go on to become a singer in the famed a capella group Sweet Honey in the Rock (figure 6). I would often have to get up at 6:00 a.m. and drive to each one of their homes to pick them up in order to be ready for an 8:00 a.m. school assembly, where we would perform our lecture-demonstration for eager youths. The students always enjoyed *The Evolution of Black Dance* because they recognized themselves and their culture in the different historical dance scenes.

In her introduction to the first paperback edition of *for colored girls*, Ntozake wrote about her experience working with me in *The Evolution of Black Dance*, even though she misnamed it as "The Spirit of Dance":

> The first experience of women's theater for me as a performer was the months I spent with Halifu Osumare's The Spirit of Dance, a troupe of five to six black women who depicted the history of Black dance from its origins in Western Africa thru to the popular dances seen on

our streets. Without a premeditated or conscious desire to create a female piece, that's what, in fact, Halifu did. Working in San Francisco and Berkeley public schools as an adjunct to Ethnic Studies, I learned the mechanics of self-production & absorbed some of Halifu's confidence in her work, the legitimacy of our visions. After some 73 performances with The Spirit of Dance, I left the company to begin production of *for colored girls.*[16]

Ntozake was correct about my lack of premeditation or *conscious* creation of a women's piece. Although it could have easily been performed with some male performers, and later was, I simply put together the best artists I could find who *happened* to be women. Little did I know that *Evolution* was helping Ntozake visualize *for colored girls,* her all-women's production that *was* about women's issues and that would cause a national controversy over so-called male-bashing. I had no idea that I was bolstering her confidence to move forward with her feminist theatrical vision; I simply always had a natural confidence in myself as a woman, and once my revolutionary black consciousness was awakened, there was no stopping me.

Financially, at that point, I was able to support myself with my teaching at Stanford and my community dance classes at a multicultural dance studio in Oakland called Every Body's Dance Studio, which would later become prominent in my life's journey. Therefore, after paying each of the dancers, I could *save* my portion of the fees from the school performances, which became the fund for my trip to Africa.

Halifu Productions, as a business, became my first chance to develop my own arts administrative skills out of necessity. NaNa and I broke up as a couple after she returned from a March 1974 trip back to Boston, and I realized that she had committed more infidelities. Donna Maynard, turned TM teacher NaNa Maynard, whom I had met on the island of Ibiza, Spain, had transformed herself from an administratively smart young New Englander. She went from being afraid to freely express herself to a freer spirit with more personal confidence in the Bay Area. As a free dancing spirit from Haight-Ashbury hippiedom, I had helped in her transformative process, while she helped me to become more grounded, learning more caution about dealings with people. But in the fall of 1974 I had had enough of the cheating and reluctantly, with much inner pain, moved out of our Telegraph Avenue flat. I moved to a North Berkeley apartment at the corner of

Prince and Grove Streets (now Martin Luther King, Jr. Boulevard). During this personal break-up I wrote in my continuing journal and used dance to kinesthetically express my emotional pain.

Dance helped me make my emotional transition because NaNa and I had been together, albeit not consistently living under the same roof, for almost seven years. Dance had become not only my career and, luckily, the way I supported myself, but also how I came to realize my life's purpose— my path of destiny. I was learning how to use dance to educate, entertain, explore spirituality, and now to process my personal emotions. When I was alone, I would turn on music that I loved, such as the then popular "The Creator Has a Master Plan" by Leon Thomas, and dance tearfully for myself. Publicly, I became well known for the pronouncement: "Dance is Life, and Life is a Dance."

Meeting My Future First Husband

Toward the end of 1974 I continued performing *The Evolution of Black Dance* and working on my thesis for University Without Walls, when, lo and behold, I met the man who would become my first husband. Kimathi Asante (born Thomas Williams) came into town as a pot-smoking, electric bass–playing musician, with an Ohio band called the Pyramids. The Bay Area, as liberal Mecca for artists and free thinkers escaping the strictures of midwestern culture, attracted the Pyramids as a place to grow their reputation as an African-centered jazz band. Kimathi (bassist), Idris Ackamoor (saxophonist), who would go on to Cultural Odyssey fame, and his then wife Margo Simmons (flautist) arrived in the Bay Area and took it by storm as the Pyramids with a fiery jazz sound with African musical influences. The three had met at Antioch College in Yellow Springs, Ohio, and took advantage of Antioch's study-abroad program to travel to Europe and Africa (Egypt, Ethiopia, and Kenya), where they collected musical instruments and sonic influences along their journey. They had returned to the United States with a new sound that was reminiscent of the Art Ensemble of Chicago, but with an even more Africanized approach. The Pyramids immediately began to book gigs, fitting right into 1970s Bay Area exploration of non-Western cultures.

One day I was teaching a class at Every Body's Dance Studio, and Kimathi walked in and changed my life. Midway into my class, this tall, light-skinned black man with freckles like me and dressed in what I would then call hippie garb, came in and sat in the studio's side lobby to watch my class. After I finished, he introduced himself as an Ohio musician who had just arrived in the Bay Area and was trying to get to know local performing artists; Every Body's Dance Studio was recommended as a center where creative artists gathered. I happened to be going to a nearby restaurant with a few of my students after class, so I asked him to join us. I thought he could meet my students, who I knew would be interested in hearing the Pyramids' music; I always saw myself as a catalyst who could help grow the Bay Area performing arts. The Pyramids were playing that weekend at a then popular club on Telegraph Avenue called One World Family. I remember Kimathi as being very polite and gentlemanly, which impressed me, and I was definitely interested in checking out his music. I did go to the concert that weekend and loved the Pyramids' energy-filled African-inflected jazz.

Kimathi and I began dating and found that we had much in common, and he wasn't intimidated by my immediate past relationship with a woman. We both liked other cultures and were followers of African diasporic music like the Brazilian duo Airto and Flora Purim. One night we went to see them at San Francisco's premier 1970s jazz club, Keystone Korner. During the mesmerizing Brazilian jazz music, I remember looking at Kimathi and realizing that I had found a black man with whom I could really relate. He was spiritual (but not religious), college-educated and smart, built his identity on being an artist who loved to make and listen to music, and loved nature (we camped out a few times together). He *had* me even before the first time we slept together, but when he said to me poetically, "I want to see the sunrise with you," I was in love again. His sense of romance, as a Scorpio, was overwhelming, and I was a goner. After my long-term relationship with a woman, I realized that I hadn't lost my desire for, or feminine touch with, a man. We soon established ourselves as a couple and became socially known as "being together" in the Bay Area arts community.

But the primary foundation of my beginning relationship with Kimathi Asante was his preparing me for my first trip to Africa. As he had already spent time in Ethiopia and Kenya, as well as Egypt (he had a picture of himself standing on top of the Great Pyramid at Giza), he was the perfect person to orient me to the realities of being African American in Africa. He had also been to Ghana on a previous trip to West Africa. His African name, like mine, was reflective of a Pan-African sensibility—*Kimathi*, the name of Dedan Kimathi, a main Mau Mau rebel leader in Kenya's independence movement who was killed by the British, and *Asante*, the name of the main Akan group of Ghana. Born Thomas Williams in Springfield, Ohio, in 1951, he was the first child of a deaf mother, Betty Valentine, and was raised in Columbus, Ohio, along with four sisters and one brother (who was also deaf like his mother). He had grown up poor, being raised by a single mother on welfare, with college becoming his ticket out of poverty. We had a lot in common: our rebellious personalities, both defying parents and in some ways raising ourselves; we both had strong minds, artistic sensibilities, and interest in other cultures. We smoked together sometimes, and that was another link in our beginning relationship, although I had been a regular weed-smoker and now as a meditator had tapered off.

Even while teaching at Stanford and Every Body's Dance Studio, working on my bachelor's thesis, performing *The Evolution of Black Dance*, and starting a new love relationship, I also took on a new creative project. My new dance-theater production, *I Believe*, was a full-evening production as an extension of *The Evolution* that became my culminating project for my degree at UWW. *I Believe*, like *Changes, Or How Do You Get to Heaven When You're Already in Hell?* in Boston, was my attempt to bring together much of the black performing arts community of the Bay Area. The production included well-known local dancer-teachers, such as popular New York transplanted teacher-choreographer Raymond Sawyer; Jose Lorenzo, the Brazilian dancer-drummer whose Batucaje Ensemble was the first professional Brazilian dance company in the Bay Area; and Raymond Johnson, well-known dancer teaching in Oakland.

I conceived of bringing together as many dancers and musicians in unity to create a large statement of "the way the dance of black people has co-incided with the moods of each historical period—from Africa up to the present day," as the Halifu Productions press release read. *I Believe* was presented on both sides of the Bay—Friday, May 9, 1975, at Martin Luther King Jr. High Auditorium in Berkeley, and Saturday, May 10 at Roosevelt Jr. High in San Francisco, the latter venue being the middle school I had attended. Tickets for the shows were $2.50 in advance, and $3.50 at the door, commensurate with mid-1970s prices. Other artists in the production included Aisha Kahlil, Elvia Marta, my sister Brenda Miller, Jamal Hamilton, a dancer with Raymond Sawyer's group, and Paula Moss, who would go on to become the first choreographer of *for colored girls* in New York; Ntozake had already left the Bay Area for New York. The two shows of *I Believe* were sold out and created a lot of community buzz. In 1975 *I Believe* was a galvanizing force for both Bay Area black artists and the community, demonstrating the power of our culture through dance.

Stephanie Jack, who had performed in *Four Women*, was also a writer for the San Francisco black newspaper the *Sun Reporter*, with a column called "The World of Women." She wrote a full-page review of *I Believe* called "I Believe: Two Successful Words."

> The combination of historical analysis and entertainment blended well in a spiced potpourri of talent and artistry. The Bay Area's best dancers were soaring on the same stage, each shining brilliantly. Unfortunately this rarely occurs, and when it does[,] not enough of the Black community is seen in the audience. . . . [A]ll those who attended can testify that it was an evening of high energy and high spirit. Halifu must be congratulated for her dancing and choreography and most importantly for doing her homework. . . . [I]t is beautiful to know that [she is] beginning to document the history of [our dance] expression.[17]

I had proved that Bay Area black performing artists could transcend individual artistic egos and unify to make a major statement about the power of our collective culture. In my production of *I Believe* the major black dancer-choreographers in early 1970s Bay Area truly unified to dance in *blackness*.

With the accomplishment of *I Believe* I finished my degree at University Without Walls. I received credit for codirecting and choreographing for my Danish dance company, Magic Lotus Dance Theatre, my one-year teaching tenure at the Balettakademien in Stockholm, performing with the Rod Rodgers Dance Company, choreographing and directing *Changes* in Boston, as well as teaching jazz dance at S.F. State and Stanford University since I had returned to the Bay Area. I also got units for writing and directing *Four Women* and choreographing and directing *Body 'N Soul* and *Ours in Spirit*. My transcript distinguished between work done before and "Work Done While at UWW-B." Those credits listed in the latter category were: Essay on dance history—"The Evolution of Black Dance"; Lecture-Demonstration—*The Evolution of Black Dance* including accompanying videotape; and *I Believe*—"Culminating Project." My academic transcript read: "Halifu Osumare's work included choreography, directing, setting production, costuming, producing, and dancing." Barbara T. Christian was listed as my supervisor, and the B.A. degree was awarded in dance and theatre arts on November 13, 1975. I felt like this was a signpost in my career that acknowledged all of my hard work up to that point and allowed me to complete what I had started in 1965, when I first entered S.F. State University.

Later in 1990, when I decided to enter an interdisciplinary master's program at S.F. State, full professor Barbara Christian, had by then, unfortunately, been diagnosed with cancer. But she wrote me a letter of recommendation that documented her evaluation of my work at UWW-B and my value as a student.

> UWW-B was an attempt to provide, particularly for people of color, an alternative to Higher Education that did take into account diverse cultures, approaches and experiences at a time when this was not fashionable. . . . Because faculty like myself (I was not the only one from UCB) knew that we had to validate our existence at UWW-B we were more rigorous with these students. I am sure, given anyone's standards that the time, quality, and duration of the study Halifu Osumare and I shared were far superior to that of [other] graduate students at UCB with whom I worked. Ms. Osumare is eminently qualified to enter any graduate program in African/Afro-American Studies, based on the work we did.[18]

I indeed felt honored to have such a respected scholar of African American studies as Barbara Christian as my UWW-B supervisor, and I would take my bachelor's degree and use it the next year at the University of Ghana, Legon.

With my newly minted degree and three years of solid creative work in the Bay Area that established me as a major artistic player, in early 1976 I began to make plans to *reverse* the transatlantic journey—to visit the Motherland for the first time. I had saved enough money from the school performances and negotiated several letters of recommendation from African studies scholars to support my mission to go to Ghana and study dance in Africa, the source of what I had been choreographing and writing about. I knew a couple of African American friends who were in Ghana, and I had written to them about my pending trip so I could have someone meet me at the airport. But now I had to prepare my family for yet another long-term trip, as I was planning to stay a minimum of a year. My mother, Tenola, was now used to her first-born going off to "places unknown" and was less traumatized this time. My father, Leroy, simply told her, "You know Janis has got to do what she's big enough to do." Even though we maintained separate abodes, I had now been with Kimathi for about six months, and he had been preparing me well for the psychological and cultural impact of being on the African continent.

Kimathi and I spent almost every day together during the last month I was in the Bay Area, as we were starting to realize the reality for which he had prepared me—I was getting ready to leave him. A week before I left in March 1976, we camped out at S.F. Beach, waking up to the sound of the Pacific Ocean and clinging to each other. We were trying to be emotionally strong, but we both realized that we had strong feelings for each other and that the separation was going to be emotionally challenging. We had known each other for less than a year but had made a commitment to each other and now would have to separate. As he saw me off at the San Francisco airport, we were both in tears. I was stopping in New York for a week to see Ntozake and congratulate her on the success of *for colored girls* on Off-Broadway before taking off for Ghana; Kimathi and I promised to talk each day by phone before I left for Ghana. I had bought a lot of audiocassette tapes, not only for my fieldwork but also to make personal tapes and send back to him so that he could hear my voice and not feel so separated from me.

When I arrived in New York, I stayed at the famous Hotel Chelsea, located in the Chelsea district on Twenty-Third Street between Seventh and Eighth Avenues. As one of the first long-term residence hotels in New York built in the nineteenth century, it became a NYC landmark in 1966 and made the National Register of Historic Places in 1977, a year after I stayed there. The week I was there I imagined myself among the famous writers, musicians, actors, and artists who had stayed at the hotel.

I visited Ntozake at her apartment, and we marveled over what had happened to the poems that she had woken me up in the middle of the night to share and that I had improvised to in her readings at places like Minnie's Can-Do Club on Haight Street in San Francisco and the Bacchanal women's bar in North Berkeley. What a journey those twenty choreopoems had made, and now they were making the big transition from Joe Papp's Off-Broadway Public Theater to the Booth Theatre on Broadway that September, becoming the second play by a black woman to be performed on Broadway after Lorraine Hansberry's 1959 *A Raisin in the Sun*. Ntozake herself was a part of the *for colored girls* cast, along with Paula Moss and

Trazana Beverley, who received a Tony award as the Lady in Red. *For colored girls who have considered suicide/when the rainbow is enuf* received an Obie Award for Distinguished Production in 1977. But I would not see the Broadway production of the choreopoems, with which I had been so intimately involved since its very inception, until I returned from Ghana.

A couple of days before I left New York for Ghana, Kimathi flew to New York to see me one last time. This really impressed me, letting me know that we really had something that could be sustained over the course of the one year I was planning to be in Africa. He stayed with me at the Chelsea, and I remember sitting with him on the windowsill of my room, with the Chelsea district looming large outside and him asking me to marry him when I returned. I was a bit surprised, but I said, "Yes," and immediately told him I wanted him to wait for me. Sealing our relationship was important before I left, and our time in New York reinforced our love and commitment. With our strong pledge, I left for Ghana in early April 1976 to embark upon my pilgrimage to the Motherland, looking for Africa through dance.

5

ѴѴѴѴѴѴ

Dancing in Africa

We bend ourselves low to raise ourselves high.

AFRICAN PROVERB

My journey to comprehending Africa started on the plane ride, literally and figuratively. Taking off from New York on April 29, 1976, on the now defunct Pan American Airways, I was surrounded by young Peace Corps volunteers, white American seasoned travelers to Africa, and, of course, Africans (mostly Ghanaians), who talked and laughed furiously throughout the trip. Among the Africans were big-hipped, buxom women with wigs and straightened hair, which I naively didn't expect. I was already getting an up-close-and-personal lesson about "modern" Africa on the plane ride. I had done a little research on African religions and prayed to the Ewe deity Afá, the god of divination and destiny, attempting to enter an African cosmological universe before I arrived on the anticipated sacred land. I was also thinking about Kimathi and what I had left behind, praying that this journey would give me what I wanted and bring me safely back home to him. Global intersections of contemporary African dynamics mingled with my African American youthful naiveté and real-life personal emotions.

Carletta, a Bay Area friend, thankfully met me at Accra's Kotoka International Airport and took me to her small apartment near the University of Ghana, Legon (UG), about seven miles from Accra. The feelings of a black American arriving in Africa for the first time cannot truly be explained in words. The mental conception one has of four hundred years of history underpinning the ancestral pilgrimage "home" floods the immediate consciousness with so many emotions. One sees, hears, and smells the West

African experience of black people everywhere, not as a minority, but as the majority. I was speechless with awe at seeing black people in every capacity, from the highest airport official to the baggage handlers, simply trying to take it all in as much as I could. I was so glad that I had Carletta's help negotiating airport customs, Ghanaian English accents, and crowds of hustlers trying to sell me everything from chewing gum to African cloth. She got me out of the airport, into a taxi, and to the shelter of her place within one hour of my arrival.

I rested for three days, basically staying around the university campus and Carletta's apartment until that Sunday, May 2, when two male friends of Carletta took us to their nearby village. Mike and Fargos were two young Ghanaians whom she had met around the university campus, and who lived in Christian Village, which would turn out to be "my village" in Ghana. Christian Village, located between the university and the famous upscale Achimota Secondary School, is named for an Ewe elder whose surname was Christian. Mr. Christian had led the villagers from neighboring Togo, settling with his Ewe entourage in the current site near the UG campus. There were red dirt trails running through the campus to the village, which I walked many times during my stay. Fargos (birth name Asu Atiso), who would become my Ghanaian guide and bodyguard, was one of those unemployed young Ghanaians who hung around the campus looking for Americans or Europeans for whom they could become guides for a price. So, even though the Ashanti were the largest ethnic population, with their Twi language as the lingua franca and English as the official language of the country, Ewe culture, through Fargos and Christian Village, became my immediate experience of Ghana.

Dancing in Christian Village

I had a basic knowledge of some of the well-known Ghanaian traditional dances from studying with C. K. Ladzekpo at the University of California, Berkeley. I had prepared for Ghana by studying with C. K., one of the famous Ladzekpo drumming brothers, along with his brother Kobla at UCLA. He had been in the Bay Area since 1973 and almost immediately joined the UC Berkeley music faculty, heading the African Music Ensemble in the Department of Music at that institution until today. Having performed with the national dance company, Ghana Dance Ensemble (GDE) that formed at the University of Ghana, he was adept at presenting all of the major ethnic groups' dances. I had studied *adowa* of the Ashanti and *agbadza* and *gahu* dances of his own native Anlo-Ewe in the Volta Region of Ghana. But I was still learning the dances' nuances with the music and welcomed continuing my study of Ewe dances in their natural setting in Christian Village.

During my first time in the village that Sunday I witnessed agbadza as a social dance. The dance is so foundational to Ewe people that they form agbadza clubs, and the May 2 dance-drumming event in Christian Village was actually sponsored by a neighboring village's club. In my journal I chronicled my first time seeing agbadza in Ghana:

> *Total lack of inhibition within a very set structure reigned. Sweat pouring, colorful cloth, intense facial expressions all communicate a kind of "getting down" that was basic. They are sisters and brothers expressing their energy of life; singing, drumming, dancing, and pantomime that tells age-old stories of family relations, personified into a grand drama of life through which their life energy flows, and relationships are expressed. Mother Africa is beginning to teach me of her ways through the dance.*

Ten days later I was back in Christian Village at a funeral where the agbadza dance was again central. On this second occasion of the dance I ventured to join in the dancing to test what I had learned from C. K. Ladzekpo back at UC Berkeley. Fargos introduced me to the villagers as an American friend, which opened a certain degree of acceptance, but it was my own *dancing* that released the floodgates of their unconditional reception of me as foreigner into their community. Before I danced agbadza, I was this light-skinned, skinny (125 lbs., five-foot, seven-inch), small-breasted woman who wore more than one pair of earrings (I had three holes on the left ear and two on the right), which all denoted *difference* to Christian villagers. But my dancing obliterated this perceived dissimilarity and brought me closer to the center of the village family. Rosa, Fargos's disabled friend, who had one leg shorter than the other and who lived in the next compound, had wrapped my head properly and given me some cloth to tie around my waist, so I was traditionally dressed and prepared to participate.

Even though I knew the *movements* from studying with C. K., it was the music that I needed to understand more fully. In Africa, dance is a complex that includes the movements, the rhythms, and the accompanying songs; those three components comprise the *dance complex*. If one does not know at least the first two, then one does not know the dance. Fargos had shown me the agbadza rattle (*axatse*) rhythm so that I would be more familiar with the music itself. I was therefore instructed on how the axatse rhythm fit with the *gankogui*, or bell, and the main battery of drums—*sogo, kidi*, and *kaga*—all led by the master drum, the *atsimevu*. Musicologists have noted that Ewe drumming is some of the most complex in West Africa, and I would go on to study it at UG, but I knew enough of the basic time keeping of the axatse and gankogui that I could venture to perform the dance with the villagers. Agbadza is often humorously called the "chicken dance" because the lower arms are held close into the body, with the elbows flexed outward or behind, moving up and down to the counterrhythm of the feet, and one must know exactly where to place each step within the complex polyrhythms.

Before I knew it, a woman grabbed me by the arm and yanked me into the dance circle, facing the drummers at one end. The community clapped and sang, giving themselves more and more over to the spirit of the occasion. As I danced agbadza, the Christian villagers began to yell and scream at my execution, embracing me and giving me thumbs-up. I felt that I had been preparing all my life for that moment—my first African dance in a traditional setting—and receiving the approval of the people from whom the dance came. When I finished my dance with the proper thrusting of the elbows toward the drummers on the correct beat, Fargos smiled at me and came to escort me back to the perimeter of the dance circle; I had gone through a dance rite of passage and come out the other side.

He then asked the drummers if I could join them in playing the axatse rattle. Before I knew it I was seated in the percussion section playing the rattle with the Christian Village drum orchestra. I focused with all my might, because continual rhythmic repetition is not easily accomplished with vigor, keeping one's own part while listening to how it fits into the other rhythmic parts. Musicologist John Miller Chernoff explains the particular cultural *sensibility* to rhythm within the complexity of a particular African drumming experience:

> We can think about the difference in sensibilities as the difference between perceiving a rhythm as something to "get with" or as something to "respond to." Rhythms which cut across each other are also dynamically coherent. . . . Ibrahim felt that his isolated beating was meaningless without a second rhythm, but more than that, he could not even think of the full range of stylistic variations he might play

without the beating of a second drum. [Otherwise] there was no conversation.[1]

African drumming is about community not only in the social context but also within the actual music itself. One's part only really makes sense when one is in "conversation" with the other parts; only then can true improvisation evolve from the base of the interlocking rhythmic construction.

However, with my novice ear, I could only focus on my part, occasionally allowing myself to "feel" the whole. So, I watched the other axatse players and followed them, not really listening to the atsimevu because that surely would have thrown me off. I was not that good; I had to depend upon the others to know when to stop and start, but still I had crossed a musical barrier. I was now speaking the "language" of Africa. I had danced a traditional dance and played a traditional rhythm that had been passed down for centuries. I had conversed in the dance and music language of the Ewe people, and they recognized it. Through the dance and music I experienced my Africanness within, and I knew why I had come to Ghana.

African Dance and Western Cultural Hierarchy

The joy of my dance experience in Christian Village is, unfortunately, shrouded in the denigration of Africa as the "Dark Continent," with the narrative of Africa as uncivilized evolving partially from Europeans' perception of its dance. Robert Farris Thompson was one of the first scholars to conceptualize the complex social and cosmological principles at the basis of African dance aesthetics with his "ten canons of fine form."[2] He proved his counternarrative in his seminal *African Art in Motion* (1974). Africa had been vilified partially through the assessment of its dance as lewd, lascivious, uncontrolled, and uncivilized but also as ubiquitous. This latter assessment unwittingly testified to the continent's focus on dance and music as primary socialization tools. Moreover, its dance was rightfully viewed as the antithesis to European dance and culture. Hence, Africa had to be demonized as unsophisticated; its dance, central to its thousands of cultures, became a part of the overarching hierarchical evolutionary schema Europe constructed to justify colonialism and the vicious exploitation of its natural resources.

Curt Sachs's *World History of the Dance* (1937) was one of the early texts that articulated the resulting evolutionary paradigm of dance through his use of expressive movement of the so-called "primitive," with African dance as prime example. He essentially naturalized and exoticized African dance as one stage above the animal world. As African dance theorist Francesca Castaldi notes: "Sachs establishes two models and interpretative frameworks that he employs in his world history of dance. Sachs's first model, applied to 'primitive' societies, conceived of dance as movement; his second model, applied to 'civilized' societies, conceives of dance as art."[3] "Movement" is posited as dance outside of culture, where forms of bodily expression of animals, particularly apes, and the primitive (read African, Polynesian, etc.) are *precultural*. Their expressive movement is primal, not yet refined through the cultural sophistication of dance as art. Hence, the representation of dance by various culture groups followed the hierarchical separation of the world's human (racial) groups, purposefully primitivizing Africans and their dance forms while rationalizing colonial control over them.

Castaldi positions the emic and etic aspects of African dance succinctly at the very beginning of her *Choreographies of African Identities* (2006): "Dance and Africans have a long-standing association that has been nurtured through the last two centuries of colonial histories and anticolonial struggles. On the colonial side of history, the coloring of the African body with the heavy tones of racist discourse and the devaluation of dance as a prediscursive form of expression concurred to make African dance a powerful icon of primitivism."[4] The historic positionality of dance in Africa would also become the basis for the assessment of the dance of black Americans and eventually the lens through which black choreographers would be viewed, even when the Africanist elements were blended with European ballet and approximated "white" modern dance forms. The primitivist analysis is what plagued Katherine Dunham from the late 1930s, Alvin Ailey in the 1960s, and Jawole Willa Jo Zollar in the 1980s and 1990s, prompting my national dance initiative, Black Choreographers Moving Toward the 21st Century (chapter 6). The dye had been cast centuries ago in Africa, and black dancers and dancemakers had to continually negotiate the racist minefield of Western assessment of the black dancing body at different periods on different continents.

But Castaldi also offers the other side of the equation, the emic insider perspective of African dance: "On the anticolonial side, African dance allowed for the articulation of indigenous cultural beliefs and the expression of historical continuities, making dance also a powerful medium of indigenous resistance against the European colonizers."[5] This is what I experienced in Christian Village on that Sunday afternoon at the funeral: a continuity of "the articulation of cultural beliefs" through the body and rhythm. Ewe dances often tell of their migrations, some of which were due to the mass fleeing of slave catchers. In fact, the Anlo-Ewe of Ghana's Volta Region migrated to their current "cluster of island settlements surrounded by the salty waters of the Keta lagoon" off of the Volta River, specifically to escape slave catchers, with their dances actually chronicling their migration to the region as resistance. C. K. Ladzekpo notes:

> The memory of these raids and the loss of entire settlement populations have been deeply imprinted on the *Anlo-Ewe* consciousness through the holdings of oral tradition such as folklore, myths and songs. A mass migration northward and the establishment of lagoon island settlements began as a necessary security against becoming a slave in some strange land. The *Keta* lagoon became central to the early evolution of the *Anlo-Ewe* traditional state. Its shallow waters were not navigable by the large slave ships and provided a much needed buffer-zone between the settlers and the aggressive slave traders.[6]

The Ewe Christian villagers were originally from Togo, like the Anlo-Ewe. The memory of the slave trade and its effects historically have been passed down through the dances and songs that continue to inculcate the historical resistance to colonialization and its precursor in the slave trade that created the African diaspora, the Black Atlantic.

Castaldi accurately notes that Western writers on African dance must lodge contemporary positionality in "the space between personal and social histories," and *Dancing in Blackness* is an ode to this authorial model. As a *white* American, Castaldi notes about herself: "I turn white as I step into African dance; I turn white like my dead ancestors who invented the tones of racialized discourse."[7] This honest subjectivity is where white and black American dance scholars separate: as an African diasporan, I turned African when I stepped into the agbadza circle in Christian village, dancing and reveling in my blackness.

When I visited Ghana in 1976, the resistive Black Power and Black Arts movements had affected the entire world, including the Caribbean, South America, and Africa itself. But I found "old [indigenous] values [still] maintaining their tenacious hold" on several generations of Ghanaians, including UG students, who were feverishly debating the imposed colonial British epistemology while glossing over their own ancient traditions. The hierarchical world order was alive and well among many educated Ghanaians who had been brainwashed by the British colonial system, while traditional dance and music was viewed ambivalently as an antidote to the imposed European class-ridden order. I was there partially because I understood that African dance and music promotes an important counternarrative to the hegemonic Western discursive order. This embodied knowledge transcends the rational mind, allowing participants to engage emotional and ancestral spiritual dimensions, like we did that Sunday at Christian Village.

The School of Music, Dance, and Drama (SMDD, now the School of Performing Arts) at the University of Ghana, Legon, became an important institution for promoting and elevating indigenous cultural beliefs carried by Ghanaian dance, music, and traditional theater in late-1970s Ghana. This department, founded by the eminent musicologist J. H. Kwabena Nketia, in its institutional history represents two sides of this overarching history between Africa and Europe: promoting the skills and values of traditional African dance and music while being subject to pushback from its own university, a premier educational institution in West Africa started by the British before Ghanaian independence. SMDD became my home on many levels during my nine-month stay in Ghana.

Dancing at the University of Ghana, Legon

Within a few weeks of arriving in Ghana and temporarily staying with Carletta, I knew I had to establish a formal relationship with UG so I could legitimately take dance classes in the SMDD. In order to enroll as an official university auditor, I had to make the long trek up University Avenue to Legon Hill at the very top of the campus, where the university's administration offices are. University Avenue, as the main thoroughfare of the campus, moves pass Balme Library and the University Bookshop, and past Legon and Volta Hall dormitories. The campus has interesting architecture for an African university, because the architectural design of many of the buildings, particularly the roofs, has an Asian pattern. I was told that Kwame Nkrumah, Ghana's first president, had an agreement with China and the Eastern Bloc to send expert architects and construction workers to the country in the 1960s. The Asian architectural design of some of the buildings on the campus was the result of Chinese designers. Globalization and cultural connections did not start at the end of the twentieth century but in fact were well established long before, particularly in Africa during the Cold War.

I paid a nominal fee for the remainder of the spring 1976 semester and became a part of UG with an official ID card. I took my paperwork to the SMDD and got a schedule of the weekly dance classes from the secretary. She told me that I should visit Professor Kwabena Nketia, as the director, and he could advise me about which classes were open to me. I didn't really know of Dr. Nketia's esteemed reputation at the time, but I found a very gentle, soft-spoken, and unassuming man who was graciously helpful. He welcomed me to Ghana and asked about my academic and artistic background, wanting to know why I desired to learn traditional Ghanaian dance. I had no idea I was meeting one of the world-renowned scholars of African music, as he exuded complete humility. He was delighted that I already had a degree in dance and some experience with Ghanaian traditional dances. He outlined the SMDD program, which would only be available for one month before the semester ended. I assured Professor Nketia that I was serious and that I would begin again in the fall, because I was planning to stay until the end of the year.

As one enters the Main University Gate off of Dodowa Road, which connects the Legon campus to Accra, the SMDD was and is conveniently right at the entrance to the campus. The SMDD was built as several compounds of offices and classrooms surrounding courtyards, similar to a village compound. The music classes were held in classrooms, while the dance classes had one large hall with an elevated stage that doubled as a theater space for performances. None of the rooms were in really good shape, with rickety desks and chairs and lots of dust from the outside unkempt, dirt-filled courtyards. But the Ghanaian students made do and were grateful to be enrolled at the university. For African dance, all one really needed were competent drummers and knowledgeable bodies to create transcendent magic, which happened in almost every class.

The curriculum in dance and music was built on a Western model of dance technique courses, along with ancillary foundational theater arts courses. Students enrolled in a Certification Program, Diploma I, Diploma II, or Diploma III degrees. The one-year Certificate allowed one to teach as an assistant for the arts in the public school curriculum. The Diploma programs required more study, with the highest degree, Diploma

III, taking three years of study, qualifying one to become an assistant lecturer at Legon or other tertiary institutions. The curriculum consisted of various traditional dance and music techniques of the major ethnic groups: Ashanti, Fanti, Ewe, Dagomba, Lobi, Dagara, and others. Supplementing this foundational dance and music curriculum were courses in labanotation, dance composition, principles of choreography, arts of the theater, stage lighting, folk songs, acting technique, and even in African literature and mass media.

I was impressed to find such a comprehensive curriculum and soon realized that the faculty of the SMDD at UG was from two backgrounds: those educated in Western dance, music, theater; and traditional experts from throughout the Ghanaian regions. Professor Nketia, born in 1921, had studied at the University of London and Trinity College of Music, as well as Columbia University, Julliard School of Music, and Northwestern University in the United States. Once Nketia returned to Ghana he was on a fast track to become the foremost musicologist of African music and was promoted to full professor at UG in 1963. His *The Music of Africa*, published in 1974, established his international reputation and remains one of the most comprehensive texts on the subject today.

Other faculty members were equally qualified. Albert Mawere Opoku, the head of the Dance Division, had gone to Julliard in the 1960s and studied with Martha Graham. Dr. William Ofotsu Adinku was one of the first students of SMDD, who then, in 1971–73, furthered his dance studies at the University of Illinois at Urbana-Champaign, earning a master's degree in dance and later going on to the University of Surrey in the United Kingdom to earn a doctorate in dance studies in 1988. Nii Yartey started as a diploma student in the program, 1969–71, and then went to University of Illinois in 1972 for his MFA. Ms. Patience Kwakwa, lecturer, was teaching in the United States the year I was studying at SMDD, but I heard of her reputation as an original member of the Ghana Dance Ensemble (GDE) and a U.S.-trained dance educator and ethnologist. We would meet decades later in 2008, when I was a Fulbright scholar teaching in the Department of Dance Studies. All these SMDD faculty members had Western university degrees yet were steeped in their traditional culture, bringing the best of both worlds to the students at UG.

Having expert traditional practitioners from throughout the ten regions of the country was equally important and validated the authenticity of the traditional curricula. I was able to take Ashanti dance from the stately and patient Auntie Grace Nuamah from the Kumasi area, and xylophone (*gil*) lessons with the tall and lean Kobom from Lawra in the West Upper Region. Ewe dance and drumming was taught by Kwashi Amevuvor from the Volta Region; he would eventually move to Los Angeles and teach at UCLA. As I was planning to travel the country during the summer months to do field observations of the various dance styles in their specific ethnic regions, being able to study with expert practitioners from those very regions was priceless. When one walked into Auntie Grace's class, one felt the environs of Kumasi, learning the stories, proverbs, and meanings behind the hand gestures so prominent in the adowa, *kete*, and *fontomfrom* dances from the Ashanti area. When the Ewe dance class happened, students from the science and social science departments from all over the campus would come and stand by the door to watch the dynamic *atsiagbekor* war dance, with its intricate syncopated steps, turns, and jumps, or the fun gahu circle dance that really worked the hips. No other department on campus called the spirits of the students the way the drums of the dance classes in SMDD on Legon's campus did. I was in "dance heaven," studying traditional Ghanaian dances in such an organized structured manner.

There was another African American student, Ronnie Marshall, a Diploma III student in his second year with whom I became friends. He was a good tap dancer from Los Angeles, having studied with Gregory Hines, as well as being an actor who had appeared in a few Hollywood movies, including the famous 1975 coming-of-age film *Cooley High*. Ronnie, having studied in Ghana for two years, was already doing all the traditional dances, as well as assisting the drummers in the classes. He proved that the intricacy of the traditional dances and the drumming could be mastered by a non-Ghanaian, and the Ghanaians were proud of him for his disciplined dedication. He had already been given a Ghanaian name, Yao Tamakloe, which is what I always called him. We became each other's support system at the university, and Yao became my brother for life.

History of the Institute of African Studies, SMDD, and Ghana Dance Ensemble

During the colonial period and the subsequent independence movements in Africa, including Ghana's seminal independence in 1957 led by

Pan-Africanist Kwame Nkrumah, culture was a contentious realm that both furthered African nationalism and promoted subjugation, depending on the colonial power.

Nkrumah, newly independent Ghana's first prime minister, had a progressive consciousness regarding the place of culture in Ghana's newly independent efforts. This translated into his Institute of African Studies as early as 1961 at the University of Ghana. In a 2008 interview I conducted with Professor Nketia, he recounted the history of the Institute, the SMDD, and later the GDE:

> They all came in succession during the first years of independence. In 1961 Nkrumah set up an international committee to look at the university and change it from the University College of the Gold Coast [established in 1948 by the British] to the University of Ghana, and he had the idea of the Institute of African Studies at the same time. Although the university wanted just a small office and bureau for research, he wanted an institute, and Nkrumah actually wanted it bigger than the university.
>
> So it was deemed that we would have an Institute of African Studies that was semi-autonomous. But we arranged for it to be an integral part of the University of Ghana in terms of programs and faculty and so forth, because the university could provide more financial support. Then it was our idea to branch the performing arts to be separate. So I wrote a letter to Nkrumah that we wanted to set up this program in the arts, and he wrote back saying, "Approved," directly on my letter. And that was just how we set up the school [SMDD].[8]

Yet, often politicians have to be coerced into fully committing to institutionalizing and funding cultural and artistic enterprises. I asked Professor Nketia whether it was difficult to convince Nkrumah of the need for the SMDD as a part of the Institute of African Studies. This was his response:

> No, because they had already seen what we could do in the area [of the arts]. I was part of the ceremony that celebrated independence and the [new] Republic. I brought drummers and the fontomfrom drums that were for the kings, and the traditional horn blowers, and we changed the signature of the ceremony. Nkrumah was very impressed by this [display of African culture], because in his autobiography he mentioned that this [cultural display] had happened. Inde-

pendence was also about African identity, and so Nkrumah set up a committee to have an interim Arts Council to plan for important events. And of course that was the first time we had brought groups from all over Ghana to Accra. It was a big thing. And from then on we had an Arts Council that was associated with the university. That's when dance and music became a part of it, and then it was easy to do academic programs in that area. It was easy to make the arts a part of the push for African studies.[9]

Hence, Nketia's efforts to establish an African studies research institute and an arts department at the University of Ghana in the early 1960s, during the beginning of Ghana's independence, were facilitated by a sympathetic Nkrumah and the powerful demonstration that traditional Ghanaian dance and music brought to the independence ceremony itself on March 6, 1957. Politics and culture were literally and symbolically wed at that seminal ceremonial performance of Ghana's liberation from the British. Nketia would parlay that moment into the Institute of African Studies and the School of Music, Dance, and Drama as a quintessential model for the transmission of African culture in Ghana's higher education.

The importance of Nketia's efforts toward the development of African studies with an attendant arts program, all supported by Kwame Nkrumah, cannot be overstated. Nketia had a knowledgeable new prime minister who understood the importance of a school of the arts within the Institute of African Studies. He took the approval of Nkrumah's administration and established both the SMDD and the GDE. This was the well-honed African-centered department in which I enrolled in 1976, just ten years after its establishment under Professor Nketia's directorship.

The late Albert Mawere Opoku was the dancer-ethnologist who forged the dance curriculum of the SMDD. Having studied at Julliard, he had a thorough knowledge of Western theater arts and the developing U.S. modern dance scene, but he also came from the Asante royal court and had a deep reverence for the *classicism* of Asante/Akan dance. Professor Nketia told me that "Opoku started giving formalized dance training at the Cultural Center in Kumasi [capital of Ashanti Region] with no government support," so he began experimenting with Western dance training techniques in Ghanaian traditional dance even before he came to the university. He brought Auntie Grace Nuamah to Legon, as he had worked with her at the Arts Center in Kumasi. Nketia also told me that "her emphasis on the smooth transition between movements became the model for how to do adowa even back in Kumasi." In this way, the SMDD began to *standardize* traditional dances from different Ghanaian regions into trainable styles that could be taught to anyone from anywhere in the world, and this is the setting in which I began to hone my Ghanaian dance skills at SMDD.

Opoku was also a researcher-scholar who wrote several treatises on Ghanaian dance, including his seminal *Festivals of Ghana* (1970), which investigated the context of dance and music of many Ghanaian regions and ethnic groups. Only a trusted member of the culture could have recorded the meaning behind the rituals and ceremonies for the first time from an emic perspective. Opoku says in the acknowledgments to his text, "The chiefs and their various functionaries, the priests and their attendants who so understandingly allowed me into the sacred preserves deserve more than ordinary mention for praise."[10] Opoku was a cultural arbiter who wedded the best of Western theater and dance theory to a reverence for and insight into traditional Ghanaian dances and their contexts. I feel privileged to have studied and dialogued with him during my 1976 sojourn.

Nketia and Opoku were determined to establish a unique model for both the school and the dance company. Nketia assesses their original motivations in comparison to Guinea's national dance company:

> We wanted to do it differently than the Guinea Ballet [Les Ballets Africains de la République de Guinée] that focused on already-skilled dancers. The Guinea Ballet was founded by Keita Fodeba and people who had been to France, and then they became completely a government project. We wanted young dancers who had a facility for dance, but that we could train. We used highlife music for our rehearsals because we thought that the dancers who were recruited from all regions could relate to that *one* music. We looked for dancers who had the aptitude. Besides our training in the various ethnic dances, we took them to the various regions so they could get the atmosphere of the [different] dances. We were also interested in what [and who] each community thought was particularly good.

Nketia's reminiscence reveals several important issues about starting national dance companies in West Africa during the transition from colonialism to independence. Les Ballets Africains, which had become the model for African dance companies touring in Europe and the United States (chapter 3), was actually started by Guinean choreographer Fodeba as early as 1952 in Paris. With the advent of Guinea's independence from France in 1958, a year after Ghana's, the dance company was incorporated as a wing of the government and became an official cultural ambassador. That dance company, in effect, became the cultural propaganda arm of newly independent Guinea. Nketia's assessment of their difference alludes to the fact that Nkrumah gave them relative autonomy to develop as they saw fit rather than immediately attaching them to the state. After all, as the newly developing independent African countries were emerging almost every year, national dance companies were viewed as an expedient means to join the global market by showcasing African culture and earning crucial foreign monetary exchange.

Nationalistically, these new African dance companies were also a mechanism to attempt unification of the various ethnic groups that had been configured by Europe under these "new" African countries established by their colonial masters, the polities of which had not existed before colonialism. As dance and music were common cultural markers for all African ethnic groups, rehearsing recruited dancers to showcase the different ethnic groups' dance and music traditions could help create a sense of national unity through culture.

The development of the Ghana Dance Ensemble was no different and became a model of a unique approach in creating national identity through dance and music. For example, Nketia's focus on highlife music in rehearsals, such as the common West African pop music that had originated in Ghana, was an acknowledgment of the need to start with *common* popular culture until the different ethnic dancers could learn other regional cultural styles. Nketia informed me that the music followed a similar process as the dance, "recruiting the best master drummers and having them learn the supporting drums of another ethnic group, [although the lead drummer was always native to the specific music culture performed]. In that way they all became proficient at the various music traditions of Ghana as a whole." In general, Nketia and Opoku had an "incubation" approach that focused on teaching and training, allowing the first GDE members to develop at a comfortable pace. Nketia remembered: "The first two years we did not perform. We wanted them to focus on training, and they became a cohesive group in that manner. The concept of the integration of different African cultures became an advantage rather than a disadvantage."[11]

But the SMDD and the GDE, as parts of one of the premier educational institutions in West Africa, were not without their detractors. Fashioning traditional Ghanaian dance and music into an accredited discipline, within an institution established in the mid-twentieth century by the British to deliver a Western classical education, was antithetical to the cultivated mind-set of many professors and students. Nketia notes: "The Institute of African Studies became a different model *because* of the music and dance. Through the performing arts, the Institute, which also dealt with the humanities and research, became visible. But it was the students in the early days that ridiculed us with the term 'dondonology.' This was due to the university in general being based on Oxford classical education, but the *community* supported us."[12] "Dondonology" as a discursive joke refers to the Northern Ghana Dagomba drum, commonly called *dondon* or talking drum (in Dagomba called *lunga*). The general university students ridiculed the institute and SMDD's efforts to elevate traditional music and dance to an academic pursuit, and this was indeed what Nketia and Opoku were focused on doing.

However, the general campus perception was that indigenous Ghanaian culture was *beneath* Western academic knowledge and that Nketia and Opoku were making a mockery of their prestigious educational institution. Ironically, the dondon drum, chosen as a tool for this mockery, was in fact the Dagomba people's means of transmitting messages, including history, hence the concept of it being a "talking drum" attuned to the tonal language of the people. Colonialism had alienated educated Ghanaians from the wisdom and depth of their own traditional cultures, and the leaders of the institute, the school, and the dance company were attempting to restore this knowledge base through a Western-modeled educational system. Fortunately, today the university's public assessment of the current School of Performing Arts (SPA) with its departments—Dance Studies, Music, and Theatre Arts—is that it is an important and integral part of the liberal arts education of the University of Ghana.

Professor Nketia has been a distinguished visiting professor at UCLA and Harvard, and in 1993 he established the International Centre for African Music and Dance as a research arm, because "I wanted the centre of gravity of African music to be in Africa itself."[13] When I interviewed Nketia in 2008, as a professor emeritus with nearly fifty years of university accomplishments, he said, "And now I see that students are registering for the African studies freshman course by the hundreds." Today, students from all over the world come to study traditional Ghanaian dance and music in a structured academic environment, vindicating Nketia's overall mission that started in the early 1960s. Yao Tamakloe (Ronnie Marshall) and I were two of only a handful of Americans consistently taking classes in SMDD in 1976, but today the university has hundreds of academic relationships between U.S. and European universities that send thousands of students yearly to study at the SPA. Now, that university unit represents the dominant academic interest of those international students, because they want the "real" Ghanaian *cultural* experience when coming to West Africa for the first time.

The Power of Dance and the Ghana Dance Ensemble

The GDE eventually became the most visible artistic product produced by the SMDD. The dance company's repertoire represented years of research and artistic creativity that had transposed Ghana's cultures to the proscenium stage. Professor Opoku, as its first artistic director, had a visionary philosophical perspective on dance and Ghanaian culture that enabled the GDE to go far beyond good theatrical spectacle, approaching a distillation of the essence of each of Ghana's regional culture groups. As Opoku said:

> To us Life, with its rhythms and cycles, is Dance; and Dance is Life. The Dance is Life expressed in dramatic terms. The different dances speak to the mind through the heart, and the dancer is like a spiritual medium sensitive and receptive to the impressions and feelings around him and is capable of demonstrating these communal feelings with power to the people around him. In Africa the dancer is his own choreographer, able to express what he feels through his own body movements.[14]

Although variations on Opoku's powerful sentiments have been recorded in several texts, the above statement is taken from the notes that I took as Opoku spoke in 1976 in the dance hall in SMDD, now posthumously named after him. They demonstrate a thoughtful perspective on the mental, emotional, and spiritual nexus created by African dance, positioning *the dancer* as a powerful receptor of environmental, cultural, and cosmological influences, as well as becoming his/her own inspired choreographer through improvisation.

As mentioned, from the beginning the GDE had the advantage of being initiated by Western-educated, yet culturally reverential and knowledgeable artists—Nketia and Opoku—who brought the best of the West and

Africa together in their approach to staging the national cultures. Anthropologist Katharina Schramm captures this dual foundation of the company: "By narrating the history of the Ghana Dance Ensemble, I would like to argue that the formation of national culture has always been determined by local as well as global parameters."[15] The dual global-local lens is a way of denoting what I observed in classes at SMDD and performances by the GDE during my summer of fieldwork in Ghana. The cultural and artistic negotiations necessary to deliver the sensitive repertoire that I witnessed, as well as how the Ghanaian audience responded, meant that the mediations between Western theatrical exigencies and Ghanaian cultural necessities were masterfully constructed. As Beatrice Tawiah Ayi says: "Migration of traditional Ghanaian dances from rural spaces to urban pedagogical stages has produced a significant change in the world of dance in Ghana."[16] The GDE shifted the Ghanaian audiences' perception of their own cultures through the sensitively constructed repertoire of dance-theater representing several regions of a country with more than twenty-five different language groups.

The foundational repertoire of the GDE had been established with regional dances from Asante (Ashanti), Ewe (Volta), Kasena (Upper East), Bamaya (Northern), and Ga (Greater Accra), as well as Togo Atsea from Togo and Dahomeyan Dance Suite from the drilling motifs of the French colonial soldiers in the Republic of Benin. The repertoire therefore reflected not only Ghanaian dances from several key regions but also from neighboring West African countries.

This basic Ghana Dance Ensemble repertoire that Opoku had established was transferred to the late Nii Yartey (1946–2015), who became heir apparent the year that I was in Ghana. I was lucky enough to arrive and study with Opoku for the last few months before he retired from the University of Ghana and went to the United States to teach at State University of New York, Brockport. I witnessed the transition from Opoku, as the world-renowned Ghanaian dance authority, to the young, fledgling artist Nii Yartey, who was just returning from his master's program at the University of Illinois, Urbana-Champaign. In a society where age and experience are paramount, the transition from the elder Opoku to the thirty-year-old Yartey, who had been away from Ghana for the previous two years, was no small thing. Looking back in a 2008 interview, Yartey assessed his then new position:

After I had finished my Diploma at SMDD and before I left for my Master's Degree in the U.S., Nketia took me to Opoku to become his assistant. So really I served Opoku in that capacity—as his stage manager, his personal manager, and his deputy, and so on. So when finally I took over the whole thing, everyone said "but he's so young." All the dancers and drummers were people who were used to teaching. They were people old enough to be my father, and they were all in the company.[17]

It is obvious that the then thirty-year-old Nii Yartey was perceived to have particular qualities that made him competent to become the second director of the GDE. Back then, I remember Yartey only peripherally, as I was traveling around Ghana conducting my fieldwork just as he was making his transition back home into his much-envied position of artistic director of the GDE after Opoku. But, as he had just returned from the United States, and as my age-peer, we did have a few talks about the future of African choreography and the potential for new creative directions.

Indeed, setting a new course of direction for the GDE with a new contemporary African choreography is exactly what Nii Yartey set out to accomplish. He innately understood that "traditional" is relative, particularly when village dances are put onstage:

Generally, what are described as "traditional dances" are the result of both individual and community effort. As a result of being performed in public year after year, these dances become part of the group's repertoire, handed down from generation to generation. Since no community or tradition exists in isolation and since dance movements can be learned or "purchased," there is exchange of inspiration either because of aesthetic appeal or because of the religious or recreational value of a dance.[18]

Yartey saw the traditional dances performed by the GDE as in a process of flux, and hence he was driven by the vision of "new choreographic forms" that could continue to develop the artistic potential of the GDE and *staged* African dance in general.

His contribution to contemporary African dance became a new phase of development of the GDE, which he called, "observation and research . . . used to form the basis of work to inspire the present and the future."[19] Yartey's observation and research became a part of what he calls Ghana's movement toward "experimentation" that allowed for the GDE's repertoire to be "relevant to the contemporary world." One of his first experiments in contemporary African dance was *The Last Warrior*, choreographed in 1976, the year he took over the directorship of the GDE when I was living there. The dance work was based on a Ewe warrior who was killed in battle, with movements based on the *agbekor* war dance. He described his artistic process thusly: "New movements were carefully created to bridge the gap between the abstract and the concrete movement of the original dance; they kept in mind the characteristic movements found among the Ewe people, both in their villages and when they were in [urban] Accra. From all this was derived material that could lend itself to developing the story line."[20]

In this way Nii Yartey began to develop an approach to his contemporary choreography based in knowledge and respect for the traditional dances that were already a part of the GDE's repertoire. In fact, what Yartey was doing was a development of the experimentation begun by Opoku himself. *The Last Warrior* was based on Opoku's "Lamentation for Freedom Fighters," which was a community dirge for those lost in that same Ewe war and represented a cross-fertilization aesthetic. Because of Nketia's and Opoku's original intent for the GDE, Yartey's experimental approach in developing contemporary African choreography fit well within a research approach to the dance company's unique mission. Nketia's and Opoku's visionary objectives gave Yartey permission to become one of West Africa's important voices in today's contemporary African dance movement.

Eventually the GDE split into two entities, with the Ghana Dance Ensemble staying on the campus and the Ghana National Dance Ensemble becoming the resident company of the National Theatre of Ghana built in Accra in 1992.[21] Nii Yartey became the latter's artistic director, and under that auspice created many well-recognized works, such as *Solma* (1995) as a collaboration with French choreographer Jean-François Duroure and sponsored by the French embassy in Accra. Unfortunately, quite suddenly Nii Yartey fell ill in India while on tour with the Ghana Dance Ensemble, and he died in November 2015 as this book was being written; but his legacy lives on.

Over the decades Nii Yartey became the respected elder of dance in Ghana, as the head of the Department of Dance Studies, the Ghana National Dance Company, and the artistic director of his own Noyam Dance Institute and Company, which served as his personal choreographic vehicle before his death. Noyam was a part of a growing neotraditional contemporary African dance movement throughout Africa, which includes choreographers like Senegal's Germaine Acogny and her L'Ecole des Sables, Democratic Republic of Congo choreographer Faustin Linyekula and his Les Studios Kabako, and Adréya Ouabma of Congo-Brazzaville, who has collaborated with noted African American choreographer Reggie Wilson. Pan-Africanism and globalization are forces that are impacting contemporary African dance, and Nii Yartey kept Ghana in this developing dance mix as he trained the next generation of Ghanaian dancers to do the same.

What evolved into the School of Performing Arts at UG-Legon, from its origins in the Institute of African Studies, SMDD, and the Ghana Dance Ensemble, continues as a well-organized school for African dance, music, and drama in which I had the good fortune to study during its heyday, when its world-famous founders were still in charge. As I will elucidate later, Nketia would eventually hire me to teach African American dance forms during the fall semester of 1976. When I returned thirty-two years later, in 2008, as a recognized academic, I would teach lecture-based undergrad and grad courses as a Fulbright scholar while studying Ghanaian hip-hop. But my 1976 field study as my introduction to Ghana initiated a lifelong relationship with what I now call my West African home.

Settling into UG-Legon, Christian Village, and Accra

After I'd spent one month living at Carletta's apartment, she began preparing to return to the United States, and I had to find another place to live. I had submitted paperwork to get one of the university studio apartments in South Legon near the campus, but it would take another two weeks before one would be made available. Fargos and I were getting friendlier, but I was staving off his amorous advances; I kept telling him I was engaged, showing him Kimathi's picture, and making it a point to talk about my fiancé frequently. But an African man interested in a woman is not going to continue to take no for an answer if you continue to hang out together. He told me that he understood I was engaged and that he respected my relationship, but if I was going to stay in Ghana as an unmarried woman, I would need his protection. As an unemployed hustler, Fargos saw me as source of income, but he had also proven himself to be a reasonable and trustworthy man who was simply trying to survive in a poor country. He even paid for *some* of our excursions into Accra. Plus, I actually liked him a bit, because he was funny, easy to get along with, and always accommodated my needs. When he knew I needed a temporary place to stay, he offered his house in Christian Village. I knew what that meant: if I went to stay with him we would become lovers, but it also meant that I would learn firsthand what it was like to live in a village without electricity or running water. So I said yes, and went to live with Asu Atiso, better known by his nickname, Fargos.

By now everybody knew me in Christian Village and assumed that Fargos and I were already "together." The social adjustment was easy, and I could walk to my dance and music classes at SMDD in about twenty minutes. I adjusted to the lack of modern urban amenities fairly well and fashioned myself an anthropologist roughing it in the "field." Going with the women in the morning to the central pump for a bucket of water for my morning bath was fun, and reading by a kerosene lamp at night wasn't that bad either. I didn't even mind going out, with toilet paper in hand, to the nearby bush.

For me, the worse thing was bathing with cold water behind the dirt mound bath area that Fargos had created in the yard. When I complained about that, he warmed my water over a coal pot fire each morning and made sure I was as comfortable as I could be during my short stay in the village. Fargos had a two-year-old son, Kudjo, by a woman in a neighboring village; he would bring Kudjo over frequently, and I would help take care of him. My female friends in the village taught me how to tie Kudjo with cloth onto my back and carry him around like they did their children. But I was never very good at it, and Kudjo was always slipping down my back, as the village women laughed in amusement.

Settling into the village, I got more into Ewe dance and drumming and started taking private Ewe drumming classes. Fargos taught me more Ewe songs, as well as how to play the *televi*, a popular hand-held percussion instrument. Because the villagers were so impressed with my dancing, they recruited me into a Christian Village dance group and asked me to perform with the group at an Ewe festival in the Volta Region. Although I didn't feel totally confident, I agreed; I felt I was being used as a novelty because I was American, and people would be drawn to see our group because of me. However, I traveled with the group and Fargos to a town in the Volta Region called Dzodje to perform the Ewe gahu and *kpeglisu*. In Dzodje we stayed in a private home, and I began to feel a little more Ghanaian and not as much an outsider. The performance was well received, and the crowd went particularly wild when I performed the kpeglisu war dance with a male partner. This was another rite of passage, as I was experiencing another part of Ghana.

When we returned to Christian Village I was honored to meet the founder of the village, Mr. Christian, who granted me an interview about the history of the village. He was a small, slight man with gray hair who wore a black toga cloth and small black apple hat. He carried himself in the dignified manner of an elder, and although he spoke English, he chose to speak to me in Ewe with Fargos interpreting. I also met the female priestess of the village, who told me that my "grandfather" was watching over me and guiding me, which was very interesting because I never knew either my paternal or maternal grandfathers. She also offered me an amulet "for protection," but I refused it, saying that God was watching over me. She was not offended and told me it was as I wished, saying I would receive a blessing before I left Africa. I was penetrating deeper into the culture of Ghana through living in Christian Village.

It became obvious that the Ewe of Christian Village, as well as the Ewe throughout West Africa in Togo and Benin, were still very invested in their traditional religion, with its attendant music and dance. I regarded myself, at that time, a "participatory skeptic"; I didn't know if the traditional religion of the people I was living among was effective, but I did know it was real for them and that much dance and music evolved from the sacred. Therefore, I was interested, wanted to observe, and to a limited extent, participate. Like my future dance-spiritual mentor Katherine Dunham in Haiti, I was caught between the roles of participant and observer, between wanting to know the insider perspectives on African culture while being the uncommitted objective observer-scientist recording all that I saw and experienced.[22] Even though I was raised Catholic, I was no longer a practicing Christian, yet I still maintained a healthy skepticism about African religious traditions.

While living in Christian Village I was also invited to participate in the akpé secular youth dance, a favorite of the villagers. I danced akpé with the girls' group in an outer circle, while the inner circle consisted of small boys with the drummers in the center. This configuration of concentric circles of dancers moving counterclockwise around the drummers was a typical floor plan that, once I traveled to other African countries, I realized was ubiquitous. Each full circling of the drummers intensified the dancers' feelings, both individually and collectively. I was in the thick of the building energy—what I would later, as a dance theorist, discuss as "repetition with critical difference." Within the movement parameters of the dance itself, one was free to express one's feeling through one's own individuality within the rhythm. No one was expected to be uniform and look like the next person but instead to show one's honest feelings through the body. Although akpé was a social dance for the youth, I began to perceive that they were also invoking the spirit of their deceased friend from the previous week's funeral. I realized the dancers where inserting the deceased's name, a youth like them, within the songs. I saw firsthand how the secular and the sacred are interwoven without any sense of a dichotomy between the two.

My two weeks in Christian Village flew by, and I left when I got my studio apartment with a private bath in South Legon. The South Legon complex was built for visiting university faculty and students, and my room was a part of an enclosed semi-circle of screened-in apartments built around a common courtyard with huge palm trees. I soon realized this was a small *important* community that I was joining. My friend Yao also lived in the South Legon compound, as well as another African American female student, Dashenaba King, who was also studying dance at SMDD. There was also a Gambian *kora* master musician, Foday Musa Suso, from a renowned griot family. He was hired by Professor Nketia to teach the famous twenty-one-string kora instrument in the SMDD music program. Once I was able to set up my apartment with my own decorative aesthetics, along with a little two-burner hot plate to cook my own meals, I felt established in Ghana and ready to dive even deeper into the country and its dance culture.

The South Legon community of expatriates and non-Ghanaians from other parts of Africa became a support network, and we often went to each other's rooms in the evenings to share meals and how we were processing living in Ghana. One night Suso came to my room to eat and play his kora. Before this evening, I had not realized the depth of his knowledge and expertise as an oral historian. He began to talk to me about his family and training as a kora master. His playing accompanied hundreds of years of history, recounting empires and kingdoms of West Africa. I began to comprehend that I was befriending one of the musician-historians that I had only read about—the griots, or *jeli*, of Francophone West Africa who kept the history of their people through song and music.

Suso began to sing the history of the thirteenth-century Malinke king Sundiata Keita, the famous founder of the Mali Empire. I wanted to record this phenomenal experience on my little tape recorder, and when I asked his permission he simply said, "But of course; this is a gift for you." That night I gradually became aware of what a rare and precious gift this indeed was. Foday Musa Suso is the direct descendent of Jali Madi When Suso, the griot who *invented* the kora more than four centuries ago. I recorded hundreds of years of history that he had memorized since childhood, and witnessed this powerful way of telling a people's history; the place of the traditional African historian manifested before me in my own little room at South Legon. Years later I would see Suso again in concert in San Francisco; after he moved to Chicago in 1977, he formed his own band, the Mandingo Griot Society. Since coming to the United States, Suso has performed with jazz greats Herbie Hancock and Pharaoh Sanders, becoming the first kora player to establish a solo career in the States. But it was our time at Legon that would establish our friendship forever; I had come to Ghana at a seminal time, and I was reaping the benefits.

But by this time, I was also missing Kimathi, and I used that same cassette tape recorder to make love tapes for him. I normally ended my day recounting on tape what had happened, trying to share with him the phenomenal experiences I was having in Ghana. I would lay in bed with a candle lit, my tape recorder on, and looking at the nightstand photo of him standing on top of the Great Pyramid of Giza, wishing we could be together physically. But I made do with his picture and my tape recorder. My most cherished moments were when I would get a "care package" from him through the unreliable Ghanaian mail. He sent me goodies from home and his own audiocassettes, which I would then listen to over and over again.

Many of the things Kimathi had told me to be prepared for came true in Ghana, like issues of "race" and skin color. For example, I had to deal with the Ghanaians, who were predominantly very dark-skinned, calling me "white woman," or *obruni*. Educated Ghanaians understood my ancestral connection with them as an African diasporan, but the majority of poor "illiterates" had no conception of me, a light-skinned, freckle-faced woman, being African like them. This again led me to the concept of the relativity of "blackness." Was blackness about culture, imagined self-perception, or the result of an imposed socialized racialization process inherited from a racist Western history? Sitting next to black Ghanaians on covered flatbed trucks called *tros-tros* going to and from Accra, I began to wonder myself about whether I was "black" like them. But when I *danced*, I knew I was an African descendant; there was no denying it, and that was why I was there.

I was searching for the roots of my black culture in Africa through dance. My purpose became clearer and clearer—my blackness was lodged in our *cultural* connections.

So much has been written about the journey of African diasporans to Africa, including its meanings and its representation on both sides of the Atlantic. I myself have written about this historically loaded and contentious experience elsewhere in response to other scholars' accounts. Saidiya Hartman's *Lose Your Mother: A Journey along the Atlantic Slave Route* (2007), for example, created much discussion about the meaning of the journey back to the so-called Motherland, and whether it is really possible to go "back home" to Africa. Hartman's future journey to Ghana was different from mine:

> I had come to Ghana in search of strangers. The first time for a few weeks in the summer of 1996 as a tourist interested in the slave forts hunkered along the coast and second time for a year beginning in the fall of 1997 as a Fulbright scholar affiliated with the National Museum of Ghana. Ghana was as likely a place as any to begin my journey, because I wasn't seeking the ancestral village but the barracoon. As both a professor conducting research on slavery and a descendant of the enslaved, I was desperate to reclaim the dead, that is, to reckon with the lives undone and obliterated in the making of human commodities.[23]

Purpose and mission often yield to what one will find when going on a journey. Hartman came to Ghana to "reclaim the dead" in the wake of the Atlantic slave trade and the horrendous history that had ensued, of which we both are products. But I *had* come to find my "ancestral village" in a way, as the dance allowed me to claim the *spiritual* power found often only in village sites.

I came to Ghana to claim the *living* and my connection to them culturally. Therefore, I encountered a whole other side of Africa that could only be experienced by celebrating through the body. As I said in my *The Hiplife in Ghana* (2012), while using Hartman to reflect on my 1976 Ghanaian sojourn: "Unlike S. Hartman, for whom 'neither blood nor belonging accounted for my presence in Ghana only the path of strangers impelled toward the sea,' I did come searching for 'belonging,' but neither for 'blood' nor the slavery connection. I had little interest in tracing my specific bloodline, but *cultural* belonging is what I was desperate for, and I discovered it through Ghanaian dance and music."[24] Although I am very aware that, as Hartman puts it, "perils and dangers still threaten[ed] and that even now lives hung in the balance,"[25] my mission in 1976 as a dance artist was to illuminate the expressive mechanisms of African peoples that allowed not only for survival through slavery and colonialism but also an expressive transcendence that elevates our spirits and fortifies us to often fight back.

The Haitian Revolution, with its dependence on the drum rhythms brought from West Africa (Rada) and those created for the New World experience (Petro), is but one example of the power of culture. In this instance, the embodiment of resistance through war dances became the fait accompli that even Napoleon's navy could not overcome. On the celebratory side of the black historical experience, using the late cultural critic Albert Murray, dance historian Jacqui Malone captures the vital essence of African expressive culture that provided/provides the foundation for thriving in perilous times: "Through art we celebrate life. As Albert Murray says, 'Our highest qualities come from art; that's how we know who we are, what we want, what we want to do.' The attainment of wholeness rather than the amassing of power, is what ultimately makes people happy, and the goal of art is to help achieve that wholeness by providing humanity with basic 'equipment for living.'"[26] Even though we may have lost our "Mother" physically, we have kept her in our culture, and definitely in our motor behavior, our dance, and our rhythms. I was vitally aware that African-derived dance and music was indeed "equipment for living" that continued to help diasporans endure and celebrate. I wanted to have that understanding reinforced by being at its source; that is why I had come to Ghana to dance in blackness.

As time progressed, I also became involved with the Ga people of Accra through a friendship that I developed with musician Victor Nortey, who played in one of the highlife music bands called Wulomei. I don't remember exactly how I met Victor and his wife, but he became my inroad into Accra's main ethnic group, the Ga-Adangme people. Even though the Ga were not the majority ethnic group in the country (the Akans were), they *were* the majority population in Accra, the economic and cultural center. One day Victor asked if I would like to see one of the sacred Homowo ceremonies at the home of the Nai Wulomo, the high priest of the Ga people. Of course I jumped at the chance, and he told me to wear white in reverence to the sacred occasion. When the day arrived, we went to the Bukom area of Accra, near the district of Jamestown, with its old Portuguese colonial handiwork and the famous seventeenth-century Fort James and lighthouse built during the colonial era near the Atlantic shoreline.

We trailed off Accra's main streets into narrow, back-alley passages, entering a whole other world that I had not seen in the capital city; we were entering Bukom proper, which unescorted tourists rarely visited. I began to see more people dressed in wrapped white cloth, with white chalked faces. Victor told me that these were the priests, and that the white chalk on their face, arms, and legs represented sacred markings for this libation day for the ancestors, all for the purpose of a good harvest. The corn harvest each year yielded a ground white cornmeal mixture called *kpokpoe* or *kpekple*, which was mixed with palm soup, becoming a part of the offering during the ancestral libation.

At one point the Nai Wulomo himself appeared and walked down the isle of priests lined up for his blessings. He was a dark-skinned stocky man who looked to be in his forties and was wrapped in white cloth with a white-fringed headdress. He carried a calabash full of some kind of liquid, from which he sipped and sprayed the liquid from his mouth onto the face and upper body of each priest; this was their blessing and cleansing from him called *ashitutu*. From my twenty-something Western perspective, I first thought it an insult for him to spit on them, but I soon realized the meaning of "cultural relativity" and comprehended the indigenous meaning of the proceedings. Victor narrated the significance behind every aspect of the ceremony unfolding before me.

After the cleansing ashitutu ceremony of the priests by the Nai Wulomo, the kpekple mixture was poured on the earth, and then all the priests, led by the Nai Wulomo, made a procession to the nearby sacred grove, where a huge yam was placed on the earth as a culminating symbol of the bountiful harvest that they expected in the fall. After the ceremony had ended, Victor led me back to one of the compounds in Bukom to a feast of kpekple and palm soup. This was one of my first traditional Ghanaian meals, allowing me to hurdle another African rite of passage.

On the secular side of Accra, I often went to see Victor perform at Wulomei concerts, popular in 1976 with several albums to their credit. The band's mission was to include more Ga traditional music into their highlife pop sound, to which their name for the Ga high priest alluded. They categorized their music as "Ga cultural highlife," which was part of a neotraditional popular music movement in the mid-1970s. Hence, Wulomei had great cultural currency in the capital city. Wulomei's sound blended traditional Ga music with familiar guitar melodies and danceable beats, and I enveloped myself in the neotraditional culture they represented. Even before the Internet and its so-called shrinking of the planet, conscious musicians were negotiating how local Ghanaians were consuming global culture and assessing whether they were forfeiting their own indigenous cultural production. Negotiating meanings, uses, and appropriations of black dance and music has never been apolitical, and being in Ghana began to awaken me to this reality from an international perspective.

As the capital, Accra in the mid-1970s was a little over a half-million people (today it has expanded to 2.7 million) and undergoing an influx of migrants from rural areas throughout the country as it continued to industrialize. It was and is a site of global and indigenous cosmopolitan confluence. The seat of the government in the district of Osu, Christiansborg Castle, for example, was built by the Danes in the 1660s, testifying to early European influences. Black Star, or Independence, Square, with its great black star atop Independence Arch, looms large, reminding diasporans of Marcus Garvey's Black Star Line, an early twentieth-century shipping enterprise that tried to economically connect Africa with the diaspora. I had just missed, by a month and half, the annual Independence Celebration that happens every March 6 in Black Star Square, symbolizing the beginning of Africa's independence movement.

The Arts Council of Accra was a part of the network of arts councils throughout the country established by Nkrumah to preserve and promote the indigenous cultures of Ghana. Just as the Ghana Dance Ensemble used dance, music, and theater to promote national unity, so too did the various arts councils throughout the country offer classes in different ethnic dances and music traditions, as well as organizing showcases of local performing ensembles. I got to know C. K. Ganyo, a master drummer and director of the Accra Arts Council, and I took several of his dance and music classes. Little did I know that we would meet again twelve years later in East St. Louis at Katherine Dunham's annual dance seminars, where he taught Ghanaian dance and music, assisted by my friend Yao Tamakloe (Ronnie Marshall). Accra provided many traditional and international experiences for my cultural consumption.

But whether I was experiencing long-standing Ghanaian traditions or new waves of influential global culture, I could not ignore the political atmosphere and economic hardship that Ghana was under with Colonel Ignatius Acheampong's military government. As I eventually stated in *The Hiplife in Ghana* (2012):

> In 1976 Colonel Ignatius Acheampong, who in a military coup had overthrown the IMF-friendly Busia government in 1972, was Head of State in Ghana. Acheampong's National Redemption Council "adopted measures aimed at legitimizing his illegal seizure of political power . . . by reversing the Busia government's devaluation of the currency" that, in turn, raised the [Ghanaian] cedi's value by 21.4 percent. The result was that the price of foodstuffs and consumer goods were equally as high as they were under the International Monetary Fund policies of the Busia government. I, along with many Ghanaians, suffered long cues [*sic*] for simple consumer items.[27]

Even though I then had no idea about the manipulations of the World Bank and the International Monetary Funds (IMF) of Third World countries like Ghana, I definitely felt their effects, as well as President Acheampong's severe governmental corruption.

Fargos told me that most Ghanaians did not like Acheampong because they knew he was siphoning off the country's wealth, but governmental repression did not allow them to hold public protests. Fargos was old enough to have been in Nkrumah's Young Pioneers brigade of boys and girls. The Young Pioneers, an organization of youths between the ages of eight and sixteen, pledged their allegiance to Osagyefo Kwame Nkrumah, and Fargos told me that they were trained to help with various infrastructure projects.[28] Although some felt that Nkrumah's efforts with the youth were pure indoctrination, Fargos told me that he had felt appreciated as a young boy having a national purpose because it made him feel a part of nation building, as opposed to his time under subsequent governments, when unemployment and a lack of belonging were rampant among the youths.

All I knew at the time was that when my care packages came from Kimathi, I was temporarily relieved from the long lines at the store for basic consumer items like toilet paper that I had taken for granted in the United States. After I left Ghana in early 1977 things got even worse, and Acheampong's own military overthrew him in 1978. When Lt. Jerry John Rawlings took over the government in another military coup in 1979, Acheampong was executed by firing squad. My focus on the trip was cultural, but it was hard to ignore the mounting economic hardship, and I had a pre-monition that the government in power would not end positively.

As the spring 1976 semester at UG-Legon was ending, I relished my six weeks of formal classes at the SMDD, the dance opportunities that living in Christian Village had provided, as well as my rapid exposure to traditional and popular culture of Ghana in Accra. Now I wanted to use my summer to travel throughout the country to experience more of Ghana. I had a meeting with Professor Nketia to obtain a letter from the SMDD that introduced me as a student of Ghanaian traditional dances and that requested I be exposed, where possible, to the dances in their indigenous settings. He also suggested I contact the local arts council in each major city that I visited, so that the director could give me an orientation to the local culture and expose me to dances and the elder culture bearers whom I should interview.

This seemed like a solid plan, and armed with my letter from the nationally recognized Nketia, I made plans to begin in the Cape Coast region, where the (in)famous slave castles are. I also wanted to visit the family of Nana Nketsia in Sekondi-Takoradi, the anthropologist-chief whom I had met five years earlier in Boston (chapter 3). Although Ghana was actually one of the safest countries in West Africa, I also felt somehow protected because I had a mission as a self-motivated "dance anthropologist" without any credentials except my personal confidence and sincere interest.

The Diasporan Ambassador: Traveling throughout Ghana

The trip through several regions of Ghana turned out to be not only about dance fieldwork but also about being an ambassador, of sorts, from the African diaspora. I became an unwitting representative of those who were "lost" across the Atlantic Ocean centuries ago. Starting in the Central Region, before I visited the Door of No Return at the famous slave castles of Cape Coast and Elmina, I actually started my adventure in a small Fante fishing village called Arkrah on the Atlantic coast. Arkrah allowed me to start not on the familiar note of slavery but on a kind of "ambassadorship" and the celebration of my connection through dance.

In New York, before I left for Ghana, I had visited a few black scholars who had given me recommendations for particular towns where they had contacts. Art history professor George Preston, who had researched *asafo* military art among the Fante, suggested I visit the coastal village of Arkrah, located between the city of Cape Coast and the town of Anomabo. The Arkrah asafo officials had made him a chief; so in the village, the letter of introduction from him I had with me carried a lot of weight.

As Arkrah was on the way to Cape Coast, I figured I had to stop and bring Professor Preston's greetings from the United States. Leaving Legon on July 22 at 11:00 a.m., the trip of about sixty miles took all day and two lorry rides, including a long wait between two transports; I did not actually arrive until 6:00 p.m. But as fate would have it, while waiting on the second lorry at the depot, I met a Fante man, Mr. Quarshie, who knew Nana Nketsia's family in Sekondi-Takoradi. Once he realized I was friend to the esteemed Nketsia and that I was doing research on Ghanaian dance, Mr. Quarshie decided to make sure I got to Arkrah village safely and had a proper introduction to the villagers. This represented a central theme on my trip: genuine humbling hospitality and respect were accorded me everywhere I went. In 1976, Ghanaians were appreciative of any sincere interest in their culture from foreigners, and they were particularly impressed that a single woman would come so far to conduct this kind of extensive research on their dances.

When Mr. Quarshie and I arrived in Arkrah village, which was literally right on the sandy Atlantic shoreline, the chief's council and the village asafo organization of men were just in the process of starting a meeting about village communal labor. I was invited immediately to make a speech, and so a chair was brought for me to sit among the male decision-makers of Arkrah village. I sat taking it all in: sand under my feet and the ocean lapping upon the shore, palm trees flowing in the cool Atlantic breeze, and beautiful black men adorned in earth-tone African prints looking at me with rapt attention. They waited attentively for what this foreign American woman who had just walked into their village and interrupted their meeting was about to say. I had the seat of honor and was the main focus of attention. Everything was done in proper protocol, with the village chief explaining that they would forgo their meeting in order to explore this visit from the foreigner. Mr. Quarshie was a godsend in that he spoke in Fante to them, being my linguist and explaining my purpose and intentions before it was my turn to give a speech.

I recognized the position I was in, and very quickly my initial fear left and a feeling of pride and regality came over me; I eased into my role as diasporan ambassador. When I told them that I was a friend to Chief George

Preston from New York, all the men unanimously started smiling, and saying, "aah," and everything opened up for me. Mr. Quarshie interpreted my introduction, telling them I was a professional dancer who had been studying at the University of Ghana, Legon, and now wanted to see the traditional dances for myself in their village origins. I then asked if I could see the Fante version of the adowa dance. Immediately, the chief summoned the head of the women's organization, and a middle-aged barefoot woman in African cloth appeared. The village chief communicated what I wanted, and she agreed to arrange a dance event the next morning on the beach for me to film. I then made a short speech affirming my African ancestry and my pride in seeing traditional African government in action with the chief's council and the asafo military organization. I also mentioned that it was important that the women had their own organization to make decisions for themselves. The chief thanked me and said that they would provide the best house in the village for me to sleep in that night and that some food, including fresh fish from the ocean, would be brought to me after such a long journey. As he wished me a good night's rest, I knew Mother Africa was embracing me, teaching me of her ways, and enfolding me in her spirit.

I did sleep really well that night after initiating my new role as diasporan ambassador in the village of Arkrah, and I awoke to a symphony of shorebirds as the sun rose. After dressing I waited patiently for the women to come and get me for the dance. The woman, who had appeared at the men's meeting the evening before, came to my door and beckoned me to come outside. When I emerged from my relatively modern home, I saw throngs of African women outside, some standing on the sand and others seated on benches brought for the occasion. No men were present; this was definitely going to be a women's event. Gourds, bells, and rattles lay on the ground and the benches, waiting to be awakened. The leaders of the morning dance event were the women's auxiliary leader, who had been summoned the prior evening, and the female village priestess, the latter of whom wore a white headdress distinguishing her from the others who wore African-print *geles*. None of the women spoke English very well, but with their little English and our gestures, we communicated well. Once the dancing started, we needed no other form of speech.

The women's dance and music that I was allowed to record on film is called *adzewa*. Some scholars view the Fante dance as a variation of the Ashanti adowa, with others view it as a distinct dance-music form of its own. Music scholar Kingsley Ampomah documents both of these dance-drumming traditions—adowa and adzewa—as originally associated with women's culture, particularly as a pastime during women's vigilant waiting for the returning asafo warriors.[29] As the Fante and the Ashanti are two of the main ethnic groups of the Akan clan, sharing similar verbal languages, it is not inconceivable that these dances could be different "dialects" of the same root form.

When I saw the women begin to perform adzewa on the sandy ground, I noticed steps similar to those of the Ashanti adowa, but there were also some differences. It had the same subtle walking step, delicate hand gestures, and intricate polyrhythmic hip and torso isolations. The differences were the degree to which the Arkrah Fante women bent their backs, lowering their center of gravity so that the whole body was closer to the earth. The Asante adowa is usually more upright and regal in carriage, with only a slight bending of the waist, along with the torso isolations. The Arkrah priestess, for example, was bent low and focused on her feet rhythms and hand gestures, while communicating with the female musicians creating intricate rhythms on plain gourds and rattles, all accompanied by songs that seamlessly transitioned one to the other.

I was very excited zooming in and out with my Super 8 video camera, recording all of the adzewa movement intricacies, but after about fifteen minutes of filming, the priestess pulled me into the dance circle. I had no choice but to participate, and fortunately because of my adowa studies, along with my keen eye for recognizing the differences in the adzewa dance while filming, I was prepared to dance with the women. I kept my movements subtle, which is not easy for an American, as we tend to think dance means large exhibitionistic movements; the subtlety of the isolations and small steps of adzewa helped me to instantaneously shift my understanding of what constitutes dance. My successful *imitation* of the Arkrah women that morning on the beach was testimony to my expanding dance repertoire. I went back and forth between observation and participation, as the intercultural experience became a joyous occasion for them and me. I got what I had come to Arkrah for, and in the process the Fante women's dance culture was affirmed and reinforced by an African diasporan who came from thousands of miles away. We were all celebrating life, dancing in our collective blackness.

The blackness to which I am referring, now forty years later, is complicated within the context that I experienced that morning in Arkrah. My sharing of "black" performance on the beach that morning with the Fante women, as DeFrantz and Gonzalez note, was "situated performance[,] not only as folklore or political identity."[30] It was situationally located in the way DeFrantz discusses blackness as "action engaged to enlarge capacity, confirm presence, to dare."[31] We indeed did affirm each other—I confirmed the validity of their dance culture, and they corroborated my being a part of them as African women through dance—and in that sense we enlarged each other's existence as black women in the world, but beyond that, as *human beings that matter*. This is the humanistic capacity made possible through performance as a rejoinder to the construction of blackness resulting from colonialism and slavery that our ancestors had both endured. As DeFrantz reveals, the power of "performance emerges in its own conscious engagement, and it is created by living people."[32] Participating in the Fante adzewa dance with the women on the Arkrah beach that morning was indeed a transformative *human* experience.

If only that was my sole memory of the Fante. After Arkrah I went on to the experience drawing most African diasporans to Ghana—the subject of Hartman's book, the memory of slavery and the notorious slave castles in the Fante Central Region of Ghana. At the peak of the slave trade in the eighteenth century, there were more than fifty slave forts along Africa's west coast, built by the Portuguese, Dutch, British, Danes, Swedes, French, and Germans, with the former Gold Coast having the majority of them.[33] Because of their geographic coastal locale, the Fante were the dominant ethnic group interacting with Europeans during the infamous transatlantic slave trade. In the history of Gold Coast colonialism, the British conquering of the Asante in the early eighteenth century is the seminal event. However, as Preston says: "But this [British battling the Asante] began to happen only after the decline of the confederated Borbor Fante, who prior to the rise of Asante, had controlling interests in much of the slave marketing along almost the entire coast of present-day Ghana between Accra and the River Prah, and northward up to the Twifo-Praso."[34] Any coastal African cultural group, such as the Fante, would have had to play a prominent role in international trade, including that of human cargo.

As I visited the famous Cape Coast Castle, which in 1993 would become the site of the indie film *Sankofa* by Haile Gerima and starring my actress-priestess friend Oyafunmike Ogunlano, I had my diasporan experience of spiritual shadows. I felt the Africans who passed through those dungeons to the Door of No Return onto the ships bound for the so-called "New World." One of the most horrific moments for me, as a black woman, was when the tour guide took us to the upper areas of the fort to the captain's bedroom, with its trap door in the floor through which slave women were brought to his bed. I realized white male rape of African slave women started even before they left the African continent, continuing throughout slavery in the New World. During this sobering moment, I fully realized the Fante were not only complicit with this horrific history but actually facilitated it. Preston records Fante shame today when during his research he asked a seminal question of one of his Fante informants:

> I asked captain Obuokwan Sam, why the word *sika* (gold) concealed the word for slaves. His reply was that they would not put the word for slave in their greeting. "We trafficked in slaves so that we could get gold and with gold we could get anything. The Asante had the gold but the slaves had to pass through us to get to the trading depots and castles at Winneba, Apam, Anomabo, and Ogua."[35]

I experienced a dual reality with the Fante in the Central Region of Ghana: warm hospitality enhanced by connective performance in Arkrah, as well as the unavoidable memory of slavery. They were the primary Gold Coast arbiters of the slave trade with the Europeans, and Cape Coast Castle was a primary site of the historic crime.

The memory of that "historic crime" intensified with the other major slave castle as tourist attraction in Ghana's Central Region, the smaller and older Elmina Castle, built in 1482 by the Portuguese as St. George of the Mine. The name alludes to the way religion and the pilfering of West African gold mines were conflated as a rationale for building all the forts on West Africa's coast. Elmina Castle became the first trading post along the Gulf of Guinea, thus becoming a crucial site in the history of transatlantic human trafficking, passing from the Portuguese to the Dutch and then to the British. Today, decades later, I look at my saved entrance ticket to the slave fort, which reads: "Ghana Museums and Monuments Board: West African Historical Museum, Fee Charged for Visiting, Admit Bearer, 25p [25 pesewas or 10 cents], #1030." I was the 1,030th person admitted to the castle that year, but I wondered how many Africans bound for a completely new life experience had passed through the same place I was visiting as a tourist and whether one of them was biologically related to me. I wrote in my journal that Tuesday, June 22, 1976:

I sit on the balcony of a motel near Elmina, looking at the castle. I feel this coastline where ships sailed centuries ago when the mighty Atlantic brought the first Europeans to Africa, with the castle a testimony to deeds that cannot be erased—a history that screams of depravity and man's egotism. The sickness of humankind's need for power is actually slavery to materialism. The human spirit cries out in pain from the wounds inflicted by human hands upon other human beings.

The castles on the coastline are all being used today as monuments to this horrific history. Life continues with black people here and from the diaspora, created from this history. We live out our own contemporary lives, cultures, and destinies. But this history is still with us. All our ancestors sit on their spirit stools watching our continuing human struggles.

I was very aware that the current-day people in the town of Elmina did not have the kind of connection that I and other diasporans had to Elmina Castle. Like American history books that purposely limit the history of the slave trade and slavery to a few heartless pages, so too were Ghana's history books written primarily by the British at that time. I am even more aware today of this omission, which continues to create the casual and callous attitude about the slave trade on both sides of the Atlantic. Monuments I experienced at Cape Coast and Elmina Castles mean a very different thing to the diasporan descendants of Africa than to the contemporary people in those towns who benefit from our pilgrimage tourism.[36]

I continued my exploration of the Atlantic coast with a one-day visit to Sekondi-Takoradi in the Western Region. The coastal twin city of Sekondi-Takoradi is the capital of the Western Region near the Côte d'Ivoire border. I had a letter from Nana Nketsia that contained the names of his mother and brother still living in their royal family compound. The family had a chieftaincy in the Ahenfie stretch of Essikado town in Sekondi, about twenty kilometers from Takoradi. Everyone knew the Nketsia family, as my mentor-friend Nana Kobina Nketsia IV was the Omanhene of Essikado; so when I asked at the bus station for his mother, a queen mother of the area, I was immediately taken to the Nketsia compound. Again I found myself acting as an emissary from America, and in this case a former student of Chief Nketsia. Therefore, I was treated like royalty, fed well, and put up for the night. His mother and younger brother talked with me about the family position in Sekondi-Takoradi as Fante royals, and posed for pictures.[37] I was considered an emissary from the United States and accorded all of the privileges of a diplomat—a bridge between their world and Nana Nketsia's, who as they saw it, represented them in the West. I remember how stately and regal Queen Mother Nketsia was, and I thought of the Afrocentric posters that I had seen in the 1960s of great queens of Africa; here, I was in the presence of a real one.

After Sekondi, I traveled inland and ended up spending the next three days in the forest town of Twifo-Hemang in the Lower Denkyira District of the Central Region, receiving the same royal treatment from Nana Kyei Baffour II, the Omanhene of Twifo-Hemang.[38] With my letter from Professor Nketia, Nana Baffour became an arts council director of sorts, giving me a sense of this inland part of the Central Region, which he told me was once a kingdom that predated the Asante Empire. The one cultural event I attended was a Sunday worship service at the Jesus Memorial Healing Church, where I witnessed how African traditions and Christianity blended in Ghana. A battery of traditional drummers were stationed at one end of the open-air room with wooden benches, while the congregation sang, clapped, and danced vigorously for the Lord. If I didn't know better I would have thought I was at a traditional Ewe religious ceremony back in Christian Village, except for the "Prophet and Founder" church pastor wearing a Christian-type white robe.

On July 1, I arrived in Kumasi, the capital of the Ashanti Region and the second-biggest city in Ghana. Located near Lake Bosumtwi in the Ghanaian rainforest, Kumasi is lush and green, about one hundred miles north of the Gulf of Guinea. This city became the capital of the Ashanti Confederacy under the honored consolidating ruler Osei Tutu, the first Asantehene, king-chief of the Asante people. Osei Tutu, along with the priest Okomfo Anokye, whom legend has it received the Ashanti Golden Stool from heaven, solidified their confederacy in 1701, when they conquered Denkyira, the area I had just left. Their reputation as great warriors is notorious and can be seen in the symbolic hand gestures of the adowa, *sikyi*, and fontomfrom dances.

I spent my first day in Kumasi at the famous Kumasi National Cultural Center. My immediate contact was Kwabena, a young student from UG-Legon who had told me to contact him when I came to Kumasi during the summer. Kwabena took me to the cultural center that also housed the Kumasi Arts Council, which turned out to be the center for Okomfekrom, an

Asante holiday in process. The festivities happened all day and combined both Asante and Ghana state symbols in its celebration. Young boys sang the Ghana Young Pioneer song that I had heard Fargos repeat, and young girls carried white dolls on their backs representing the deceased relatives of their families. With their belief in the *kra* (the spirit or soul) of the Asantehene embodying the Asante nation, they have a complex Asante kingship art that merges the political and the spiritual. This was the Gold Coast group the British had to conquer to completely colonize the Gold Coast. The Anglo-Ashanti Wars lasted from 1823 to 1896, ending with the capture of the Asantehene Ageyman Prempeh, who was sent with an entourage to the Seychelles Islands in the Indian Ocean. Interestingly enough, the holiday festivities ended with a play about Kwame Nkrumah, as an example of how the Asante Kingdom and the Ghanaian state intersect.

After the dance experience of adzewa with the Fante women in Arkrah village, I had the chance to witness and dance adowa with the Asante at a funeral. One of the master drummers at the Kumasi Cultural Center was hired to drum for a funeral in the village of Kaasi, five miles outside of Kumasi, and he invited me to come along (figure 7). My sincere interest in the culture motivated many invitations such as this one throughout my trip, and I was honored to attend my first Asante funeral to observe how the dance and music I was learning in classes at UG-Legon actually operated within the people's lives. My initial journal entry outlining the funeral setting is particularly descriptive:

> *The communal and family-like feeling was dominant with the participants dressed in variations of black and red, the Asante mourning colors. The floor plan of the outdoor village square was set up in a large semi-circle, which gave me an unusual amount of distance from which to set up my camera, as I was given permission to film. The social pecking order was Chief, Queen Mother, Sub-Chiefs, and Linguist, who became the main arbiter between the funeral organizers and me, and to whom I gave my monetary contribution to the deceased's family for filming. Then there were the drummers and singers situated together, and spectators who were seated further away from the music. As there were no official dancers, dancing was left up to anyone feeling the call of the drums.*

The best dancers that afternoon showed controlled grief along with the profound feelings of personal and collective pride, all executed with subtlety and grace. The people who danced adowa at the funeral that afternoon made it clear that facial expressions are as much a part of the dance as knowing the correct steps within the complex rhythms, the subtle torso isolations, or the symbolic hand gestures. Adowa, as a solo dance, gives the individual maximum freedom to use any of the traditional proverbial variations of movements that one chooses. The dance was not abstract movements but rather the bodily expression of deep inner moods made visible. They were *dancing* adowa, not *performing* it, and I saw the difference.

While I felt the spirit of dance at the Kaasi funeral, I also saw the ego that can cause unwarranted jealousy among the Ashanti, and perhaps African peoples in general. As the obvious foreigner at the funeral, everyone expected me to honor the grieving family with what they anticipated would be my *novice* rendition of the adowa dance. But my knowledge base of the dance, and my personal feelings for the dance in particular, made me confident; however, I was reluctant to dance because I did not want to appear to be showing off. When I entered the dancing circle all eyes were on me, and I performed adowa with everything that I had learned, showing the basic walking step, and the fast variations that I had also been taught, all while trying to penetrate to my own inner feelings, trying to *dance* the Ashanti signature dance. I must have done well, because as I recorded in *The Hiplife in Ghana*:

> The famed dance-anthropologist Katherine Dunham has said that dance and the body is one of the most "tenacious cultural traits to survive the ravages of slavery." So, is that why back in 1976 the Queen Mother in the Ashanti village of Kaasi, near Kumasi, asked, "How can that white woman know how to dance like that?" when I humbly, and reluctantly, danced the signature Ashanti dance adowa that day during the funeral celebration that I had come to witness. Yet the translation of her "royal" question, by my Ashanti male escort who had brought me to the funeral in 1976, had the dreaded word, Obruni (white stranger).[39]

Being considered a "white" woman as I danced adowa in Kaasi was not the worst of it; there was spiritual *juju* used against me in reaction to my dance as well. As we were leaving the funeral, my drummer friend told me that the queen mother was so taken aback by my natural ability with dancing adowa that she thought I was challenging her, and she tried to put a negative spiritual spell upon me. I was told that in order to protect me, someone who had observed the attempted spiritual power at work had blocked her spell, but he never said who that person was, and I always suspected it was my escort himself.

I was completely surprised that my dancing ability had caused that kind of jealous reaction resulting in a spiritual battle. My successful execution of the dance was not taken as a compliment but as a challenge by the village queen mother. Understanding what I had caused in Kaasi that afternoon not only made me more aware of the various potential perceptions of my mission to learn Ghanaian traditional dance but also of the level of jealousy within the culture, which has many potentially deleterious ramifications. At its basis, the incident that my dancing caused in Kaasi taught me the power of dance in a culture where bodily expressiveness is at the core of people's collective and individual identities.

After one week in Kumasi I returned to Legon to regroup for a second trip. I met with Professor Nketia and members of the GDE who were from the Northern Region in order to prepare me for a journey to that part of the country. The GDE had several very good dancers and drummers from the North, with whom I had studied the *damba* and *takai* men's dances, as well as the northern hip-swiveling *bamaya* dance done by both sexes. After two weeks preparation at the university, I left for Tamale, the capital of the Northern Region, 370 miles north of Accra as the seat of the predominantly Muslim Dagbon Kingdom. Interestingly enough, when Nkrumah made his famous 1957 speech in Black Star Square announcing Ghana's independence, he and his cabinet members wore traditional northern smocks to symbolize their unity with Ghana's northern ethnicities, including the Dagomba.

Arriving in Tamale on July 18, I got a room at the Atta Essibi Hotel for 5.50 cedis (two dollars) per night. The Dagbani language, a very different sound, was spoken everywhere. I also noticed that there were fewer attempts to hustle me for money as an American. Even though the North is culturally different, there have always been gestures of unification by the dominant South: cultural symbols like Nkrumah's Independence Day garb and inclusion of the region's dances in the GDE repertoire. Today, political candidates for president, who are usually from the South, choose a northerner as a vice-presidential running mate to reinforce the unity of the country within each administration. Ghana's regional and religious divisions are nothing like the severe split in Nigeria between the Christian South and the Muslim North, which was one of the factors causing the actual capital of Nigeria to be moved from the notorious Atlantic coastal city of Lagos to the constructed central city of Abuja, the current capital. Ghana's ethnic disunity is not comparable to Nigeria's near-crisis regional divisions, because as a Ghanaian taxi driver once told me anecdotally, "In Ghana we like peace; Nigerians live by war."

That Sunday, July 19, I awoke to the sound of the *muezzin* chanting the Koran in the early morning, reminding me of Morocco almost ten years earlier, but the poetic beauty of Islamic singing now had the spirit of black Africa. The women were dark-skinned with kohl makeup accenting their eyes, and over their African-print geles wore chiffon scarves draped over their shoulders, beautifully blending a West African and Islamic aesthetic. Some of the young girls wore a painted dot on their "third eye" at the middle of the forehead, and the men wore the grand bubu and skullcap, as well as the famous woven smocks, called *bingba* by the Dagomba. This was indeed a different part of Ghana with a distinctly different culture.

Even though it was Sunday, I went to Tamale Arts Council and met with the director, Mr. Bamford, to get a sense of what aspects of regional dance and music culture I could experience. Mr. Bamford was my first experience with those whom Ghanaians call "half-breeds," being of Ghanaian and German descent. That very day he took me to a *petol* bar, where musicians play all day for food and whatever tips (*dashes*) they can collect from people who come to drink the traditionally made petol alcoholic beverage. There were two musicians who were actually from the Upper East Region of Ghana playing *duringa* and *bima* music of the Bussi (or Grunis) and Frafra peoples from Bolgatanga. Coming from even farther north, they demonstrated the interpenetration of the cultures and regions of Ghana and allowed me to witness music and dance from the Upper East Region, which I was not planning to visit. In fact, Mr. Bamford told me that one of his goals for the Tamale Arts Council was not only to showcase traditional culture from the Northern Region but also to increase intercultural ethnic appreciation through dance and music from other distant Ghanaian groups in the area. The arts councils and their directors in the various regions of Ghana were all overworked with the task of showcasing the indigenous cultures and trying to maintain them for the next generation in their respective regions; but the focus on cross-cultural exposure was unexpected, and I recognized how this followed the model of the GDE at a local level. Dance is a crucial sociopolitical tool when it is central to a people's identity, and Nkrumah's original model of regional arts councils was working.

The Bolgatanga musicians fit right into the Tamale petol bar and did their jobs, luring people into the establishment and entertaining them. The melodic musical instrument they played was the duringa or *gonje*, a one-string gourd instrument, accompanied by players of the *synyagre*, a gourd with seeds placed inside to create rhythmic percussion. In their duringa songs they blended their indigenous language with that of the Dagbani, and I could hear the beautiful guttural Arabic sounds within the Dagbani language. The songs were in traditional call-and-response form with the gonje player leading the singing and the gourd players singing the chorus in response, creating a constant repetitious droning effect that was infectious.

I observed the dance that both women and men performed to the duringa/gonje music. One variation was to stand without moving the feet, shifting the weight with the hips in a double-time motion like a more intricate version of the 1950s' American twist, arms held close to the body with hands moving near the breasts. When the music signaled a change, dancers would break into the bima section with stamping foot patterns that were an exact replication of the rhythm being played. One popular variation during this stamping bima section was a double stamp on each foot while scooting backward as each foot struck the dirt ground. The men had a variation of jumping and hitting the right side of their chest with their right knee, which added an extra sound to the rhythm.

The social setting was casual, with people standing and joining in the dance with their own style when the spirit called. The dancing happened in relatively short phrases, as if they were writing a short paragraph of an ongoing dialogue. Scholars of Africanist performance, like Roger Abrahams, have brought attention to this short text-like tendency of Africanist performance: "[There is a] circular, vertiginous organization of performing groups; heavy emphasis on involvement through repetition of sound and movement; retreat from closure in favor of the ongoing and open-ended; tendency to break up performance into short units or episodes, each of which is a whole, related to the other units because of intensity of contrast."[40] Indeed, the rhythmic dancing "text" that I saw at the petol bar that Sunday afternoon created language-like phrases that were related to each other. Indeed, a chapter in the ongoing story of Dagombaland was being written through dance and music.

As the participants got more inebriated and socially connected, the dancing and singing got more intense. Many of the dancers ended their danced text in front of me, as the obvious guest at the bar. This was a form of "challenge," to which I did occasionally respond by jumping to my feet, imitating the gonje stationary dance, but not the more rigorous bima dance mostly danced by the men. As time passed, I relaxed, as I too got a little tipsy from the petol we were all drinking, and became a part of the ongoing danced dialogue in motion.

The next day in Tamale it rained torrents, so I stayed at the hotel, which gave me some time to contemplate my experience of the previous day at the petol bar. During one of my attempted solos after a dance "challenge," a young girl had stood up with me to share my dance, and we had a particular embodied connection (figure 8). I wrote in my journal that morning: *The joy I saw in her eyes and that I felt while we danced together expressed everything: our bodies felt the rhythm together, our inner beings met, and we felt our cultural connection.* Was this an experience of embodied blackness, simply a human connection, or both? Is what I experienced with the young Tamale girl what DeFrantz and Gonzalez call "the expansive mutabilities of being black?"[41] I also wrote in my journal that morning: *A relaxed naturalness is the primary quality of all the Ghanaian dances I've seen. Nothing is contrived about African movement; the source of the dance always comes from tuning into a feeling, even the display of prowess and strength.*

Were the girl's and my feelings, expressed through our bodies in culturally appropriate expressive ways, an aspect of what we call "black dance"? I think DeFrantz and Gonzalez are on to something when they say, "In all these maneuvers, black sensibilities—stylized ways of being in relation to each other and our environments—become wellsprings of creative tactics employed consciously and subconsciously as resources of strength, resistance, and in unexpected pleasure."[42] I certainly know that the gonje dance we performed that day bound us together in "unexpected pleasure," but in ways that were probably different for each of us. However, the fact that we connected through our black expressive bodies in a very internal manner is the key aspect that allows me to remember the experience until today, forty years later.

From Tamale I moved on to the town of Lawra in the Upper West Region because it was the home of Kobom, my xylophone (gil) teacher at Legon. I really tuned into the melodic rhythms of the gil and had learned a few songs from Kobom during his classes at the SMDD. He had told me about his hometown of Lawra, and how I could see the real *bawaa* or *nandom* danced there. So from Tamale, instead of visiting Wa, the capital of the region, I went northwest to the town of Lawra, very close to the border of Burkina Faso (then Upper Volta). The perception of Ghanaians in Accra was that the Upper Region was "backward," so I was interested to see how I felt about the people there. I wrote in my journal: *There is an attitude of intelligence and progress here just as in the other regions. People are obviously poorer, but government organizations in industry, education, and culture, like the Arts Council, are pushing development and the people seem to really appreciate it.*

Indeed, Lawra people were gracious and kind, and when I mentioned Kobom's name, it opened all the doors I needed, including leading me to his uncle. The elder Kobom sold me one of his best gils, which I carted back to Accra to show Kobom and to continue playing and learning. I was given a small house to stay in, and in the evening I was lulled into a deep sleep by the rhythmic melodious music coming from various gils played throughout the town. When I asked Kobom's uncle why they like the xylophone so much, he said: "We like melody with our rhythm. It creates a softer feeling."

The people of this area are called Dagaaba; they speak the Dagaari language and historically belong to the Mossi Kingdom of Burkina Faso and Upper Ghana, along with the Frafra, Dagbani, and Casim. Their area of what became Ghana was never colonized directly by the British but was annexed into the Gold Coast. After the Anglo-Ashanti Wars, the British traveled north and negotiated a peaceful treaty with them. Even before British annexation, the Dagaaba were victims of the slave trade, with the Ashanti raiding their region and transporting them to the Fante coast. Visiting the Dagaaba in Lawra, I was very aware of their peaceful hospitality but also of their past as a marginalized people in the political history of Ghana; in many ways that marginalization has continued in the postcolonial era.

Kobom's uncle became my chief culture-bearer informant, with the help of a young translator. I found out from the elder Kobom that the GDE was conflating the words "bawaa" and "nandom" as the same dance. Bawaa is the dance, and Nandom is the name of Lawra's sister city closer to the border of Burkina Faso. I also learned that the bawaa dance in Nandom is called *sekpere*, and that in reality bawaa was a dance from the Upper East Region, although the Dagaaba did perform it in Lawra. My fieldwork definitely gave me more accurate cultural information, and I realized that African national dance companies often combine dances and musics from disparate regions of their countries, which is not always precise. I spent several days with the elder Kobom, discovering the many secular dances of the agrarian Dagaaba people. *Kobina*, for example, is a strong and vigorous dance performed after planting the crops, and it requires wearing iron anklets for percussive effect; while *sebre* is a postharvest festival that uses the *pira* hand castanets that I had learned to use in dancing bawaa at Legon. Dancers, among the Dagaaba, become musicians while dancing to the gil and the *kuor* drum.

On my last day in Lawra, I had a chance to witness the bawaa dance performed by a youth ensemble for the townspeople and me. The organized group gathered in the community hall in the town, dressed in blue and white denim cloth: the boys in short pants with a multicolored belt around the waist and the girls in short skirts of the same material covering short underpants, with a matching halter top, showing their midriff. They all carried the pira hand castanets and performed the vigorous dance to two gils and a kuor drum in sweltering heat and humidity. Their performance was spirited and sincere, and it followed many of the variations I had learned at Legon. The excellent dancing and musicianship prompted me to put cedi bills on the sweaty foreheads of the musicians and several dancers, as is the traditional acknowledgment of appreciation of a well-done performance all over Ghana. I felt fulfilled from my trip to Lawra, having learned some of the complexities of Dagaaba culture, which I could have never gotten in Accra. And I loved taking my own authentic gil back to Legon with me and eventually to the United States.

I had learned on my excursions throughout the country how many different language groups exist in Ghana, and how different their cultures are. But one thing bound them as a nation: their love of dance and music. On July 30 I returned to Tamale to get a bus back to Accra.

Reconnecting with Greater Accra and Journey to Togo and Nigeria

I spent my first day back at my apartment in South Legon just resting and digesting the experience-filled and physically taxing one-month trip throughout five regions of Ghana, to which many living in Greater Accra had never been. I needed to take a day to let all of my cultural dance experiences sink in. I had deepened my knowledge of Ghanaian culture, dance, and music, as well as realized my personal ability to relate to all of Ghana's culture groups. My sincere interest in Ghana's cultures had been acknowledged, and I had been allowed into several inner circles as much as an outsider could. I had now been in Ghana for three and a half months, which was as long as Kimathi had spent in East Africa before we met. I had to admit I was really missing him, and the only thing that helped was to record love poems to him that I sent every few weeks.

The next six weeks were spent in the Accra-Legon area reconnecting with Christian Village and Fargos, attending international cultural events, and hosting an American friend who came for a two-week visit. On my return to Christian Village, Fargos and Rosie made me my favorite Ghanaian food, groundnut (peanut) soup with fish and *fufu* (pounded cassava and yam), and I felt at home. Allison Jacobs, who ironically had been Kimathi's college girlfriend and whom I had met in the Bay Area, arrived from the United States. She stayed with me at South Legon for two weeks, and I tried to show her what Accra was all about. I took her to jazz music concerts, to the few movies showing in town, and to Aburi Botanical Garden in the hills of Akuapem, about fifty miles from Accra. I also assisted a Ghanaian teacher of Transcendental Meditation with a few lectures at UG that Allison attended, and we went to a Peace Corps Crossroads program lecture. After Allison left, there were several important Accra festivals, including the end of Homowo in Bukom and Labadi, as well as the Ga Twins Festival.

I began to feel I also needed to gain a comparative perspective of West Africa by traveling to other neighboring countries, and everything lined up for Fargos and me to take a trip outside Ghana together. As his people were from Togo, he told me that a major Ewe festival would be happening near Lomé, the capital, and that we could also go to Nigeria, where his twin sister lived as the first wife of a Nigerian man. Fargos could not only be my escort and bodyguard, but he could allow me to penetrate past the tourist veneer and actually live with native people. I jumped at the chance, telling him that I would cover most of our expenses but that he had to provide some of his own money. We made an agreement to travel as a couple, and I was off to see Togo and Nigeria.

After getting my hair braided the day before the trip, Fargos and I left Accra by bus on September 8 for Lomé, 125 miles from Accra. It was a stressful trip with lots of hassles at the border, which was filled with predatory hustlers. I was so glad that I had Fargos with me to speak Ewe and get us through the border customs. Because we were planning to stay in Togo on the way back, he booked a bus immediately to Lagos, which was an ordeal in itself. At Togo's border I occasionally used my rudimentary French, but for the most part, I let Fargos handle the transportation negotiations.

Arriving in Lagos on September 10, one could feel the difference in intensity with more cars, traffic, and no road rules. There was construction everywhere in preparation for FESTAC, the second world black arts festival, coming that January. Black folks from all over the world were about to converge onto the city. I wrote in my journal that first day:

> *The gods of Nigeria welcome me; the spirit of this land is deep. I can feel it in the crowded super city of Lagos—more cars and traffic than New York, but not as neurotic. Wide-awake, alert Yorubans fill the streets, and skyscrapers and new buildings are going up everywhere in preparations for FESTAC. My first day in Lagos is very promising: meeting with University of Lagos contacts and with the U.S. Information Service Cultural Director about the possibility of a university lecture tour in Nigeria on Black Dance; then going to the National Museum, where we witnessed an Ogbani Society regional meeting of chiefs, as well as viewed a cultural film on Benin. There is more of a sense of a Pan-African awareness here, and the average street people have treated me like a black diasporan sister, and not as a white foreigner as in Ghana.*

It was amazing how different Nigeria—the other major Anglophone West African country on the Gulf of Guinea—was from Ghana. As the most populous African country (with Lagos itself having about 17.5 million people) and one of the most vigorous economies outside of South Africa, the level of hustle and collective intensity was quite overwhelming.

Nigeria's ethnic groups are much more diverse in appearance, with many variations of indigenous coloring from caramel to blue-black; therefore I fit right into their scheme of what an African could look like, and they called me Fulani girl rather than *oyinbo* (Yoruba for white person). I felt like I had entered a much larger intellectual arena of discourse about the black world; I wrote in my journal: *Lagos seemed like a black New York.* Although Ghana had been the home of Nkrumah's Pan-Africanism, with his ouster in 1966, the powers that be had definitely backtracked with a more myopic and localized political agenda. Additionally, the majority of Nigerian men dressed in traditional cloth rather than trousers and Western shirts as in Ghana; the pride in one's Africanness was much more noticeable. I also felt a more male-oriented *aggressive* social atmosphere, which I attributed to the Yorubas' patrilineal descent, as compared with the Akans' matrilineal inheritance that positioned women as more central. As a female in Lagos, I was definitely aware that I needed Fargos as a buffer, which I did not in Accra. Nigerians also asked me about my last name, Osumare. "How did you get that name, and do you know what it means?" they would ask. When I answered correctly, they said, "Well, you are most welcome." I felt like Osumare, the orisa (deity) of the rainbow, was enfolding a protective arc over me.

Going inland that Sunday, September 12, Fargos and I left Lagos for Ibadan, the capital city of Oyo State, and from there on to the sacred town of Ile-Ife, touted by Yoruba cosmology as the home of all creation. Ibadan, about eighty miles from Lagos, is the third-largest city in Nigeria with more than 3 million people. We found a fairly cheap motel and spent the next day at the University of Ibadan, one of the most prestigious universities in the country. We also went to the Ademola Art Studio, as Nigerians have produced many world-class visual artists.

We traveled on to Ile-Ife that Tuesday, 135 miles inland from Lagos and a part of Oshun State. The fact that many of the southwestern states of Nigeria are named after Yoruba orisas is indicative of how strong the Yoruba traditional religion is in this part of the country, and Ile-Ife is the home of that cosmology. In the Yoruba creation myth, the orisas have human characteristics and are not above certain foibles, but there are checks and balances that accomplish the ultimate goals of the Supreme Being, Olodumare. Fargos and I visited several of the shrines for the orisas scattered throughout Ile-Ife, and although Christianity was also prevalent, I was in awe of the publicness of the traditional Yoruba religion.

While in Ile-Ife we also continued our odyssey to discover Nigerian contemporary art and met with Muraina Oyelami, one of the artists of the Oshogbo Art School, whom I had helped bring to the Bay Area in 1974, and who today is a chief of the nearby town of Iragbigi. After Nigerian independence in 1960, several visual artists working in batik, woodcut, collage, and other media created the Oshogbo Art School, which caught international attention with the help of German scholar Ulli Beier.[43] Muraina Oyelami, living in Ile-Ife at the time, met with us and gave us an orientation to their art studio in Oshogbo, the capital of Oshun State, where we traveled the next day.

Muraina introduced us to the Department of Dramatic Arts (DDA), one of the oldest academic units at the University of Ife, now Obafemi Awolowo University. The DDA had a particularly strong theater component, with traditional music and dance classes. Muraina had started teaching traditional drumming at the department a year earlier. The highlight of the visit to the DDA was meeting the late Ola Rotimi (1938–2000), one of Nigeria's leading playwrights and theater directors, who founded the Ori Olokun Acting Company. Rotimi was best known for his play *The Gods Are Not to Blame*, first produced in 1968 and published in 1971. Professor Rotimi graciously showed us around the two-story facility with its rooms of drums and theater equipment and gave us a sense that, in Nigeria, theater was the central art that cohered dance and music, as opposed to music seeming to be the organizing art form at Legon. Although the fall 1976 semester had not started yet, one could feel the activity that was generated by the dance, music, and theater classes, rehearsals, and productions emanating from the department. I remember Rotimi as a small man who was big in character, with wide-ranging ambitions for the possibilities of Nigerian theater arts springing from his international training and his belief in the depth of Yoruba culture. Nigeria was turning out to be a very stimulating trip.

Fargos and I moved on to Oshogbo on September 15 and ended up spending three days in the enchanting town that is the home of the Yoruba deity Oshun, the goddess of love. Muraina's orientation to the Oshogbo Art School made us fairly conversant with their history and artistic approach, so when Rufus Ogundele met us at the studio on Main Street in downtown Oshogbo we were prepared to partake of the various artists exhibiting at the gallery. The exhibition was a feast of batik cloth, canvas painting, woodcut prints, and sculpture with a "found objects" aesthetic, all of which we thoroughly enjoyed.

But the Oshogbo highlight was the shrine to orisa Oshun. As a house constructed in a forest grove right off the Oshun River, which runs through Oshogbo, the shrine is a mecca for Yoruba religious practitioners, common town folks with a cursory belief in the goddess, and tourists alike. The river's water is touted to be healing, and simply to wade into it and splash some of Oshun's elixir on one's body is supposed to be therapeutic. As we walked along the river and felt its energy, all of a sudden some young Yoruba women came upon the river to pay homage to Oshun. Oshun is said to give blessings to women to bear healthy children. As the women walked out into the river to receive the blessed water, I went with them and felt I was participating in a sacred women's ritual. Although I did not want children, I did want my future *projects* to bear fruit when I returned to America after this life-changing trip to the Motherland; I prayed for fruitful results from the abundant knowledge I was gaining. Indeed, I realize that many of my envisioned projects, resulting from that African pilgrimage, did come to manifest.

Our last day in Oshogbo was spent at the secular end of the cultural spectrum: visiting the pop music star and visual artist Twins Seven-Seven (1944–2011) and his many wives. Twins Seven-Seven was born Olaniyi Osuntoki of royal blood, being the grandson of the king of Ibadan in the 1890s, making him a legitimate prince. He changed his name to represent the fact that he was the "sole surviving child of his parents' seven sets of twins. 'They believed that I was the reincarnation of twins they had lost,' he told the *Baltimore Sun* in 2001."[44] He was one of the original artists of the Oshogbo School discovered by Ulli Beier, and his work reflected traditional Yoruba mythology and culture, some of which was hanging around his colorful home that Fargos and I visited that day. This was the first time I saw polygamy in action, with several of his wives catering to our needs with food, drinks, and marijuana. Yes, we got high with this thirty-something artist, a celebrity Afrobeat musician who helped develop the musical genre along with Fela Kuti and others.

Twins Seven-Seven could have easily fit into the Bay Area black-hippie arts scene of which I was a product, but he was also a child of his traditional culture. He was simultaneously cosmopolitan and entrenched in his culture, and we had fun hanging out with him that day and observing his unique mediations between the two. After the casual day of smoking, drinking, listening to his music, and viewing his art, Twins, two of his wives, Fargos, and I went to a dynamic King Sunny Adé concert of jùjú pop music. Adé was in good form with his famous guitar riffs, talking drum rhythms, and traditional Yoruba praise singing. The concert, which included dancers and choreography, allowed me to observe how the traditional arts were integrated into the popular music of the day, with the use of traditional instruments, specific indigenous dances, and the visual design of traditional costuming and makeup. This was the perfect ending of a day with a famous artist/musician, allowing me to experience the prolific creativity of young Yoruba artists of my generation who were creating a kind of 1970s Pan-African artistry and lifestyle that incorporated the diaspora, their cultural traditions, and personal cosmopolitanism.

So far the Nigeria journey had been about *my* cultural interest and research, but we still needed to visit Fargos's twin sister, who lived in a small town called Offa in Kwara State. We crossed into Kwara State, northwest of Oshun State, while still remaining in Yorubaland with a smattering of Nupe and Hausa peoples. Although a small town, Offa did have a significant history, being the railway terminus before it was extended northward to Kano and Nguru. I had been interested in visiting a smaller Nigerian town that was not as central to Yoruba culture and that would also allow me to live in a family home. Fargos's twin sister, who looked just like his female counterpart, had left Ghana and moved to Offa with her Nigerian husband when they got married. Her husband had taken a second younger wife a year before our arrival, and Fargos had not met the new wife yet; I was interested in seeing how the polygamy lifestyle worked, and his sister's home gave me that opportunity. As the Yoruba are patrilineal and patrilocal, it was a given that Fargos's sister would have to move to Offa with her husband, and they had two children. As her brother, especially twin brother, Fargos was culturally part of her nuclear family, and as his traveling partner I was accorded all customary courtesy as a family member as well.

The household was set up in a traditional compound setting, with each wife having her own separate house within the compound. The two women seemed to cooperate very well together, taking care of household duties and the children in a peaceful and efficient manner, as well as talking and laughing together throughout the day. I helped the second wife sometimes during our two days in Offa, allowing Fargos and his sister to have some leisure time to relax and talk. The husband seemed even-handed and congenial as the patriarch of the compound, and in general the household seemed harmonious. I have no way of knowing whether the congeniality I observed was a performance or genuine, or whether the seeming harmony was indicative of polygamous households in an agrarian-based society. I just remember being comfortable in the compound that appeared workable.

After leaving Offa, we retraced our journey, moving through Oshogbo, Ile-Ife, Ibadan, and finally back to Lagos to exit Nigeria and head back to Togo. But before leaving, I had a few more significant cultural experiences: an intellectually stimulating meeting with Fola Soyinka, the wife of award-winning playwright Wole Soyinka; another meeting with Ola Rotimi, who had arranged for me to purchase an *iya ilu,* the mother talking drum in the Yoruba *bata* battery; a pilgrimage to the gates of Fela Kuti's compound and attendance at a concert at his Afrika Shrine nightclub in Lagos; and witnessing the end of Ramadan as a national holiday. I had continued filming with my Super 8 video camera and had gotten some significant footage of the entire trip. In general, Nigeria had provided me with a Pan-African experience, allowing me to connect with important contemporary artists and intellectuals, all of whom reinforced my key purpose for making this pilgrimage to Africa. I wrote in my journal on my last day in Nigeria, three months before FESTAC was to take place:

> In Nigeria I have been made to feel I have a place here as a black person—that I too belong to Africa, if only I feel Africa within me and am willing to help in what they are working toward artistically and intellectually. Thank you Nigeria! You have given me what I came to Africa to find. Your awareness has embraced me and you are truly ready now to be the host of the world's Black Arts Festival (FESTAC) that will be one of the great links in bringing our people closer together.

On Sunday, September 26, Fargos and I left Lagos by bus for Lomé, staying in the capital overnight, and the next day enduring an arduous trip by bus and canoe to the remote village of Kpegedi in the Abobo area of Togo to visit his father and older brother. I will never forget this trip because it was the first time I had to put my belongings in a small canoe to sail across a lagoon to get to my accommodations. I felt privileged to be a part of Fargos's Ewe family compound for two days, becoming more privy to how the traditional village family unit lives. Fargos was always called by his birth name, Asu, and I began to see him differently as he showed deep respect for his father, a tall, stately, gray-haired man who was a respected Ewe elder. Asu's brother was taller, like his father, and could have easily fit into the "hipness" of Christian Village, though he chose to stay in this remote family compound in Togo. I also learned that the family name was Ahadzi and not Atiso, Asu's assumed surname back in Ghana. With this trip to the Abobo area, I was being given a deeper insight into the man who had become my guardian companion during this West African sojourn. His family did not judge our relationship but accepted me openly as Asu's foreign companion and treated me with respect.

The primary event during our two-day stay in Kpegedi Village was our receiving a ceremonial spiritual blessing. When I first arrived, I had no idea that his father was a practicing priest, because Asu was a man who lived a totally secular life. But in Kpegedi he began to orient me to the ceremony that his father wanted us to receive for life blessings; I began to understand how many Africans surreptitiously carry these spiritual tenets within but rarely expose their traditional religious upbringing. The Ahadzi compound contained a shrine that housed the family's protective deity, Azo, whom I was told had saved the family from cholera and other diseases. The shrine also housed another spiritual force, represented by a snake. I knew of the snake deity Damballa, representing universal wholeness, within Haitian vodou. The Ewe are indeed one of the primary ancestral ethnic groups in Haiti and are directly related to the Fon of Benin, the acknowledged source of Haitian vodou.

I thought about the many times I had danced *yanvalou* for Damballa in Miss Beckford's Dunham-Haitian classes in Oakland, where my low-bent back had to represent the undulations of a snake. Now I was in Damballa *culture* about to experience a snake ritual as a part of my relationship with Asu. I was no longer *imagining* Africa and its underlying cosmological beliefs behind the dances that we studied in Afro-Haitian dance classes; I was in Kpegedi Village, and Damballa became a living principle practiced by the Ewe.

I was told the high priest of the village would conduct a cleansing ceremony—*eshilelu* (bathing)—the following evening for Asu and me. The ritual Asu and I experienced with his father and the high priest was indeed very powerful and included prayers, water pouring, and a ceremony of cleansing for each one of us separately. I felt as if I was going through another baptism, as I had done twenty years ago in the Catholic Church in San Francisco. Even though I could not understand the language of the prayers, I sincerely felt the power of the ceremony and was completely at peace with no trepidation. I realized how much the stereotype of vodou and African religion in general in the West never took into account the deep uplifting spiritual aspects that I was experiencing in the ceremony. I was experiencing a serious cleansing ceremony of baptism. After the ceremony of eshilelu was completed, I wondered whether what I had just experienced was the blessing that the female priestess back in Christian Village had told me I would receive before leaving Africa.

I slept well the rest of the night and woke with a true sense of renewal. I was definitely getting more than I had ever imagined in coming to West Africa, and I realized that it was in divine order that I had met Asu (Fargos), as he had become an unwitting gatekeeper to my deeper experience of Mother Africa and a spiritual revitalization. Of course, I gave a monetary offering for what I had been given, but at no time did the Elder Ahadzi or the high priest ask for any money. It was left up to my own heart to give, and I realized that being with Asu had brought me deeper into the inner sanctum of African life. The next morning, with a renewed sense of purpose, I took a formal portrait picture of the stately Elder Ahadji seated in front of the shrine on a Ghanaian stool wearing his white imprinted *adinkra* cloth, and that photo remains with the family until this day.

That afternoon we left for Lomé, where we stayed at one of Fargos's relatives' compound. Togo was truly his country, testifying to the extent to which different ethnic groups like the Ewe were dispersed across the European-created borders while continuing their familial and cultural ties regardless of the nation-states that had been constructed around them. In Lomé, where the traffic was far more manageable than in Lagos or even Accra, I did some shopping and got my hair rebraided.

The next day we traveled to the town of Adangbe for the Adifozan festival that showcased young girls coming out of their initiation into womanhood. They danced with bare breasts adorned with trade bead necklaces, loincloth wraps, and hanging waist ties. The young girls carried horsetails that moved gracefully with their newly perfected movements of the Adifozan dance at the center of the festival.

The minister of Parliament for that area of Togo was a guest at the festival, and hence a traditional female rite-of-passage ceremony and a state occasion were united. This meant that the media with their cameras were there, allowing me to set up my own tripod in the center of the outdoor arena alongside the state television cameramen. The Adifozan festival became an important lesson in how modern and traditional Africa created a twentieth-century rapprochement in the 1970s. I saw several people I knew from Christian Village, as I found out that Adangbe was the original Togolese hometown, from which they had all migrated to Ghana. The festival became a grand reunion with Fargos's uncle and several elders from "my" village; I felt like I was becoming a part of a large family that spread across two West African countries. As I danced akpé with the Christian villagers in Adangbe, I realized they had become my Ghanaian family. Driven by the constant command of the drum and the accompanying akpé trumpet, I was one of them, feeling and expressing the rhythm because I knew the language of the akpé dance from dancing with them back home in Christian Village. I was speaking their embodied language, and that made me family.

Teaching at UG-Legon and Preparing to Return to the United States

After returning to Ghana and Legon from my excursion to Nigeria and Togo, I needed to resume my dance studies at SMDD, my private drum classes, and attempt to realize a dream of actually teaching African American dance there. Dashenaba King, the African American female dance student who was also at UG, and I began to work on a proposal for an "African American Dance Forms" course for Professor Nketia's evaluation. We hoped he would include it in the fall 1976 SMDD course schedule. Dashenaba had been trained in curriculum development, and along with my practical experience in teaching dance in Europe, Boston, New York, and my own Bay Area, our combined expertise came together in a ten-page proposal for why black American social dance forms should be taught in the Dance Division of SMDD. Nketia had a strong Pan-African consciousness from working in the United States at UCLA and other institutions; with our articulated course rationale containing specific black American dance units, he was able to convince the dean to allow the scheduling of this non-Ghanaian dance class. Our black American dance class was included on the "Lecture Time-Table 1976–1977." As I filled out the payroll forms as an assistant lecturer at UG-Legon, I realized that this was an important change in my status in Ghana, and I wrote in my journal:

> I am deeply into my work here with people beginning now to see me differently. My first dance class taught at Legon was October 12, changing my status. I have gone from student auditor to lecturer, and it is blowing minds. In such a traditionally status-oriented African culture this shift became very significant. Teaching dance and lecturing on the cultural history of American black folks will be intense all the way to the performance I am supposed to present at the end of the semester.

The course was simply listed as "Dance Technique," and I was the instructor. As I already had my B.A. in dance and theater arts, and Dashenaba had one more semester to complete her degree, I was listed as the instructor of the course and positioned to teach most of the classes. With my previous research in historical periods of black dance used in *The Evolution of Black Dance* lecture-demonstrations, along with my increased knowledge of Ghanaian traditional dances, I was well poised to teach a comparative Pan-African dance class that explored the relationship between black movement forms across different cultures. I used Dunham Technique as warm-up exercises and then taught the remainder of each class in a big circle, focusing on different periods of black American social dance with an improvisational circle method. The course, held at the end of the day from 4:00 to 5:30 p.m., proved to be a big hit not only because it was a different experience than the familiar traditional Ghanaian dances but also because the Ghanaian students themselves comprehended my main objective and helped me "teach" the class.

As I taught my Ghanaian students about different U.S. black dance historical periods and the movement styles, they clearly saw the historic recycling of various Ghanaian dance styles in the American social dances. The 1920s Charleston was a big hit, although there are actually more Central African Congolese origins to that particular dance. My students still found specific movements in certain Ghanaian dances that are similar to the feet-crossing and relaxed polyrhythmic torso isolations of the Charleston, which had begun to "Africanize" white U.S. dance culture in the 1920s Jazz Age. The 1930s lindy hop, too, was a great lesson in couple partnering in relation to the fast-paced feet movements that reminded them of several steps in the Ewe war dances.

But it was the 1970s dances made famous on Don Cornelius's *Soul Train* TV show that most animated the students, because at the time they were contemporary for their generation. Many of them remembered the U.S. Soul-to-Soul touring concert that came to Accra five years earlier. Held on March 6, 1971, in Independence Square, the fourteen-hour Soul-to-Soul performance, as the name suggests, was a showcase of American pop music with a variety of styles, including R&B, soul, rock, gospel, and jazz. The artists included Wilson Pickett (called Soul Brother #2 in Ghana after James Brown), Ike & Tina Turner, Les McCann and Eddie Harris, the Staples Singers, Santana featuring Willie Bobo, Roberta Flack, and ending with the Voices of East Harlem. I could only imagine what a "reunion" that had been, and I literally saw how much effect that live concert still had on my students who were only young teenagers five years earlier.

When I introduced a simple 1970s Soul Train dance called "the bump," where one touches one's partner's hip or other body parts with one's own hip on syncopated beats, they all said, "That's *touré* from Bamaya." We recruited the Tamale-born Fatima from the Ghana Dance Ensemble to properly demonstrate the touré, and it was an exact replica of the bump. These were the kinds of embodied black dance connections we learned through my "Dance Technique" class at SMDD. In an interesting way, the course extended the sociocultural work established by African Americans in Ghana before me during the Nkrumah era, like Maya Angelou and Shirley Du Bois, as well as her husband, the pioneering Pan-Africanist W. E. B. Du Bois himself. I felt very fulfilled teaching my dance course, which also prepared the entire SMDD for my Ghanaian production of *The Evolution of Black Dance*. I had included the production in the proposal as a culminating performance for the course, scheduled for the end of the semester.

October was spent teaching my dance students and starting to rehearse *The Evolution of Black Dance*. At the same time I still continued my established Legon activities, like visiting Christian Village and assisting the TM teacher Nii Padi with his TM lecturers at the university. Fargos's birthday was in mid-October, and I organized a special party for him at his house in the village with the help of next-door neighbor Rosa. Even though he knew that my heart was still back in the United States with Kimathi, I wanted him to know how much I really appreciated his being there for me during my West African sojourn. My rehearsals for *Evolution*, with chosen dancers from my class and drummers from the school, started at the end of month in small groups for each historic period, and GDE costumer Auntie Maggie volunteered to make costumes for me, for which I was grateful.

Being aware of my impending return to the United States, in November I made two short weekend trips to other Ghanaian regions to see dance and music festivals. In early November I traveled to the Volta Region for the first time to attend the Ewe Hogbetsotso festival in Anloga, the capital of the Anlo-Ewe traditional state.[45] This major annual festival testifies to the Ewe ethnic group's geographical spread across three countries—Ghana, Togo, and the Republic of Benin—each supplying Ewe dance troupes to the festival. Hogbetsotso represents a prime example of the strength of ethnicity in postcolonial Africa, with Ewes across hundreds of miles celebrating their common culture regardless of the borders established by the Anglophone and Francophone colonial powers.

Later that month another use of dance and music as resistance happened when I went back to Kumasi to attend the fiftieth anniversary of the Asante Kotoko Society, established in 1916 to unify the Ashanti as a nation during British rule. Their program booklet for the occasion gave the rationale for the society: "The British supposed that the Osei-Poi Dynasty had vanished with Nana Prempeh I, and that the two-centuries-old kingdom of Asante was no more to exist. Yet the Asante had hopes of future unity in the failure of the British to capture the Golden Stool, in which they believed the soul of the Asante nation to be eternally enshrined." Therefore the *durbar* (festival) that I attended at the Kumasi Cultural Center was a display of political resistance, demonstrating how the Ashanti did not allow themselves to be *culturally* subjugated by British colonialism.

The Asantehene high chief, Opoku Ware II, with his full regalia of gold headdress, bracelets, and anklets, held court under a covered dais, along with several representatives of the Acheampong military government. The lower Omanhene chiefs and the queen mothers from the various districts of Ashanti Region came to pay tribute to the Asantehene using *atumpan* and fontomfrom drumming and dance, each approaching the dais with dance to honor the Asantehene. As this was both an Ashanti cultural and state governmental public event, the media was out in full force. With my little movie camera, I situated myself among the male journalists as the only woman, foreigner, and wearing traditional cloth. I positioned myself with the television men, including the BBC, to document the auspicious occasion. A memorable moment for me came when Opoku Ware, a UK-trained attorney, visibly noticed me as the only foreign female recording the event; when our gazes met, he gave me a slight nod. I interpreted that moment of royal acknowledgment of me as a show of approval of my iconoclastic role at the fiftieth anniversary of the Asante Kotoko Society, a commemoration of Asante resistance against colonialism.

Back at Legon in November I continued to rehearse *Evolution*, using as many dancers and musicians from the school as would commit to my schedule. But I was distracted by the fact that I was really missing Kimathi, and both our birthdays were approaching. Although I was tempted to tell him that I needed to stay through January to attend the historic FESTAC event in Lagos, he had already told me that if I didn't return to the Bay Area by January, he could not guarantee that he would still be there waiting for me. I had pushed my intended nine-month stay in Ghana to the limit, and my intuition told me that he was seeing someone else; if I was serious about our relationship, I had better return sooner rather than later. I decided to schedule an international phone call to talk to him for his birthday.

Unlike in modern Ghana, with its twenty-first-century mobile cell phone technology, in 1976, making a call from Ghana to the United States was extremely primitive. I had to make an appointment in Accra at the central telephone headquarters a week ahead of time to make the call on the date I wanted. I went into Accra on the appointed day with my paperwork, and after I gave them the number in Oakland, California, to call, I was shown to a phone booth to wait. When I finally heard the phone ring in the booth, my heart started beating fast. All I had were the audiocassette tapes that we exchanged through the mail; I had not heard his voice in real time since April. But the long-distance phone conversation was actually anti-climactic: there was so much static that we spent most of the time yelling into the phone and asking, "What did you say?" Even though the sound quality was poor, I wished him a happy birthday, told him that I loved him, and that I was definitely not staying for FESTAC and was coming home in January. He affirmed his love, reinforcing that my return in January was a necessity. I understood and realized that my personal life finally had to take priority over my dance mission.

I had my thirtieth birthday in Ghana that November 27, 1976. By choice I spent the day mostly by myself to reflect on the mission that I had been on since I first left the Bay Area in the summer of 1968 for Europe. In eight years I had traveled throughout Morocco and southern Europe, started a dance company in Copenhagen, taught for a year at one of the most prestigious dance schools in Stockholm, danced in a professional New York Dance Company, returned to the Bay Area and galvanized the dance and theater scene there with my original dance theater, and was now teaching dance at the University of Ghana thousands of miles away in West Africa. With that much whirlwind artistic activity, I needed to take stock. I felt "called" by my mission and was following that cultural-spiritual vocation. But I realized that once I went back home, I needed to settle down, plant roots, and establish something for the long term, including a family.

As a part of my birthday life reflections, I reread the poem that I had written the previous month about how I felt about being in Africa. I had written it while sitting on Registry Hill looking out over the campus and listening to Herbie Hancock's *Maiden Voyage* on a cassette tape:

We Come Back

We Come Back
Back to Mother Earth
Weaving our melodious rhythms
in the land of their origins

We Come Back
Different now, yet Africa dwells within
Uncovering our essence

Often camouflaged in a blue note
Blowing African polyrhythms on a horn
Telling the story of a throbbing history

We Come Back
God's Children of the Heart
Expressing the rhythms of nature in continuing forms
Like the wind that scatters the seeds
Fertilizing the Earth
For it to feel itself
Planted deep into different lands
We sprout and grow to come back Home
and make Home fuller

We Come Back
Prodigal Sons and Daughters
Searching to find our way
Back to the Womb of Life
As Mother Africa is made happy by our coming
To better know the spirit of her essence
Only then can we all know
The Wound of Earth's longing
and the Patience of God's Love

These life reflections on my thirtieth birthday gave me important insights, but the next day, Sunday, I had a party on Labadi Beach with many of the African American and Ghanaian friends that I had made, including my dear buddy Ronnie Marshall (Yao Tamakloe). Some drummers came, and we all celebrated, letting me know that I had created a family of sorts at Legon. I was happy dancing on the beach with my Ghana friends for my thirtieth birthday, but I knew it was time to go home.

Everything that I had been working for in Ghana came to pass on December 17. My culminating experience—the Ghanaian presentation of *The Evolution of Black Dance*—took place in the Dance Hall of SMDD. I told my version of our story to Ghanaians using African American and Ghanaian artists, and it was a big success. The dance hall was packed with folding chairs, and every seat was filled. I put much of what I had learned about Ghanaian dance into it, including dancing adowa myself during the opening Africa section. Cheers and applause accompanied that solo as I validated Ghanaian dance as a "technique" that can be taught to anyone. Yao performed part of the Ewe agbekor, as well as a full tap dance solo in the 1930s American section. The Ghanaian audience was mesmerized, and I felt validated that they got the message—that they understood their cultural connections to us as African diasporans. Professor Nketia congratulated me after the performance, thanking me for what I had brought to SMDD. Little did I know then that we would remain colleagues and friends for years to come, with him decades later endorsing my second book, on Ghanaian hiplife pop music, which wouldn't evolve until the mid-1990s.

After paying many bribes to get my musical instruments and Ghanaian artifacts and souvenirs packed into a wooden crate and shipped to the United States, I left Ghana on January 2, 1977. It was an emotional leave-taking between Fargos and me, but he helped negotiate all of the necessary transactions, including all the *dashes* that had to be paid to get me on that plane. I was so appreciative of him, fully realizing how much he had helped me through many cultural obstacles in Ghana and during our West Africa travels. I was grateful, but we both knew that our relationship was over, and I was going home to be married. On my Pan Am flight, with a stop in Dakar, Senegal, I wrote in my journal. I reflected on how both traditional and modern Africa were in negotiation with each other for the future of Ghana. I wondered how Africa was going to mediate these powerful forces of so many long-held cultural traditions with global modernity, moving into the last decades of the twentieth century. I had no answers, only hopes and wishes. But I did know that I had received the cultural and spiritual validation I came for and that I had also given back to Mother Africa.

6

Dancing in Oakland and Beyond, 1977–1993

Dance is a survival art: rhythm is a refuge, movement
is medicine, and energy is a language. Feet that listen
to the Earth are moved by her song.

GABRIELLE ROTH

I arrived in New York from Ghana on January 3, 1977, in the dead of winter. It was so cold I could see my breath in the crisp winter air, and for a person just coming from the tropics of West Africa and who grew up in the Bay Area where it never snowed, the experience of this kind of cold was over-whelming. But it was not only the climate change that had me disoriented; culture shock also hit me hard. I had been living almost a year in a culture where no one is "touchy-feely" and everyone felt a part of each other. In Ghana people were truly socially connected to each other for better or worse, but in New York I immediately felt the cold, icy social distance that creates intense individual alienation.

I was back in the United States—thrust again into the social, cultural, racial disconnect that is often palpable, intensified by the fact that I had just left a society that is the opposite. Ethnic and cultural difference might be social divides that Ghana was trying to overcome, but "racial" difference, as we know it in the United States, did not compute. I had experienced a re-prieve from the alienating effects of racial othering for almost nine months, and New York in the winter of 1977 was a stark reminder of the home en-vironment that I had tried to escape. The day after returning from Ghana,

I wrote the following poem to express the culture shock I felt, allowing me to really see America through a different lens:

America, We Came

America, We Came
from the glow of tropical sun
and the sweet scent of bright flamboyant trees
flowing in the sensual breeze
To the starkness of high-rise brick
a concrete jungle
And the stillness of winter

America, We came
from the pride of a defined tradition
To the black weariness of tired eyes
that look at tomorrow as another demon to conquer

America, We Came
From "This I Am"
To the question of "Who Am I?"

We came, yet we were brought
We fought, yet we were brought
Brought to this land of Promises
of the Grand Human Laboratory:

5 cups of the British
2 cups of the Irish
4 tablespoons of the Jews
a dash of the Italians

Throw in a little Rugged Individualism
And Manifest Destiny

And mix it all up with the juice of the Blacks
Make it all come together and rise with Sweet Blackberry Juice

Optional:
For Spices from the East, you can always add a pinch of
Chinese, Japanese, East Indian, and South East Asian

And for those who like it muy caliente
How about a little Chicana or Latino Tabasco on top?

While the Bowl that you use for the entire Mixture
belongs to the Indian and the Hawaiian, the only Native Americans

The Recipe for world salvation?
The Mixture of Hope for universal Humanhood?

America!
We came to this Prosperous Wasteland
And now here we stand!
Trying to get our share of the Prosperity or the Waste!

Yes, America, we came, we were brought
We fought, yet we were brought
Children of the Heart, the Sun, and of Rhythm

We came in sorrow—the only unwilling Immigrants
forced to build the house
that Jack then claimed

We came in terror, forced to be the quintessential Other
enslaved, whipped, raped,
Yet, sang, danced, prayed, . . . and rebelled

And in the process forged links
Where there was no thread except human breath

America, we came
We came to add the Heart, the Soul, the Conscience
We came to add the beat of the human heart
To the shaping of the Universal Man & Woman!

Yes, winter in New York in 1977 provided a lot of food for reflection on the nature of America and black folks' place in the scheme of the country's development. I had missed the U.S. Bicentennial, but I was always reflecting on its history. I conceptualized black Americans' position as the "glue" that holds the culture together. In the midst of the vast multicultural society that had become more like a tossed salad than a melting pot, black folks were the salad dressing that made the various cultural ingredients coalesce as much as was possible in the late 1970s. Little did I know then that a new black cultural phenomenon was brewing in the South Bronx—hip-hop— that would take this analogy to a whole new level in the latter part of the twentieth century, with global capitalism and black popular culture becoming near synonymous.

At the beginning of 1977, the United States had just emerged from a grand Bicentennial, celebrating its two-hundredth year as a nation, forged from conquering the indigenous nations that had been here for thousands of years, and building its economy to become number one in the world through nearly 250 years of slave labor. I considered it poetic justice that only a month after I returned from Ghana, *Roots*, the most-watched television miniseries at that time, appeared on television nightly for a week. It was based on Alex Haley's book *Roots: The Saga of an American Family*, which placed the story of enslaved Africans in the historical context of the United States, something that was new to U.S. popular television. I was glued to my TV set every night, remembering that I had just returned from my ancestral African journey and knowing the country really needed this black history lesson that the education system had avoided for so long.

I ended up staying in New York for one week, met with Ntozake, and got comp tickets to the Broadway production of *for colored girls who have considered suicide/when the rainbow is enuf*. To see the choreopoems, for which I had helped develop some of the movement concepts, now on the Broadway stage was nothing short of miraculous. To see Ntozake and Paula Moss, who had also danced with me, as Broadway actors on the stage performing the poems I knew so well, along with other talented women like Sarita Allen, Trazana Beverley, and the late Laurie Carlos (1949–2016), was truly inspiring. Having gone from Joe Papp's Off-Broadway Public Theater just four months earlier to Broadway's Booth Theater was phenomenal, and the play ran for 742 shows until July 1978. I was truly happy for Ntozake, but she was also caught up with the negative feedback she was getting from black males for so-called "male-bashing" and "airing our dirty laundry." I advised her to bask in her newfound glory, realize that she had merely exposed her actual personal experience, and that the truth would set her free.

I also hooked up with NaNa, who was spending some time with friends in New York and teaching Transcendental Meditation. She and I had made amends and realized that we would be friends for life; we moved on to what our relationship was really meant to be. She realized that I was in love with Kimathi and we were to be married. I left New York on January 11 to return to the Bay Area and Kimathi, filled with a new sense of responsibility.

On my flight to Oakland I realized that I was going to the next stage of my life and my first major relationship living together with a man that would lead to marriage. Kimathi met me at the airport, and we were overjoyed to see each other and to finally get time to be together. He drove me to his new North Oakland flat, and we spent a solid week together without leaving home or contacting anyone: making love, talking incessantly, eating, watching television, and then starting that cycle all over again. It was like we were inside of each other, penetrating deep into our mutual love. We needed that time to reconnect on a deep level, and we took it.

When Kimathi and I were ready to come up for air and rejoin the world, I called my mother to announce I was back from Africa. I went to see Mama and my sisters in San Francisco, which was a loving reunion. I was back, reconnecting to my personal life, and was finally ready to lay down *roots* in my home area again, after many global *routes* of self-discovery.

Kimathi had rented the top level of a two-story house on Sixtieth Street in North Oakland right near the border of Berkeley, a historic part of the East Bay with many black landmarks. Just a few yards from his house was Lois the Pie Queen, the famous soul food restaurant owned by Lois Davis, a former gospel singer and the mother of famous gospel singer Tramaine Hawkins. The restaurant was known for its southern-style breakfast, biscuits, and fried chicken, and when Jesse Jackson ran for president in 1984 and came to campaign in Oakland, Lois the Pie Queen's fried chicken was a must. Our home was also a couple of blocks from the old Merritt College, where the Black Panther Party started in 1966. Back in 1973, before I left for Ghana, this was the college where I had taken my first black history courses—Grove Street College, after Merritt College had moved up to the Oakland hills. The community had lobbied to keep educational activities in those historic North Oakland buildings. So we lived in a strategic area where Oakland, Emeryville, and Berkeley converged, which gave me access to many geographic and historic spots in the East Bay. The Sixtieth Street house was Kimathi's first rented home, and he was glad to have his own place where I could come home. Little did I know that the house would eventually become the first home we owned and the key to our financial future.

However, I soon noticed that there was trouble in paradise. After our initial week together, I began sensing that something was not quite right; Kimathi seemed distracted and slightly agitated. Noticing this "disturbance in the force," I confronted him and he confessed: he had had an affair with a young Filipino girl, Gloria (named changed), that had become fairly serious, and he could not shake off the relationship. I could not be totally angry about this situation, as I had just left an affair with Fargos in Ghana. But I rationalized that I always knew where my heart was and never gave *myself* in my Ghanaian relationship; Kimathi had obviously gotten his heart involved with his affair, and that was different. I was proud of my reaction, because without any anger or "drama," I calmly told him that he needed to figure out whom he really wanted, and quickly. I realized I had put my cultural mission in Africa before our relationship, and now I could potentially lose him. At that time it never entered my consciousness that men put careers and their purposes before their personal lives all the time, but something in my developing feminist consciousness did know that I had done the right thing for *me*. Kimathi met with Gloria and came back and told me that he was still in a dilemma; I again showed courage and told him that I would give him one month to make up his mind. I moved into my own place to give him some space to do just that.

By early April I was living in my own house on Fifty-Fourth Street, six blocks from Kimathi's flat. In my journal, I called my new home my place of refuge and expansion. I was really proud of myself for how I was dealing with this personal crisis, and I actually felt inner peace knowing that I was ready to deal with any decision that Kimathi made. I was ready to become his wife or move on with my own life. Because he had waited for me, I felt he deserved a small window of time to make this important decision, but secretly I wondered, without any humility, how he could give up this experienced woman of the world who was becoming a well-known artist; I didn't even consider that these very facts might intimidate him as a man.

As Kimathi was making his decision, I continued my work and waited patiently, summoning all the personal discipline that I learned through meditation. I resumed my dance career, performing at La Peña, Berkeley's Latin American cultural center, giving a solo version of *The Evolution of Black Dance,* which was becoming my signature performance piece. My patience and self-control paid off, because within my one-month time limit, Kimathi came to me one night on Fifty-Fourth Street and told me that he was finished with his relationship with Gloria, and he wanted us to be together. I continued to live on Fifty-Fourth Street for the next six months and eventually moved back with him on Sixtieth Street to start the rest of our lives together.

Everybody's Creative Arts Center as Representative of Oakland and Bay Area Consciousness

While our personal drama was playing out, an opportunity came to me that would set the agenda for the next stage of our lives and my career, as well as the cultural destiny of Oakland. I went back to Every Body's Dance Studio (chapter 4), the rental dance studio located at the corner of Broadway and Fifty-Second Street in Oakland, to rent a dance-class slot again. I made an appointment with the two dancers who owned the studio: modern dancer Ferolyn Angel (whom I had met at a summer workshop in Stockholm) and belly dancer Shiraz (Sharon Arslanian). We discussed what days and times might be available for me to teach some of the Ghanaian dances that I had spent nearly a year learning. Their dance studio was a funky, community-oriented place that was typical of the egalitarian, multicultural postrevolutionary, posthippie 1970s climate of the Bay Area. Every Body's Dance Studio housed various dance styles from Afro-Haitian to Middle Eastern, and from freestyle improvisation to jazz and African dance techniques. In 1977 Ferolyn and Shiraz had been running the rental space for about seven years and had built a good reputation within the East Bay dance community. Most classes, taught in the evenings and on weekends, were well attended in the large, open dance space that they had created in the makeshift old abandoned mattress warehouse at that busy corner of Broadway and Fifty-Second Street, near Rockridge Shopping Center, not far from the California College of Arts and Crafts.[1]

But to my surprise, Ferolyn and Shiraz also wanted to talk to me about selling the business, not just renting studio space. This meeting took place in February, only one month after I had returned from my West African sojourn. Why they thought I would be interested in becoming the owner of the studio I do not know, but I supposed they saw something in me that I didn't recognize in myself.[2] Running a daily arts business was surely different than producing and booking the previous Bay Area dance theater productions for which I had become known. My first reaction was that I was still in culture shock and certainly did not have the energy to run a business—even a dance studio—and plus I was experiencing a personal crisis that needed my attention. However, my second thought was that

I shouldn't be too quick to turn down the offer, so I thought about it and conferred with Kimathi and my family. I realized immediately that an affirmative answer would affect not only my life but everyone close to me as well. Kimathi saw the possibility of realizing some of his own artistic dreams in having such a space. He said he could see concerts as well as classes at the studio, which already happened at Every Body's Dance Studio with theatrical lighting instruments already set up. He also discussed starting a music program, giving musicians time slots to hold private and group classes. We could have African drumming classes, as well as Western instrumentation including piano lessons on the studio's upright piano that came with the purchase. An artistic dream began to take shape in our imaginations.

Ferolyn and Shiraz told me they wanted to sell the seven years of community goodwill and reputation of Every Body's Dance Studio, along with all the equipment that included flooring, mirrors, the piano, dance barres and all of the fixtures, for two thousand dollars. In 1977 this was no small amount for a poor dancer without a job; therefore, if I did accept, I would need financial help. I went to Mama and Herman and Bubber (my biological father's nickname) to discuss the business possibility with them and to see if they could loan me some money to pull it off. Mama, forever cautious, asked me if I thought I could handle such a responsibility, especially since I had just returned from a nearly one-year trip abroad. But she said if I decided to buy the business, she and my stepfather Herman could loan me five hundred dollars. Bubber thought it was a great idea, and said he could match the five hundred dollars, giving me half of what I would need to purchase the dance studio.

These negotiations took place in March and April, and on April 30, after making my offer to Ferolyn and Shiraz, they chose me to become the new owner of Every Body's Dance Studio. I was humbly grateful, but I was still baffled by their choice since I knew they had another offer from Boni Grove, a dancer who was trying to expand from her smaller studio on Telegraph Avenue called Full Spectrum; after all, she obviously already had proven business acumen running a dance studio. As it would turn out, tragedy struck: Boni's boyfriend murdered her the very next day after I bought the business. Many things happen in life that we can never truly explain but only accept and know that they are beyond our control. Our choices within the circumstances with which we are presented determine our destinies. My celebration of my new ownership of Every Body's Dance Studio was tempered by the untimely death of Boni Grove, my main competitor for the studio and a beloved member of the Bay Area dance community.

I began seriously thinking through what I really wanted to do with this new wide-open arts business opportunity. The easiest thing was simply to continue the dance classes already scheduled at the studio. We called it "Everybody's," now emphasizing an "all the *people*" concept, rather than the "all *bodies*" concept of "Every Body's." Kimathi and I had decided we would be a couple and run the studio together as our mutual community arts project. But I also knew that I would need more help, and in true community-oriented Bay Area style I asked several of my dance students and friends to join me in forming a collective to brainstorm the creative possibilities. I needed help with the initial implementation of a new *scope* of dance classes and services at Everybody's.

The Everybody's committee I formed consisted of dance students and emerging activists, some of whom would go on to become community leaders. Fania Davis, a dance student of mine and the sister of prison activist Angela Davis, became an integral part of the initial community collective. As a third-year law student at UC Berkeley's Boalt School of Law, Fania wrote the by-laws and articles of incorporation to create a tax-exempt, non-profit organization. Today, she is an attorney and the executive director of Restorative Justice for Oakland Youth, a non-profit focused on healing justice for indigenous communities of color. Toni Meriah Kruse, also my dance student and who worked as a bank teller at Chemical Bank, became our business manager, our first part-time paid position. She was hired at three hundred dollars per month before I paid myself anything. Today Meriah is a holistic movement specialist and certified Feldenkrais Method practitioner in Louisville, Kentucky. Candice Martin was an attorney and TM teacher who had gone on the Ethiopia Teacher Training Course with NaNa (chapter 4). Carolina Gonzalez was another dance student of mine, who also drafted her then husband, Manuel Gonzalez, a Chicano political activist, into our collective. Another Mexican female activist, Alaciel, also joined our collective and later married Manuel after he and Carolina divorced. Sadika, a Caucasian freestyle hippie who was also my dance student, simply said, "I'm willing to do whatever I'm needed for." Along with Kimathi and me, this group became the motley crew of sincere community people who helped me start what would become, over time, an important defining cultural institution in Oakland and the Bay Area.

As I had always created and produced my own dance theater works, never seeking to fit into the existing larger (white) Bay Area concert dance scene, starting my own dance studio was actually an extension of my track record as a communalist-oriented artistic iconoclast. I saw myself as a cultural activist who was not the product of the elitist-trained concert dance world. I had first emerged from the cultural activism of the West Coast Black Arts movement (chapter 1), with political sensibilities leaning toward the politics of the Third World Liberation Front that had formed around the San Francisco State Strike. Even though I had *not* stayed in the United States to participate during the heat of the strike, my politics developed from that sense of black cultural power in solidarity with other communities of color. Therefore, my Everybody's Collective of black, Chicano/a, and politically progressive whites was in alignment with a Bay Area tradition of reformist cross-cultural politics, as well as my own sense of individual rebellion.

If one studies the historical development of California as a state in the Union, one finds pioneers, scoundrels, and bold, self-made characters, and the initial Everybody's Collective viewed itself through the lens of the *former*, pioneering a kind of "politics of recognition"[3] through dance and the arts in the East Bay cultural scene. I was determined that black dance, representing the marginalization of *all* dance cultures of color, was no longer going to be peripheral; instead, it would be recognized as central to the Bay Area artistic scene. Having just returned from Ghana, after studying traditional African dance and drumming in one of the premier West African performing arts schools in higher education, and conducting my own dance fieldwork, I was ready to claim *the dance of black people* as fundamental, not marginal, to American culture. The foundation of my various productions of *The Evolution of Black Dance* had now been enhanced by the direct experience of the Motherland. I was ready to show the often-arrogant Bay Area white modern dance scene that black dance forms and the dance of other cultures of color were going to take their rightful place in the circle of human cultural production.

Every Body's Dance Studio already had the reputation for being an inclusive model of Third World dance. The roster of dance classes in the business that I had bought was known for multiculturalism, but I set out to create an even wider cultural scope. Ferolyn Angel told me at the signing of the bill of sale that they chose me because they knew I would keep the diversity of dance classes in which they believed, and I intended to do just that at an expanded level. We had Congolese dance with Malonga Casquelourd from Congo-Brazzaville, C. K. Ladzekpo taught Ghanaian drumming, Luisah Teish held Afro-Haitian dance classes, and even the famous Harold Nicholas taught tap dance for a while. I booked qualified instructors to teach classes in Mexican folk dance emerging out of the growing Ballet Folklórico in the La Raza movement in California, Middle Eastern belly dance, and even Balinese dance. We had a few classes in the dance staples like ballet, modern dance, and jazz dance, but my emphasis was on the many cultural forms reflecting the diversity of the Bay Area and the world.

The collective that I had created set about turning Every Body's Dance Studio into Everybody's Creative Arts Center (ECAC). Now that we had a studio/performance space, Kimathi and I talked incessantly about our dreams for what it could become, and we set about turning those dreams into a community reality. Sadika changed the look of the place, installing tie-dye cloth that had become the face of Bay Area counterculture gone mainstream, along with colorful creative signs of studio rules and regulations, as well as photos of the Everybody's Collective. Meriah established a simple accrual bookkeeping system for all the income and expenses in a hardback ledger (computers and bookkeeping software were ten years away from regular use), and I was very proud of ECAC's professional bookkeeping system because it gave us a sense of being a *real* business. Fania, with some help from Candice, started interviewing Kimathi and me to see what organizational parameters should be contained in the by-laws that we wanted for the board of directors that would become the caretakers of the pending 501(c)(3) non-profit organization. The Everybody's Collective became the first board of directors, as we did not want to give that power to any outsiders. Of course, as the organization continued to grow and professionalize, all that would change, but in the beginning we were the motley crew that birthed a center for the performing arts in Oakland, and it was all ours. One day Meriah and I drove to the capital in Sacramento to file our non-profit paperwork. It had taken six months to get our official IRS tax-exempt status, but now we were legit.

We named the new non-profit Everybody's Creative Arts Center (ECAC) officially in the articles of incorporation, with a vision to expand the performing arts offering by adding music and theater classes, as well as to emphasize more studio performances. Although we knew dance was the staple artistic offering ("product" or "brand" in current twenty-first-century parlance), we definitely wanted to add a music program directed by Kimathi. As a musician himself, he could pull in many of his music colleagues to teach piano, saxophone, bass, drums, etc. Theater was something to which I was partial, as I always created interdisciplinary productions that included scripted text to create what today is called "edutainment." We created and marketed the new multidisciplinary image but quickly found out that the general public wanted to participate in a program that specialized in *one* art done well. We realized within the first year that we could dream about all the arts under one umbrella, but as a *community* art center, the community itself is always the other crucial factor. I had hired my old S.F. State drama major friend Judith Holten to teach improvisational theater, but the classes never really caught on. Kimathi's music classes had one, two, or three students—not enough to make it worth it for the teachers. Most of our clientele could not afford the cost of a one-on-one single music class, so within six months we realized that dance classes would remain the main art on which we had to focus, while producing more concerts to emphasize the other performing arts.

Kimathi established a goal of presenting unique music performances at ECAC to underscore our multidisciplinary approach. We purchased about fifty folding chairs, and for the larger concerts borrowed another twenty-five. The chairs were set up in the dance studio, leaving enough space for a performing area, with the audience facing away from the small lobby where people entered the building. I was thrilled when Kimathi announced at our bimonthly collective meetings that he had gotten an affirmative from the famous Art Ensemble of Chicago to perform at Everybody's, and that his band, the Pyramids, would open for the internationally famous quintet, giving his own group more exposure. He assessed that we would have to hold two concerts in order to accommodate the size of the anticipated audience in our small space. We were all excited, knowing the reputation of the well-known free jazz music ensemble that had come to prominence during the 1960s Black Arts movement. We knew they would bring music critics as well as community attention to our newly established arts center.

The Art Ensemble of Chicago consisted of five well-known musicians: Lester Bowie (trumpeter); Roscoe Mitchell (saxophonist); Joseph Jarman (saxophonist), with whom I had danced as a teenager at the Black House in San Francisco (chapter 1); Malachi Favors (bassist); and Famadou Don Moye (drummer), whom I had met in Europe. Their artistic focus was to go beyond what they considered to be the confines of jazz to *performance art*, with instruments from all over the world and the use of costumes and face paint. Their operating motto is "Great Black Music: Ancient to the Future." This was also the creative focus of the Pyramids, and the two sold-out shows at our small studio on Broadway and Fifty-Second became a historic event that helped put the new multidisciplined Everybody's Creative Arts Center on the map.

ECAC's second major music concert, which particularly attracted the Latino community, was the touring Cuban group from Havana, the famous rumba band Los Papines. In his music circles Kimathi had heard about a rare U.S. tour of the renowned Cuban conga drummers, who had traversed the red tape of the Cuban government and the U.S. Immigration and Naturalization Service to book a tour in America. I don't know how Kimathi got ECAC as the venue for the East Bay concert of Los Papines instead of La Peña, *the* East Bay Latin American cultural center, but he did. And again we scheduled a two-show appearance of these famous Cuban musicians. Born in Marianao, Cuba, Los Papines consisted of four brothers from the famous Abreu music family; the Marianao area also produced the great Chano Pozo, one of the early Cubans in the United States who helped established Latin jazz with Dizzy Gillespie.[4] Our concerts of Los Papines would become indicative of occasional touring Cuban groups who managed to come to America during the intensity of the U.S. embargo of Cuba since 1961. The two shows were again sold out with standing-room only, announcing to the East Bay community that we were truly multicultural in our approach to the arts. Kimathi's oral introduction of the group those evenings drew the important African diasporan connections between the United States and Cuba, and in this way, through our initial music concerts, the "creative arts" concept of ECAC became a reality, expanding beyond the mere "dance studio" image.

Of course, we also continued dance performances in the space as well. We hung four pipes from the ceiling and draped black hanging cloth for stage "wings" on each side of the area that defined the performing space, allowing for stage entrances and exits. One important early dance performance was marketed as *Gathering Together,* an evening of my choreography along with that of Raymond Johnson, who had performed with me in my *I Believe* production in 1975 (chapter 4), and a newly arrived black dancer from New York, Evelyn Thomas. Evelyn came to the Bay Area with her husband and daughter, after already performing with George Faison and Rod Rodgers (chapter 3), as well as doing commercial work in the Broadway and national touring companies of *The Wiz.* She would eventually go on to found her Nuba Dance Theater, which still performs today. Evelyn,

Raymond, and I created *Gathering Together* by choreographing solos, duets, and trios with each other in the evolving black modern fusion dance of the day, emphasizing our unique individual styles: I, with my African-inflected improvisational style; Evelyn, with her long extensions evolving from her elegant six-foot frame; and Raymond with a strong masculine approach to his jazz-inflected modern style. *Gathering Together* became a representative dance performance of ECAC's intention to become a professional dance center where both supportive communalism and creative individuality could evolve in relation to each other.

During the summer of 1977 Kimathi and I took a break and drove across the country in his old Harvester Scout, the forerunner to the SUV, to his Columbus and Yellow Springs, Ohio, homes. This was the first time that I would meet his family, and the trip provided the opportunity for me to get to know him on a deeper level—to understand the family roots that shaped his personality. The cross-country trip was a scenic drive across the mountains of California, the salty flatlands of Utah, the Rocky Mountains, the wide-open plains of Wyoming, and the large boulders of Colorado to the cornfields and farmland of Kansas, Missouri, Illinois, Indiana, and finally Ohio. Although he had told me, I began to realize the actuality of him going to Yellow Springs High School and living with the white middle-class family of George and Rae Dewey, parents of a high school friend who took him in after he left his mother, Betty, in Columbus and moved back to his Yellow Springs birth town. The Deweys generously treated him like another son (they already had two sons and two daughters) and also helped him get through Yellow Springs College; on that trip they accepted me as a daughter-in-law. It was a revelatory experience of the often deeply personal relations between the races hidden behind the racist societal veneer of America.

In Columbus I met his mother, Betty Valentine, and immediately loved her because she was a bold deaf woman who had insisted that her first son, Thomas (Tommy), be a full participant in society and not be held back by her so-called disability. Talking with his sisters Rosemary, Kathy, Pauline, and Susan about their upbringing was also a revelation in how a single black deaf mother kept her family together against the bureaucratic onslaught of the welfare and deaf services systems that wanted to take her children away and put them in foster care. The only one she lost to "the system" was her only deaf child, her son Allen. Kimathi still had raw feelings as the big brother who couldn't save his younger brother from that system.

The trip to Ohio drew us closer, allowing me to experience more of the background of the man with whom I was fulfilling my career dreams and was about to marry.

Upon returning to Oakland, several managerial bombshells hit almost at once, coming after all of the administrative and artistic developments of Everybody's Creative Arts Center that had happened within the first six months. First, a corporation had bought the prime real estate property at the busy commercial corner where our building was located; and second, the IRS want to audit the organization only six months after we had received our tax-exempt status. I called an emergency meeting of the collective to discuss and strategize these two major administrative challenges. Our Everybody's Collective became even more important, and we formed subcommittees to divide the tasks and tackle the next steps. Meriah, the business manager, oversaw the IRS audit; Fania, Kimathi, and I formed a subcommittee to explore rental facilities that could accommodate the needs of a dance studio, and we decided to concentrate our property search closer to downtown Oakland.

As we searched for a new dance studio and performance space, it occurred to me that we were establishing a community that was indeed about human transformation and exchange. For example, several of our students did various services for the studio in exchange for dance classes. We established a barter system with some of our regulars because they were so sincere about studying the arts and the particular way we delivered them. One such student was Selimah Nemoy, who had been my student at Every Body's Dance Studio before I left for Ghana. When I returned, she immediately came back to my dance classes and approached me with a deal to offer her talent as a calligrapher in exchange for dance classes, making publicity signs and class flyers for Malonga Casquelourd and me. She was a Jewish woman who grew up in Los Angeles and studied with her famous calligrapher father, Maury Nemoy, who had done much of the calligraphy for early Hollywood films. I loved her handwritten script for many of our advertisements for classes and performances and was glad to make this kind of mutually beneficial exchange.

Over time she became one of my closest friends, and she reminisced with me for this book about the 1970s Oakland dance scene. She told me: "We all invested in each other; we all believed in each other. You weren't just teaching dance, but were teaching us about transformation and community—this value that we all had for one another, and the joy that we could share."[5] As we continued on the phone to recall those "good old days," I realized I had been trying to share with the Oakland dance community the social and spiritual connection that dance and music can engender, which had been vitally reinforced in my own direct dance experiences in West Africa.

Dance, in its purest context, is a socializing and a healing tool, and at its very core, that's what Everybody's was all about. It attracted people like Selimah who were looking for that kind of experience with other like spirits to form a community of caring and supportive people. As we continued our discussion of the Everybody's experience, Selimah said:

> The perfect metaphor was the circle at the end of your dance classes. When I was challenged to go into the center of the dance circle [to improvise what I learned], I was being pushed to be the fullest of who I was, while being encouraged by the other dancers and the drummers. [When I was in the center,] I understood we were carrying something from Africa. I remember you talking about transformation for a common good, and we were inspired to pursue that together in the dance class. Now I can see we were investing in each other, and what you gave lives on.[6]

In our phone conversation she illuminated the era of late 1970s in the Bay Area, which by that time had become a ten-year crucible of "the revolution"—attempted social, cultural, political, and sexual counterculture activism. The arts—theater, dance, music, and visual—were crucial in that attempted societal makeover in the Bay Area.

Selimah's insights allowed me to see that Everybody's Creative Arts Center was a microcosm of the larger effort for social and cultural transformation in the entire Bay Area. My work with Everybody's was an important continuation of the cultural revolution I had been part of since my college days at S.F. State. Noted theater director Thulani Davis has said it best:

> The challenge is to make theater a public space where many private worlds can be seen and heard; to make a public space where the fictional boundaries of the past can be our metaphors, rather than our prisons. American theater is the natural public space for a society no longer able to keep its fictional fences standing. It is a space of creative energy that is a shelter where people try to understand a world in which we are all materially, spiritually, elbow-to-elbow interde-

pendent. People living at the periphery of society are the translators, the boundary crossers, moving back and forth from main to margin, making autonomy in the shadows.[7]

At Everybody's we were creating a world that was important to our immediate community: consciously nonmainstream. We were establishing an artistic and cultural "shelter" where people tried to understand their interdependence and tear down the "fictional boundaries of the past" of race, class, gender, and sexuality that were unfortunately still so present. And the drum, used in so many of our classes, was the call of the spirit to make that understanding possible, if only for a one-and-a-half-hour dance class.

ECAC's special confluence between dance technique and spiritual connectedness did not go unnoticed by the larger society, particularly because our students lobbied local media to cover the sociocultural synergy being created at our dance studio. One of my students, Italian journalist Vita Lee Giammalvo, wrote an extensive profile of me that was published in a 1981 issue of *City Arts*, a now defunct San Francisco monthly. Her article not only described the personal artistic trajectory that had brought me to that point in my career but also captured the cultural and spiritual aspects of what we at ECAC were creating for the general public:

> Halifu Osumare wears a big smile as she signals her sweaty class to spread into a circle. She leads them into a final series of African gestures and movements, telling the dancers to focus their energy towards the earth. Two conga drummers, keeping the spirit going for an hour and a half, gradually fade into familiar rhythms. The circle, a familiar closing to Osumare's classes, moves closer together, the dancers reaching their arms around each other in a bright moment of camaraderie.[8]

The article included a photo of me in a dance position reversed into a creative photo-negative graphic: I stood in a fourth position turned-in jazz contraction, arms stretched diagonally upward, head tilted upward, with my face in an expression of ecstasy with eyes closed. The message: I was spiritually connected to my body through my dance. This kind of media attention put both ECAC and me on the cultural map of the Bay Area.

This was why we couldn't let Everybody's die with a mere building loss, and when Kimathi, Sadika, Meriah, and I walked into the ground-floor open area of a downtown Oakland office building at the corner of Webster and Twenty-First Streets, we looked at each other and knew that was our new studio. We negotiated to lease the new space, and because it was an old office building with few tenants, the owners, whom we never really met, were glad to have ECAC as a lessee to bring in some needed funds for a relatively vacant four-story office building. The Webster and Twenty-First Streets space had an even larger studio with a small stage for music and speeches. Most importantly it had a hardwood sprung floor, crucial for dance. It also had a smaller studio space with a linoleum floor where we could hold simultaneous children's classes, as well as shoe classes like tap and flamenco. It also had a second-floor open space with rugs that would be used as a student lounge, as well as two office spaces adjacent to that open area.

The new space offered needed opportunities for growth. At the old studio, we had one tiny room off of the lobby that served as an office, and I knew that we needed real administrative offices for the next stage of our development with a paid staff. We all pitched in painting our two new offices, and we were soon ready for business. By March 1978, ECAC had made the physical transition from the outskirts of Oakland at Fifty-Second and Broadway to the heart of downtown Oakland at Twenty-First and Webster.

The opportunities of the new studio brought new artistic and administrative developments. Within the year we had received our first major grant from the San Francisco Foundation (TSFF) of twenty-five thousand dollars, which, for a one-year-old organization, was phenomenal. The TSFF is one of the oldest and largest community philanthropic foundations in the country, founded in 1948 to serve the entire Bay Area. Arts and culture luckily was one of their primary foci, with their website stating that they emphasize the arts because they help people "to imagine and create a better world." This was the foundation of my own mission in dance, and I felt that what we had created in less than a year fit their mission for the arts exactly, and so did they.

While in our first building I had invited the grants administrators of TSFF to one of our signature days of classes, "Free Day" at Everybody's Creative Arts Center. One of the ways I increased dance class attendance was to run classes in seasonal sessions; so, the spring session, for example, was started on a Sunday of free dance classes taught by teachers for that session. Students experienced one-hour shorter dance sessions, each hour featuring another teacher and dance style, all for free. This publicity day became a signature of ECAC, with hundreds of people coming to the studio throughout the day. Free Day generated tons of community goodwill and really showcased the quality and energy of our dance classes. Malonga's Congolese classes, for example, created both physical and emotional heat that was palpable: his Congolese singing, call-and-response chanting, dancing, and drumming re-created a Sunday African village–like dance event, reminding me of those in Ghana and Togo (chapter 5). When the TSFF administrators saw this kind of energy and the community response in large numbers, along with my growing grantsmanship, ECAC received the twenty-five-thousand-dollar grant that transitioned the organization to the next level in its second year.

With that first major grant from the TSFF, other funding sources took notice, and we expanded our contributed income, allowing us to hire paid staff, including me. Now ECAC was financially able to pay me a salary as executive artistic director of Everybody's Creative Arts Center. We grew in reputation very quickly, obviously serving a community need, and I learned to articulate our ability to meet that need in grant proposals. I applied for and received three positions during the last few years of the Comprehensive Employment and Training Act (CETA) under the Carter administration, designed by the federal government as a decentralized job-training program for the long-term unemployed. Through this program we were able to hire Kimathi as the publicity director, Barbara Martin as a full-time business manager, and Kate McKean as part-time bookkeeper; the latter two were both white dance students in our classes. Our pool of employees usually came from our own student body, which made it easy for our staff to fit into the mission of the organization, as they were already a part of the cultural atmosphere of the ECAC community.

Barbara developed the idea of extending the concept of our barter system to a formal work-study program to run ECAC. After the administrative staff had worked all day, we did not want to stay into the evening registering students into classes. I had negotiated with the teachers to take a percentage of class fees rather than renting space from ECAC. This financial arrangement created a better cash flow for the organization and more control of the services, but it also increased our financial administrative duties. Barbara's idea to have trained students register other students for classes in exchange for a certain number of free classes became the answer to our problem, and our famous Work-Study Program began. The ECAC Work-

Study Program became an extension of the community exchange philosophy at the basis of ECAC's mission and helped some students continue their dance training.

Growing Everybody's Creative Arts Center

As the founding artistic director, one of my main tasks was to envision new programs that showcased the mission and objectives of ECAC. Even as we were preparing to move to the downtown Oakland location, Kimathi and I decided we should rent a large auditorium to end our first year of operation with a concert that would showcase the dance companies and individual artists teaching at ECAC, as well as include music groups that would again make the statement that ECAC was about *all* the performing arts, with dance at the center. We also wanted to make sure that the multicultural "everybody's" concept remained central to such a concert. Therefore, in December 1977, we produced the first annual ECAC Multicultural Festival of Dance and Music. That first year, it was held at the Berkeley Community Theatre, compliments of my old friend, Berkeley High School teacher Richard Navies (chapter 4). We presented a wide array of dance cultures and performing artists, including Malonga and his Fua Dia Congo dance company, Batucaje Brazilian dance ensemble with Jose Lorenzo, an East Indian dance group, Ruth Beckford dance protégé Naima Gwen Lewis, and my choreography performed by a group of my advanced students that included Fania Davis and Meriah Kruse. Kimathi also pulled together a group of musicians to perform some of his original music compositions. The concert attracted nearly a thousand people, signaling that what we were doing was not only appreciated but also served a community need that reflected the tenor of the times and our local region. See a photo of the finale of the show in figure 9.

Subsequent ECAC Multicultural Festivals of Dance and Music became more professional, with regional and nationally known artists, while continuing to showcase dance and music on the same program. Moving into downtown Oakland, we began to produce the concert at the Oakland Auditorium Theater, a union-run venue at Tenth Street and Fallon (now known as the Calvin Simmons Theater). In 1979 we assembled an all-star jazz band that included Ed Kelly (piano), John Handy (saxophone), our friend Eddie Marshall (drums), Bill Summers (congas and percussion), and Mel Martin (woodwinds). Given the artistry and reputation of this specially assembled jazz ensemble, the concert would have sold out on the music alone, but we featured some of the best dance companies in the region as well, allowing them a larger audience exposure. The dance companies included Jose Lorenzo's Batucaje, featuring Jacque Barnes, Mexican folk dance with Ballet Folklórico Jalisco, modern dance with Kathy Sanson and dancers, and jazz dance with the Panamanian Marta sisters, Elvia and Cecilia. For this particular end-of-the-year show we even had well-known radio deejays, Roy Lee of KRE and Joanne Rosensweig of KSAN, as emcees for the evening. Blues singer Taj Mahal, Latin percussionist Pete Escovedo, and the late R&B singer-songwriter Syreeta Wright headlined subsequent festivals.

In this way ECAC began to professionalize the multicultural approach to dance and music, becoming a well-known presenter of performing arts throughout the Bay Area, moving beyond merely our mainstay dance classes. We proved that community-orientation and professionalism in the arts were not mutually exclusive. ECAC also revealed the wide-ranging dance cultures of the Bay Area that went far beyond the San Francisco and Oakland Ballets and a couple of predominantly white modern dance companies, which usually got most of the arts funding.

Although we emphasized high-quality artists in our big-venue performances, we did not neglect our community base, providing them a year-round dance class schedule and special student concerts. ECAC's annual student concerts were where regular serious students could perform in our studio theater for family, friends, and the general public. Students loved experiencing the end product of their "sweat equity" acquired during three months of intense dance training. The excitement behind the scenes during the ECAC Annual Student Concert night was palpable. Secretaries, lawyers, community activists, city government staff workers, and college students, by day, became *dancers* for a night; they felt like artists too. I ran ECAC like the Zimbabwe proverb: "If you can talk, you can sing; if you can walk, you can dance." Everybody's Creative Arts Center established itself as *the people's dance studio* with high-quality instructors producing a community-oriented artistic product. I had learned a lot from my time in Ghana about dance and music as a socialization tool and their place in integrating a community. I transferred my familiarity with the structured curriculum of the School of Music, Dance, and Drama at the University of Ghana, Legon, and my participation in the transformative power of dance and music in Ghanaian villages (chapter 5) into the mission of Everybody's Creative Arts Center—my own dance school and cultural center. But in the early days, I still could not fully comprehend ECAC's potential to evolve into a defining institution for Oakland, the East Bay, and the Bay Area as a whole.

The Wedding and My First U.S. Dance Company

Kimathi and I got married the same year that ECAC moved into the second location. The year 1978 was a life-altering one with moving the organization in March and legally solidifying our personal relationship in August. Kimathi and I conceived of the wedding as an extension of our community artistic and cultural work and decided to ask many of our dancer and musician friends teaching at ECAC to perform as their wedding gift, creating an all-day arts festival. Always the consummate organizer, I called together three of my girlfriends—Fania Davis, Selimah Nemoy, and Allison Jacobs—to help me plan the details. Instead of a paid wedding planner, I had girlfriends who volunteered to take responsibility for various tasks.

However, Kimathi and I had to make some serious relationship adjustments in order to reach that wedding day. I had moved back into his Sixtieth Street upstairs flat while we were intensely working together administering ECAC, he as publicity director and me as artistic director. The pressure of living and working together on a daily basis brought out negative aspects of our personalities. We were both hot-tempered, creating an imbalanced, volatile mix. We perceived ourselves as equals, yet I was administratively "the boss" at ECAC; this took its toll on our personal relationship and disturbed the administrative peace of the office. One day Kimathi and I got into a screaming match about an administrative decision in the inner office while Barbara and Kate were in the adjacent office, with only a thin door between us. When he and I finished our argument, the two women both had red faces and could hardly look at us. I knew then that he and I might not be able to continue our dual relationship.

That night at home we coolly discussed our situation: we were about to be married and we worked together in an often-stressful non-profit organization. Could we do both successfully? If we had to eliminate one of our relationships, which one would it be? Many couples cannot live and work together, and we were obviously one of those. I told him that our personal relationship was more important, and he agreed. We decided that night that I needed to continue as artistic director, and he would get another job to save our more important pending marriage. He vowed to continue to consult on the music program and the overall mission of the organization from afar, and I promised that I would always give him credit as co-founder. Soon Kimathi got a job in the advertising department of the *East Bay Express*, a weekly newspaper that became like the *Village Voice* of the East Bay. His working at the newspaper gave us more separation, allowing us to come together at the end of the day to say, "How was your day, Dear?" Although we were both still "hot" in temperament, simplifying our roles helped tremendously, and we continued on with the wedding plans.

Thomas Williams (Kimathi Asante) and Janis Miller (Halifu Osumare) were married at the Cascades in Joaquin Miller Park in the Oakland Hills on August 27, 1978, a bright, hot, 90-degree day. The ceremony was not a traditional wedding but instead a Bay Area multicultural arts festival that brought together many artists in a grand community celebration. Kimathi brought his family by bus from Ohio: Mama Betty and his sisters Kathy, Pauline, and Susan (the oldest sister, Rosemary, could not come, and his brother Allen was in a home for the deaf). He also brought his father, Charles Valentine, who was a bit estranged from the family. They all arrived a week before the wedding and remained for a week afterward, sleeping in makeshift beds in the living and dining rooms.

My wedding planner friends were lifesavers because everyone knew their tasks and performed them well. Selimah created our wedding invitations in beautiful calligraphy printed on blue parchment paper that I sent out to friends and family, and Fania became the mistress of ceremony, keeping everything moving like a performance on the day of the event. The Cascades was a developed area of the park that could be rented for occasions such as this, complete with a man-made waterfall that Allison was in charge of making sure was turned on at the beginning of the wedding march. There was a wading pool encircled by a concrete area with stairs terraced down to a lower area. Kimathi was in charge of getting the sound system and the ceremony musicians, hiring his friends, a local band called the Sons and Daughters of Light, headed by Bazuki Bala. They played an original composition, "Let the Sunshine In," for the opening wedding march, as Kimathi and I walked in together from the lower level to the top of the wading-pool circle, where we then separated, walking around the circle as our respective family members filed in behind us, all meeting in front of the Cascades waterfall for the marriage ceremony.

As we had already officially married at the Oakland City Courthouse a few days earlier with Mama Betty and Kathy as witnesses, the August 27 ceremony was our spiritual ceremony and celebration for our community. We had survived nine months apart while I was in Ghana, as well as the stresses of starting a non-profit organization together, and we felt we deserved a big wedding celebration. My wedding outfit reflected my true Bay Area multicultural hippie background: white Balinese wraparound pants with a dragon motif, white Mexican-lace halter top with matching midi-length lace jacket, cornrowed African hairstyle dotted with gold beads and thread, and Egyptian Isis earrings. Kimathi wore a three-piece white suit, salmon-colored shirt, and white tie (the jacket eventually had to come off in 90-degree weather). I had written our vows, memorized my part, and after realizing that he had not done the same, feverishly wrote down his part of the vows on index cards. During the ceremony, he alternated between looking into my eyes and down at his cue cards, while sweating profusely.

Some aspects of the wedding ceremony were actually traditional, but only a few. It was a beautiful and meaningful ceremony, emphasizing love and commitment without binding each other. TM teacher Don Coles performed the ceremony, using passages from my various researched sacred scriptures. Mama and my stepfather, Herman, stood behind me as my parents during the processional, with my father, Leroy, in the background. (He always took a back seat in deference to Herman, who actually raised me.) Betty and Charles stood behind Kimathi, and in this manner the two families were united as we were joined in holy matrimony. We did have a traditional cake-cutting ceremony, but it was a healthy carrot cake with cream cheese icing dotted with fresh strawberries, all in the image of a layered pyramid. The pyramid-cake concept echoed Kimathi's trip to the Pyramid at Giza in Egypt, the photo of which stayed on my bedside nightstand the whole time I was in Ghana.

The artists who performed at the August 27 marriage ceremony represented the visionary artistic goals of ECAC itself. Rick Willis, who taught in the ECAC music program, played solo classical and flamenco guitar as guests entered the Cascades. Percussionist Baba Duru played East Indian tabla drums, and Malonga assembled several African drummers, who jammed after the ceremony for various spontaneous African dance solos, including members of my newly formed dance company, Aquarius Rising Dance Theater.

My seemingly endless youthful energy allowed me to actually form Aquarius Rising in January of that year, even during the ECAC move. It consisted of my dance students and therefore was a student, rather than professional, company. Up to that point, I had mostly choreographed concept dance-theater with text that told a specific story—*Four Women, I Believe, The Evolution of Black Dance*. After starting ECAC, artistically I felt that I needed to begin choreographing *individual* dances for which I could become known. Therefore, I choreographed two dance works that symbolized the cultural aesthetic of the late 1970s for Aquarius Rising Dance Theater: *The Movement of Ja's People* used a suite of music by Bob Marley and the Wailers, in which I performed a character called "The Force of Unity" costumed in a unitard that was black on one side and white on the other; and *Fiesta*, to music by Argentine saxophonist Gato Barbieri, featuring a solo by me with a finale by the company.

Aquarius Rising Dance Theater reflected the racial makeup of the student body of ECAC—black, white, Asian, and Latino. Some of the notable student dancers were Roger Dillahunty, who actually became a founding member of ECAC's eventual professional dance collective; Meriah Kruse, our original ECAC bookkeeper; Cyril Tyrone (Babe) Hanna, who played congas for many of my early Bay Area classes before Ghana; and Jackie Burgess, who eventually became dance faculty at Laney College in Oakland; as well as student dancers Michele Wong, Zebia Pecot, Samaki Pecot, Tabu, Monica Thomas, and Kathy Calderaro. One of the company's first large performances was at the annual Oakland "Festival at the Lake" on Lake Merritt. An *Oakland Tribune* news article for that performance described the company: "Aquarius Rising reflects both Halifu Osumare's insistence on technical mastery and her interest in and encouragement of mutual cultural respect and appreciation."[9] This media statement succinctly summed up my focus for ECAC and my new dance company. At the wedding, Aquarius Rising members did spontaneous, energetic solos to Malonga's infectious Fua Dia Congo drummers' rhythms as the wedding celebration continued.

Kimathi really liked Middle Eastern belly dance, and our belly dance teacher at the time, Khadija Rabanne (now Khadija Leverette), got two other excellent belly dancers to perform solos and a finale trio. Mary Ellen Donald and Baba Duru accompanied them with live *doumbek* drum rhythms, with each dancer performing in front of Kimathi and me as we sat in our shaded seating area under a tree. As the sensual belly dancers performed, he was in heaven, smiling and playing his tambourine.

As evening approached, the day ended with Malonga's drummers and my Aquarius Rising dancers leading a parade of all the remaining guests around the wading pool in the continuing unrelenting heat. By that point everyone was into the outdoor celebration of it all. I remember my sister Brenda dancing in the parade, with our sister Tenola's daughter, little Theresa, perched on her shoulders. Mama, Herman, my younger sister Tracey, Leroy and his girlfriend at the time had already left, testifying to me that they had truly enjoyed themselves. It was an untraditional, but enjoyable, wedding that reflected our growing cultural influence in Oakland and the Bay Area.

To Kimathi's and my surprise, Allison came up to us at one point in the partying and gave us an envelope with a one-night gift certificate to the Bridal Suite at the top of Claremont Hotel in the nearby Berkeley Hills, with a panoramic view of the Bay. She had taken up a collection from our friends for this expensive wedding gift. We had originally planned to spend our wedding night at home with Kimathi's visiting family, but instead we simply drove down the hill to the Claremont Hotel with this surprise gift certificate that allowed us an unforgettable wedding night alone.

The Growth of Everybody's Creative Arts Center

Over the four years ECAC remained at the Twenty-First and Webster Street second location (1978–81) the reputation of the organization grew with increased programing, along with new teachers and performers from the African diaspora, all of which attracted more funding. Even with its wide-ranging multicultural offerings, the Center became known particularly for the world's best *black* teachers and performers. The Bay Area, as a home for many immigrants from throughout the diaspora, provided easy access to artists not only from West and Central Africa but also Cuba, Haiti, and Trinidad and Tobago. Jackie Artman, a Trinidadian native, began teaching Trinidadian dance at the Center, as well as Wilfred Marks, the founder of Dance Kaiso Company in San Francisco. Jackie Artman drew more Caribbean students to ECAC and eventually became the founder of Carijama, an Oakland Caribbean carnival parade and festival happening in conjunction with the annual San Francisco Carnival held in May. A Panamanian ECAC instructor, Adela Chu, along with musician Marcus Gordon, founded Carnival San Francisco. Our dance-cultural center had become very influential, attracting the best of the African diaspora.

Just as in the first building, I thought ECAC should also continue producing studio concerts, and I created a performance series called Spotlight on Culture that featured professional dance companies, musicians, and actors. *The Evolution of Black Dance*, this time with a subtitle of *From Africa to the 80s*, was one of the first performances in the series in May 1980. It included new artists who were either teachers or students at ECAC, such as Leon Jackson, Linda Goodrich, tap dancer Fred Ferguson, and students Soyinka Rahim, Gaynell, and Charles McNeil (figure 10). I began to take this version of the lecture-demonstration into the Oakland public schools again, establishing an official ECAC school outreach program.

As new Caribbean artists came to live in the Bay Area or were on tour, I booked them into the Spotlight on Culture series. ECAC became one of the first venues where Conjunto Cespedes, a Cuban musical family trio, performed in the Bay Area. They were a part of the Mariel boatlift migration in the 1980s,[10] and became known in the Bay Area for their traditional Cuban *son* music, with melodic vocals, accompanied by guitar, and small percussion instruments. They initially consisted of the late Luis Cespedes, his sister Gladys "Bobi" Cespedes, and their nephew Guillermo Cespedes. Conjunto Cespedes became known regionally and nationally in the United States as important musicians, but when they performed at ECAC they included son and rumba dances with their show, helping to introduce Cuban music and dance to the Bay Area. I was always on the lookout for new artists from the diaspora to produce.

Another important Caribbean group appearing in Spotlight on Culture was the Astor Johnson Repertory Theatre of Trinidad and Tobago, produced at ECAC in 1981 when they were touring the United States. I did not know it at the time, but they were one of the leading contemporary dance companies in the Caribbean, founded by the late choreographer Astor Johnson in 1972. As their website states, their repertoire "is based on Afro-Caribbean dances in the region, and seeks to embrace a fusion of indigenous Caribbean and modern dance styles."[11] I remember them performing two sold-out shows that put the Spotlight on Culture series on the regional map and made Astor Johnson a lifelong friend of mine. His company was well-rehearsed and costumed, presenting a vision of Caribbean modern dance that several islands were establishing. Astor had studied with Trinidadian contemporary dancers, as well as the Dance Theatre of Harlem in the United States. The fact that the company has continued until today is a testament to the professional foundation that Astor Johnson laid. When Kimathi and I visited the island nation in 1984, he graciously hosted us, showing us his beloved Port-of-Spain capital, where the dance company currently resides.

Because of our comprehensive program of dance instruction, the performance series, and occasional school outreach programs, ECAC became a regional cultural institution with which to reckon, and the media began to take notice. In 1979, Charles Shere, staff writer with Oakland's main newspaper, the *Tribune*, stated: "Osumare directs Everybody's Creative Arts Center, a downtown cultural center at 354 21st St. where housewives and office workers can learn West African dance—and where a dancer from the National Ballet of Cuba can drop in to tune up his entrechats. Intense but calm, lithe, intelligent and attractive, she hovers—at 32—over three activities: dancing, teaching, administration."[12] He actually left out choreographing, because I was doing it all and being fairly successful with all of these roles, from the artistic to the administrative. This news article focused on my personal background, and I was able to recount my story from S.F. State to Europe, and from New York City's Rod Rodgers Dance Company to receiving my African name from Ntozake Shange, as well as my dance studies and research in Ghana. Major media coverage allowed the Bay Area to understand more of my personal career trajectory within the context of our growing dance and cultural center.

After the wedding festival and during the increasing visibility of ECAC, Ohio dancer Linda Goodrich became an important part of my and ECAC's story. Growing up in the Midwest in Columbus, Ohio, she became an integral part of the Oakland dance scene. She arrived in October 1978 with her preteen son, Lamar (now Achebe), and a boyfriend who had convinced her to move to Oakland where he had friends rather than go to New York where she had periodically received her professional dance training.

A couple of years younger than I, she had come of age in a more diluted midwestern manifestation of the 1960s revolution, and she wanted a more vigorous dance scene than Columbus, Ohio, offered. Columbus had only ballet and tap with little modern or jazz dance, so she eventually became one of the only modern jazz teachers with her own dance company at the Paul Lawrence Dunbar Center in the Columbus black community. Luckily her city of birth was close enough to New York as the nation's dance center, and she began making excursions to New York to take a larger scope of dance classes. At New York's Clark Center, she studied modern jazz dance with important figures in black dance like Fred Benjamin, Diane McIntyre, and Thelma Hill. When she arrived at ECAC, she immediately recognized that, "It had a similar energy as the Clark Center where I had been studying, and that convinced me to stay in Oakland."[13]

She remembers the exact class that was being taught when she first came to the Twenty-First and Webster Street location, persuading her that Oakland was the place for her, a decision that changed the trajectory of her life. She says it was Bayan Jamay's modern jazz blues dance class that often utilized popular top-40 R&B music, inspiring an emotional modern jazz style: "When I walked into Bayan's class, I thought I was back in Fred Benjamin's [New York jazz] class. Little did I know then, that she, too, had studied with Fred. Everybody's became an extension of my study at the Clark Center, and I knew I had found my dance home."[14] The Clark Center was started by Alvin Ailey in 1959 "as a multi-racial, multi-ethnic arts community in New York City."[15] Social inequality affects every aspect of society, including the arts, becoming a destabilizing factor at every level. Luckily in dance there were pioneers, like Ailey, who were able to envision new institutions that could address that inequality, allowing black dancers and others to find their artistic voices.

When I started ECAC in the late 1970s, I was aware of continuing marginalization of black dancers and the black dance aesthetic, and I had the same proactive motivation that Ailey felt in the Civil Rights era of the late 1950s and early 1960s (chapter 3). It was no surprise that Linda Goodrich felt the same kind of energy at the ECAC as at the Clark Center, because the programs and services represented the same motivating mission. I, too, had studied at the Clark Center when I danced with the Rod Rodgers Dance Company in 1972, but I had not really made that connection between what I was initiating in Oakland and the famous dance center in New York. ECAC was becoming the West Coast Clark Center, and it took someone like Linda Goodrich from another part of the country to put what we were doing in Oakland into national context. It wasn't long before Linda became a member of the teaching staff, a frequent member of pickup dance groups for my choreography, and eventually a full-fledged member of the ECAC professional dance company, discussed below. Figure 11 shows Linda and me dancing together in the studio in 1979.

Shere's 1979 *Oakland Tribune* news article was seminal in articulating my mission and vision for ECAC, as well as my philosophy of black dance that grew from the times in which I came of age:

A born arts administrator, Osumare talks easily about art and society—and about social issues: "The 1960s were waking up—an awareness period. Lately there's been a sort of counter-reaction. People are more concerned with material values now, with getting theirs. The struggle during the '60s brought out more solid values. In a multicultural society like ours it's important for every part to be available to all. The melting pot is going to come about gradually. It's important to look back—and to look forward, too."[16]

I suppose my intellectual, academic side was always there, lying semi-dormant in my prescient intuition, waiting to be nurtured and honed by graduate school, which lay in the future.

CitiCentre Dance Theatre and the Third and Fourth Venues

Everybody's Creative Arts Center lasted at the Twenty-First and Webster location for four years, and then it again became the victim of the shifting, volatile Oakland real estate market. In early 1982 ECAC moved to the Jenny Lind Hall at the corner of Telegraph Avenue and Twenty-Seventh Street, remaining in the downtown Oakland area. We were becoming more entrenched in Oakland city politics through members of our board of the directors, who were lawyers, corporate executives in major Oakland businesses like the Clorox Corporation, as well as administrators in city government itself. People like corporate attorney Barbara Parker, City of Oakland deputy director of economic development Jeff Tucker, Port of Oakland attorney Rene Benjamin, and corporate executive Pat Collins constituted a cadre of high-powered overseers of the non-profit organization I had cofounded, helping to obtain more corporate and City of Oakland funding. I developed a relationship with the first black mayor of Oakland, Judge Lionel Wilson, and he personally made sure, even before the city's annual competitive arts funding cycle, that ECAC got city funds for our annual Multi-Cultural Festival of Dance and Music.

The Jenny Lind Hall, one of the American concerts halls built for the touring nineteenth-century Swedish opera soprano, became a venue where our administrative staff, students, dance faculty, and the Spotlight on Culture series continued to develop. The facility met our usual needs of two studios, the small one on the first floor and the large studio-performance space on the second floor, with an elevated small stage, like the old facility.

By this point, ECAC was receiving funding from the National Endowment for the Arts' Expansion Arts Program, and this new funding source allowed us to occasionally hire nationally recognized dancer-choreographers to give special workshops. The famous choreographer Donald McKayle gave a one-week dance workshop at ECAC in August 1983, coming up to Oakland from southern California.[17] His workshop became a real boost to our professional instruction program. Donny and I became lifelong friends, with our artistic paths crossing many times.

Spotlight on Culture as a performance series expanded in the Jenny Lind Hall, with artists coming from the commercial center of Los Angeles, as well as evolving experimental Bay Area artists. Veteran actor Beah Richards (1920–2000, the mother to Sidney Poitier in the 1967 film *Guess Who's Coming to Dinner*) came up from Hollywood to perform her *A Black Woman Speaks* one-woman show, and emerging Berkeley theater artist Whoopi Goldberg performed her *Spook Show*, which became the foundation of the Broadway performance that propelled her to international fame. I met Whoopi at Soul Brother's restaurant on Telegraph Ave one afternoon to buy her lunch and "negotiate" a $250 contract for her one-woman show in our Spotlight on Culture series. Little did I know at the time that I was talking to a soon-to-be Academy, Tony, and Emmy Award–winning actor-comedian.

I always had a strong sense for good artistic work, and Spotlight on Culture became an important small studio venue for quality performing artists. I used my theatrical and personal connections to fill the yearly roster with the best dance, music, and theater artists available. The performance series attracted a larger audience than our daily dance students, as well as several donors. Just as her *The Color Purple* novel was being turned into a Steven Spielberg film, Bay Area novelist Alice Walker became an important contributor. She was aware of ECAC's important multicultural artistic work and contributed one thousand dollars to our organization, mailing in a check, along with the filled-out contributor's form that had the category of "Patron" changed to "Matron." She hand-wrote the feminist correction on the form, and thereafter I always called Alice Walker our "Matron" when thanking our contributors.

We had started gathering many of our dance teachers into professional faculty concerts in the old building, and our first one in the Jenny Lind Hall was called *"Mixed Bag": ECAC's Annual Faculty Dance Concert: A Tribute to Katherine Dunham* on May 21 and 22, 1982, which garnered a lot of public attention. One featured dance piece was called *Calenda,* by choreographer Lenwood "Lenny" Sloan, who had reconstructed an early twentieth-century traditional *calenda* dance as a duet between him and me. This traditional African-derived dance had a checkered history in the Americas, having been deemed indecent by European observers, a point I made about the clash of cultures through dance between Africans and Europeans in chapter 5. Dance historian Lynne Fauley Emery recorded some of the European assessments of the calenda: "The Calenda seemed to be the favorite of the blacks. Most white observers thought it indecent. Labat believed that the Calenda came 'from the coast of Guinea and, by all indications, from the Kingdom of Arda.' By 1724, . . . the slaver owners had banned the Calenda, partly because of its immodesty and partly because they feared uprisings among large gatherings of blacks."[18] This latter point calls up many early black dances during and after slavery in the Americas as not only celebratory but as forms of resistance.

E. Patrick Johnson explores this dual purpose of black performance in his "Black Performance Studies: Genealogies, Politics, Futures" (2006). He quotes bell hooks: "Performance was important because it created a cultural context where black people could transgress the boundaries of accepted speech, both in relationship to the dominant white culture, and to the decorum of African-American cultural mores."[19] Johnson then notes that, "Following this logic, we might concede that black performance is at the interstices of black political life and art, providing the lynchpin that sustains and galvanizes arts and acts of resistance."[20] Indeed the calenda dance might easily be positioned in this context of a popular galvanizing celebratory occasion, as well as an act of resistance because of the public disdain by whites of the day. The calenda dance definitely had African origins because it was performed throughout the Americas, in Haiti, Barbados, Trinidad, and other islands. Lenwood Sloan's version for the ECAC faculty concert took a carnival approach, using hip movements along with processional progressions, and we danced calenda in elaborate carnival costumes and props that included large hats and umbrellas.

In our 1982 Faculty Concert, I was attempting to make connections between Katherine Dunham's pioneering dance works and what we were doing at ECAC. That connection was recorded in an advance article for *Mixed Bag* in the May 1982 issue of *City Arts Monthly*: "'You have to be a pioneer,' Halifu Osumare says, referring to Dunham's adventure and to the performance potential for dancers in the Bay Area. 'There's not a lot of ready-made work.' Like Dunham, the black dancer must examine culture and create extensions of their own experience: 'You have to be a pioneer.'"[21] I was attempting to make a connection between Miss Dunham's groundbreaking technique and choreography, already a foundation of black dance in the Bay Area through Ruth Beckford and similar work we were doing at ECAC in the 1980s.

By 1981 I had disbanded Aquarius Rising Dance Theater and was choreographically focusing on solo dances for myself. One such work was *St. Louis Blues: Portrait of a Woman,* which was my exploration of the iconic blues woman, represented by Josephine Baker, Bessie Smith, and Billie Holiday. The music started with Bessie Smith's well-known 1929 "St. Louis Blues" with me seated in a chair costumed in sequined leotard, wraparound dance skirt, and feather boa. I distilled movements of sorrow and loss, yet with a firm resignation moving to a place of self-empowerment. Angela Davis recognizes this kind of black female empowerment by the 1920s and 1930s blues woman in her *Blues Legacies and Black Feminism*: "If we were beginning to appreciate the blasphemies of fictionalized blues women—especially their outrageous politics of sexuality—and the knowledge that might be gleaned from the lives about the possibilities of transforming gender relations within black communities, perhaps we also could benefit from a look at the artistic contributions of the original blues women."[22] This was exactly what I was attempting in my choreography and performance of *St. Louis Blues: Portrait of a Woman,* and it felt empowering to perform as bold, sexy, and audacious as I wanted.

This was my first artistic period where I wanted to focus on my own individual choreography, but my role as ECAC artistic director necessitated that I generate income through outreach programs in the schools that increasingly helped keep the organization solvent. Hence, I created a new lecture demonstration called *Dance around the World* that emphasized the multicultural nature of our dance classes and faculty. This school program included jazz, African, flamenco, and Polynesian dances, with each cultural dance form performed by an ECAC faculty member. Linda Johnson performed West African dance; jazz was represented by Leon Jackson and Debra Floyd, who had now risen from dance student to faculty member; there was a flamenco dancer, whose name I cannot remember; and Polynesian dance was performed by Ricalda Uchiyama (now Mehalani), an African American woman who had become a master in several South Pacific dance forms while living and performing in Hawai'i for many years.

I choreographed the overall structure of the piece, and each dancer was responsible for her/his solo, creating a "dance cultures around the world" theme. I reprised my "Force of Unity" character from *The Movement of Ja's People*, serving as a unifying character who wove the various cultures together. *Dance around the World* became a much-sought-after performance that not only dynamically represented our mission as a dance center but also brought in needed revenue for ECAC that supplemented dance class tuition as our staple earned income.

But it was the founding of CitiCentre Dance Theatre (CDT) in 1983 that become a major professional vehicle for my choreography. Two of the long-term teachers at ECAC—Leon Jackson and Linda Goodrich—and I discussed the need for a professional company that represented the core black dance aesthetic and philosophy of the center. We felt that a small democratic *collective*, rather than an artistic director–focused company, was the structure we wanted. As several of our advanced students—Roger Dillahunty, Debra Floyd, and Daniel Giray (whom Linda had married a year earlier)—had become quite proficient dancers, they were asked to join our company, and the six-member dance collective was born. CDT was inaugurated during two weekend debut concerts in October 1983 at Laney College Theatre in Oakland and the Victoria Theatre in San Francisco. Because our new fledgling dance company consisted of some of the most popular modern and jazz dance teachers in the East Bay, CDT became a hugely anticipated artistic venture, and the 1983 performances, billed as CDT's grand debut, was a success, with sold-out houses for all four concerts.

The debut of CitiCentre Dance Theatre announced to the Bay Area that there was another serious dance company that was showcasing the black contemporary dance tradition. We did not perceive CDT in competition with Dimensions Dance Theater, which had started in the late 1960s; rather, we conceptualized that the addition of CDT to Oakland's professional dance scene said something about the demographics of the Bay Area, where two professional contemporary black dance companies were now residing in Oakland. CDT was another testament to black arts evolving out of the social and cultural reality of Oakland being a predominantly black city at the time.

The CitiCentre Dance Theatre repertoire grew quickly with the collective approach, with each of the three experienced choreographers developing new dance works. Leon Jackson (ca. 1950–1990) choreographed a popular favorite, *Lost but Not Forgotten,* that he performed with Debra as a duet about loss of love through death. In hindsight, this dance became Leon's own memorial, as he was one of the early Bay Area victims of the AIDS crisis. Linda Goodrich set her *Bag Lady* (1981) on the company, for which she had won a Bay Area Izzie Award, as well as *Somebody's Mama,* about the plight of abused women, of which, little did we know, she was a victim in her marriage with Daniel. I reconstructed my ode to female power, *Feminine Trinity* (1980), on CDT. It was originally cast with Alleluia Panis, Evelyn Thomas, and Sara Newton, and in its new incarnation Linda, Evelyn as guest artist, and I danced it.

I continued to churn out choreography for CDT. I created *The Journey* (1982) about the Middle Passage—the transatlantic slave trade—as the major turning point for African peoples plunged into their destiny in the Americas. *The Journey* became the CDT piece that we performed in the 1984 Olympic Arts Festival in Los Angeles. I also choreographed the group work *All This Jazz* in 1983, eclectically exploring the blues of Sonny Boy Williamson and the classic jazz of Horace Silver and the avant-garde jazz of Cecil Taylor. In 1984 I returned to my choreographic focus on solo work for myself with *Rites of Passage,* a dance exploration of the major transitions in human life from birth to childhood, and from puberty to adulthood and death.

CDT became an artistic mandate to develop my choreographic repertoire, enabling me to focus on my creativity in the midst of daily administration of an arts organization. Somehow I found time to choreograph a new work each year, and in 1985 I made *Wonderland,* a suite of dances as a tribute to the developing musical legacy of Stevie Wonder. This piece began with the operatic overture of "The Secret Life of Plants" that segued into several of his top-40 classics like "Ribbon in the Sky." CDT became a vehicle for me to finally develop as a choreographer of significant dance works, beyond my previous focus on black history through dance. Of all my choreographic works of this period, I am most proud of my twenty-minute solo *Rite of Passage.* The CDT Company became an important choreographic vehicle, particularly for Linda, Leon, and me.

While promoting ourselves as the people's studio—"The Oldest Multicultural Dance School in Oakland," the CitiCentre Dance Theatre Company became a showcase for the *professional* standards in dance that ECAC was setting. The name of our new dance company grew out of ECAC's identification with the development of Oakland's district near the Oakland City Hall called City Center. In the mid-1980s Oakland was focused on attracting new business for the commercial development of downtown. The ECAC board of directors wanted to identify with that thrust toward business growth and wanted to position our new dance company within the city's emphasis, making the statement that arts and culture were just as much a part of the projected city growth as entrepreneurship. Thus "Citi-Centre" became the creative spelling of Oakland's "City Center" development project. We even had a logo created with a dancer looming over and cradling downtown Oakland buildings. The marketing message was: Everybody's Creative Arts Center's professional dance company, focused in the black dance aesthetic, was an *Oakland* dance company that was a part of the city's growth.

Although the six-member CDT collective was Oakland-identified, we were not provincial by any means, wanting to be viewed as a touring professional dance company. Our two-concert seasons per year consisted of two weekends, one usually slated for San Francisco at the Victoria Theater in the Mission District (see CDT's first publicity photo in figure 12). We hired professional dance trainers and choreographers, pushing ourselves to be an important *repertory* dance company that could become the repository of great choreographic works by other recognized dancemakers as well. For example, we hired Alonzo King, who had just started his now world-famous Lines Ballet Company, as our ballet master. He came from San Francisco over to Oakland to give us classes, and I remember working hard during his ballet barre: "You have to love every inch of those muscles in that developé," he would quietly say; "love is the key to beautiful movement." His approach to ballet was unique, positioning dance within an understanding of nature itself.

Alonzo set a piece on the company, as well as several other noted choreographers. The local Hassan Al Falak set his *Nommo II* and his *Sweep/Spiral/Trash* on CDT, and we commissioned the internationally recognized Diane McIntyre and Talley Beatty to create works for us as well. Talley choreographed *Runagate,* about slavery and escape on the CDT Company (figure 13). We always hired the best community-oriented lighting designers and costumers. The lighting designer who creatively lit many of my dances and whom I brought into the CDT Company was Stephanie Johnson, now associate professor of sculpture, installation, performance and public art at California State University, Monterey Bay. Her vast knowledge of lighting, particularly for dance, always gave CDT's performances the professional polish that pushed our reputation within a short time period.

During the five years the CDT company was in existence, we accomplished one regional tour and one international tour, both of which received a great deal of publicity. In the summer of 1984 the Olympics came to Los Angeles, with an Olympic Arts Festival accompanying the games. Within the arts festival was a major dance festival that was directed by Bella Lewitzky (1916–2004), the former lead dancer with the Lester Horton Dance Company, where Alvin Ailey started his dance career. Bella had the forethought to break up the dance festival into several cultural components and subcontracted a Black Dance Festival to Lula Washington, artistic director of the LA-based Lula Washington Dance Theatre. Lula and I were California dance colleagues, as she had founded her company in 1980 with her husband, Erwin Washington. Just as Ailey had done in New York two decades before, Lula had established her company in Los Angeles, as her website states, "to provide a creative outlet for minority dance artists in the inner city."

CitiCentre Dance Theatre was Lula's choice to represent northern California in the Olympic Black Dance Festival, alongside dance companies from other parts of the country, including the Rod Rodgers Dance Company. Although we had kept in contact over the decade since I danced with him (chapter 3), I was particularly eager for Rod to see my choreography as an example of why I had the courage to leave his New York company at the height of my New York professional dance career and return to the Bay Area to realize my own artistic goals. CDT's performance of my piece *The Journey* was a big hit at the Olympic Arts Festival, and I remember Rod winking at me from the backstage wings as we came offstage. I had not only begun realizing my choreographic dreams but had built a noted dance center and dance company as well. At the L.A. Olympic Black Dance Festival in 1984 I felt vindicated by my rejection of a New York dance career. Figure 14 is Leon Jackson and me dancing together as a part of a CDT performance.

CDT's one international tour was to the eastern Caribbean island of Martinique in the Lesser Antilles. We were the only American dance company in the thirteenth annual "Identité et Culture" Martiniquan arts festival. Perhaps surprisingly for a small island with fewer than a half-million people, Martinique, with its strong emphasis on culture, is known as the "Paris of the Lesser Antilles." Along with Guadeloupe, it is still an overseas department of France rather than an independent nation. Of course, Aimé Césaire (1913–2008), as its world-famous poet-mayor, had a lot to do with the island's internationally recognized arts scene. When we six members of CDT, along with Ursula Smith as our stage manager, arrived in the Martinique capital of Fort-de-France, we immediately felt the intense tropical heat, as well as an accompanying Caribbean hospitality. The local government-supported modern dance company Companie Contemporaire Corail was designated as our official host. The company members spoke only a little English, so I got a chance to practice my rudimentary French during the entire week we were on the island. The mandatory immersion in my second language allowed me to improve my French-language skills, as we took class with Companie Contemporaire Corail during their daily rehearsal routine and got to know the dancers—Surmac, Allen, Christine, Michélene, Carol, Susie, and others—quite well. They accompanied us everywhere we went, including showing us Martiniquan nightlife after our evening performances.

We had contracted to perform two nights at the "Identité et Culture" festival because of the then Oakland-based anthropologist Sheila Walker, who was an American consultant to the festival. She had been impressed with our debut concerts just a year earlier, and we were honored when she approached us as her choice to represent American dance at the annual Martiniquan festival. We thought hard about the CDT repertoire that we would present and chose Leon's *Lost but Not Forgotten,* Roger's new work *Sign of the Times,* and my *The Journey* and *Rites of Passage.* When I partnered with Roger, during our evening performances on the outdoor stage, he would sweat so much in the humid heat that I had a hard time holding on to him during our lifts. I also had to watch the stage areas where he had just danced, because of the slippery sweat puddles he left in the swelteringly hot night air. The reviews in the morning newspaper after each of our two performances showed us that the general public and critics alike loved our choreography and performances. In fact, we were "treated like nobility," I wrote in my journal, "the way we should be." There was a distinct difference in how Martiniquans viewed their artists and art itself. We were in a very different culture that revered artists and truly supported them. We were in the home of Aimé Césaire, one of the architects of *Négritude,* and I felt as if CDT, in some small way, was part of the realization of his exploration of black cultural identity first articulated in his famous 1947 book of poems and essays, *Cahier d'un retour au pays natal* (*Notebook of a Return to the Native Land*).

After the CDT Company returned from our triumphant international Caribbean tour, the fall of 1984 brought another organizational crisis. Real estate prices in downtown Oakland were rising, and our Jenny Lind Hall landlords increased our rent, pushing ECAC to relinquish our first-floor small studio that serviced our evening and weekend children's classes. The *Tribune* dance critic, Janice Ross, wrote a story on our financial crisis in relation to Oakland's City Center development, with which our board of directors, headed by attorney Barbara Parker, was grappling:

> Barbara Parker, president of the board's executive committee, noted sadly that Jenny Lind's owner is asking just over half a million dollars for the building, a price that puts ownership out of reach for the company, which subsists on $15,000 budget for projects like this fall [dance company] season. "We're in a real dilemma because of Oakland's renaissance," Parker said, noting the irony. "As the renaissance draws people into the city—new audiences—it also forces up the cost of spaces. A building like our current home could well be rented out for more money as offices if the trend continues."[23]

Even with an active, fund-raising, and high-powered board of directors headed by Parker, ECAC still had a rough time financially negotiating the changing mid-1980s business climate in Oakland.

The pressure of being both the chief administrator of a non-profit arts organization *and* dancer-choreographer in its dance company became more than I wanted to continue managing. In March 1986, after nine years at the helm of ECAC, I resigned as artistic director. A local arts administrator, Angela Johnson, was hired with the title "artistic/program director" to take over the administration of ECAC in my place. She had a B.A. in ethnic studies and mass communications from UC Berkeley and had worked for the UC Berkeley Jazz Festival and as publicity director of a Bay Area record company. On the ECAC spring 1986 class schedule, a message to the public about my leaving said the following:

> Halifu Osumare along with her husband Kimathi Asante founded ECAC in February 1977. For the past nine years she has worked diligently as artist and administrator to create a place where the study of dance and the presenting of the performing arts could flourish in a multi-cultural, warm and encouraging environment. ECAC is a testa-

ment to nearly a decade of dreams and hard work. She now moves on to use her skill in administration as a free-lance consultant to the arts with her own business called Expansion Arts Services. She continues to choreograph and perform with CitiCentre Dance Theatre. She also remains an active member of the Board of ECAC. She is still very much with us.

In order for the organization to grow in the changing economic times of the era of 1980s Reaganomics, ECAC needed high-powered businesspeople on the board to navigate the increasing complexity of surviving the non-profit arts world. The community-oriented, feel-good community dance center that I had started nine years earlier was now changing into a professionally administered Oakland arts institution with a professional dance company that needed increased funding to produce two quality dance seasons a year. I began to feel I could become more of a hindrance than an inspiration for the needed administrative growth of ECAC. Organizational survival and growth was more important, and I finally admitted I needed a break from running a daily arts business for the general public.

I had begun teaching again at Stanford University (discussed below) and had made enough contacts in various Bay Area arenas that I could continue doing arts administration as a hired consultant with my Expansion Arts Services, which I began to market while still dancing and choreographing with CDT. And most importantly, I remained on the voting governing board that increasingly directed the organization's growth. While the above public statement was one perspective, I wrote the following personal statement about leaving ECAC as director in my journal:

> *I begin to let go of "Everybody's," a relationship that started in 1977, after just coming back from Africa. Thrust into the world of business, fundraising, marketing, and organizing artists, nine years as Artistic Director has been the catchall title for being Mother to ECAC. And now Mother lets go of her adolescent child and hopes for the best. She lets go to allow her child to find out who it is on its own. She lets go for the child to find if it can make it in the world without Mama—to prove to itself that it can. "Everybody's" has a strong woman spirit; it will survive. I let go in order to find out who the Mother has become after all the years of loving, caring, tending, laughing, prodding, urging, and most of all dancing. Who am I now? What has the child taught me?*

The year I turned forty years old and gave up the helm of ECAC—the non-profit dance center I had nurtured—the world, in fact, did not stop. The CitiCentre Company continued, expanding its touring with run-out performances to the Mendocino Dance Festival and Stanford University's Dinkelspeil Auditorium (figure 15). As an arts consultant, I now had the time to get involved with larger regional arts initiatives. I negotiated a major contract to produce the Bay Area Ira Aldridge Acting Competition, a black actors' contest founded by noted City of Los Angeles arts administrator James Burks. The mission of the competition was to give emerging black actors a career boost. Turning my nine years of arts administrative experience into a new role as a consultant for hire, I began to receive small contracts for arts projects that helped supplement my salary as a dance lecturer at Stanford.

I also began focusing on the developing California multicultural arts movement initiated by the California Arts Council and began adding my voice to the developing push for arts funding equity for communities of color. The "California Dialogue" in March 1986 at the Asilomar Pacific Grove Retreat Center was the beginning of this movement that would develop the fledgling Multicultural Advisory Panel for the California Arts Council in Sacramento under the chairwomanship of Gloriamalia Flores Perez. As Los Angeles congresswoman Maxine Waters said at the Asilomar meeting, "We are starting a network and a vehicle by which we can have assistance for the multi-cultural arts that will help to seek funding for many of the groups and individuals who have been left out of the process."[24] I began working with my colleagues from Oakland, like Benny Ambush, of the Oakland Ensemble Theatre; Majigiza, the then executive director of Dimensions Dance Theatre; and my former S.F. State dance teacher Nontsizi Cayou, of Wajumbe Cultural Institution (chapter 1), as well as visual artist Alonzo Davis of the Los Angeles Brockman Gallery. Now that I was freed up from running a day-to-day dance organization, I was able to focus on the crucial issue of statewide arts funding equity. I had been a cultural activist in Oakland to garner municipal support for ECAC, but now my activism opened out to the state of California, and even the growing *national* multicultural arts movement.

The year 1986 was a transitional one, not only because I resigned as director of ECAC but also because, after four years at the Jenny Lind Hall, the next venue transition for ECAC became necessary. Oakland's so-called "renaissance" was pushing downtown real estate rentals beyond what any non-profit organization could afford, bringing us the now familiar news: the Jenny Lind Hall was being sold. This time it was not a white man in a suit bringing the news but a group of Asian men who announced to ECAC that they had bought "our" building and they were going to turn it into a Buddhist temple. The ECAC board of directors had been discussing the possibility of our facility being sold, and some of them had been attending Oakland City Council meetings, with discussions about the large building that had been an old YWCA at 1428 Alice Street, near the corner of Fourteenth Street, becoming a city-owned arts facility. That building functioned as a six-story residence facility, where the top three floors were rental apartments and the first three floors had large wide-open spaces that were not in use. It was a perfect space for a multitenancy arts center, and community arts administrators and city officials began to focus on the facility as a possible venue for the arts. An Alice Arts Center could actually be the solution to several Oakland arts organizations' space problems, potentially becoming a cultural boon to the city-focused renaissance.

Throughout that year many arts groups had been in discussion with city officials individually, but because we had already formed the Oakland Arts Alliance, this group became the perfect arts lobbying collective. With the movers and shakers of our respective boards of directors, we tried to convince the City of Oakland to buy the building on Alice Street and rent the first three floors to arts organizations to create a real *center* for the arts in Oakland. Competition became fierce for which organizations would be the main "anchor tenants" of the building. Although there were many small rooms for office spaces, there were only three large spaces for classes and performances; therefore only three organizations could be the *primary* tenants. Because I had assembled an influential board before I stepped down as director of ECAC, our board members lobbied hard for ECAC to become an Alice Arts Center anchor tenant, and we won. Everybody's Creative Arts Center, along with the Oakland Ensemble Theater, the only professional black theater company in the city, and the Oakland Ballet became the three anchor tenants, and in early 1987, ECAC moved to the second floor of Oakland's new Alice Arts Center.

Over the next year, the city began to renovate the first three floors. Our second-floor large and small studios were sanded, and theatrical lighting and pipes for wings were hung in the large space, allowing us to have our usual two-studio format, with the large studio doubling as our performance space. The major renovation took place on the first floor, where a two-hundred-seat theater was created for the Oakland Ensemble Theater. The third-floor studios were designated for the Oakland Ballet, and we all moved into "The Alice" with renewed hope for our place in the development of Oakland as a major center for the arts. Offices were given to Dimensions Dance Theater and Concepts Cultural Gallery, the jazz music organization originally cofounded by Kimathi and his old college friend Edsel Matthews. "Concepts," as we called it, had begun on the third floor of the Jenny Lind Hall and had quickly made a name for itself in the world of small-venue jazz cafés. Kimathi, however, only lasted as its codirector for one year, and by the time the organization moved into the Alice, Edsel Matthews was its sole director.

In 1987, when ECAC moved into the Alice Arts Center, the organization was celebrating its tenth anniversary, and the board decided that we needed to commemorate that milestone with a performance spectacle. On September 12, 1987, ECAC held its "A Salute to Dance: The Celebration of Life," the tenth-anniversary gala at Oakland's Calvin Simmons Theatre in the Henry J. Kaiser Convention Center. We went back to the venue where we had produced the last few of our annual Multicultural Festivals of Dance and Music before we had begun to focus on the CDT Dance Company. This gala anniversary event also served to announce the next phase of the organization by officially changing the name of the non-profit to "Citi-Centre Dance Theatre." We felt the concept of "Everybody's" was a 1960s and 1970s appellation that spoke to our beginnings in social change. Now we were in the phase of *being* that change, which the organization's mission had accomplished: we had now become a major arts organization in Oakland. We identified with Oakland's bourgeoning renaissance, and the organization was now taking the name of its resident dance company—CitiCentre Dance Theatre (CDT). We used the tenth-anniversary event to make this name change announcement to our community.

A Salute to Dance: The Celebration of Life functioned to position the organization that I had founded as a major player in Oakland and the entire Bay Area. Mayor Lionel Wilson gave the renamed CDT organization a city proclamation, calling September 12, 1987, "Everybody's Creative Arts Center—CitiCentre Dance Theatre Day." The 8 × 10 glossy audience program proclaimed the organization's new thrust:

Everybody's Creative Arts Center has served the community well during the last ten years and looks to a second decade of providing quality professional programming to meet the needs of the community while advancing the cultural life which is uniquely Oakland's. Our specific mission in the coming decade is to foster the development of contemporary Black American dance and to create employment and training opportunities for professional as well as emerging Bay Area dancers. In order to more appropriately reflect this commitment to the development of dance art, and to reflect our commitment to a very contemporary aesthetic, The Board of Directors has selected to change the center's name to CitiCentre Dance Theatre. Look for our new name and logo starting October 1st.

The tenth-anniversary event, which was professionally produced by Ronda White-Warner, who had been on the staff at Festival at the Lake, had civic and corporate sponsors and donors, as well a "Honorary Gala Advisory Committee" that included Benny Ambush, director of Oakland Ensemble Theater; C. K. Ladzekpo, my former Ghanaian dance teacher (chapter 5); activist Angela Davis, who had become a dance student in our classes, including my own; Congressman Ron Dellums; Danny Glover; Alice Walker; Lenny Sloan; County of Alameda supervisor Doris Ward; and others.

We also used the gala event to honor particular long-term dance artists who had created the black dance legacy in the Bay Area. We paid tribute to Ruth Beckford, Nontsizi Cayou, our own Leon Jackson and Malonga Casquelourd, tap and jazz dance teacher Geraldyne Washington, and myself as founder of the organization. We even had a special presentation to noted Hollywood dancer-choreographer Paula Kelly, who came from Los Angeles just for her award. Between these acknowledgments of the black dance legacy, dance performances were showcased, including two of my works, *The Journey* and a new non-narrative ballet called *Streams,* danced by the CDT Company. There was also choreography by Hassan al Falak and Latina choreographer Priscilla Regalado, and a performance by Malonga's Fua Dia Congo Dance Company. The grand finale featured award-winning Oakland vocalist Linda Tillery with her band, bringing all the artists onto the stage as one big artistic family.

The gala event also provided the opportunity to announce our new administrative structure. The job that I had been performing for nine years needed to be divided into several different positions. Linda Goodrich was introduced as the new artistic director of the CDT organization, having started as student, then becoming a popular teacher, and finally cofounding our CDT company. Angela Johnson had now become solely program director, with noted Bay Area arts administrator Lynn Rogers as general manager. Our business manager, Barbara Martin, resigned, and Kate McKean became ECAC operations manager, while Ursula Smith was hired as registrar and volunteer coordinator over the continuing work-study program. In subsequent years there were a series of executive directors of the organization, including dancer-administrator Karen Ransom, Aishah Bashir, and eventually, in the early 2000s, Ursula Smith, who had served the organization in so many previous capacities. The former Everybody's Creative Arts Center became CitiCentre Dance Theatre, with a five-member administrative staff, a donation of Mac computers from the Apple Corporation, a powerful board of directors that had negotiated our position into the Alice Arts Center, and the regional clout to bring the entire Bay Area dance community together to commemorate our position in the development of black dance in northern California for our tenth anniversary. Ten years of hard, grinding work in Oakland community arts had paid off.

Part of the reason I was so driven in my work ethic is that I simply never wanted to be a "starving artist." To have a regular paycheck, I realized, I had to learn grantsmanship, marketing, administrative staff coordination, board development, and long-range planning, all in the name of community arts, while dancing, teaching, and choreographing. The conjunction of these multiple roles is what it took to build an arts institution, around which my and others' art could flourish within an inequitable dance field. Instead of assimilating into the larger Bay Area dance community, I built my own arts institution—using models like the Rod Rodgers Dance Company (chapter 3) and the School of Music, Dance, Drama at the University of Ghana, Legon (chapter 5). I had built a community dance center that was now strong enough to survive without me, and with my developed administrative skills I moved on to my Expansion Arts Services consultancy.

Teaching, Choreographing, and Administrating at Stanford University

But even while executive artistic director of ECAC, I felt I needed a larger salary than the organization could provide, so I took a part-time adjunct dance position teaching at Stanford University. Located in the city of Palo

Alto approximately fifty miles from Oakland on the peninsula, in what became the home of hi-tech Silicon Valley, Stanford was a one-hour-and-fifteen-minute drive that I did two to three days a week, all while running ECAC. Teaching dance at Stanford, I developed important artistic and academic relationships that would last a lifetime. Stanford also would help hone my intellect and motivate me to go to graduate school, which would eventually determine my future academic second career.

As I already had taught dance at Stanford in 1974 and 1975 before going to Ghana (chapter 4), I was acclimated to the commute and its Ivy League of the West university culture. So in fall 1981 I accepted a new Stanford teaching position, with my appointment again in the Committee on Black Performing Arts (CBPA) and the Stanford Dance Division. John Cochran had left Stanford, and his protégée Sandra Richards, having received her Ph.D. in dramatic literature in 1979 from Stanford, was now assistant professor in the Stanford Drama Department and director of CBPA. Again my job description was to teach two dance classes per quarter and provide necessary choreography for any dramatic productions directed by the CBPA director. As Sandra usually directed a play only once a year, the majority of my time was spent in the Dance Division, which then was under the Athletics Department in Roble Gymnasium, just yards away from Harmony House, the home of CBPA near the Stanford Black Community Services Center.

The director of the Dance Division was the late Susan Cashion (1943–2013), a Ph.D. in anthropology who had also become a specialist in Mexican and Latin American dance along with modern dance. As a white artist-scholar, she was focused on Mexican folk dance and founded Ballet Folklórico de Stanford in 1972, the first resident student Mexican folklórico troupe in the United States. Susan was a special person who truly believed in the equality of human cultures, hence her choreographic focus on dance south of the U.S. border. Like me, she believed in dance not merely as steps and movements but as embodied representation of rich cultural legacies that expressed the adaptation of a people's social and political history. She was pleased to have me in the Dance Division and accorded me all the courtesies of the full-time dance faculty, whose appointments were lodged directly in the Dance Division itself.

Even though I was not a scholar, she immediately recognized our common interest in joining practice and theory—dance and its cultural context—and we exploited that mutual interest in several concerts and artistic projects. Our first joint dance program was in April 1982, "Moving Together: A Montage of Afro-American, Jazz, Modern, and Traditional Mexican Folk Dances." The title of the concert—Moving Together—said it all: our choreography of black dance, Mexican folk, modern, and jazz was performed by our dance students, mingling a representative potpourri of American culture, just as I had at ECAC in Oakland. The Stanford Dance Division was the kind of dance department that I could invest in because Susan Cashion's curricular focus reflected inclusiveness and respect for all forms of dance.

As a result, Susie's and my artistic relationship and personal friendship developed over my twelve years at Stanford. I slowly became more involved with the departmental decision-making like the full-fledged faculty members, furthering my choreography through participation in the Dance Division's yearly concerts. Susie and I often shared dinners at her home, where we discussed our mutual priorities for dance in higher education. Susan Cashion's visions set the tone for the entire dance program, the faculty members of which were modern dancers Tony Crammer and Diane Franks, ballroom and social dance teacher Richard Powers, and dance historian and theorist Janice Ross, who was also then the *Tribune* dance critic in Oakland.

Two major dance projects, spearheaded by Susan Cashion, and with which I was involved, showed her commitment to the African diaspora within Latin America. In 1993, the Stanford Dance Division hosted the famous rumba ensemble Los Muñequitos de Matanzas for two days that brought Cubans and Cuban dance enthusiasts from around California. It even drew the San Francisco–based master *rumbero*, the late Francisco Aguabella (1925–2010), who played with Los Muñequitos, making the entire two-day residency a historic event. I was able to hone my rumba dance skills by dancing directly with these master Cuban dancers touring the Bay Area.

But two years earlier, a longer Cuban dance and music Stanford residency was even more influential. In 1991, Danza Nacional de Cuba, the main Cuban contemporary dance school located in Havana, which blends modern dance and Afro-Cuban folkloric dance styles, was in residence at Stanford for a two-week intensive. As dance anthropologist Yvonne Daniel assessed: "This occasion marked a historic meeting of Cuban dance and music specialists from the western United States who teach Cuban dance/ music. . . . All the Cuban dance and music specialists were there from the Bay Area and nationally."[25] This Cuban dance residency was the culmination of a year and half of Susie's work with U.S.-Cuban immigration and university policies, becoming the first dance exchange with the United States since the Cuban Revolution.

Cuban folkloric dances, like U.S. African American social dances, are retentions and revisions of African movement styles, including the Central African congo dance with its pelvis- and shoulder-centered movements. Always being the amateur dance researcher, during the residency I interviewed Manuel "Manolo" Vasquez Robaína, the director of the company and school.[26] Manolo gave me several insights into Cuban modern dance as a blending of Graham technique with Cuban folkloric roots. As Manolo compared the African movement contributions to Cuban contemporary dance with its basis in Graham Technique, the question became, What is cause and effect? Searching for the answer, Gottschild has masterfully noted: "A home truth is described as 'an indisputable fact or basic truth, especially one whose accuracy may cause discomfort or embarrassment.' . . . Africanisms are home truths in European American culture."[27] Did Martha Graham's technical emphasis in the pelvis and solar plexus for her expressive and percussive contractions evolve from cultural "permission" already lodged contextually in U.S. society's black *social* dance vocabulary?

The dancers and musicians of Danza Nacional de Cuba's residency at Stanford with their Cuban modern dance provided another example of the power of black dance and the implications of its appropriations throughout the Americas. Gottschild recognizes that U.S. modern dance pioneers were not unaware of these borrowings. In building her argument she used an assessment about nonwhite artists by Louis Horst, Graham's composer and piano accompanist, who had this to say: "'The primitive did not create works of art, but magic weapons.' Like his peers and colleagues and in keeping with the tenor of his times, Horst believes that these appropriations are not really appropriations . . . but, instead, an elevation of the status of primitive raw materials to a higher, cultured, European aesthetic standard of excellence."[28] As I analyzed in chapter 5, Africanist dance has been viewed through this racist evolutionary perception, partially precipitating the cultural and historical revisionism in several black dance initiatives in which I was involved in the late 1980s and early 1990s (discussed below).

Susan Cashion always showed her commitment for creating these kinds of cultural dance exchanges, such as Danza National de Cuba residency and the Los Muñequitos workshop, which demonstrated the rich Africanist dance material in Latin America and helped dispel the long-held myths about Africanist dance styles.

The other side of my Stanford position was the Committee on Black Performing Arts, where I played the roles of choreographer, program coordinator, and eventually acting director, utilizing both my artistic and administrative skills. One of my most memorable choreographic collaborations with Sandra Richards, as the CBPA director, was a Nigerian play by Femi Osofisan in spring 1987, *Farewell to a Cannibal Rage*. Sandra had made contemporary Nigerian dramatic theater her academic research emphasis, and Osofisan's work in particular. She eventually published *Ancient Songs Set Ablaze: The Theatre of Femi Osofisan* in 1996. My Stanford position stimulated my curiosity about academic research and exposed me to several seminal intellectuals such as Richards and Osofisan.

To choreograph *Farewell* I had to become conversant with Nigerian myth and ritual as metaphorically used by Osofisan, as well as with an overview of Nigerian postindependence history. The time I had spent in Ghana and the side trip I had taken to Nigeria gave me insights into the cultural underpinnings of the play. My personal life experiences and academic appointments were informing each other in practical ways, and now, at forty years old, I could easily recognize that synergy in my career. Sandra and I worked very well together in rehearsals, where I focused primarily on *narrative* choreography, providing the student actors with a conceptual movement vocabulary that worked for their character development, as well as actual choreography for scenes that necessitated dance. Working on this production allowed me to reconnect with my own West African sojourn ten years earlier, and I was able to meet Osofisan when he came to the premiere of *Farewell*, and directly receive his feedback and appreciation of my choreography.

I also played an administrative role with CBPA as program coordinator starting in 1986, the same year that I resigned as executive artistic director of ECAC. I then began juggling teaching in the Dance Division, administratively supporting Sandra Richards as program coordinator of CBPA, rehearsing and performing with CDT in Oakland, and continuing to serve on the ECAC board of directors. I was stretched thin but thrived on this level of career activity because it was all about the promotion of black dance and culture that had become my life's mission, and CBPA had become an integral part of that mission.

When I assumed the position of program coordinator of CBPA, we began to plan even more relevant programing. To accommodate more administrative activity we obtained more funding to hire an office manager, a position that was filled by East Palo activist Elena Becks, who became an integral part of the CBPA operations. We tried to create a sense of the history of CBPA with the entirety of 1991 becoming our fifteenth-anniversary year. There was a Meyer Library exhibit of CBPA history, as well as off-campus excursions for students, including a trip to see the American Conservatory Theater's production of August Wilson's *Fences* in San Francisco's Curran Theater. That was the same venue where I had performed in *Show Boat* as an undergraduate nineteen years earlier (chapter 1).

During my tenure as program coordinator of CBPA I created several new projects. In 1990 I founded the *Black Arts Quarterly* newsletter to communicate the purpose of CBPA and its yearly projects. In later years the newsletter became a major black literary and cultural voice edited by students, but during my tenure as editor, I articulated the history of CBPA that had gotten lost. For example, the winter 1991 issue recapped the 1987–88 CBPA school year, when we initiated the first statewide black theater conference in ten years called "Black Theatre: Moving Toward the 21st Century." I wrote in my journal after the conference: *It was one of those monumental tasks that took me to the precipice, the brink of exhaustion. It is an impossible job that so many small black arts operations (be it community or academia) attempt with so little staff and funds; yet somehow pull it off with some modicum of quality and success.* We had convened some of the main players in the black theater movement in California, such as Luther James and C. Bernard Jackson from Los Angeles, and Benny Ambush, and Stanley Williams and Quentin Easter of the Lorraine Hansberry Theatre in the Bay Area.

In my twelve years at Stanford University, I was stimulated by black intellectuals who served as role models and, without my realizing it, kindled my desire to go to graduate school to hone my own intellect for an eventual academic career. World-renowned sociologist, anthropologist, and Pan-Africanist St. Clare Drake was finishing his long, distinguished career at Stanford, and I was able to meet him while attending his retirement reception. Historian Clayborne Carson initiated the Kings Papers Project while I was there, having been selected by Coretta Scott King to edit and publish Dr. Martin Luther King Jr.'s papers. Spanish professor Sylvia Wynter was a great inspiration as an academic, who simply had me in awe with her ability to connect philosophy, history, anthropology, biology, and African diaspora studies in groundbreaking lectures. I also worked closely with Sylvia Wynter on her 1973 play *Masquerade,* which Sandra Richards directed in 1984, allowing me to learn much about the history and characters of Caribbean carnivals.

But it was a January 20, 1987, Stanford symposium commemorating the newly established Martin Luther King Jr.'s birthday as a national holiday that became a major Stanford event where 1980s black intellectual and political activism came most into relief. The event was meant as an acknowledgment of white historian David Garrow's book *Bearing the Cross: Martin Luther King Jr. and the Southern Christian Leadership Conference* (1986). Poet June Jordan, then professor at SUNY Stony Brook, was a respondent to Garrow's reading from his eight-hundred-page opus that had won the Pulitzer Price for biography that year. The Stanford event became a historic black intellectual event with Angela Davis and Alice Walker in the audience, along with Bay Area black television journalist Belva Davis. When Garrow espoused the main tenet of his new award-winning book—Martin Luther King Jr. was a reluctant leader who could have been replaced by any number of other leaders, such as Andrew Young or James Abernathy—I remember a controversy occurring. Garrow argued that it was the times and the Civil Rights movement itself that had created the social change, and not necessarily the persona of Rev. Martin Luther King.

June Jordan, as well as her black sister colleagues in the audience, became worthy intellectual adversaries of Garrow's argument, deftly refuting his stated thesis. Jordan analyzed Garrow's "the leader versus the movement" dichotomy as a misreading of the obvious reality of the symbiotic relationship between the two. Angela Davis added her challenge by questioning the ethics and validity of Garrow's FBI wire-tapping sources underlying the proof of his thesis. Then Alice Walker administered the final rejoinder with *her* definitive personal account of why *she* went back to the South and risked her life to work in the Civil Rights movement. In her typical soft-spoken style, she added, "It was not because of Andy Young, but because Martin Luther King said come back and work." Even I ventured to add to the debate by articulating a cultural argument, emphasizing black history as indeed *American* history, and that the sooner historians acknowledged that fact, the sooner the entire country would be able to embrace King as one of our greatest American leaders and thinkers of the twentieth century.

This was an important Stanford public debate in the mid-1980s, after the fierce battle since the late 1970s to establish MLK's birthday as a national holiday. David Garrow did not stand a chance with his thesis that diminished the importance of Martin Luther King Jr. to the Civil Rights movement with that convocation of black female intellectuals gathered at Stanford to commemorate the new hard-won national holiday. In the era of Reaganomics, the 1980s were becoming a fight against regressing from the enforcement of the previous era's civil rights laws, as well as an escalation of the South African anti-apartheid divestment movement in major cities across the country. Stanford, as the private Ivy League academic institution of the West, was an incubator of black intellectual production with black studies and human rights issues at the center of the public discourse.

My administrative position shifted again in the winter 1989 quarter to Acting Director of CBPA, as Sandra Richards moved on to become associate professor of theatre and African American studies at Northwestern University. This put me at the helm of CBPA just at the time of what I assessed as my major accomplishment during my twelve-year tenure at Stanford: the historic May 1989 Katherine Dunham Residency. This project included Miss Dunham teaching dance, accompanied by the famous Senegalese drummer Mor Thiam, and anthropology classes, a Dunham "Stanford Centennial Symposium" coordinated by Yvonne Daniel, a major public lecture–demonstration named "A Walk Through Katherine Dunham's Life" at Memorial Auditorium, public community classes in the neighboring community of East Palo Alto, and an exhibit of Dunham's books and costumes in Meyer Library (figure 16). This Stanford Dunham Residency was a major event that took two years of fundraising, as well as organizing Stanford professors and staff, along with community leaders, as an official Dunham Residency Planning Committee. The 1989 Stanford Dunham Residency became a major one-month event that galvanized the entire campus and surrounding community and led to Stanford awarding Miss Dunham a writing fellowship the next year, which I also coordinated.

My acting directorship of CBPA lasted during the national search for a new drama professor to replace Sandra Richards, which eventually brought noted theater scholar Harry Elam in the 1990–91 school year. One of Elam's first administrative efforts, as the new CBPA director, was the East Palo Alto Project, a research-to-performance design that investigated the history and evolution of the city of East Palo Alto. The research led to two original plays written by an African American and a Chicana playwright—Charles "OyamO" Gordon and Cherríe Moraga. The East Palo Alto project became very important in bridging the elite Stanford campus and the wealthy city of Palo Alto with its adjacent poor black and Third World community of East Palo Alto. The East Palo Alto project was a success, with the plays being performed on campus, and an eventual video documentary of the entire East Palo Alto Project as a model in university-community relations.

My artistic and intellectual experiences at Stanford inevitably led to my decision to attend graduate school, and in spring 1991 I left my Stanford administrative position at CBPA to pursue a master's degree in dance ethnology. I wrote the following in the winter 1991 *Black Arts Quarterly*:

> Although I am remaining on the Stanford dance faculty and the CBPA Steering Committee, I am leaving this administrative position to pursue graduate studies in anthropology. Feeling the panic of age, I am beginning my academic program in the Spring Semester [at S.F. State University]. Why anthropology? When I exam my approach to the teaching, performing, and choreographing of dance, it has always been from a strong cultural basis. The relationship of dance to culture and society's development (or lack of it) in relationship to its attitude toward the non-verbal expression of movement has always been key to me. I look forward to combining anthropological cultural theory with dance theory in relation to the cultures of the African diaspora.[29]

In reality I was following in Katherine Dunham's footsteps. I wanted to find the late twentieth-century marriage between dance and culture, the way she had explored the connection in the 1930s during American anthropology's initial developments at the University of Chicago.

I entered San Francisco State University's Special Major program, positioned in the Graduate Studies Office, in the fall 1990 semester. That major allowed me to combine anthropology, ethnic studies, and dance as a uniquely self-designed master's program. This was ideal for me as an older graduate student who knew exactly what I wanted to study to enhance my established career. Anthropology became my major subject, with 75 percent of my coursework in that department; 15 percent of my studies in the

College of Ethnic Studies, which had now become the prototype of ethnic studies in the country; and 10 percent in the Dance Department, where I took Jerry Duke's dance ethnology and labanotation, and Malonga Casquelourd's Congolese class that included lectures on Congo culture, dance, and songs. Professors like Bernard Wong in anthropology, Wade Nobles, Jose Cuellar, and the late Laura Head (1958–2013) in ethnic studies were all key in helping me develop my theoretical perspectives in my chosen interdisciplinary field.

I graduated with my master's degree in the spring of 1993 and resigned my dance position at Stanford after the fall of 1993. Kimathi and I had been planning a major life transition since buying property on the Big Island of Hawai'i in 1990. After resigning from my Stanford teaching position, we moved to Hawai'i, where I would continue my graduate education, eventually receiving my doctorate in American studies in 1999 from the University of Hawai'i–Manoa. Considering my twelve years at Stanford, along with the previous two years in the 1970s, I wrote the following about my leaving the university in the winter 1994 issue of *Black Arts Quarterly*:

> Spanning three CBPA directors and many changes in the Dance Division since 1974 has given me a breadth of vision of Stanford. I've always known that to the greater university, a *dance lecturer* is a rather non-entity. But that never bothered me, because being black, a woman, and a dancer, one learns early on about the vicissitudes of being a triple minority. I have developed thick skin and the strength to be inner-directed, following my own path. Now that my husband and I move on to our lives in the Hawaiian Islands, I thank Stanford for the opportunity to hone my skills. Hopefully in that honing I have contributed something to the quality of our lives on campus and a better understanding of ourselves.[30]

I was only partially aware then that Stanford University had actually prepared me for my future in academia, to which I would transition after my artistic career as a dancer six years later.

Run-Out Artistic Projects, 1981–1993

During the time that I was directing ECAC and teaching at Stanford, I also participated in several artistic projects that are important to explore because of their significance to my artistic career and the field of black performance. I call them "run-out projects" because they were temporary artistic ventures that interrupted my job duties at both institutions. At the same time they furthered my artistic career while linking previous parts of my personal life. They also brought more prestige to those institutions where I was employed.

Several run-out projects between 1981 and 1985 reconnected me with my work and friendship with Ntozake Shange. Ntozake (Zake) called me in April 1981 to see if I would come to New York and perform in a new performance piece she had written called *Mouths: A Daughter's Geography*, about a black couple who journeys through the African diaspora reflecting on particular sites of black history, while they also work out issues in their personal relationship. It was to be a one-week intensive of all-day and night rehearsals with Ed Mock, my former S.F. dance teacher (chapter 1), and Elvia Marta, my friend and ECAC dance instructor who also performed with Zake in my *The Evolution of Black Dance* school programs back in 1974 (chapter 4). To convince me, Zake added that *Mouths: A Daughter's Geography* would be directed by Thulani Davis, choreographed by Diane McIntyre, and premiering two nights at the famous experimental performance venue the Kitchen in Soho. And for good measure, she revealed that she would be playing the female lead herself, partnered by Hollywood actor Richard Lawson as the boyfriend/lover/travel partner. I immediately said, "Come on Zake, you know I can't turn this down." Although it was to be one month before ECAC's Mixed Bag II Faculty Concert, where I was premiering my newly choreographed *Feminine Trinity* with an original score played by live musicians, I said "yes" and was off to New York to dance in a historic Ntozake Shange premiere at the Kitchen.

To premiere a full-evening production with only one week of rehearsals, even with the professionals Zake had assembled, was ambitious, but we pulled it off royally. We rarely slept that week, with Richard and Zake rehearsing their lines and scenes at her apartment all day long, while Ed, Elvia, and I rehearsed at the Kitchen with Diane the entire day. When we three dancers arrived back at Zake's apartment late in the evening, she and Richard were usually rehearsing feverishly in the next room, and we fell asleep to them drilling lines from the play. By Wednesday, Thulani pulled us all together in the evenings at the Kitchen to see the totality of what she had, and it was very rough at first. But by Friday April 24, the premiere day, she had a production ready for the sold-out two days of performances, with hundreds of people turned away.

Diane McIntyre was a sensitive choreographer whom we all respected, and we loved the duets and trios that she created for us. She choreographed an especially poignant solo for Ed Mock playing Jean-Jacques Dessalines, who led the Haitian Revolution to victory after the deportation to France of Toussaint L'Ouverture. Zake titled that particular poem "Une Nuit Noire en Haiti," and Ed danced it fiercely to Lester Bowie's "The F Troop Rides Again." Ed Mock died in May 1986, and Zake paid a tribute to him in *Attitude: The Dancers' Monthly*: "One of the most inspiring and encouraging teachers of contemporary Afro-American dance I have ever had, whose choreography was intellectually, politically, and aesthetically exhilarating, Ed Mock's death is a stunning bombardment of my senses just as his classes were."[31] His teaching had been the same for me in the late 1960s when I was contemplating a dance career, and he helped me make that decision to become a dancer. Dancing with Ed Mock at the Kitchen in 1981 was my last dance experience with him, and Zake made it happen.

In the 1980s I became known in the Bay Area as a choreographer and director of Ntozake Shange plays, a reputation that grew from my work with the Lorraine Hansberry Theatre (LHT), the premier black theater company in San Francisco. Because of my close personal relationship with Zake and past work with her poetry (chapter 4), Stanley Williams (1950–2010), the artistic director of LHT, hired me as a choreographer for several of Ntozake's work that he staged. The first was a premiere of Shange's *Boogie Woogie Landscapes* in January-February 1984, directed by Williams and with original music composed by Idris Ackamoor, the saxophonist who was the cofounder with Kimathi of the Pyramids.

The following year I choreographed Ntozake's well-known *Spell #7* for LHT in February 1985. This Shange play is about a group of black actors in an after-hours bar processing what it means to be black in contemporary American theater, complete with a looming blackface minstrel mask as background prop. Stanley hired Keryl E. McCord as director and me as choreographer, and I used my research from *The Evolution of Black Dance*, particularly the cakewalk dance associated with blackface minstrelsy. The dance had survived from a slave plantation dance of derision to a turn-of-the-twentieth-century Victorian-era high-society social dance craze.

My choreographic experience with Ntozake's plays paved the way for commissions to actually *direct* two of her theater pieces, with which I already had extensive experience. In 1988, San Francisco State University's Department of Theatre Arts hired me to direct and choreograph *for colored girls Who Have Considered Suicide When the Rainbow Is Enuf.* Larry Eilenberg, then chair of the department, knew of my history with Zake and this particular play, and felt I was the best to direct it, giving me the opportunity to implement my own vision for the choreopoems, having been involved in so many aspects of the play from its Bay Area inception in 1973 to its Broadway run in 1977. I strayed away from the script, breaking up the poems assigned to one actor into more of a dialogue between several of the women. Hollywood actor Gina Ravera, who would later star in films like *Soul Food* (1997) and *The Great Debaters* (2007), was an undergraduate in theater at S.F. State at the time and played the Lady in Red. I also had the pleasure of casting and working with Dominique DiPrima, the daughter of famed writers Amiri Baraka and Diane DiPrima, and who is now the host of the early-morning talk radio show *The Front Page* on Los Angeles radio station KHLH. *For colored girls* won the Theatre Arts Department's "Best Play" of the season that year, allowing me to come full circle with Zake's best-known play.

In the summer of 1985 I directed a second play of Ntozake's with which I already had experience: a new version of the 1981 play *Mouths: A Daughter's Geography*, renamed now as *From Okra to Greens: A Different Kinda Love Story*. Ntozake called me and asked me if I would direct and choreograph the play for the University of Mississippi's Festival of Southern Theatre. Zake was sick and begged me to take the job, saying she had complete confidence in me to direct the play. I consented and received a contract from the head of the Theatre Department at Ole Miss, with a significant fee and all expenses paid. I agreed with apprehension, because although I was born in Texas, as a black person I had never been to the Deep South, which in the collective black consciousness is associated with deep terror and fear.

The two and a half weeks I spent rehearsing *From Okra to Greens* became my first and only experience with the university where James Meredith became the first black student to be enrolled under federal court order just twenty-three years earlier in 1962.[32] During the summer of 1985 the university was trying to show how far it had come from its racist past by holding a Toni Morrison festival with a conference on her novels, and the Theatre Department was a part of that reconciliation gesture by including an Ntozake Shange play in their summer offerings. This is the situation in which I found myself that summer of 1985 in Oxford, Mississippi, where they still held an annual Ku Klux Klan parade.

Like the 1981 New York rehearsal period of *Mouths*, the short rehearsal period necessitated rapid auditions and casting, along with a marathon of day and evening rehearsals. Thank goodness the casting call was regional and not limited to the small town of Oxford or even the university theater department. To have a polished production within two weeks, I worked two actors and five dancers harder than they had ever been worked before, with a rehearsal schedule from 9:00 a.m. to 10:00 p.m., with breaks only for meals.

On July 30 and August 1, 1985, *From Okra to Greens: A Different Kinda Love Story* was performed in Fulton Chapel on the University of Mississippi's campus. As I had come to suspect, the Oxford theatergoing audience was not ready for this deeply sensual and political African diasporic journey. They may accept the veiled homosexuality of Tennessee Williams or the surrealism with pastoral blacks of Oxford's own native son William Faulkner, but they had no real-world references for Ntozake's interrogation of a fully engaged worldly black couple, Okra and Greens, who were exploring the meaning of the Haitian Revolution in Port-au-Prince and engaged in the sensual revelry of Brazilian carnival in Rio de Janeiro. After intermission, half of the audience did not return for the second part. And once word spread, particularly about the last scene, "The Last Revolution" with all of the performers pointing fake wooden rifles at the audience in a fantasized guerilla war against the "reactionary worldwide exploiters of black people," our second night barely had an audience.

Kimathi arrived to meet me on the day of the last performance, and I remember feeling like he was my *black* knight in shining armor, coming to rescue me from the forces of evil. The very next day we left and went to New Orleans for a one-week vacation. I was so glad to get out of Oxford and to be in New Orleans, where black culture, though often exploited, was at least celebrated. I felt like I had come back to the light of day out of the forest of deep ignorance, from the real "heart of darkness."

Another run-out project of particular note during the 1980s was my choreographing of August Wilson's *Joe Turner's Come and Gone* for San Francisco's American Conservatory Theater (ACT). In January 1988 this classic of Wilson's ten-play cycle of black life in twentieth-century America premiered at the Curran Theater. ACT had contracted with the smaller Lorraine Hansberry Theater (LHT) to produce the play; this was the way the premier theater institution of the Bay Area was diversifying its organization in the 1980s. Claude Purdy, a longtime theater colleague of Wilson's, was hired to direct the play, and Stanley Williams of LHT suggested that I choreograph the production.

Choreographing *Joe Turner's Come and Gone*, a Wilson play taking place in the post-Reconstruction 1910s, was an opportunity for me to work with some of the best black actors in the business. The late Roscoe Lee Browne (1925–2007) played the part of Bynum Walker, a "conjure" man who is a freed slave from the South, while Anna Deavere Smith, then a celebrity faculty-member of the Stanford Drama Department whom I knew, played the part of Molly Cunningham, a young, strong, and independent woman, who does not believe in black spirituality. My job was to choreograph what Wilson called in the script directions a "Juba" dance, which was to take place in the kitchen of the boardinghouse where the itinerant wanderer, Harold Loomis, was briefly staying while looking for his wife, from whom he had been separated while serving a seven-year sentence on a chain gang. However, once I read the script and discussed it with Claude Purdy, I knew the scene around the kitchen table was actually supposed to be a "ring shout," a Christianized counterclockwise African ceremonial to call down the ancestral spirits. My job was to get the boardinghouse characters in the scene, who represented several black generations, to understand the meaning of a ring shout and to get their minds, bodies, and spirits to embody the old-time American revision of an African ancestor reverence ceremony. With some work I was able to get the actors to reenact an old southern ring shout that became the transformative crescendo of the entire play.

August Wilson (1945–2005) himself attended the postpremiere reception, held on the actual stage of the Curran Theatre. This man, who had won two Pulitzer Prizes and one Tony Award for several of his plays, was standing off alone from the crowd at this own reception for *Joe Turner's* San Francisco premiere. I walked over to him, introduced myself, and told him what an honor it was to work on his play. I also was bold enough to tell him that the scene I choreographed was a ring shout and not a juba dance, and that I was very familiar with both from my black dance research. He thanked me for my knowledge and correction, said he agreed, and told me that he was glad I was able to work on *Joe Turner's Come and Gone*, to capture what he wanted from that scene. Our brief interchange at the reception was professionally validating.

Later in 1993, before moving to Hawai'i, I choreographed another play for ACT called *Pecong* that Benny Ambush, from the old Oakland Ensemble Theater, directed. This Caribbean-like production had many dance scenes, for which I hired real dancers to supplement the cast, and I won a Bay Area Critics Circle Award for Choreography that year for my work in that play. These kinds of dance experiences within theatrical dramas utilized my research knowledge of black dance, along with my choreographic skill, and the synergy between the two built my larger artistic reputation in the San Francisco–Oakland Bay Area.

Dance Black America, 1983

Looking back, one run-out performance project was a turning point in my career: Dance Black America, a 1983 landmark dance festival at the Brooklyn Academy of Music (BAM) held April 21–24. Dance Black America presaged the way I was destined to make my mark in black dance and culture. Those four days at BAM became a virtual Who's Who in black dance with all the living legends—Katherine Dunham, Pearl Primus, Talley Beatty, the Copasetics hoofers; the established choreographers—Alvin Ailey, Donald McKayle, Charles Moore, Rod Rodgers, Eleo Pomare, Louis Johnson; and the then current trendsetters—Garth Fagan, Blondell Cummings, Diane McIntyre, and New York's breakdancing Rock Steady Crew. And there I was, Halifu Osumare, dancing in the festival with Leon Jackson from Oakland's CitiCentre Dance Theatre.

Dance Black America, dubbed "A Landmark Festival of 300 Years of Black Dance," was presented by BAM and the State University of New York, and produced by Mikki Shepard (until recently the executive producer of the Apollo Theater). BAM hired Shepard as festival director and Harold Pierson (1934–2000), former artistic director of the Philadelphia Dance Company, as artistic director of the dance programs featuring the major dance companies. My friend Lenwood "Leni" Sloan was the conceiver and artistic director of the Street and Social Dance concert, in which I performed.[33]

Besides being able to hobnob with all of my dance heroes, what made this festival so influential on my future career was the fact that it was so comprehensive, including master dance classes and panel discussions. Dance classes were taught by Walter Nicks, Lavinia Williams, Chuck Davis, Fred Benjamin, Honi Coles, Henry Le Tang, and Professor Albert Opoku from the SMDD in Ghana (chapter 5), then teaching at SUNY, Brockport.

The foremost scholars of black dance and culture—Zita Allen, Joe Nash, William Moore, Bernice Johnson Reagon, Sally Banes, VèVè Clark, Brenda Dixon Gottschild, and Julinda Lewis—were in discussions with the choreographers. The Dance Black America humanities component was impressively strong, with the festival booklet containing essays by Leonard Goines, Julinda Lewis, Sally Banes, and Zita Allen. This was the first time that I had been a part of a black dance program that convened dance with humanities in a thorough way, and this fascinated me. It planted an internal seed that would eventually allow me to start my own comprehensive black dance initiative by the end of the decade.

There were two different dance concerts on BAM's Opera House stage with all the recognized concert dance companies, Program A and B, as well as the Street and Social Dance concert by Leni Sloan as Program C, presented on the adjacent Playhouse stage. Leon and I danced in Program C, performing choreography by Leni, whose connection to the Bay Area was responsible for us being a part of the historic dance event. We performed his reconstructed nineteenth- and turn-of-the-twentieth-century period dances: the *Juba* solo by Leon, and the *Cakewalk* duet by both of us. Thus, the Bay Area was represented in a major way at this landmark black dance festival through our participation.

Dance Black America even impressed jaded New Yorkers, because never before had there been such an assemblage of all the notable black choreographers from several generations. The *New York Times* dance critic Jennifer Dunning assessed it this way: "The worlds of African ritual, New Orleans Congo Square, the modern dance studio and [rapper/graf artist] Fab 5 Freddy of street corner fame may seem very far apart in geography and time. But they are really one world, and that is the message of 'Dance Black America.' . . . The festival covers more than a century of black American dance and cultural history in performances and free lecture-demonstrations, films and seminars."[34] Dunning then quoted Harold Pierson (1934–2000): "What we're talking about is a continuum. . . . These powerful and pioneering dances all came from African roots. We're dealing with the soul of black people as it expresses itself in dance, and exploring what it means about the past, present and future, and the part it played in shaping American culture. The dances aren't an end in themselves, but part of a whole."[35] For me, the "whole" was in having so many of my dance heroes and heroines, as well as mentors with whom I had worked, from Professor Albert

Opoku to Rod Rodgers, all in one place. When I wasn't rehearsing for the cakewalk, I spent all of my time attending every dance class, performance, and panel discussion, while taking copious written and mental notes.

The panel discussions whetted my appetite for the many issues implicit in black dance that I would later frame in various ways as a producer-presenter, symposia convener, and scholar of black dance, which was destined to be the next stage of my career. Panels such as "The African Heritage" and "Dance as Liberation, Protest, Celebration and Affirmation" were provocative, paralleling the trajectory of my own dance career. Professor Opoku sat on the former panel and literally held court with his knowledge of dance cross-culturally. "The meaning of classicism is decorum and graciousness, and is not inherently connected to Europe; In Ghana we have court dances of the Ashanti that exhibit these same qualities," declared Opoku authoritatively. He also complicated the relationship between Africa and African American cultures with, "improvisation does not translate exactly across the Atlantic, because Africa always deals with structure." Here, I could have debated him, because jazz music, for example, does the same thing: riffing off of classically and *structurally* established melodies and harmonies.

But this was the exciting part about Dance Black America: the authorities were all together, with heated debates and attempted clarifications happening in the hallways and lobbies of the theaters. I gathered as many autographs in my copy of the glossy, bound program booklet as I could, and today it is one of my treasured archives. I vividly remember the second time I met Alvin Ailey, in the lobby of BAM's Opera Stage, where he sat on a lounge couch with dance students gathered all around him. I managed to wedge in and introduce myself, letting him know that I was a former student of his friend Nontsizi (Delores) Cayou, and that I had taken a jazz class with him in the late 1960s at S.F. State University (chapter 1). He remembered the class but not me. It didn't matter; I was sitting and talking casually with Alvin Ailey himself.

Bernice Johnson Reagon, the founder and then artistic director of Sweet Honey in the Rock a cappella singing group, as well as the then director of the program in black culture at the Smithsonian Institution,[36] was a major intellectual force on several panels. I remember my notes from her talk:

We [blacks] seek balance; we are not of this insanity. It's the cultural expression that allows us to manifest ourselves as a different people.

Don't get too far ahead of the spirits because they make the way; know where your foundation is, [like in music] the bottom is your ground, Mama Earth. In Black America the only way to hold a stance is too keep moving.

This was food for my soul, connecting my lifelong journey of dance and the arts as "cultural expression" to the foundation of black survival.

In covering the Dance Black America festival Dance critic Elizabeth Zimmer captured the overall sociopolitical context of black dance companies in the 1980s for the *Village Voice*:

> The major racial issue in the American theatrical tradition used to be stereotyping, as a look at the available collection of rare film clips so readily showed. Now it's more likely to be suppression, as scarce resources and prejudice squeeze blacks off the concert stage. Black critics and presenters, as well as a number of white writers and scholars, were vehement in their resolve to create an informed community which would appreciate and support these artists, traditional and contemporary.[37]

It was this kind of sociopolitical dance awareness that Dance Black America generated, inspiring me tremendously. This was a career turning point for me, allowing me to witness how thinking-conceptualizing and dancing-performing were cut from the same cloth in the context of black people's historical and contemporary dance. Zimmer alludes to this when she paraphrased one of Professor Opoku's pearls of wisdom: "They were reminded by Ghanaian artist Albert M. Opoku that in Africa, even statesmanship required the ability to dance."[38]

Between Leni's Street and Social Dance concert on the Playhouse stage and the concert dance classics featured on the Opera House stage, the breadth and depth of black dance was embodied and explored. There were excerpts from Ailey's *Revelations*, Katherine Dunham's *Shango*, Asadata Dafora's *Awassa Astrige/Ostrich*, Louis Johnson's *Forces in Rhythm*, Eleo Pomare's *Junkie* and *Las Desenamoradas*, Talley Beatty's *Road of the Phoebe Snow*, Rod Rodger's *Box*, Blondell Cummings's *Chicken Soup*, Diane McIntyre's *Etude in Free*, and the "coming out" performance of Garth Fagan's *From Before*, a study in blending modern and Africanist dance styles that became the festival's crowd-pleaser. I was able to see one of the Opera stage programs on Thursday, April 21, when our show was not being performed, and I sat in the audience in awe, viewing the dance classics that I had only read about.

Our Street and Social Dance program was as much a lesson in black culture behind the scenes as it was onstage. I hung out with Philadelphia's Arthur Hall and his Afro-American Ensemble, which performed a New Orleans second-line dance with a live brass band; with Chuck Davis's company members, who "tore up" the well-known West African dances *lenjengo* and *mandiani*; with Mama Lu Parks's lindy hoppers performing with the Copasetics; and with elder hoofer Chuck Green. It was also a treat to check out the early 1980s New York hip-hop generation: the Jazzy Double Dutch Jumpers, rappers Fab 5 Freddy and Afrika Islam, graffiti artist Dose, and the Rock Steady Crew breakers, about whom I would write fifteen years in the future. It was fun joking and improvising moves backstage with any number of these performers. The experience was black culture in motion, and one always had to be ready for a spontaneous moment in a dressing room or hallway. When the concert was in progress, Leni was constantly coming backstage telling us to keep our voices down and to be respectful of the current act on the Playhouse stage.

Within this rich black cultural context, Leon Jackson and I performed Leni Sloan's reconstructed turn-of-the-century exhibition cakewalk, "Darktown Stutter's Ball—Strut Miss Lizzie," and Leon, a nineteenth-century juba (forerunner to tap dance) originally performed by Master Juba, or William Henry Lane. Several other Everybody's Creative Arts Center artists were a part of the creative team creating these two dances: Linda Goodrich as labanotation consultant to Leni during rehearsals in Oakland, and lighting designer Stephanie Johnson, who came with us, designing the entire Street and Social Dance concert. ECAC had sent out an April 1 press release announcing: "ECAC Performance Unit Goes to New York for Dance Black America Festival." Although Leni had rehearsed us in Oakland, Leon and I had to also rehearse in New York with the live musicians who were to play for our cakewalk dance. We had several rehearsals with the pianist Neal Tate (1927–2005) and singer Ruth Brisbane. Their rendition of the 1917 classic song "Darktown Stutters' Ball," historically used for exhibition cakewalks, was perfect, and Leon and I loved the inspirational energy that their live music gave the dance.

Performing "Strut Miss Lizzie" was actually fun, and we gave it everything we had. When it came time to step out onto that stage in my long red period dress, complete with bustle, which I had purchased myself in San Francisco and brought with me to New York, Leon and I *became* an early twentieth-century cakewalk couple, kicking high and strutting proudly. We tried to portray the shifting social context of the former slave plantation dance becoming the embodied aspirations of the black middle class of the turn-of-the-century era. There were a lot of tricky syncopated steps that Leni loved to throw into his choreography, along with many partnering turns. Leon and I worked well together and loved partnering each other. At his hospital bed in April 1990, when he passed from AIDS, I whispered in his ear, "We will cakewalk in heaven together," and even though at that point he couldn't talk, he smiled.

Dance Magazine hired Ntozake to write a review of the entire conference, which appeared in their August 1983 issue, and she started it with her own journal entry #692 written in her own signature constructed writing style:

What does it mean that blk folks cd sing n dance?
Why do we say that so much/we don't know what we mean/
I saw what that means/good god/did I see/like I cda
Walked on the water myself/I cda clothed the naked and fed the
    hungry/
With wht dance I saw tonite/I don't mean dance
I mean a closer walk with thee/a race thru swamps that fall
Off in space/I mean I saw the black people move the ground
& set stars beneath they feet/so what's this mean that
black folks cd dance/well/how abt a woman like dyane harvey who can
    make
her body the night riders & the runaways/the children hangin
on they mama's dress/while they father's beat to death/
the blood/from the man's wounds/his woman's tears/the night riders
going off in darkness/the silence of the night[39]

Yes, those four days of the Dance Black America landmark festival were indeed a spiritual well spring of past, present, and futuristic never-to-be-forgotten black dance and cultural experiences.

Two years later, Pennebaker Associates released a VHS video of the BAM Dance Black America festival, complete with interviews with many of the artists, which aired as a PBS Great Performances television special. On Friday, January 25, 1985, the entire Dance Black America experience could be viewed by the whole nation as it premiered on public television. The film is directed by D. A. Pennebaker and Chris Hegedus and narrated by Geoffrey Holder (1930–2014), with his unforgettably powerful West Indian voice. For marketing purposes, they switched the Alvin Ailey American Dance Theater's performance from Ailey's *Revelations* excerpts to Louis Johnson's *Fontessa and Friends*, a comedy spoof featuring then Ailey principal dancers Donna Wood and Gary DeLoatch (1953–1993). Leni Sloan's *Juba* and *Cakewalk* made the cut, which meant that Leon and I are in the video documentary of Dance Black America still on sale today on DVD. Out of all the performances and choreography that I have done throughout my career, the approximately one-minute excerpt from our cakewalk dance in Dance Black America, spliced with vintage archival footage of turn-of-the century competition cakewalkers, remains the main recorded dance for which I am known today. People continue to ask me, "So that's you as the Lady in Red performing the cakewalk?" One never knows what moments will become one's historic footprint after a long dance career.

My reputation in the Bay Area definitely grew from dancing in Dance Black America. The *San Francisco Chronicle* interviewed me in January 1985 for the premiere of the PBS special, summarizing my personal and professional life, starting from my childhood in Galveston, Texas, to San Francisco's George Washington High School and S.F. State University, continuing to Europe and Africa, and finally to my founding Everybody's Creative Arts Center in Oakland: "Halifu Osumare, the energetic founder of Everybody's Creative Arts Center in Oakland, and cofounder of its multi-ethnically oriented resident CitiCentre Dance Company, did not start out with the aim of championing black dance per se."[40] That journalist, Calvin Ahlgren, was right: I might not have started with this purpose, but my mission found me, and by 1985 I was well on my way toward illuminating this complex, multidimensional artistic expression that we simplistically call "black dance."

Another big performance opportunity also came from Leni's "Black Street and Social Dance" show. The concert, as an educational and entertaining black cultural statement, was turned into *Sweet Saturday Night: A Celebration of Street and Social Dance* and toured State University of New York college campuses for six weeks in January-February 1984, ending with a reprise at BAM on March 6–11. Not all of the former acts were brought into this touring show, but as Leon and I were performing Leni's choreography, we were sure to become a part of the touring *Sweet Saturday Night*.

This was actually my first time performing on a tour of one-nighters, traveling to different SUNY campuses, such as Binghamton, Albany, Buffalo, and beyond, and it was a very taxing experience. We had a tour bus, and those of us who became the smaller touring *Sweet Saturday Night* show got even closer: Mama Lu Parks (1929–1990) and her lindy hoppers were hilarious, and Chuck Green (1919–1997), sixty-five years old at the time, was quiet, but when he started showing a complex rhythmic step backstage, he would come alive. Al Perryman (1945–1985), who played Earl "Snake-Hips" Tucker, was paired with former Ailey dancer Loretta Abbott (1933–2016) to form a larger cakewalk number with Leon and me. As disco dance and music was still popular, Leni pulled in Eddie Vegas and Lourdes Jones to perform the disco hustle. Of course the continually evolving hip-hop culture of the early 1980s had to be presented; the Rock Steady Crew and the Double Dutch Champions were included as well. The publicity for the tour's culminating show at BAM marketed the entire touring show stereotypically as "HOT." It also used one of Jennifer Dunning's *New York Times* quotes: "It was party time at the Brooklyn Academy of Music, when the Dance Black America Festival's Street and Social Dance program erupted on the stage of the Playhouse." It was a lively show, but I reveled more in how the entire program communicated a history of "how we got over"—how black folks survived the often-devastating American experience through our expressive culture, and the power of dance and music as healing forces.

Becoming an Arts Advocate and Published Dance Journalist

Throughout the 1980s my ability to negotiate various roles around dance and the arts was growing, from dancer-choreographer to arts administrator, and from community cultural activist and national arts advocate to budding black dance scholar. For example, after the *Sweet Saturday Night* tour, I went to Washington, D.C., to the National Endowment for the Arts (NEA) to lobby for our ECAC grant proposals that were pending with both the Dance and Expansion Arts Programs. In this way BAM paid for my lobbying trip to the East Coast while I also worked for my ECAC organization. At this point in my multiple careers I was well beyond being afraid to advocate for my mission with black dance. Making myself known at the NEA paid off, because in the latter 1980s I was asked to be one of the reviewing grants panelists for both programs to which ECAC applied for grants. Expansions Arts, led by the famous jazz music scholar A. B. Spellman, was particularly rewarding because I got a chance to become familiar with the many national arts groups of color doing phenomenal projects in the arts but who were usually passed over for tax-based funds because of the overarching racist national arts hierarchy.

The large-budget municipal arts companies—operas, symphonies, and ballets—got the majority of the relatively small amount of government funding that went to the arts; this was the arts version of what today is called the 1 percent versus the 99 percent that became the short-lived Occupy Wall Street movement. I became a major spokesperson in the "multicultural arts movement" at the national as well as the state level, with the California Arts Council (CAC). Mentioned earlier, at the CAC we formed the Multicultural Arts Advisory Committee to create policy that would ensure more equitable distribution of tax-based arts dollars. African dance companies, ballet folklóricos, Chinese operas in the Chinatowns across the country, and emerging Native American contemporary dance companies all started getting a bigger piece of the pie. In the process, I got to know the movers and shakers with a strong social conscience in the arts-funding arena, like A. B. Spellman in Washington, D.C., and Juan Carrillo at the CAC in Sacramento. In California, this was my motivation to make the trek from Oakland to Sacramento (which was to become my future home) to advocate for cultural justice in the arts. I also became a NEA site visitor for many cultural institutions around the country, and our efforts in the 1980s and early 1990s helped change the funding landscape for the arts. I was both artist and administrator simultaneously and was excelling in both arenas.

My role as dance scholar was also progressing but was far less developed. During this period, I was becoming a journalist, publishing several articles on issues of black dance and black choreographers. One such article was "Black Dance in America: A Reevaluation of History" published in San Francisco's *City Arts* magazine, May 1981. I started the article with:

Black Dance has always been more than African dance, or the many Afro-Caribbean derivatives—tap, vernacular, social dance, or modern jazz dance. No matter what the specific form, the essence of it has always been beyond the form. The essence of Black Dance has always been about the expression and particular spirit of the individual dancer at the movement he or she is dancing. One may say that this is true of any dance form; but in Black Dance it is the basis, the foundation, the *raison d'etre* behind every dance, and every piece of choreography.[41]

Other published essays in the 1980s followed: "Black Choreographers in Contemporary Dance" (January 1987) in *In Dance*, newsletter of the S.F. Bay Area Dance Coalition; on the national level, "Black Dance: To Be or Not to Be," the *Crisis*, journal of the NAACP (October 1988); "Katherine Dunham, Where African, Caribbean and African American Dance Converge," *Unity Newspaper* (September 29, 1989); and upon his death as another victim of AIDS in the dance community, I wrote the obituary for Alvin Ailey, "The Legacy of Alvin Ailey," for the *San Francisco Bay Guardian* (December 1989). I began to understand that I had a responsibility to educate the dance audience and larger public about my chosen mission— black dance and culture.

My reputation as a dance journalist who could interpret the black dance experience grew to a national level with dance articles that followed in the 1990s, while I was still teaching at Stanford, advising CitiCentre Dance Theatre as a member of the board of directors, and working on my master's degree at S.F. State. I continued writing articles on black dance for the *Crisis* and was commissioned to write audience program essays for the Cleo Parker Robinson Dance Ensemble and the Lula Washington Dance Theatre's appearances at the "Dance Women/Living Legends," a project of New York's 651 Arts, held at the Aaron Davis Hall in the late 1990s.

But the turning point in juggling my many roles happened in 1986 after I resigned as executive artistic director of ECAC. I began concentrating less on my dance and choreographic career (although I didn't stop altogether) and started emphasizing what I considered to be the larger issue of my mission: exploring and elevating the complexity of the *discourse* on black dance. The 1983 Dance Black America project had awakened a new sense of my mission, and I began to regard the ability to articulate the *issues* of my art form as more important. There is no better source to enunciate the aesthetic, historical, political, and policy advocacy contexts of dance than someone who is an actual practitioner. As I developed my writing and advocacy careers, I began to view my dancing and choreography as providing an insider perspective, which gave me an advantage as a spokesperson for dance in the larger arena of social and cultural justice.

Dancing in Malawi, Southeastern Africa

These growing artistic and spokesperson roles led to a major international commission that took me back to the continent of Africa. In 1990, when I was well established in my dance and arts administration career, I was commissioned by the then United State Information Agency (USIA) to work with the national dance company of Malawi, the Kwacha Cultural Troupe. It was my affiliation with Stanford University that brought me to the attention of USIA. The July 5, 1990, *Stanford University Campus Report* published a notice that succinctly captured the essence of my commission in Malawi:

> Halifu Osumare, Program Coordinator of Stanford's Committee on Black Performing Arts and a lecturer in the Dance Division, has been chosen by Arts America of the US Information Agency for a one-month commission in the southeastern African country of Malawi. Osumare will assist the Kwacha Cultural Troup in staging their traditional dances. Her commission is for choreographic staging, production values, and management consulting for international touring. The troupe is seen in Malawi as a symbol of national unity for the many ethnic groups within the country.[42]

Although Malawi was very different from West Africa, my 1976 residency in Ghana (chapter 5) prepared me well to deal with official diplomacy, African cultural nuances, and common sociopolitical conditions on the African continent, all aspects of my Malawian residency and particularly my work with the Department of Cultural Affairs.

I left San Francisco on July 17, 1990, on Pan Am Airlines for London and then Kenya, the "New York" of East Africa, in order to arrive in Lilongwe, Malawi, on July 20. Kimathi averted his eyes when I left him at curbside at SFO airport, avoiding that pregnant moment of separation again for a full month. I was going to miss him, but I was happy to be leaving the United States and going to Africa again, having been more entrenched in the daily routine of community arts building for the last fourteen years than I could have ever imagined. I stayed in London for one day and traveled to Oxford to see a Stanford colleague working at the University of Oxford for the summer.

When I arrived on a Boeing 747 in Nairobi, Kenya, on July 20 with Brits, white and black South Africans, and black and Indian Kenyans, I realized that I was now an "African American" in Africa again. This was a relatively new term that Jesse Jackson had just introduced in the United States, moving America away from the appellation of "Afro-American" that had been in vogue for several decades since the 1960s revolution. Ghana was an engraved memory, but I was experiencing my initial reconnection with the African continent all over again, fourteen years later. I noticed the cosmopolitan atmosphere of Kenya from the airport and made a note that I would spend a little time there on the way back home. I transferred to another flight to arrive in Lilongwe, Malawi, the same day.

As I was an official representative of the United States government assigned to the Cultural Affairs Department of Malawi, this trip was worlds apart from my Ghanaian sojourn. I was picked up at the airport by officials from the government and driven to the Lilongwe Hotel, comparable to a three-star hotel in the United States today, but in 1990 Malawi it was considered high-end. Every place I went—to rehearsals with the national dance company, excursions out of town, and official meetings with Cultural Affairs—a chauffeur drove me. I took this as a measure of how far I had come in my dance and administrative careers, and although the luxury made me a little uncomfortable, I tried to relish my newfound status. The day after arriving, I met with Mr. Serman Chavula, the senior Cultural Affairs officer, and the choreographer of Kwacha Cultural Troupe, Mr. Bernard Kwilimbe, who became my main contacts for the entire one-month residency.

Malawi had gained its independence from England in 1964, and as a relatively new government was still building its institutions with culture and the arts as a part of that nation building. The Kwacha Cultural Troupe was formed in 1987, and Mr. Chavula told me: "The main criteria for choosing the dancers were that they must have completed Standard 8 [equivalent to the tenth grade in the United States], speak English, and could perform and teach at least one dance from their ethnic group." It was these dances from the main ethnic groups—Chewa, Tumbuka, Lomwe, Yao, and Ngoni—that I was to observe and restage for international touring.

Over the next three days I was given a thorough orientation to my job and taken to my first Malawian village to view one of the dances in the Kwacha troupe's repertoire, which would inspire me enough to become the subject of my master's thesis. It was necessary not only to view the company in rehearsal and performances but also to see several of the dances in their indigenous settings. I was grateful for the few hinterland excursions because I knew that I had to strike the right balance between traditional intent and Western staging techniques that would attract an international audience. I assured them that I was there to learn as much as to instruct. Mr. Kwilimbe mapped out a three-pronged plan. He told me that my main duty was to train the dancers and develop the repertoire of the company itself, but he also needed me to develop a written three-year plan for the department and to promote cultural exchange by teaching the Kwacha dancers some American culture and African American dance. As these duties fell within my time-tested experience, I assured him I could handle all three expectations (figure 17).

But as I set about a rehearsal schedule, I immediately noticed a gender difference in the thirty-nine-member company's reception of me. My initial rehearsals with the Kwacha Cultural Troupe was mixed. The majority of the young men were eager to see what restructuring I had for the exclusive men's dances and immediately practiced the new formations, entrances, and exits that I choreographed. But the women looked at me askance with their arms akimbo (Where had I seen this attitude before?). Malawi was far more traditional regarding women's roles than I had experienced in Ghana. The Kwacha Cultural Troupe was not used to a woman being the "boss"; hence I was a novelty to the men, amusing them as they played along with the temporary *official* policy of a woman being in charge; whereas the women's reluctant attitude said, "Where does she come off telling us what to do? She's just a woman like us." Although the dancers had to have a textbook knowledge of English, the majority of them were not very proficient in the language, which became another barrier. To be understood I had to speak slowly and enunciate clearly, while engaging gestures and psychic communication. But the gender difference in Kwacha's reception of me was pronounced and had to be met head-on.

I decided that I had to engage the women from a different perspective if I was going to get the best work out of them. One lunch break I decided to go with the young women to where they gathered to eat their food and just hang out with them. They brought cooked food, including the staple *nsima* cornmeal all Malawians eat, and shared it with me; this casual eating experience helped us get more familiar with each other. I also asked one of the women to come to my hotel to braid my hair, and three of them showed up and did a beautiful job. These "female activities" were icebreakers in my relationship with the women of the Kwacha Cultural Troupe, reducing me to the same level and allowing them to see me as another female like them, who could transcend the obvious cultural barrier. The gender differences in my initial reception by the dance company, and the female rituals in which I engaged to gain the women's trust, prompted me to write an essay upon my return to the United States about this particular aspect of my Malawi experience. "Viewing African Women through Dance" was published in the fall 1994 issue of the now defunct Spelman College academic journal *SAGE, A Scholarly Journal of Black Women*.[43]

The first village trip on my itinerary was to Chimbalanga Village, near the town of Salima in proximity to Lake Malawi. Chimbalanga was a village of Yao people living in the Chewa ethnic area, the largest ethnic group in Malawi. The fact that the Yao were cooperative with the coastal Swahili and Arab slave traders in East Africa has everything to do with the *beni* dance that I had come to observe in Chimbalanga. Beni is a unison military-like dance developing from East Africans' participation in World Wars I and II, syncretizing precision European military marching with African war dances. The inland region of what became Malawi was a large source of slaves for the Indian Ocean slave trade. The subsequent colonial railroad infrastructure, built by the British as the colonial masters of Nyasaland (the colonial name for Malawi), was a later connection between inland ethnic groups like the Yao and Chewa peoples with the coastal cultures during the world wars between England (Kenya) and Germany (Tanzania) in East Africa. The beni dance, developing out of this East African history, traveled from Zanzibar Island and the coastal city of Mombasa to the central African regions of Malawi. In 1990 there were several variations of Malawi beni that were performed in rural and urban areas, becoming popular enough to be a major dance in the Kwacha Cultural Troupe's repertoire.

The men's beni dance performance that afternoon went on for hours, with an intermission that became an interlude for me with a women's dance. During the break from Beni, I was called over to another section of the village square, where the women had gathered in a circle for their less formal dance. A young boy who had been dancing in the men's beni dance circle became the drummer for the women and girls, accompanying their syncopated rhythmic hand clapping. *Chitalela* is the circle challenge dance in which I participated, with each female taking a turn in the center. Back in the United States, I had the songs accompanying the dance solos, which I recorded, translated. I realized that each woman or girl entering the circle was identified by the kind of vegetable that she cooked in her home to go along with *nsima*. In African dance, the accompanying songs are just as important as the movements themselves, and when I realized this important music structural relationship with the dance, I used it in my rehearsals with the Kwacha company. I changed specific dance formations, or a stage direction of a particular dance, as the accompanying songs changed. This made it easy for the dancers to grasp the choreographic reorganization.

Chitalela's emphasis was on a two-count rhythmic butt release that punctuated a bent-knee, relaxed torso backward shuffling movement. As the drummer played the two-count accent, the dancer would bend lower and protrude the butt, accenting the rhythm. Those who could perform the butt accent the hardest and most humorously were complimented with laughter and cheers. Two young girls, who looked to be about ten years old, were the hands-down winners, but my inevitable turn in the center even trumped those girls' virtuosic performance. I wrote in my journal: *They didn't know that for me the chitalela dance was merely another variation of "Da Butt" that Spike Lee had made famous in his film School Daze, becoming a 1988 U.S. dance craze, particularly among black college fraternities and sororities.* When I moved into the center, I bent low, and knew exactly when to execute the two-count butt accent. The women forming the circle and the men observing from outside started yelling and cheering at my successful chitalela performance, becoming the crescendo of the entire dance. The Chimbalanga village experience prepared me for the second Malawian village experience in Njombwa near the Kasungu National Park. At this second village excursion I witnessed the four-hundred-year-old mask dance, *Gule Wamkulu* (Great Dance) of the Chewa, but even the viewing of this important ritual secret cult dance could not match my personal experience with the women's dance in Chimbalanga.

One other excursion away from my job with the national dance company was truly a memorable one, because I got a chance to have a private meeting with Malawi's head of state, Life President Dr. H. Kamuzu Banda. Like several of the original prime ministers of newly independent Anglophone African countries, Banda was educated in Britain and the United States. He was a medical doctor who in 1958 had been invited to return from Britain back to the old Nyasaland, which was a part of the Federation of Rhodesia and Nyasaland. Through the Nyasaland African Congress, Banda led the protest against English rule and to lobby for independence. He became the prime minister in early 1963, and complete independence was achieved in 1964. By 1966 Banda established a one-party system, having deposed all of his detractors in his cabinet, and by 1970 he had proclaimed himself the president for life. When I was in Malawi there was palpable fear in the air about saying anything against the "Life President," or the government, as so many dissenters had been killed or fled into exile. When I was asked by my Malawian friends if I would like to return to Malawi after my consultancy, I promptly said, "Probably not, because I'm the type who might say something against the government and get myself in trouble." They immediately understood.

So how did I get a meeting with the Life President Hastings Kamuzu Banda? It was all due to Katherine Dunham. In early 1990 I had obtained a writing fellowship for her at Stanford University after the success of her May 1989 Stanford residency mentioned above. When she heard that I was scheduled to travel to Malawi, to my surprise she said, "Oh, you're going to Hastings Banda's country; you must take a letter to him for me." My mouth fell open, and I said, "You know the president of Malawi?" Banda had attended the University of Chicago in the 1930s as a premed student when Miss Dunham was there as a student in anthropology. As two of the few black students attending the university at the time, they of course knew each other. Her story about their relationship during those days was humorous: "Banda used to chase me around the cafeteria table saying, 'As I am of royal blood I can only sow my seed in royalty.' Of course, I never let him catch me." Although this story was hilarious, I was more focused on her giving me a letter that I would have to deliver to the president of Malawi, which I did not relish. Miss Dunham dictated the letter to Jeanelle Stovall, her administrative assistant, and gave it to me in a sealed envelope a week before I left for Malawi. I had a lump in my throat the whole time I carried the letter.

After arriving in Malawi, it took me a week before I told Mr. Chavula that I had a letter for the Life President. Just as I had suspected, when I mentioned the letter, all conversation stopped and everyone stared at me. I explained my friendship with one of Banda's old college friends and showed them a photo of Miss Dunham. Anything having to do with Banda was like walking on eggshells; even mentioning him was always guarded. They opened the letter to make sure it was appropriate, created a cover letter to Miss Dunham's note, and passed it up the chain of command in the government. Two days before I was to finish my dance assignment with the company, I was told that I would be driven to Blantyre, the older Malawian city of commerce in the south, to meet with the president in his main palace residence. I had read several biographies of Banda and felt like I knew what to expect. On August 20, 1990, the day of my chauffeured drive to the presidential palace, I was calm and resigned to the task at hand, writing in my journal, *I look forward to meeting "The Old Man" [as he is affectionately called by everyone], one of the few remaining African liberators.*

My meeting with an African head of state was definitely something to remember. Mr. Chavula accompanied me as Senior Cultural Affairs Officer, and as we approached Sanjeka, Banda's Blantyre Palace (he had many throughout the country), the chauffeur drove on the restricted road through three guarded gates. Each time a gate was opened by a white-jacketed guard in a red beret, and the driver announced, "Mrs. Janis Miller-Williams has an appointment with the Life President"; although Cultural Affairs officials called me Halifu Osumare, meeting the president required the use of the legal name on my passport. After circling up the hill to the palace overlooking the city, we reached a small courtyard with a nonrunning fountain in the center. An attendant opened my door, and we were led into a small waiting room inside the palace. Ebony and ivory statues graced small mahogany tables, with the center coffee table lined with Malawi magazines that had covers of Banda meeting various international heads of state.

After about fifteen minutes, the principal secretary, Mr. I. C. Lamba, joined us, giving me instructions as to the protocol of meeting President Banda. He told me that Malawi had been misunderstood and that the world was beginning to rethink Banda's "pacifist approach." I simply listened and nodded my head. Then, in walked the Honorable Maxwell Pashane, the chief of protocol, to tell me where I would sit in the presidential meeting hall and what would be the order of protocol for the meeting: I would need to rise and bow when Banda entered the room, and I should speak first, telling him that I was grateful for him giving me an audience. I was instructed to refer to him as "His Excellency" or "Life President," but there was no need to use his full title and name. Lastly, I was told that I should refrain from any controversial statements: "Keep it light and pleasant." However, Pashane did tell me, "If you have any matters that might be considered controversial and that need clarification, you can talk to me afterward." During these instructions, Mr. Chavula looked extremely nervous, tapping his foot and frowning. I realized that his job and reputation was on the line because of my meeting with Banda. Finally, a guard opened the door, and I, Mr. Pashane, Mr. Lamba, and Mr. Chavula rose to be taken to meet Banda.

The presidential meeting hall was filled with tapestries of the official government, complete with the national emblem—the lion and the leopard, symbols of jungle rivals who can peacefully coexist. This symbolism was echoed by two taxidermy animals—one a full-sized lion standing on a granite-like stand, facing the huge oval conference table at which we sat. The other was a leopard skin with the head still on it, mouth open, baring its teeth, lying flat in the center of the conference table, and facing the chair in which Banda would sit. The no-nonsense ferocity of the symbolism was palpable, and I began to get nervous again. But when President H. Kamuzu Banda entered the room and we rose in respect, he reminded me of my beloved uncle James Evans, brother to my maternal grandmother. He looked exactly like him—short, medium-brown skin, and a close-cropped short haircut, impeccably dressed in a gray three-piece suit, with crisp white starched shirt. Purported to be ninety-two years old at the time, he walked slowly but securely, assisted by a carved ebony cane. Banda sported a confident smile and walked directly over to me, reaching out his hand warmly; we stood about two feet apart and shook hands as I slightly bowed. The photo taken of that precise moment of our greeting was on the front page of the *Malawi News* the next morning (figure 18).

We all sat down at our official positions at the state conference table, with the Honorable Pashane, Principal Secretary Lamba, and Senior Cultural Affairs Officer Chavula on the far side, Banda at the head of the table with the leopard head pointing toward him, and me on the opposite side of the table from the officials and close to the head of state. Banda immediately called for me to move even closer so that he could be sure to hear me. I then opened with a greeting from Miss Dunham and summarized her history after their 1930s time period at the University of Chicago, making sure he knew about her Caribbean dance research that led to the world-famous Katherine Dunham Dance Company. Banda was very interested and appreciative to hear of his former colleague's successful artistic career. Of course I thought of Miss Dunham's story about Banda "trying to sow his royal seed" and smiled to myself. I ended my presentation to Malawi's president on the work I was doing with the Kwacha Cultural Troupe and the culminating performance that was just presented that past Saturday in Lilongwe, which I discuss below. I concluded by emphasizing that it was important to preserve traditional African culture through the dance and music, and he nodded approval. I had immediately taken noncontroversial command of the meeting, and the officials across the table looked more at ease.

After my official presentation to Banda, he took over, responding to my presentation and asking more about my experience in Malawi. He told me that he was very happy to hear of Katherine Dunham's achievements, and how few "black faces" there were during that time at the University of Chicago. He mentioned how much the black students had to stick together and that his generation had to be very strong. He then asked me whether I had been to his home village near Kasungu to see the secondary school he had built there. When I told him that I had not, he looked sternly over at the officials and told them to see that I got a chance to see his academy and his village before I left the country. This actually extended my intended stay by three days, but what Banda commanded always happened.

The Life President then went into a surprising discourse on the ancient history of the Greeks and the Mesopotamians that ended in a lesson on the origins of the Brits. After reflecting on Banda's history soliloquy, I wrote in my journal: *In hindsight, I analyze this seemingly unrelated history treatise as a demonstration of his academic knowledge, as well as to show the Anglo-Saxons' cultural origins pre-dating Britain's relative recent colonial history. This revealed Banda's preoccupation with the Brits, with whom he had a love-hate relationship.* Banda had punctuated this history discourse with humorous anecdotes, each time looking at his government officials and laughing; like clockwork, they too responded with their own nervous laughter. Banda definitely had everyone under his thumb and ruled with absolute authority.

At the end of our official meeting, he presented me with two pictorial books on Malawi for Katherine Dunham and me. Both were signed and gold-embossed with "Compliments of the Life President H. Kamuzu Banda." He finished by again welcoming me to Malawi, taking my hand, and looking in my eyes while imploring me to return and get to know more of his country. I remember this final moment as he showed genuine generosity, and again I had the strong father feeling from him that reminded me of my Uncle James. As he rose from his chair, so did we. Mr. Pashane took Banda's cane and handed it to him while kneeling. Banda bid me farewell and turned to walk out, but before he left the room, he turned once again to look at me and waved. I waved back, and he walked out. I wrote in my journal: *That last wave seemed to say, "Well, if I don't see you again, go in peace and farewell." I had been prepared only to feel a benign respect, but came away with a full heart after viewing a world leader who had the courage do it his way.*

On the way out of the palace, Mama Kadzimira, the country's "Official Hostess" and Banda's unofficial wife, about twenty-five years my senior, met us in the hallway with wrapping paper for the book for Miss Dunham. She talked to me like an elder aunt whom I was meeting again after a long time, and she inquired about Miss Dunham's health and thanked me for bringing her greetings to Banda. It was a warm exchange between two black women of different generations. As we drove down from the presidential palace into downtown Blantyre, I heard my name on the government's news radio station. I had had one of only two presidential meetings that day; the other was with the ambassador of Brazil. Instead of a nervous, politically constrained meeting that day, my audience with Malawi's dictator president actually turned out to be a "family" experience and another occurrence of "dancing" in blackness.

Two and a half weeks before my trip to Sanjeka Palace, I had started intense all-day rehearsals with the Kwacha Cultural Troupe to restage some Malawian traditional dances, as well as the cultural exchange part of the residency. I taught the troupe African American and diasporic dances for a culminating performance. Additionally, it so happened that Mr. Kwilimbe, the choreographer, had to take a trip to London for a black dance choreography workshop. Along with Waliko Makhala, the troupe leader, this put me in charge of the company. I usually split up the rehearsal day with the American dance rehearsal in the afternoon after the lunch break. The company dancers were most excited about my teaching U.S. African American dance, as this dancing denoted cool "modern" dance that connected them to the outside world.

As I was to present my culminating performance at the Kamuzu Institute of Youth on August 18, with a VIP performance for the American ambassador the previous afternoon, I focused on teaching the troupe members choreography to a specific U.S. pop song that would conclude my culminating presentation. My "American dance" was to the then immensely popular 1990 hip-hop radio hit, MC Hammer's "U Can't Touch This" on his album *Please Hammer, Don't Hurt 'Em*.[44] The dancers loved it and jumped with energy every time I put on the music. When we rehearsed "U Can't Touch This," I recognized the power of American popular culture on the entire world. It made them feel like they were internationally cool dancers, not merely Malawian traditional dancers. I also recognized the influence my concert with the Kwacha Cultural Troupe would have on the entire country. I wrote in my journal:

With several other countries' ambassadors and Malawian government officials at my performance, I am in a unique position and under pressure. However, I am treating it like any other of my major projects, even though it has diplomatic and international implications. I not only have a chance to make a major impact on Malawi's cultural plan for the near future, but also to plant seeds of cultural and artistic cooperation between various consulates represented in Malawi.

Having in mind my usual theme of *The Evolution of Black Dance* that I had developed throughout my career, I titled the entire production *Africa Around the World*. The theme allowed me to use several traditional Malawian dances, and in that regard, I was warned by Cultural Affairs to make sure I used representative dances that covered several Malawian ethnic groups so as to avoid giving any cultural offense; dance was extremely political in "tribal" Africa. I diplomatically chose the most dynamic dances that I had been rehearsing from Malawi's diverse cultures: (1) *ngoma-msindo-ingoma* of the Ngoni, who had migrated from the Southern African region into Malawi; (2) *vimbuza*, a sacred healing priest dance of the Tumbuka (Mr. Chavula's group); (3) *chitoto, gynayasa,* and *indonda* dance complex of the Chewa, Malawi's most populous ethnic group; and (4) a choreographic ethnic medley developed by Mr. Kwilimbe called "AAW," that included movements and sequences from various Malawian dances woven into one piece.

The big hit of my *Africa Around the World* performance was, hands-down, my "U Can't Touch This" dance. Although I also taught the dance company the popular Ghanaian *kpanlogo* dance and Haitian *merengue* that the dancers liked, my "U Can't Touch This" dance was the part of the performance the dancers most enjoyed. Yet, being forty-four years old at the time, I had never focused on the continually shifting hip-hop dance styles, so I used basic black social dances that I knew, along with a few of Hammer's movements from his music video, depending on my choreographic expertise to congeal the dance moves. I particularly employed the popular "running man" move, along with Hammer's side-scooting step with rotating torso circles during the chorus hook, "a-ho, a-oh, a-oh, here comes the Hammer." I choreographed the most difficult movements into solo and duet sections, giving them to particular Kwacha dancers who learned the hip-hop choreography fastest, while the rest of the company performed generic black social dance moves in unison choreography that flanked the featured dancers. One unison section of the dance included the dancers pointing at the audience, while verbalizing the song's refrain, "U can't touch this," drawing thunderous audience laughter. The department had contemporary costumes made for my dance, which included dark-green pants and skirts and African-print dashikis that the dancers loved. *African Around the World* started in Malawi, went to Ghana, then Haiti, and ended in the United States with "U Can't Touch This" as the show's finale. The entire performance, and particularly the finale, was a huge hit with the Malawian general public, the Malawian government dignitaries, and the foreign diplomatic corps alike.

Leaving Malawi was heartwarming, demonstrating to me how much the Cultural Affairs Department officials and the dance company appreciated what I had accomplished. They threw a party with presentations and informal performances for me in the reception room at the Lilongwe Hotel that I really appreciated. One gift they gave me was a treasured African outfit—a long wraparound skirt and top made from the cloth used for the costumes for "U Can't Touch This" dance. The next day, the entire troupe stayed at the airport in Lilongwe until I boarded the plane, and as it took off I could see them on the outdoor balcony waving touchingly at the rising plane.

I left Malawi on August 23 to fly to Nairobi, which by contrast to Lilongwe was like New York or Paris. In Nairobi I went to the famous Nairobi Hilton with its sky-high circular rotating restaurant overseeing the downtown area, I attended a theatrical play about the Mau-Mau rebellion leader Dedan Kimathi (the namesake of my husband, Kimathi, with whom I had stayed in touch via a weekly official phone call paid for by the government), and went to the famous Bomas of Kenya, the cultural village built to showcase the dances of Kenyan ethnic groups. I had a personal tour of that major tourist attraction by the director, who escorted me around the grounds to the Massai, Samburu, and other simulated ethnic villages. The entire trip to East and Southeastern Africa gave me a strong sense of the diversity of the continent, which increased my knowledge base of African dances underpinning my dance career.

Black Dance Initiative: ADF's Black Tradition
in American Modern Dance

Before my Malawi trip toward the latter part of the 1980s, I began to take black dance organizing to a national level. The big transition from focusing on performing and administrating my community school to that of national arts administration happened in 1988; having turned forty years old two years earlier forced the realization that I could not maintain dancing and administrating equally any more. As age began to catch up with me regarding physically performing, I created an adage for myself that I wrote in my journal in 1988: *We are constantly juggling our desires and visions with reality.*

It was time for me to make a major statement as an arts administrator and black dance advocate at the *national* level. Ever since my undergraduate San Francisco State University days, during the beginning of the big student strike for ethnic studies, I had chosen activism through *dance* rather than direct political action. Now, at forty-two years old, dance and the arts continued to be the vehicle through which I contributed to American social justice. After accruing ten years of arts administrative acumen, along with the many contacts that I had garnered from performing, serving on NEA and CAC arts panels, and networking with other arts administrators and black dance companies throughout the country, I was ready to make my own major statement through a national black dance initiative.

I had been sensitized to the national level of black dance organizing and its potential impact by my participation in Dance Black America, but I still needed more training about *how* to combine the arts and humanities— black dance performance and its contextual issues. This necessary preparation came with the American Dance Festival's (ADF) Black Tradition in American Modern Dance project. ADF is the oldest organization for modern dance in the United States, having started at Vermont's Bennington College in in 1934 with four modern dance pioneers—Martha Graham, Hanya Holm, Doris Humphrey, and Charles Weidman. Bennington was the beginning of the institutionalization of this new American art form, although with one German, Hanya Holm (having evolved from Mary Wigman's German expressionist dance), it is debatable that modern dance was strictly a new *American* form of dance. As the *New York Times* dance critic Jack Anderson opines: "Some observers may claim that modern dance is indeed fundamentally American. But that argument overlooks both the diversity of modern dance and much of its history."[45]

Although it is speculative that modern dance is solely American in its origin, it is not at all hypothetical that the dance form is not all Euro-American in its origins. At the time that the Big Four—Graham, Holm, Humphrey, and Weidman—were teaching that summer in Bennington, Katherine Dunham was applying to the Rosenwald Fellowship to conduct her discipline-changing research in the Caribbean to find the roots of black dance in the Americas. Dunham and other black choreographers— Edna Guy, Hemsley Winfield, Pearl Primus, etc.—developed an expressionist dance idiom during the 1930s and 1940s that also shaped modern dance (introduction). Although critics like John Martin recognized these black dance artists' contributions to the concert stage, their dance was still viewed as ethnic, not modern, dance. Philosopher Gerald E. Myers, the project director of the ADF's Black Tradition program, had this to say about the imposed ethnic-modern divide:

> A Katherine Dunham can modify the [Haitian] *yanvalou* into an original unpredictable invention of her own, expressing in contemporary additions and subtractions the artist's rebellious respect for the inspiration that tradition supplies. If we are ignorant of what the traditional *yanvalou* is like and of how it differs from what she created by using some of its elements, then of course, mistakenly assuming that we are seeing a clone of the traditional dance, we stamp "ethnic" on it. Black dance critics and scholars, aware of this happening too often, urge non-black viewers to become more informed about the character of traditional African and Caribbean dances and about the ways, in a modern dance spirit, in which that character gets redefined in the creations of choreographers such as Dunham and Pearl Primus.[46]

The propensity for cultural bias regarding ethnic source material in the new dance expression of modern dance was all the more glaring because the white modern dancers often appropriated from indigenous dance sources as well. Ted Shawn had a strong proclivity for Native American dance. Ruth St. Denis's "orientalism," to use Edward Said's term, was blatant in her choreography inspired by East Indian and Asian dance forms, which became the first examples of "othering" the Orient in the early stages of modern dance.[47] But due to U.S. racial hierarchy, black choreographers were not truly recognized as modern dance artists like Graham, Humphrey, and Mexican dancer José Limón, who used choreographic inspiration from his own culture. ADF's Black Tradition in American Modern Dance, now based in Durham, North Carolina, at Duke University, set out to rectify this "oversight" fifty-four years later.

The American Dance Festival's Black Tradition in American Modern Dance was a three-year project (1988–90) that brought much-needed attention to the plight of black modern dance legends and their choreographic works. The initiative happened at a time when ADF itself had grown to international stature, with an annual summer festival of classes and performances that drew students and audiences from all over the world. I heard about this pioneering project by ADF and knew I had to go to its inauguration in 1988. ADF's stated purpose for the project was: "To broaden public awareness of the intellectual and artistic contributions black Americans have made and are making to the development of modern dance; to present and preserve historically important dances by black choreographers; to initiate further study of black dance in America." This mission placed the artists, their works, and the intellectual and cultural contexts as important to augmenting public awareness of this neglected tradition in modern dance. I was eager to see how all these levels worked cohesively because when I was at Dance Black America in 1983, I had to focus on my own performance. Now I was going to ADF at Duke University in Durham to meet the legends of black dance, see some of their classic works that had *not* been viewed in performance by my generation, and listen to the artists interact with the writers and scholars on black dance.

The centerpiece of the Black Tradition in American Modern Dance (BTAMD), supported by a generous grant from the Ford Foundation, was the performances of the classic works by the legendary living choreographers working with regional professional black dance companies to reconstruct them for three concerts. On June 23–25, 1988, their choreographic works were premiered on Duke's campus at Page Auditorium: Pearl Primus's *The Negro Speaks of Rivers* and *Hard Time Blues* (both 1943), danced by Philadelphia Dance Company; Donald McKayle's *Games* (1951), performed by Chuck Davis's African American Dance Ensemble, now based at Duke University; McKayle's *Rainbow 'Round My Shoulder* (1959), performed by Dayton Contemporary Dance Company; Tally Beatty's "Congo Tango Palace" from the larger ballet *Come and Get the Beauty of It Hot* (1960), danced by Chicago's Joel Hall Dancers; and Eleo Pomare's

Las Desenamoradas (1967), performed by Dayton Contemporary Dance Company. Katherine Dunham, as a seemingly obvious omission, was *not* selected only because Alvin Ailey had recently reconstructed fourteen of her dance works in his full-evening-length *The Magic of Katherine Dunham* in 1987. As I sat in the theater viewing these classic dance works that I had only read about or viewed on film, I was humbled by the historic experience I was having. I was transported to another realm, a state of deep recognition of my history and how my ancestors survived through a commendable spiritual resilience, as well as the power of their ability to celebrate life, despite their degradation, through dance. These legendary choreographers captured the human spirit embedded in that powerful history through their artistry, now being reenacted through the young black dancing bodies of that time.

I established familiarity, and even camaraderie, with the choreographers between the formal ADF events. After going to dinner one evening with several of the choreographers, I returned to our hotel and rode in the elevator with Madame Pearl Primus. I became keenly aware of how regal and gracious she was while being down-to-earth at the same time. From the theater wings, I watched her rehearse *Hard Time Blues*, observing her showing that same grace to the dancers; there was never any yelling or diva attitude but instead quiet, thoughtful directions. Of course, it was not the same with Talley Beatty, but that is another story. Each artist had his or her own temperament, some being more unpredictable in dealing with their artistic craft than when speaking on a panel. Donald McKayle was always even-tempered and thoughtful in his assessment on the panels, adding just the right reflection at the right time, showing his great humanity. I was grateful for these formal and behind-the-scene experiences with my dance heroes.

The panel discussions were equally important, consisting of dance historians and critics, American historians and philosophers, along with the choreographers. The Sunday, June 26, 1988, panel discussion, taking place after the three concert days, was an important culmination of the project, positioning the entire dance initiative into perspective. I remember cultural and dance historian Richard Long (1927–2013), who was just about to publish *The Black Tradition in American Dance* (1990), saying at the very beginning, "The past is prologue," which opened the discussion to exploring the past through the classic works we had all just witnessed as windows into the present and future of black dance. Joe Nash, with whom I became good friends as I got more involved with the ADF project in subsequent years, said, "These artists brought 'the gospel' to the public," and now it was necessary to expound upon the "historic, philosophical, political, and economic perspectives of black dance." Joe Nash proclaimed that day, "Dance was not in isolation [from its contexts]." These pearls of wisdom opened me to what my future charge would become.

Zita Allen, the first black writer for *Dance Magazine*, also offered important insights. She noted that *Dance Magazine* had decreed that it would not review Dance Africa, a dance festival Chuck Davis started in 1977 at the Brooklyn Academy of Music. She told the panelists that the magazine did not view African dance as an art form. She offered that anecdote to emphasize the level of prejudice that black dance has had to endure, and she said, "Because of this closed door, the fabric of American dance is suffering." This was exactly why Charles and Stephanie Reinhart, the then codirectors of ADF, knew it was long overdue that their premier modern dance organization recognize this historic travesty and bring major attention to the issues of black choreographers and black dance at the end of the 1980s.

The choreographers themselves listened attentively, and each offered what he or she was currently doing with his or her work, echoing that they had *lived and danced* through the history being discussed. Talley talked about his jazz ballet *Stack Up* that he had choreographed in 1983 for Alvin Ailey, and how it reflected what he was seeing in the 1980s on the streets of Harlem. Donny was excited about reconstructing his *District Storyville* on Dayton Contemporary Dance Theater and was particularly well aware of the issues being discussed. He was one of the few dancers who wrote about their plight in his short, but poignant "The Negro Dance in Our Time" in Walter Sorell's *The Dance Has Many Faces* (1966). But it was Eleo Pomare, bad boy of the New York dance scene of the 1960s and 1970s (see chapter 3), who acknowledged that although the ADF project discussion was positive, "What are we going to do now?" Eleo was always about activist organizing, and his question was key. I took it seriously and decided then and there that in order to not repeat the past, I needed to develop a project for *contemporary* black choreographers of the 1980s going into the 1990s and the twenty-first century. I got busy developing and producing my own black choreography advocacy project in 1989, and because of my growing reputation as a black dance critic in 1990, I returned to ADF's BTAMD project as a panelist.

As a part of the humanities component of the BTAMD project, ADF published the booklet *The Black Tradition in American Modern Dance* in 1988. Among the important essays documented in the small, linear-shaped booklet were Robert Hinton's "Black Dance in American History," which would become a staple on the reading list for my dance courses at Stanford. "'Gimme de Kneebone Bent': African Body Language and the Evolution of American Dance Forms" by Peter Wood and Joe Nash's "Pioneers in Negro Concert Dance: 1931 to 1937" both unearthed little-known early black modern dancers Hemsley Winfield and Edna Guy. Zita Allen's "What Is Black Dance?" laid out the conundrum of the appellation "black dance" itself, and William Moore (1933–1992) wrote "The Development of Black Modern Dance in America," a brilliant positioning of black dance within the larger context of black aesthetic in the United States and Europe. One of Moore's arguments is that black choreographers must have "the freedom and mobility to create from the total fabric of the Black experience . . . , [meaning] the freedom of black artists to create works within and outside of their specific African American heritage."[48] This point alludes to black choreographers not being boxed into the established black heritage—to have the freedom to choreograph within and without that cultural foundation. This was key for me, and this "freedom" became part of my concept for the Black Choreographers Moving Toward the 21st Century (BCM) project that I had begun to initiate in California. The ADF project was definitely fulfilling its mission by making sure that these dance classics by choreographers without their own dance companies were being performed for the current generation.

Although ADF's three-year BTAMD project on Duke University's campus with the choreographic reconstructions formally ended in 1990, the humanities component continued. There was a second scholarly publication in 1993, *African American Genius in Modern Dance*, for which I wrote an essay, and a national ADF-on-Tour Performance with Dayton Contemporary Dance Company (DCDC) accompanied by a cadre of humanities scholars, which I joined. There were also administrative resources put to the task of producing a documentary film on the subject of black modern dance, culminating in the 2001 *Free to Dance: The African American Presence in Modern Dance*. The 1993 tour spread around the country to continue the important rejoinder that BTAMD had become to the usual Eurocentric narrative of modern dance. Art Waber, now president of Artsource Management, was the efficient ADF coordinator of the national tour who got us to the right part of the country at the right time. Geraldyne Blunden's

DCDC would perform a concert of reconstructed works on one or two nights, and we scholars—Beverly Barber, my friend VèVè Clark, Karen Hubbard, Richard Long, Joe Nash, Cynthia Sithembile West, Arthur Wilson, Peter Wood, project director Gerald Myers, and myself—would hold audience discussions on the contextual issues at postperformance talks or on separate days as their own events. I had now become thoroughly a part of the ADF Black Tradition project as a scholar.

From January through May, the tour went to Pennsylvania, Wisconsin, Ohio, Oregon, California, North Carolina, and New Mexico. Different scholars were chosen from the pool for different legs of the tour, but Joe Nash had become the official historian-archivist of the ADF project and went to all tour dates. He and I became very good friends, spending many hours in between public presentations talking about black dance history and artists. I learned so much from him and even today miss the infectious twinkle in his eye. Joe, Gerry Meyers, and I were the panelists who went to the Southwest, to Taos, Farmington, and Silver City, New Mexico—Indian country—where we interacted with the Navajo in an important cultural exchange. One of our panel discussions took place on the reservation itself, the day following a DCDC performance. The Navajo elders had refreshments for us and listened to our talk on African American dance. Then they asked, "Could you help us use this modern dance to tell the story of our Long Walk?"[49] Although it was perfectly logical, I was taken aback because I didn't expect that question. They told us that so many of their young people were losing touch with their tribal history, and after seeing the performance they thought a contemporary dance concert could better tell their own history to their young people. I realized Native Americans, too, needed to use dance to tell their story of oppression from their own perspective. Gerry Meyers promised to look into the possibility, and I recommended some qualified choreographers for such a project. I don't know if it actually happened, but it was potentially an intriguing and worthy artistic project. This was the far-reaching influence of the Black Tradition in American Modern Dance project, and the Reinharts as codirectors, along with Dr. Gerald Myers as humanities director, dedicated much of their time and resources to garner the largest possible audience.

A larger national audience was definitely reached with the *Free to Dance* film that premiered on PBS Great Performances in a three-hour series in June 2001. The documentary was accompanied by a companion website of essays, a black dance timeline, and artists' and scholars' profiles still on-line today. It took years of fundraising and finally ended up as a coproduc-tion of ADF, the Kennedy Center for the Performing Arts, and TV Thir-teen/WNET New York. ADF found noted African American filmmaker Madison Davis Lacy to produce and direct the documentary, and Zita Allen became a writer and editor of the film. By the time the film was in production, I was living in Hawai'i, and Lacy called me to see if I could fly to New York to be filmed discussing two important dance subjects: Kath-erine Dunham's legacy and late twentieth-century black choreographers, for whom I had become a kind of spokesperson because of my own BCM project.

I was flown to New York, and Lacy actually filmed me in his own New York apartment answering his poignant and penetrating questions. I appear in the second hour of the series that devotes a half hour just to Katherine Dunham, and in the third hour devoted to the younger choreographers. In the latter, I was able to give my perspective on Bill T. Jones's controversial statement at BAM's Dance Black America conference about being "an art-ist who just happened to be black." I felt honored to have my perspectives included in this definitive documentary on blacks in modern dance, and I used excerpts from the film documentary in the dance lecture classes as my academic career developed.

ADF's second humanities booklet, *African American Genius in Modern Dance* (1993), was dedicated to William Moore, who had recently died. It was a collection of scholarly essays on the master choreographers who had been a part of the BTAMD project. My essay on contemporary choreog-raphers, "The New Moderns: The Paradox of Eclecticism and Singularity," was the only exception. Gerry thought my essay was important to include, allowing the publication to encompass the then present manifestations and potential future of this great legacy. In the essay I argue for the importance of the aesthetics of the choreographers of the 1980s, who were engaged in so-called "postmodern" dance, but who were also, in fact, connected to the legacy of the black tradition in modern dance. I state that they were ex-pressing one of the components that Bill Moore revealed as necessary for a strong black dance foundation: black choreographers creating "outside of their specific African American heritage." I felt it was important to in-clude choreographers like Bill T. Jones, Blondell Cummings, Jawole Willa Jo Zollar, Garth Fagan, David Rousseve, and Bebe Miller, within a text that mostly examined the aesthetics of Katherine Dunham, Pearl Primus, Talley Beatty, Donald McKayle, and Eleo Pomare. In the essay I articulate the aesthetic of the then current generation of black choreographers as I saw it.

> Cummings, Rousseve, Fagan, Zollar, as well as Jones, and many others are completely and utterly individual in approach having no single dance aesthetic which binds them together. Yet their commonality is a willingness to be eclectic, multi-disciplinary and dense, risk the wrath of the "immoral minority" (like many of their white contemporaries), and use whatever media are necessary to serve a work's purpose. . . . Their predecessors have paved the way for them to be completely who they are as individuals.[50]

In California I had already started Black Choreographers Moving Toward the 21st Century and had actually incorporated works by some of these artists into my own national dance project. ADF's Black Tradition project had taught me well the components and logistics of transformative national dance initiatives, and now I was becoming a black dance arts advocate for the current generation of black choreographers, helping to define their contemporary aesthetic within the complexities of the era moving into the twenty-first century.

Black Dance Initiative: Black Choreographers Moving Toward the 21st Century (BCM)

The year 1989 was truly transitional for me professionally and personally. As a part of my Stanford University job, I was preparing for the major May 1989 Katherine Dunham Residency, and at forty-two years old I was beginning to feel my transition into middle age, coming into the realization that with all of the different roles that I had been playing with (black) dance, I needed to come to terms with where my professional mark was really going to be. I was past my prime as a performer, and although my choreographic career was credible, my dancemaking never really made national waves. Joan Myers Brown's Philadanco in Philadelphia had already inaugurated the International Association of Blacks in Dance (IABD) in January 1988, and she began to organize all the major regional black dance companies, including those used in the ADF project, to support each other around their own interests. It became obvious to me that my career mark was as a thinker-organizer, emphasizing the discourse of blackness within the dance field. My career focus was made increasingly important by a major national arts trend called by the buzz term "Multicultural Arts and Audiences."

As I had cut my teeth, so to speak, on ADF's BTAMD project, I put together a project proposal focusing on innovative contemporary black choreographers that would be linked to the ongoing question of "What is black dance?": How are contemporary young black choreographers dealing with the black dance legacy, within the context of their own individual artistic statements, moving toward a new century? From the very beginning I wanted the project, Black Choreographers Moving Toward the 21st Century (BCM), to focus on dancemakers and their *individual* artistic statements rather than on the conundrum of "black dance" itself. One decade away from the new millennium, I felt it was time to make a national statement about the state of contemporary black choreographers, just as ADF had done with the older dance masters and their legacy that laid the foundation. I had always been ahead of the curve, like ECAC and CDT's multicultural dance approach with an emphasis in African-derived dance classes and performances. Now I was using all of my accumulated arts organizational acumen to develop a comprehensive new national dance initiative.

In late 1988, I took my BCM proposal to one of the major theater and dance presenters in San Francisco, Theater Artaud, to see if they would enter into an agreement with me to present the first BCM project in November 1989. Theater Artaud is a part of Project Artaud, a pioneering arts complex in San Francisco's Mission District started by a group of artists in 1972 who moved into an abandoned industrial warehouse building and named it after the French avant-garde theater artist Antoine Artaud (1886–1948). Theater Artaud became the most visible part of Project Artaud, fiercely representing an experimental approach to the performing arts while developing an excellent reputation as *the* avant-garde theater presenter in San Francisco. Kim Fowler, the then executive director of Theater Artaud, who is African American, was receptive but initially skeptical about the possibility of funding for such an ambitious project, with performances by nationally recognized dance companies, symposia, and outreach classes in the public schools. I ended up writing a proposal for the BCM project to the National Endowment for the Arts that *was* funded, convincing her to put the BCM project into the theater's 1989 season.

But my plans for BCM were more ambitious than just San Francisco and the Bay Area. I wanted to make it a national dance initiative that presented what I called the "BCM Model" in Los Angeles, as the other major California city. But San Francisco was *my* town, and I had little experience with the southern California city that we in northern California call "Tinsel Town." My main LA contact was James Burks, then executive director of the Ira Aldridge Acting Competition, producer of the L.A. African Marketplace, and director of special projects with the City of Los Angeles Department of Cultural Affairs. When I took my proposal to him, he immediately set up a meeting for me with the executive director of the most prestigious presenter in Los Angeles, UCLA Center for the Performing Arts. Along with James Burks, I entered Pebble Wadsworth's office at UCLA wearing my best business suit and left with a tentative "yes" to my BCM proposal.

To a presenter, funding is key, and with a major grant from the National Endowment for the Arts, along with a ready-made project that focused on diversity in dance, this proposal offered a win-win situation. However, she rightfully felt that the black community would respond more favorably if UCLA collaborated with a smaller black arts organization. She suggested black producer Neil Barclay and his First Impressions Performances. Neil, Pebbles, and I met and constructed a collaborative organizational deal that worked for Los Angeles. Therefore, UCLA Center for the Performing Arts' Wadsworth Theater and SF's Theater Artaud became the two presenter-venues for the first Black Choreographers Moving Toward the 21st Century project in 1989, immediately establishing itself as a national dance initiative to be noticed.

My 1989 BCM project was in tune with the times because major multicultural arts festivals that featured dance were emerging, and BCM was comprehensive, presenting high-quality dance in a topical sociopolitical context. Peter Sellars's Los Angeles Festival was one year away from bringing "authentic" Pacific Rim cultural dance to Los Angeles, and Leni Sloan's Festival 2000 in San Francisco was slated to show off the best of diverse national dance, featuring Katherine Dunham as guest of honor. Preceding these high-profile events, Black Choreographers Moving Toward the 21st Century brought established or emerging black choreographers from around the country to California, along with top scholars of black dance in a series of symposia, and outreach lecture-demonstrations by the artists in public schools. Hence, BCM presented black cutting-edge dance artists, put audiences in dialogue with the best thinkers about the legacy and contemporary issues of black choreographers, and developed new audiences by taking the dance into public schools and universities. To ensure good audience attendance and the greatest community impact, I formed an advisory committee in each city representing different sectors of the community that supplemented the general media publicity.

BCM received major national and local publicity from the outset, immediately establishing it on the coast-to-coast artistic map. *Dance Magazine's* November 1989 issue recorded me as the executive producer saying, "The idea is not so much to deal with the issue of whether there is a black dance style, but rather to make a statement regarding the diversity of black choreographers." Although the project encompassed the subject of "black dance" I focused on the *diversity* of styles by black choreographers as the raison d'être of the project, debunking any stereotypic image that audiences, both white and black, might have had about black choreographers. This was evident in the ten choreographers from four different states represented in the 1989 festival: San Francisco's Alonzo King's Lines Ballet with guest artist Christopher Boatwright from the San Francisco Ballet; San Francisco's aerialist-dancer Joanna Haigood/Zaccho Dance Theater; Oakland's Dimensions Dance Theater performing a Garth Fagan work; Los Angeles's Lula Washington Contemporary Dance Company; John Pickett's Spotted Leopard Dance Company that had a Japanese butoh aesthetic; Denver's Cleo Parker Robinson Dance Ensemble; New York's Urban Bush Women and Donald Byrd/The Group. The 1989 inaugural BCM project not only made an *intended* eclectic artistic statement about black choreographers, but regionally it allowed northern California dance companies to be seen in Los Angeles and vice versa, something that rarely happened.

There's an adage that says, "Humans make plans and God laughs." We producers of BCM were definitely challenged with this metaphysical reality due to the 1989 San Francisco Bay Area earthquake happening two weeks before we were to premiere the BCM project. The Loma Prieta earthquake occurred on October 17, the strongest earthquake to hit the Bay Area since the famous 1906 quake. There were 63 deaths, 3,800 injuries, and an estimated $6 billion in property damage, including to the San Francisco–Oakland Bay Bridge when a span of the top deck collapsed to the lower deck.[51] The bridge, the lifeline of Bay Area transportation, was not operational, and the entire region was severely traumatized to say the least.

When the quake occurred I was on the Stanford campus, the only one left in Harmony House doing administrative work for CBPA. The approximate forty-mile commute between Palo Alto and Oakland that usually took about fifty minutes, on that day took two and a half hours, with no traffic lights working. Drivers were in shock and were thankfully especially courteous driving through the streets that evening. Eventually I was able to get through by phone to Kimathi, and he let me know that he and our home were fine, with only minor cracks in the walls and a few broken trinkets. But Theater Artaud and I had to have an emergency meeting about whether to continue on with the BCM festival. Even the World Series being played at Candlestick Park between the San Francisco Giants and the Oakland As was postponed for ten days.

Kim Fowler, her staff, and I decided to continue on with our plans for the November 1 opening of the BCM festival, with transportation as the major problem to be figured out. As the bridge could no longer be used, traveling between the San Francisco peninsula and the East Bay was solely through the underground BART system. As people coming from the East Bay could not *drive* across the Bay Bridge, we knew that transportation from the nearest S.F. BART station on Mission Street, at least three-quarters of a mile from the theater, would be a challenge. We decided to rent a van to transport audience members, free of charge, from BART to the theater and to return them to the station after the show. We began an immediate advertising campaign to inform the public that we would provide this theater shuttle service. Our quick thinking and administrative troubleshooting paid off with sold-out houses at Theater Artaud for BCM's premiere. I opened the concert with a special thank-you to the audience for their emergency regrouping and attendance after such a severe natural disaster: "Obviously the Bay Area earthquake could not keep you away from the opening of Black Choreographers Moving Toward the 21st Century. You have shown what strong stuff we Bay Area folks are made of. Thank you." In his review of the performance, San Francisco dance critic Allan Ulrich wrote, "Events like this 10-day celebration, organized by Artaud's Kim Fowler and Expansion Arts Services' Halifu Osumare, may be just the remedy for the doldrums into which the arts in the Bay Area sank after the Oct. 17 earthquake."[52]

With that major logistical problem solved, the first BCM project in both San Francisco and Los Angeles was a huge success, and it became obvious that the entire BCM model was what the black dance community needed, as well as the dance field as a whole. I made clear to the media my motivation for initiating the BCM festival: "At heart I am an universalist; I like people all over the world and can get along anywhere," the *San Francisco*

Chronicle staff writer Calvin Ahlgren recorded from an interview with me. "However, I could feel my own cultural roots, and when I came back [from Europe], I found myself really wanting to explore the black experience. . . . I feel like I do have a national perspective on current trends in the arts, and brought all that information and [those] contacts to bear on this project."[53] I also made it clear that the BCM model was based on ADF's BTAMD project.

The equally important humanities component of BCM contextualized the entire project with eight panels in San Francisco and four in Los Angeles. This component was solely my purview and eventually became my specialty in the annual BCM project that continued over the next five years. In the inaugural festival I brought together four scholars and one artist associated with the ADF project—Brenda Dixon Gottschild, Joe Nash, Julinda Lewis-Ferguson, William Moore, and choreographer Cleo Parker Robinson—along with key local dance and black cultural spokespersons in both cities. In the Bay Area I included many of my colleagues from over the years, such as Nontsizi Cayou, Deborah Vaughan, Linda Goodrich, and Geraldyne Washington. In Los Angeles, I incorporated local dance pioneer R'Wanda Lewis, the late black theater pioneer C. Bernard Jackson (1927–1996), Donald McKayle, and Lula Washington.

The discussions that emerged through the panels in the two cities were so rich and vital that I got funding from the California Arts Council to publish a book excerpting key panel discussions, which I titled *Black Choreographers Moving: A National Dialogue*. The 1991 book was compiled and published by me and edited by Julinda Lewis-Ferguson. As online file sharing did not exist at the time, I remember flying at least twice to New York, where Julinda lived, to work on the manuscript; during that era we were still downloading files onto floppy disks, with no storage on the average desktop computer. In the text we also included scholarly essays, such as Joe Nash's "Blacks in Concert Dance: A Step in Time" and Julinda's "Blacks in Postmodern Dance." Brenda Dixon Gottschild wrote "The Afrocentric Aesthetic," which presaged her seminal *Digging the Africanist Presence in American Performance: Dance and Other Contexts* (1996), and I wrote "The Avant Garde, Dance History and Labels." I had one thousand copies printed and personally marketed them nationally to university libraries and bookstores, hiring a personal assistant to handle the administrative details of the book marketing and mailings; all copies were sold. Yes, I worked hard on this project, and when I look back on the entire BCM effort I make myself tired. But I was on fire with my determination to make a difference in my chosen profession of dance; as I say today, my ancestors drove me.

My independent, rebellious nature revealed itself loud and clear in my BCM project. I did not hold my tongue in articulating the ultimate problem underlying the need for the BCM project: "America's a racist country," I succinctly articulated to *Los Angeles Times* journalist Martin David about BCM. But, during his interview he captured my underlying personality as more than simply indignant about U.S. political and cultural history:

> Osumare, who had the predominant hand in choosing both the performers and the panelists, sees the festival as helping to steer away from what she calls this country's Eurocentric bias. "We have to re-think our history, because our history was written by people whose visions were colored by their own upbringing and their own knowledge. . . . America has always had this vision of itself," she adds, referring to the country's pride in its melting-pot heritage, "but it's been pretty hypocritical about it." The tall soft-spoken Osumare strikes the casual observer as neither a rabble-rouser nor a harried producer whose first major festival has just become a reality. Her pronouncements come in an easy, conversational tone and her eyes are just as likely to convey flashes of humor as of indignation.[54]

I had had many experiences throughout the dance world on three different continents with ten years of directing a multicultural dance center, all of which balanced my perspective about the complex artistic and cultural history underlying the BCM project. These experiences had fired my rebellious nature but also tempered me about the reality of cultural change at the same time. I was simply telling it like it was (is), without malice. I was trying to wake up the country and the dance world to their hypocrisy with my BCM project; I wanted to see black artists treated as individuals like any other group of artists. As Joe Nash said at one of the panels (figure 19), "The dancer needs to become an intellectual guardian for his/her art form," and I was taking on that mantle.

The 1989 two-city BCM festival was such a resounding success that both presenters and the Bay Area and Los Angeles communities wanted it to happen again. Luckily, the BCM project continued through a circuitous route for the next five years, even after I moved to Hawai'i. Theater Artaud and I received an Izzie Award (the San Francisco Bay Area Dance Coalition's Isadora Duncan Dance Awards) for the BCM project, and Dr. Ernest

L. Washington, M.D., a Los Angeles black medical doctor who specialized in kinesiology and sports medicine for dancers, published several of his *Talking Drums! The Black Dance Newsletters* on the BCM project for the Los Angeles dance community. The next festival happened in 1991, giving the presenters and me a little over a year for the planning.

The 1992 festival expanded to San Diego, a third city for BCM, presented by Sushi Performance and Visual Art at the Lyceum Theater. That year's performances featured Dallas Black Dance Theater performing works by choreographers Kevin Jeff and noted modern dance master Milton Myers. We introduced the Rousseve/Reality company directed by David Rousseve, a new choreographer that focused on performance art, as well as choreographer Maia Claire Garrison, the daughter of famed jazz bassist Jimmy Garrison, with whom I danced at Ornette Coleman's Artist House back in 1972 (chapter 3). Lynn Schuette, executive director of Sushi, wrote in the San Diego program, "For the first time, Sushi will be able to offer a cultural, social, historical, and political context for the exceptional black choreographers we have previously presented."

The BCM project became a major boost to the presenters in the three cities, bringing them increased regional and national recognition, particularly with black audiences, which grew because of the project. Theater Artaud definitely became more visible to the theatergoing black community, while Neil Barclay's First Impressions organization was actually put on the Los Angeles map with BCM, as he took the project from UCLA to the Japanese American Community and Cultural Center's Aratani Theatre. As Kim Fowler resigned as executive director of Theater Artaud and Dean Beck-Stewart took over the reins of the organization, my relationship continued with the San Francisco presenter under his direction.

Dean, Neil, and Lynn then formed a coalition as presenters of the BCM project. Over time they began to organize without me, the overarching executive producer and humanities coordinator, which changed the entire administrative dynamics. When I saw a potential presenters' "coup" coming, without telling them I incorporated my project as Black Choreographers Moving, Inc. as its own non-profit organization in the State of California. In a 1993 meeting between the three BCM presenters and me, I announced the formation of the incorporated BCM non-profit organization. One could have heard a pin drop in Lynn Schuette's San Diego home, where we were meeting. All three looked at me, and Neil ventured to articulate what they were all feeling, "How could you do this without telling us?" I simply answered: "I don't need your permission to incorporate a project that I conceived, established, and initially got funded. I appreciate what you have all done as presenters to make this project what it has become, but I will not be pushed out of my own creation. Anything that happens with Black Choreographers Moving must happen with my approval." Needless to say, I stayed a part of all decision making for the 1993 and 1994 projects and only turned over the total reins of the BCM project to the presenters when Kimathi and I moved to Hawai'i.

My Mission and My Family

What I call the "mission" that drove my career obviously came first. Dancing, and all of the roles that I assumed around this calling—performer, choreographer, director, dance educator, arts administrator, community organizer, national black dance advocate—took priority over Kimathi and my family. But I did try to find some balance in the midst of such "obsession" (do I dare call it that?) with my life's calling. Luckily I was married to someone who had his own calling in music but, as I perceive it now, not nearly to the degree that I did with dance and arts advocacy.

Kimathi had organized several of his own music groups during the time that we were developing ECAC. His first group was Kimathi Asante and Something Else, but his music ensemble that made the biggest "noise" was Kimathi Asante and Umlilo, which included two members of the Uzulu Dance Theatre of South Africa, a group of South African dancers and musicians whom we helped get established in the Bay Area. The South African performers arrived in Oakland in 1983, after defecting from the South African musical *Ipi Tombi* touring the United States in the early 1980s. Thamsanqa Hiatywayo, Dingane Lelokoane, Matome Somo, and Sechaba Mokeoena became a part of the Bay Area dance and music scene, with Dingane and Matome becoming a part of Kimathi Asante and Umlilo. While working at the *East Bay Express* newspaper and helping with some of the ECAC decisions as board member, Kimathi struggled with his music career on a local level, but the Pyramids, the group with whom he had come to the Bay Area (chapter 4), remained his major performing credit that established his music reputation. Today, the Pyramids have been revived and frequently tour Europe, where their audience following continued.

During the 1980s several major events happened within both of our families. Kimathi's mother, Betty, married Lindy Woodward, who was the first deaf man she had been serious about. Betty (1931–2015) had always been with hearing men, having been a gregarious deaf woman who did not let her so-called disability define her, but with Lindy, who did not speak either, she had totally entered the deaf world. Kimathi and I went to Ohio to their joyous wedding in 1986, and I truly became a part of his family, establishing a solid friendship with his sisters Rosemary, Kathy, Pauline, and Susan, as well as a deep love for Mama Betty. Also in the late 1980s, my sister Brenda had a girl-child, Anjelica Morgan, and my second niece arrived as another strong-willed female who fit right into the family temperament (Tenola had my first niece, Theresa, when I was in Ghana). As I could not have children and Kimathi and I had decided against adopting, I began to realize that children would have been a serious challenge to the pursuit of my mission with the fervor I had pursued it. My youngest sister, Tracey, in the early 1990s created another circle in my life by marrying a Danish man, Torben Voetmann, an exchange student at San Francisco State University, where she was attending graduate school. Many previous parts of my life were reconnecting during this life transitional period.

My stepfather, Herman, passed in January 1990 at seventy-four years old, and I was grateful that I had made peace with him before he died. We had such a rocky relationship throughout my younger years. He was an "old-school" father who could not reconcile my rebellious, independent nature with what he thought an obedient daughter should be. But in the end, he realized that I had made good choices for my life's path because he acknowledged my success in the dance field and told me, in fact, that he was proud of me. At first, my mother, Tenola, seemed a bit lost after her husband of forty years passed, but his death actually opened the way for her to make her own personal decisions for the first time in her life. Like so many women of her generation, she had gone from her mother, Alberta, to her first husband, Leroy, and to Herman in rapid succession. I was so happy to see her use her newfound freedom to her advantage, starting exercise classes, becoming a TM meditator, and going to many theatrical productions with her friends.

As I look back, the period from 1977 after West Africa to 1994, when Kimathi and I moved to the Big Island of Hawai'i, had solidified my career. I had established my reputation regionally and nationally by founding Everybody's Creative Arts Center, which had become the major center in the Bay Area for African and African-derived dance with a multicultural arts focus. I had galvanized and organized the Bay Area multicultural arts movement with several annual arts concerts, including the Multicultural Festival of Dance and Music that became a prototype for subsequent Bay Area annual festivals, such as today's Ethnic Dance Festival. I had helped give a voice to the multicultural arts movement not only in the Bay Area but also statewide through the California Arts Council, and even nationally with the National Endowment for the Arts. Simultaneously, I had worked at Stanford University as dance lecturer and administrator of CBPA, teaching black dance and helping to further black studies at that institution through the arts. As an artist, I had continued to develop my choreographic craft through my early company, Aquarius Rising Dance Theater, and had matured my dancemaking craft through ECAC's professional company, CitiCentre Dance Theatre, which had briefly gained an international reputation.

As I nourished my dance career I was simultaneously developing my perspectives on black dance advocacy, gaining a national perspective as major black dance initiatives were developing in the 1980s: BAM's Dance Black America in 1983 and ADF's Black Tradition in American Modern Dance starting in 1988. By the end of the 1980s, my administrative and advocacy skills had matured to the point that I had developed my own national dance initiative, adding my voice to the end of the twentieth-century black dance advocacy movement with Black Choreographers Moving Toward the 21st Century. I had made my professional mark, not as a dancer-choreographer but as an articulate spokesperson for the multicultural arts movement in America through black dance.

In 1993 I finished my master's program at San Francisco State, an institution that had served me since the mid-1960s, obtaining a graduate degree in dance ethnology. I then wanted to parlay my master's into a doctorate in anthropology, following in the footsteps of my mentor Katherine Dunham. I had been going to East St. Louis to study directly with Miss Dunham since 1988, and utilizing my relationship with Stanford University, I had established two major Stanford residencies for her in 1989 and 1990; my relationship with Katherine Dunham had become so important and far-reaching that it deserves its own book. In the process, I realized that instead of a recognized artist, I had become a thinker and activist for black dance and culture's influence in the United States and the world, and I wanted to pursue this line of research academically. My life's mission at forty-eight years old was leading me to become a scholar as a second career. Hawai'i represented not only a personal and cultural shift with Kimathi but also a chance to pursue a doctorate degree and shift my focus to academia.

Transitioning from Dance to Academia: The Bay Area to Hawai'i

I finish this memoir with our transition to Hawai'i on the brink of my second career as a tenure-track professor. The series of community farewells for me began in October 1993 with a gathering at CitiCentre Dance Theatre (CDT) at the Alice Arts Center, now the Malonga Casquelourd Center for the Arts. A wonderful synchronicity happened on October 14, 1993: Les Ballets Africains de la République de Guinée was performing at UC Berkeley, and Ursula Smith, the CDT director at that time, decided that my farewell reception could happen along with a reception recognizing that premier West African dance company. The simultaneous receptions brought my Bay Area work full circle with the African community, because not only had I been an avid follower of the dance company since the 1960s (chapter 1), but I had produced Oakland dance workshops for their choreographer, Kemoko Sano, and members of the company, hosting them at our home and becoming good friends with Sano. The Ballets Africains reception was held in the first-floor lobby of "The Alice," and my farewell reception was held in the second-floor dance studio, with me giving commemorative speeches at both.

I realized that day that I don't do farewells very well. I work myself to almost complete exhaustion, but public "thank-yous" and too much focused recognition of my work make me uncomfortable. However, I did feel honored and wrote the following in my ongoing journal:

> To know that I am loved and held in high esteem by those who are still involved and dancing with "my baby," Everybody's/CitiCentre, which I labored over for so many years, made the CitiCentre Farewell fully rewarding. Words simply can't describe it. Many people shared their love and respect for me, and this allowed me to know how much effect I have had on the East Bay dance scene. Ruth Beckford came to speak, which was like "Mama" giving testimony to her daughter. It was beyond belief. Carlos Aceituno and Fogo Na Ropa played high-powered afoxe and samba; African dancer and friend Linda Johnson, whom I had introduced to the Bay Area dance community, spoke; other African dance teachers who had

become my friends, like Mabiba Baegne from the Congo and Zak Diouf (Senegal) and his wife, Naomi Ghedo (Liberia), also came out to say good-bye. Linda Goodrich did a dance for me to music used by Leon Jackson that became a tear-jerker. When she invited me to dance with her in the last section of her dance in honor of me, it was overwhelming. Linda had become my best friend and we danced our connected spirits for each other, going into another world. The spirit sent us from a "chasse frolic" into a "Yoruba ritual" creating a deep soul force. When our dance ended, we bowed to each other and "came back" into the room. That was my transition dance, my dance of leave-taking! There was no fear, just a willingness to be moved and journey forward.

I went through a similar parting at my other long-term institution, Stanford University. In the Roble Dance Studio on December 9, 1993, after twelve years of teaching and choreographing in the Stanford Dance Division, administrating the Committee on Black Performing Arts (CBPA), and organizing and implementing two Dunham residencies, I was leaving. Campus faculty and staff, with whom I had interacted for over a decade, came out in full force to acknowledge my contributions to Stanford. Harry Elam, director of CBPA; the administrative assistant, Elena Becks; and Susie Cashion of the Dance Division worked in tandem to organize the Halifu Osumare Stanford Farewell.

When it was my turn to speak and to show some dance class demonstrations with my current students, I was overwhelmed after a myriad of speeches about my contributions by deans, professors, and dance colleagues. Stanford University was honoring *me*, a lecturer with no clout within the academic hierarchy of the Ivy League institution of the West. I knew I would have trouble receiving these many accolades and genuine personal love. In my ending speech, I was honest and simply said:

> *For some of us, it is easier to give than to receive. But you have allowed me to grow to a new level of accepting praise, love, and gratitude in large doses. Thank you! However, the ancestors will not let me get such a swollen head over all of this, because I am acutely aware that we were all in this last twelve years together. I could not have done what I did without you—faculty, students, peers, superiors, and subordinates—we were all in it together. In honoring me, you honor yourselves!*

I packed away all of my files from CitiCentre, Stanford, Black Choreographers Moving, and my many choreographic projects, as Kimathi and I continued to ready ourselves for the big transition to Hawai'i. I spent more time with family members while preparing our "piece of the rock" on Sixtieth Street to rent. Over the years we had bought the house and taken over the ground-level apartment, opening an indoor staircase to the first floor and thereby creating a one family unit. Kimathi and I were entering a new life plateau as we prepared for the move to Hawai'i.

Although I knew I was preparing for a life transition that was not only geographical, I could not have fully understood the life changes that lay ahead of me with this move to the Pacific. I was about to transition from *dancing* to *writing dance*, as I mention in the introduction; I was destined to develop the skill of dancing across the *page* rather than the *stage*. I applied to the University of Hawai'i's Department of Anthropology, attempting to follow my dance mentor Katherine Dunham. I naively thought my master's degree in dance ethnology from San Francisco State University would qualify me to enter a formal anthropology doctoral program. In actuality, UH-Manoa's anthropology department no longer had a dance anthropologist like Adrienne Kaeppler with whom I could work, and required me to get a master's degree in anthropology itself. Needless to say, at my age I was not about to start at the master's level again.

As I was interested in dance and Africanist performance, it was the anthropology department that recommended I look into the Department of American Studies at UH-Manoa, one of only seven Ph.D. programs in the discipline in the United States. American studies is interdisciplinary, with a strong emphasis in history, literature, popular culture, and often anthropology. I researched the department's faculty members and found scholars like political radical David Stannard who taught courses on race and racism, and African American literature scholar David Helbling. I applied to the department, and to my surprise they accepted me, saying although they did not have a faculty focused specifically on African American performance, with Helbling's focus in literature, and their interest in performance's interface with American studies, they were willing to accept me with my research agenda. I felt blessed to have found this department and American studies as a discipline through which I could begin to explore black performance and its influence on the United States and the world. As a baby boomer, little did I know then that my research focus would end up being hip-hop.

Becoming a doctor of philosophy in American studies in 1999 would lead to two major tenure-track academic appointments: the Dance Division at Bowling Green State University (2000–2005) and the Department of African American and African Studies at University of California, Davis (2005–16), during the latter of which I would become a full professor, eventually retiring in 2016.

Beginning my Hawai'i sojourn, I could definitely not have fathomed that I was to become a recognized hip-hop scholar, choosing the globalization of hip-hop as the new lens through which I would continue to explore "dancing in blackness" as it manifested in U.S. concert dance with brilliant choreographers like Rennie Harris, as well as the internationalization of this influential youth culture. I could not have imagined that *The Africanist Aesthetic in Global Hip-Hop: Power Moves* (2007), with my major theoretical perspective of "connective marginality" as global sociopolitical inequalities that link hip-hop youth beyond the culture's commercialization, would put me on the academic map as hip-hop studies became a bourgeoning new academic discipline.

Five years later, my *The Hiplife in Ghana: West African Indigenization of Hip-Hop* (2012) would be the result of a coveted Fulbright Fellowship. The research for my second book would bring me full circle with Ghana, which I had experienced thirty-two years earlier as a dancer (chapter 5). My six-month Fulbright at University of Ghana in 2008 allowed me to renew my relationship with Professor Kwabena Nketia, then eighty-seven years old, and my old friend, the late Nii Yartey (figure 20). It would also spur me to make connections between Ghanaian dance, music, and culture with the current manifestation of hip-hop in Accra called hiplife, a confluence between hip-hop and highlife music. My life had come full circle, and the artist and the scholar were connecting in a vital way that yielded unique insights in *The Hiplife in Ghana*.

Personally, as Kimathi and I left to start our new life in Hawai'i, I could not have foreseen that we would eventually divorce in 2004, and I would marry a second time to my current deeply supportive husband, painter-poet-playwright Gene Howell. All of these life changes were ten years in the future, and the subject of a future memoir. In February 1994, I was leaving the Bay Area—my home area where I had finally become entrenched and focused on my mission for seventeen years. I could not help but realize that my work—my mission—had made a major difference in that community.

Today, when I go to the Malonga Casquelourd Center for the Arts at Fourteenth and Alice Streets in Oakland, I witness the continuing healing power of the dance and drumming classes for a whole new generation of young people of all colors. These sweating dancing bodies are attracted to the power of Africa and black dance, and I realize that the curative rhythms of blackness beat on over time, even in the urban gentrification of the so-called "New Oakland." I realize, in keeping with the following insight by playwright Cherríe Moraga, that I could not help but follow my mission— my path of destiny: "Finding the path to memory is my task as an artist; writing for the 'Ancestors' as playwright August Wilson has said. That's my job. To remember ancestral messages, to counter the U.S. culture of forgetfulness."[55] Today I realize that remembering ancestral messages is the process in which I have been engaged my entire career—"dancing in blackness" for my ancestors and for the future generations—for those who have the eyes to see and the ears to hear.

My ancestors gave of themselves to make sure I could continue to dance in blackness to save myself, and in the process to help save others. One important Congolese adage that Malonga's Fua Dia Congo company uses is, *Wa dia Fua Yika Dio* (What you inherit, you must add value to). I have come to understand through my *mission* that Dance is Life and Life is a Dance, and I am the Eternal Dancer.

Notes

Introduction: Dance and Blackness

1. Susan Leigh Foster, *Choreographing Empathy: Kinesthesia in Performance* (New York: Routledge, 2011), 45; Margaret Newell H'Doubler, *Rhythmic Form and Analysis* (Madison, WI: J. M. Rider, 1932), 1.

2. Karen Nicole Barbour, *Dancing across the Page: Narrative and Embodied Ways of Knowing* (Bristol, UK: Intellect, 2011).

3. Ibid., 52.

4. Clifford Geertz, *Works and Lives: The Anthropologist as Author* (Stanford, CA: Stanford University Press, 1988), 23.

5. Ibid., 9.

6. Judith Lynn Hanna, *To Dance Is Human: A Theory of Nonverbal Communication* (1979; Chicago: University of Chicago Press, 1987), 5.

7. Ibid.

8. See Robert Farris Thompson, "Toward a History of African Dance," in *African Art in Motion,* by Thompson, 29–41 (Los Angeles: University of California Press, 1974).

9. See Joe Nash, "Pioneers in Negro Concert Dance: 1931–1937," in *The Black Tradition in American Modern Dance,* ed. Gerald E. Myers, 11–13 (Durham, NC: American Dance Festival, Duke University, 1988).

10. Qtd. in Ntongela Masilela, "The Importance of the African Element in Contemporary Dance Culture," *Attitude: The Dancers' Magazine* 5 (1988): 10.

11. Ibid.

12. Joyce Aschenbrenner, *Katherine Dunham: Reflections on the Social and Political Contexts of Afro-American Dance. Dance Research Journal Annual XII* (New York: Congress on Research in Dance, 1980), 23.

13. Zita Allen, "What Is Black Dance?," in *The Black Tradition in American Modern Dance,* ed. Gerald E. Myers (Durham, NC: American Dance Festival, Duke University, 1988), 22.

14. Nash, "Pioneers in Negro Concert Dance," 11.

15. This is not to belittle Flournoy Miller's and Aubrey Lyles's genius. They were two of the most talented and prolific theater people of the vaudeville era, whose greatest achievement was *Shuffle Along* in 1921. However, their continuation of the blackface genre of performing as late as 1943 set them apart as continuing a dying theatrical image.

16. See Aschenbrenner in *Katherine Dunham: Reflections on The Social and Political Contexts of Afro-American Dance.*

17. Brenda Dixon Gottschild, "Is Race Still an Issue in Dance?," *Dance Magazine,* February 2005, 54. See also Brenda Dixon Gottschild, *The Black Dancing Body: A Geography from Coon to Cool* (New York: Palgrave Macmillan, 2003).

18. Susan Manning, "Modern Dance, Negro Dance and Katherine Dunham," *Textual Practice* 15, no. 3 (2001): 489. See also Susan Manning, *Modern Dance, Negro Dance: Race in Motion* (Minneapolis: University of Minnesota Press, 2004).

19. Manning, "Modern Dance, Negro Dance and Katherine Dunham," 489.

20. Andrew Hacker, *Two Nations: Black and White, Separate, Hostile, Unequal,* 2nd ed. (New York: Ballantine, 1995).

21. Nadine George-Graves, "Diasporic Spidering: Constructing Contemporary Black Identities," in *Black Performance Theory,* ed. Thomas F. DeFrantz and Anita Gonzalez (Durham, NC: Duke University Press, 2014), 37.

22. Melissa V. Harris-Perry, *Sister Citizen: Shame, Stereotypes, and Black Women in America* (New Haven, CT: Yale University Press, 2011), 33–43.

Chapter 1. Coming of Age through (Black) Dance in the San Francisco Bay Area

1. See Brenda Dixon Gottschild's chapter "Barefoot and Hot, Sneakered and Cool: Africanist Subtexts in Modern and Postmodern Dance," in her *Digging the Africanist Presence in American Performance: Dance and Other Contexts* (Westport, CT: Greenwood, 1996), 47–58.

2. Historian Glenne McElhinney is working on a documentary short about Zack Thompson for a Web series that highlights his contributions as a seminal jazz dance figure in the San Francisco Bay Area in the 1960s and 1970s.

3. See a 1968 kinescope KQED-PBS tape of a Ruth Beckford dance class as a DVD entitled *African-Haitian Dance Class: Dunham Technique,* distributed by Insight Media. It was a taping at Peters Wright Studio in San Francisco of an advanced class, in which I participated at age twenty shortly before leaving for Europe.

4. Amy Abugo Ongiri, *Spectacular Blackness: The Cultural Politics of the Black Power Movement and the Search for a Black Aesthetic* (Charlottesville: University of Virginia Press, 2010), 89.

5. James Edward Smethurst, *The Black Arts Movement: Literary Nationalism in the 1960s and 1970s* (Chapel Hill: University of North Carolina Press, 2005), 256–57.

6. Ibid., 286.

7. Larry Neal, "The Black Arts Movement," *Drama Review* 12, no. 4 (Summer 1968); reissued by National Humanities Center Resource Toolbox: The Making of

African American Identity: vol. 3, 1917–1968, http://nationalhumanitiescenter.org/pds/maai3/community/text8/blackartsmovement.pdf.

8. LeRoi Jones, "Communications Project," in "Black Theatre," special issue, *Drama Review* 12, no. 4 (Summer 1968): 53–57.

9. Ongiri, *Spectacular Blackness*, 94.

10. Ibid., 283.

11. Craig J. Peariso, *Radical Theatrics: Put-ons, Politics, and the Sixties* (Seattle: University of Washington Press, 2014), 4.

12. My use of the word "primitive" to describe my 1960s dance style did not have the academic connotation underlying Katherine Dunham's earlier anthropological use of the word. In 1930s anthropology, "primitive peoples" meant those without a written language or history. She frequently used the term "primitive dance" in that anthropological sense while illuminating the great sophistication of those dances. Even after the revisionism in social sciences that challenged this ethnocentric language, she continued to use the term, representing her original anthropological connotation.

13. See the development of the symbolism of the "panopticon" in Michel Foucault, *Discipline and Punish: The Birth of the Prison* (New York: Pantheon, 1977).

14. See his website at www.kennethnash.com/.

15. *Agents of Change* is a film codirected and produced by Frank Dawson and Abby Ginzberg about the 1968 S.F. State Strike that sparked a series of student strikes across the country. The film's website notes, "Agents of Change links the past to the present and the present to the past—making it not just a movie but a movement" (www.agentsofchangefilm.com/).

16. In 2006, the New Dance Group officially opened a new state-of-the-art studio located at 305 West Thirty-Eighth Street at Eighth Avenue.

Chapter 2. Dancing in Europe

1. "Many supporters tried to encourage Douglass to remain in England but, with his wife still in Massachusetts and three million of his black brethren in bondage in the United States, he returned to America in spring of 1847" (Wikipedia, source credited to Marianne Ruth, *Frederick Douglass* [New York: Holloway House, 1996], 117–18).

2. Bennetta Jules-Rosette, "Reflections on the Future of Black France: Josephine Baker's Vision of a Global Village," in *Black France/France Noire: The History and Politics of Blackness*, ed. Tricia Danielle Keaton, T. Denean Sharpley-Whiting, and Tyler Stovall (Durham, NC: Duke University Press, 2012), 248.

3. Daniel James Brown, "My Educational Life at GSU," blog entry, September 9, 2012, Word Press.com, http://danieljamesbrown91.wordpress.com/2012/09/11/discovery-of-what-it-means-to-be-an-american-by-james-baldwin-1961/.

4. Karen C. Dalton, "Baker, Josephine, and La Revue Négre," in *Africana: The Encyclopedia of the African and African American Experience*, 2nd ed., 3, www.oxfordaasc.com/article/opr/t0002/e0332.

5. Jules-Rosette, "Reflections," 250.

6. Halifu Osumare, *The Africanist Aesthetic in Global Hip-Hop: Power Moves* (New York: Palgrave Macmillan, 2007), 84–85. See also "African Influences in Modern Art" on the Metropolitan Museum of Art's website, www.metmuseum.org/toah/hd/aima/hd_aima.htm.

7. "Bustle," Wikipedia, http://en.wikipedia.org/wiki/Bustle.

8. Gottschild, *The Black Dancing Body*, 147.

9. Ibid.

10. Ananya Chatterjea, *Butting Out: Reading Resistive Choreographies through Works by Jawole Willa Jo Zollar and Chandralekha* (Middletown, CT: Wesleyan University Press, 2004), 180.

11. Ibid., 181.

12. Dave Lifton, "45 Years Ago: John Lennon and Yoko Ono Begin 'Bed-in For Peace,'" Ultimate Classic Rock, http://ultimateclassicrock.com/john-lennon-yoko-ono-bed-in/.

13. Interestingly enough, Abdullah Ibrahim is the father of the underground rap artist Jean Grae.

14. I visited the club during its original heyday, because from 1959 to 1976 it made jazz history as the European home for jazz giants like Dexter Gordon, Ben Webster, Stan Getz, and Kenny Drew. Its inviting, intimate jazz atmosphere was responsible for several artists becoming expatriates in Copenhagen. It reopened in 2010, and the current website is www.jazzhusmontmartre.dk/about-us.html.

15. Lena Hammergren, "Dancing African-American Jazz in the Nordic Region," in *Nordic Dance Spaces: Practicing and Imagining a Region,* ed. Karen Vedel and Petri Hoopu (Farnham, UK: Ashgate, 2014), 101.

16. "Thanks to Doug Crutchfield Fru Nilson Can Dance: Cincinnati Jazz Dancer Helps Denmark's Aged and Infirm Find New Joy in Living," *Ebony Magazine*, April 1970, 86–89.

17. Hammergren, "Dancing African-American Jazz," 105.

18. Besides Crutchfield, Hammergren notes that there were several other black jazz dance teachers in the early 1960s as well, including South African–born Rikki Septimus and African Americans George Mills and Henry Turner (see ibid., 107–8).

19. Ibid., 108.

20. Ibid.

21. Ibid., 114.

22. Ibid., 123–24.

23. The work of Alwin Nikolais continued as Nikolais Dance Theater under the auspice of Nikolais/Louis Foundation for Dance, Inc. The late choreographer Murray Lewis, Nikolais's longtime creative and life partner, became the director of the company until his death in February 2016. See more information at www.nikolaislouis.org/NikolaisLouis/Home.html.

24. Helle Hellman, "Der danser revolution," *Politiken*, November 5, 1969.

25. Ibid.

26. Lars Blicher-Hansen, "To USA danserinder i København: Her er provinsielt, men godt," *B. T. Frokosten*, February 19, 1970, 31.

27. In the seventeenth century, following territorial losses on the Scandinavian

peninsula, Denmark-Norway, then a single polity, began to develop colonies, forts, and trading posts in Africa, the Caribbean, and India. Christian IV first initiated the policy of expanding Denmark's overseas trade, as part of the mercantilist wave that was sweeping Europe. After 1814, when Norway was granted to Sweden following the Napoleonic Wars, Denmark retained its colonial holdings (see "Danish Empire," *New World Encyclopedia*, www.newworldencyclopedia.org/entry/Danish_Empire).

28. bell hooks, *Yearning: Race, Gender, and Cultural Politics*. Boston: South End Press, 1990, 104.

29. "History of the Balettakademien," www.folkuniversitetet.se/Skolor/Baletta kademien-dansskolor/Balettakademien-Stockholm/Om-Balettakademien/.

30. See Saroya Corbett, "Katherine Dunham's Mark on Jazz Dance," in *Jazz Dance: A History of the Roots and Branches,* ed. Lindsay Guarino and Wendy Oliver (Gaines-ville: University Press of Florida, 2014), 89–96, for a comprehensive exploration of Dunham's aesthetic influence on the recognized major jazz dance choreographers.

31. Hammergren, "Dancing African-American Jazz in the Nordic Region," 106.

32. "Walter Nicks," Wikipedia, http://en.wikipedia.org/wiki/Walter_Nicks.

33. Hammergren, "Dancing African-American Jazz in the Nordic Region," 104.

34. Thomas F. DeFrantz, *Dancing Revelations: Alvin Ailey's Embodiment of African American Culture* (New York: Oxford University Press, 2004), 16.

35. Hammergren, "Dancing African-American Jazz in the Nordic Region," 109–10.

36. Ibid., 105. Here Hammergren quotes Paula Saukko, *Doing Research in Cultural Studies* (London: Sage, 2003), 181.

Chapter 3. Dancing in New York

1. Today Boston's South End is the home of the Boston Ballet and the Boston Center for the Arts, as well as many galleries and artists' studios.

2. "New Dance Classes Offered," *Bay State Banner*, September 30, 1971, 14.

3. Foster, *Choreographing Empathy*, 7.

4. Yvonne Daniel, *Dancing Wisdom: Embodied Knowledge in Haitian Vodou, Cuban Yoruba, and Bahian Candomblé* (Urbana: University of Illinois Press, 2015), 4.

5. Foster, *Choreographing Empathy*, 9.

6. Ibid.

7. Kay Bourne, "'Changes' Stirs Old Memories," *Bay State Banner*, March 16, 1972, 10.

8. Ibid.

9. Impulse Dance Company is directed today by Adrienne Hawkins and has a mission to promote jazz dance (see http://www.impulsedance.com/index2.html).

10. Allan Tannenbaum, *New York in the 70s: Show Blues—A Personal Photographic Diary* (New York: Overlook Duckworth, 2011), 6.

11. La MaMa: Mission + History, http://lamama.org/about/mission-history/.

12. Rod Rodgers interview, "African American Legends," hosted by Dr. Ros-coe C. Brown, CUNY Television, May 10, 2000, www.youtube.com/watch?v=sl2 DREYKRgA,

13. I thank the RRDC general manager, Rachel Lubell, for providing current information about the company and its operations.

14. Don McDonagh, "Rod Rodgers Offers 'Box' Duet for Isolated Men," *New York Times*, August 1, 1972.

15. Ibid.

16. Carole Y. Johnson to author, e-mail message, February 7, 2015.

17. Ibid. I want to thank Carole Johnson for providing the details of the Dancemobile project, which started fifty years ago. After leaving the Eleo Pomare Dance Company and her groundbreaking New York City dance organizational work, she moved to Australia, where she became the founding director of the National Aboriginal and Islander Skills Development Council (NAISDA) and the founder of the Bangarra Dance Theatre. Carole was inducted into the Australian Dance Awards Hall of Fame in 1999, and in 2003 she was awarded the Australian Government Centenary medal in recognition of the contribution she has made to the Australian Indigenous community.

18. "Ernie Rodgers: A Chat with This Year's SEMJA Award Recipient," *UPDATE: Southeastern Michigan Jazz Association*, May 1999, www.semja.org/may99/index.html.

19. The American National Theatre and Academy (ANTA) is a non-profit theater producer and training organization that was established in 1935 at the same time as the Federal Theatre Project. It was established to be the official United States national theater as an alternative to the for-profit Broadway houses of the day. The ANTA sponsored touring companies to foreign countries in the post–World War II period of the late 1940s and 1950s but ultimately had a greatly diminished role in the 1980s. Today it has become the National Theatre Conservatory at the Denver Center for the Performing Arts.

20. Zita Allen, "'Revelations' and Beyond," *Free to Dance: The African American Presence in Modern Dance*, film documentary by the American Dance Festival, dir. Madison Davis Lacey, prod. Charles L. Reinhart and Stephanie Reinhart, PBS-TV, 2001, www.pbs.org/wnet/freetodance/behind/behind_revelations.html.

21. Ibid., 1.

22. Ibid.

23. Alvin Ailey, *Revelations: The Autobiography of Alvin Ailey*, with A. Peter Bailey (New York: Birch Lane Press, 1995), 89.

24. Ibid., 91.

25. DeFrantz, *Dancing Revelations*, xiii.

26. Ibid., 69–70. He quotes from the *New York Times* dance critic Jennifer Dunning's book *Alvin Ailey: A Life in Dance* (New York: Addison-Wesley, 1996), 52.

27. Dance historian Constance Valis Hill notes that *Southland*'s performance in Santiago, Chile, and Paris, France, against the wishes of the U.S. State Department caused Dunham's lack of support by the developing State Department–sponsored arts touring program, and eventually the demise of her company in the early 1960s (see Hill, "Katherine Dunham's *Southland*: Protest in the Face of Repression," in *Kaiso! Writings by and about Katherine Dunham*, ed. VèVè A. Clark and Sara E. Johnson [Madison: University of Wisconsin Press, 2005], 345–63).

28. DeFrantz, *Dancing Revelations*, 70.

29. John Parks, interview by author, June 29, 2015, University of South Florida's School of Theatre and Dance.

30. Ibid.

31. Movements Black mission statement, Movements Black Dance Repertory Theatre, Inc., 168½ Delancey St., New York, NY 10002, John E. Parks, director.

32. Lynne Fauley Emery, *Black Dance from 1619 to 1970*. 2nd. rev. ed. (Hightstown, NJ: Dance Horizons Book, 1988), 251.

33. Doris Green to author, e-mail message, January 10, 2015.

34. Halifu Osumare, "The Aesthetic of the Cool Revisited: The Ancestral Dance Link in the African Diaspora," *UCLA Journal of Dance Ethnology* 17 (1993): 1.

35. Susan Manning, "Key Works, Artists, Events, Venues, Texts, Black Dance on U.S. Stages in the 20th Century," Black Dance Timeline, Black Arts Initiative, Northwestern University, bai.northwestern.edu/wp-content/uploads/ . . . /Black-Dance-Timeline.docx

36. Bernadine Jennings to author, e-mail message, January 16, 2015.

37. Thomas F. DeFrantz, *Dancing Many Drums: Excavations in African American Dance* (Madison: University of Wisconsin Press, 2002), 22.

38. Francis Davis, "Ornette's Permanent Revolution," *Atlantic Monthly*, September 1985, 1, www.theatlantic.com/past/docs/unbound/jazz/dornette.htm.

39. Jonathan David Jackson, "Improvisation in African-American Vernacular Dancing," *Dance Research Journal* 33, no. 2 (Winter 2001): 42.

40. Ibid., 47.

41. Dana Reason, "Navigable Structures and Transforming Mirrors: Improvisation and Interactivity," in *The Other Side of Nowhere: Jazz, Improvisation, and Communities in Dialogue*, ed. Daniel Fischlin and Ajay Heble (Middletown, CT: Wesleyan University Press, 2004), 73.

42. Daniel Fischlin, Ajay Heble, and George Lipsitz, *The Fierce Urgency of Now: Improvisation, Rights, and the Ethics of Cocreation* (Durham, NC: Duke University Press, 2013), 61.

Chapter 4. Dancing Back into the San Francisco–Oakland Bay Area, 1973–1976

1. Alice H. G. Phillips, *Times Literary Supplement*, qtd. in Poetry Foundation Newsletter, *Poems and Poets: Ntozake Shange*, www.poetryfoundation.org/bio/ntozake-shange.

2. Ntozake Shange, *for colored girls who have considered suicide/when the rainbow is enuf: A Choreopoem* (New York: Bantam, 1977), xv–xvi.

3. "Vera Cruz (city)," Wikipedia, http://en.wikipedia.org/wiki/Veracruz_(city) #The_port.

4. "Coming to Texas, 1528–1836," Texas Black History Project, www.tbhpp.org. This site noted: "Approximately 54% of all enslaved Africans brought to the New World between 1519 and 1700 disembarked in Spanish America, and New Spain (Mexico) received its share through the ports of Veracruz."

5. "La Bamba," State of Veracruz, http://mexfoldanco.org/mexican/folkloric/dance/veracruz.html.

6. Sandra Richards, "Bay Area Theater History," in "Report on Black Theater" column, *Black World/Negro Digest*, April 1974, 67.

7. Ibid.

8. Ibid., 68.

9. Ibid.

10. Ibid., 69.

11. Donna Jean Murch, *Living for the City: Migration, Education, and the Rise of the Black Panther Party in Oakland, California* (Chapel Hill: University of North Carolina Press, 2010), 99.

12. Mike Sell, "The Black Arts Movement: Performance, Neo-Orality, and the Destruction of the "White Thing," in *African American Performance and Theater History: A Critical Reader*, ed. Harry J. Elam Jr. and David Krasner (New York: Oxford University Press, 2001), 56.

13. Ongiri, *Spectacular Blackness*, 89; Larry Neal, "Some Reflections on a Black Aesthetic," in *The Black Aesthetic*, ed. Addison Gayle (New York: Doubleday, 1971).

14. Rita Preszler Weathersby, "Education for Adult Development: The Components of Qualitative Change," *New Directions for Higher Education* 29 (1980), http://onlinelibrary.wiley.com/doi/10.1002/he.36919802904/abstract.

15. Barbara Christian is best known for her coauthored book *Black Women Novelists: The Development of a Tradition, 1892–1976* (Westport, CT: Greenwood, 1980), which helped establish a focused analysis on the works of Toni Morrison and Alice Walker, as well as *Black Feminist Critical Perspectives on Black Women Writers* (New York: Pergamon, 1985).

16. Shange, *for colored girls*, xvi–xvii.

17. Stephanie Jack, "I Believe: Two Successful Words," *Sun Reporter*, May 16, 1975.

18. Professor Barbara T. Christian, personal written communication, October 3, 1990.

Chapter 5. Dancing in Africa

1. John Miller Chernoff, *African Rhythm and African Sensibility: Aesthetics and Social Action in African Musical Idioms* (Chicago: University of Chicago Press, 1979), 55.

2. For a succinct typology of Thompson's ten canons of fine form, see Osumare, "The Aesthetic of the Cool Revisited," 3.

3. Francesca Castaldi, *Choreographies of African Identities: Négritude, Dance, and the National Ballet of Senegal* (Champaign-Urbana: University of Illinois Press, 2006), 40.

4. Ibid., 1.

5. Ibid.

6. C. K. Ladzekpo, "Introduction to Anlo-Ewe Culture," https://home.comcast.net/~dzinyaladzekpo/Intro.html#History.

7. Castaldi, *Choreographies of African Identities*, 1.

8. J. H. Kwabena Nketia, personal interview by the author, University of Ghana, Legon, October 6, 2008.

9. Ibid. Professor Nketia also mentioned that creating an arts unit was made easier because of "my colleague in government, Nana Kwabena Nketia [no relation]." This points to the importance of having sympathetic governmental people in key positions to facilitate the utilization of the arts.

10. A. A. Opoku, "Acknowledgement," in *Festivals of Ghana* (Accra: Ghana Publishing Corporation, 1970).

11. Nketia interview, 2008.

12. Ibid.

13. E. A. Akrofi, *Sharing Knowledge and Experience: A Profile of Kwabena Nketia, Scholar and Music Educator* (Accra: Afram, 2002), 57.

14. Albert Opoku, introduction to presentation of the Ghana Dance Ensemble, University of Ghana, Legon, June 1976 (from author's archives).

15. Katharina Schramm, "The Politics of Dance: Changing Representations of the Nation in Ghana," *African Spectrum* 35, no. 3 (2000): 339, www.jstor.org/discover/10.2307/40174857?sid=21106286961713&uid=3739560&uid=3739256&uid=2&uid=70&uid=2129&uid=4.

16. Beatrice Tawiah Ayi, "Stepping into New Places: Migration of Traditional Ghanaian Dance Forms from Rural Spaces to Urban Pedagogical Stages," http://aUSdance.org.au/uploads/content/publications/2012-global-summit/dance-learning-rp/stepping-into-new-places-migration-of-traditional-ghanaian-dance-forms.pdf.

17. Francis Nii Yartey, personal interview by author, University of Ghana, Legon, December 2, 2008.

18. Francis Nii Yartey, "Development and Promotion of Contemporary Choreographic Expression in Ghana," in *FonTomFrom: Contemporary Ghanaian Literature, Theatre and Film*, ed. Kofi Anyidoho and James Gibbs (Amsterdam and Atlanta: Rodopi, 2000), 125.

19. Ibid., 126.

20. Ibid., 127.

21. The National Theatre of Ghana was jointly built by the government of the People's Republic of China and the government of the Republic of Ghana and is located in the heart of Accra. It houses three resident companies: the National Dance Company, the National Theatre Players (Abibigromma), and the National Symphony Orchestra. There are also three youth groups: the Dance Factory, IdigenAfrika, and Vision Band.

22. See, for example, Katherine Dunham, *Island Possessed* (1969; Chicago: University of Chicago Press, 1994).

23. Saidiya Hartman, *Lose Your Mother: A Journey along the Atlantic Slave Route* (New York: Farrar, Straus and Giroux, 2007), 6.

24. Halifu Osumare, *The Hiplife in Ghana: West African Indigenization of Hip-Hop* (New York: Palgrave Macmillan, 2012), 2.

25. Hartman, *Lose Your Mother*, 6.

26. Jacqui Malone, *Steppin' on the Blues: The Visible Rhythms of African-American Dance* (Urbana: University of Illinois Press, 1996), 23. Malone's use of the phrase "equipment for living" is referenced from Kenneth Burke, *The Philosophy of Literary Form* (New York: Vintage, 1957), 253–62.

27. Osumare, *The Hiplife in Ghana*, 147. I quoted Kwame Boafo-Arthur, "Structural Adjustment Programs (SAPS) in Ghana: Interrogating PNDC's Implementation," *West Africa Review* 1, no. 1 (1999), www.africaknowledgeproject.org/index.php/war/article/view/396.

28. For further readings on Nkrumah's Young Pioneer organization, see Harcourt Fuller, *Building the Ghanaian Nation-State: Kwame Nkrumah's Symbolic Nationalism* (New York: Palgrave Macmillan, 2014).

29. Kingsley Ampomah, "An Investigation into Adowa and Adzewa Music and Dance of the Akan People of Ghana," *International Journal of Humanities and Social Science* 4, no. 10 (August 2014): 117–24.

30. Thomas F. DeFrantz and Anita Gonzales, "Introduction: From 'Negro Expression' to 'Black Performance,'" in *Black Performance Theory*, ed. DeFrantz and Gonzales (Durham, NC: Duke University Press, 2014), 5.

31. Ibid.

32. Ibid., 6.

33. Judith Graham, "The Slave Fortresses of Ghana," *New York Times*, November 25, 1990, www.nytimes.com/1990/11/25/travel/the-slave-fortresses-of-ghana.html.

34. George Preston, "Preston on Shumway, 'The Fante and the Transatlantic Slave Trade,'" *H-AfriArts: Humanities and Social Science Online*, January 2012, 2, http://daxter.matrix.msu.edu/node/12834/reviews/13043/preston-shumway-fante-and-transatlantic-slave-trade.

35. Ibid., 3.

36. An important doctoral dissertation exploring the complex issues of tourism in Ghana's former slave forts is Tometi Gbedema, "The Door of No Returns—Role of Heritage Tourism in Local Communities in Sub-Saharan Africa: The Cases of Elmina and Keta in Ghana" (PhD diss., Geography Graduate Group, University of California, Davis, 2012).

37. I learned later that Nana Kobina Nketsia IV, who died in 1995, had been an important part of Nkrumah's independence team, helping him to form his political party, the Conventions People's Party (CPP). I had been tutored in Boston (chapter 3) by one of the primary thinkers of the political transition of Ghanaian independence.

38. The *Omanhene* is the title of the supreme traditional ruler or king in a region or a large town. He is the central sociopolitical figure for those people but has no function in the Ghanaian state. The Omanhene is usually a major landowner and commits the land he theoretically holds in trust to various caretaker families.

39. Osumare, *The Hiplife in Ghana*, 2.

40. Roger Abrahams, "Concerning African Performance Patterns," in *Neo-African Literature and Culture: Essays in Memory of Janehinz Jahn*, ed. Bernth Lindfors and Ulla Schlid (Wiesbaden, Germany: Heymann, 1976) 40.

41. DeFrantz and Gonzalez, *Black Performance Theory*, 8.

42. Ibid.

43. See John Pemberton III, "Ulli Beier and the Oshogbo Artists of Nigeria," *African Studies Review* 45 no. 1 (April 2002): 115–24.

44. Williams Grimes, "Prince Twins Seven-Seven, Nigerian Artist Dies at 67," *New York Times*, July 3, 2011, www.nytimes.com/2011/07/04/arts/design/prince-twins-seven-seven-nigerian-artist-dies-at-67.html?_r=0.

45. C. K. Ladzekpo offers a concise history of Anloga: "The *Anlo-Ewe* people settled at their present home around the latter part of the 15th century (1474) after a dramatic escape from *Notsie,* an ancestral federated region currently within the borders of the modern state of Togo. The escape and subsequent resettlement are commemorated in an annual festival known as *Hogbetsotso Za.*"

Chapter 6. Dancing in Oakland and Beyond, 1977–1993

1. I thank Ferolyn Angel for some of the details included here about the origins of Every Body's Dance Studio before I bought the business.

2. Ferolyn actually believes that I asked *her* about purchasing Every Body's Dance Studio, which is not my account. The relativity of memory versus actual historical facts has been written about ad nauseam.

3. Here I use Melissa Harris-Perry's concept of the "politics of recognition" that she analyzes as the strategies by black women authors to claim space for their marginalized black heroines in her *Sister Citizen: Shame, Stereotypes, and Black Women in America* (New Haven, CT: Yale University Press, 2011).

4. "Los Papines," AFroCubaWeb, www.afrocubaweb.com/papines.htm.

5. Selimah Nemoy, phone interview by author, May 25, 2015.

6. Ibid.

7. Thulani Davis, "Theater beyond Borders: Reconfiguring the Artist's Relationship to Community in the Twenty-First Century—Moving beyond *Bantustans,*" in *The Color of Theater: Race, Culture, and Contemporary Performance,* ed. Roberta Uno and Lucy Mae San Pablo Burns (London: Continuum, 2002), 23.

8. Vita Lee Giammalvo, "Everybody's Vehicle of Expression," *City Arts,* March 1981, 31.

9. "Festival Dancers," *Oakland Tribune,* May 15, 1978, 21.

10. According to Wikipedia: "The Mariel Boatlift was a mass emigration of Cubans who departed from Cuba's Mariel Harbor for the United States between April 15 and October 31, 1980. The event was precipitated by a sharp downturn in the Cuban economy that led to internal tensions on the island and a bid by up to 10,000 Cubans to gain asylum in the Peruvian embassy. The Mariel boatlift was ended by mutual agreement between the U.S. and Cuba in October 1980. By that point, as many as 125,000 Cubans had made the journey to Florida" (http://en.wikipedia.org/wiki/Mariel_boatlift).

11. The Astor Johnson Repertory Dance Theatre of Trinidad and Tobago homepage, www.astorjohnsondance.com.

12. Charles Shere, "A Lively Culture Center for Everybody," *Oakland Tribune,* July 13, 1979, "Lifestyle" sec., B1.

13. Linda Goodrich, personal interview by the author, Sacramento, May 27, 2015.

14. Ibid.

15. History, Clark Center NYC, www.clarkcenternyc.org/571228/history-and
-mission/.

16. Shere, "A Lively Culture Center for Everybody," B1.

17. Donald McKayle is one of the most respected elder statesmen of dance with numerous awards. His autobiography, *Transcending Boundaries: My Dancing Life*, published by Routledge in 2002, was honored with the Society of Dance History Scholar's de la Torre Bueno Prize. A television documentary on his life and work, *Heartbeats of a Dance Maker*, was aired on PBS stations throughout the United States.

18. Emery, *Black Dance from 1619 to Today*, 2nd rev. ed., 21. She quotes Pére Labat, *Nouveau voyage aux Isles de l'Amerique*, 2 vols, trans. Anthony Bliss (The Hague, 1724).

19. E. Patrick Johnson, "Black Performance Studies: Genealogies, Politics, Futures," in *The Sage Handbook of Performance Studies*, ed. Soyini D. Madison and Judith Hamera (London: Sage, 2006), 452.

20. Ibid.

21. Alice Thebeau, "Everybody's Mixed Bag," *City Arts Monthly*, May 1982.

22. Angela Y. Davis, *Blues Legacies and Black Feminism: Gertrude "Ma" Rainey, Bessie Smith, and Billie Holiday* (New York: Pantheon, 1998), xiv.

23. Janice Ross, "CitiCentre Dance Board Faces Space Crisis, Tough Decisions," *Oakland Tribune*, October 13, 1985.

24. Maxine Waters, "California Dialogue," March 16–17, 1986, Asilomar Conference Center, Asilomar, CA.

25. Yvonne Daniel, *Rumba: Dance and Social Change in Contemporary Cuba* (Bloomington: Indiana University Press, 1995), 172n12.

26. Two other major teachers in the residency were dancer-teacher Margarita Vilela Creagh and drummer-singer Rejino Jimenez Saez.

27. Gottschild, *Digging the Africanist Presence in American Performance*, 48.

28. Ibid. Her quote of Louis Horst is taken from his *Modern Dance Forms* (1961; Princeton, NJ: Princeton Book Company, 1987), 57.

29. Halifu Osumare, "A Five Year Cycle," *Black Arts Quarterly*, Stanford University's Committee on Black Performing Arts (Winter Quarter 1991): 1.

30. Halifu Osumare, "Dancing through Stanford," *Black Arts Quarterly*, Stanford University's Committee on Black Performing Arts (Winter Quarter, 1993–94): 7.

31. Ntozake Shange, "You Are So Beautiful to Me: Ed Mock," *Attitude: The Dancers' Monthly* 4, no. 1 (September–November 1986): 5.

32. It should be noted that even today, racial tensions around James Meredith's historic stance in 1962 are still being enacted. An Ole Miss fraternity was shut down after a frat member confessed to hanging a noose around the neck of the Meredith statue on campus, erected to commemorate him (see Associated Press, "Ole Miss Frat Shuttered in Wake of Noose Incident," www.cbsnews.com/news/ole-miss-fraternity-closes-after-james-meredith-statue-noose-tying/).

33. The Brooklyn Academy of Music has created a digital archive of its programs

over the decades, including Dance Black America. Photos, videos, and audience programs of the festival can be accessed at http://levyarchive.bam.org/MultiSearch/Index?search=Dance+Black+America.

34. Jennifer Dunning, "Dance: Black Festival at the Brooklyn Academy," *New York Times*, April 22, 1983.

35. Ibid.

36. The Smithsonian's program in black culture has now morphed into a major new institution near the Washington Monument, the National Museum of African American History and Culture, which opened in 2016.

37. Elizabeth Zimmer, "Keepers of the Flame," *Village Voice*, May 10, 1983.

38. Ibid.

39. Ntozake Shange, "Who Says Black Folks Could Sing and Dance?" *Dance Magazine*, August 1983, 78.

40. Calvin Ahlgren, "Stretching Out to Black Dance Roots," *San Francisco Chronicle*, January 20, 1985, 50.

41. Halifu Osumare, "Black Dance in America: A Reevaluation of History," *City Arts*, May 1981, 37.

42. "Osumare Awarded Commission to Assist Dance Troupe in Malawi," *Stanford University Campus Report*, July 5, 1990.

43. In the article I had this to say about women in Malawi in general: "Women are still under the yoke of polygamy and traditional subservience, yet there is a conscious government trend toward raising the status of the women and including them in the development plans of the country." The second annual five-day National Commission on Women in Development conference was held at the Lilongwe Hotel, where I stayed during my residency, and was attended by key Malawian professional women and ministry officials.

44. Songwriting credits for "U Can't Touch This" are Hammer, Rick James, and Alonzo Miller, as the song samples James's "Super Freak." The track is considered Hammer's most successful hit.

45. Jack Anderson, "Modern Dance: A Harmonious Melting Pot," *The New York Times*, August 20, 1989, 7.

46. Gerald E. Myers, "Ethnic and Modern Dance," in *The Black Tradition in American Modern Dance* (Durham, NC: American Dance Festival, Duke University, 1988), 24.

47. For an excellent analysis of Ruth St. Denis's oeuvre from a postcolonial perspective, see Jane Desmond, "Dancing out the Difference: Cultural Imperialism and Ruth St. Denis's *Radha* of 1906," in *Moving History/Dancing Cultures: A Dance History Reader*, ed. Ann Dils and Ann Cooper Albright, 256–70 (Middletown, CT: Wesleyan University Press, 2001).

48. William Moore, "The Development of Black Modern Dance in America," in *The Black Tradition in American Modern Dance* (Durham, NC: American Dance Festival, Duke University, 1988), 15.

49. Similar to the Cherokees' "Trail of Tears," the "Long Walk" is the term used for the 1864 ouster of the Navajo by the U.S. government from their original homeland in Arizona to eastern New Mexico. Forced to walk thirteen miles per day at

gunpoint, the Long Walk is forever etched into Navajo collective memory and even today defines their identity, as we saw in our Farmington, New Mexico, interaction. Some sources say that there were fifty-three different forced displacements of Native Americas from 1864 to 1866.

50. Halifu Osumare, "The New Moderns: The Paradox of Eclecticism and Singularity," in *African American Genius in Modern Dance* (Durham, NC: American Dance Festival, Duke University, 1993), 29.

51. "San Francisco–Oakland Earthquake of 1989," *Encyclopaedia Britannica*, www.britannica.com/event/San-Francisco-Oakland-earthquake-of-1989.

52. Allan Ulrich, "L.A. Dancers Shine in Black Fest," *San Francisco Examiner*, November 6, 1989, B1.

53. Calvin Ahlgren, "Black Choreographers Fly High at Festival," *San Francisco Chronicle*, October 29, 1989; Datebook 1.

54. Martin David, "Seeing Black Dance in a Universal Context," *Los Angeles Times*, November 12, 1989, 8. Life had come full circle; the author of this article, journalist Martin David, was "Mardav," the former husband of my Copenhagen dance colleague Diane Black. See chapter 2, "Dancing in Europe."

55. Cherríe Moraga, "Sour Grapes: The Art of Anger in América," in *The Color of Theater: Race, Culture, and Contemporary Performance*, ed. Roberta Uno with Lucy Mae San Pablo Burns (New York: Continuum, 2002), 128.

Bibliography

Abrahams, Roger. "Concerning African Performance Patterns." In *Neo-African Literature and Culture: Essays in Memory of Janehinz Jahn*, edited by Bernth Lindfors and Ulla Schlid, 32–40. Wiesbaden, Germany: Heymann, 1976.

Ailey, Alvin. *Revelations: The Autobiography of Alvin Ailey*. With A. Peter Bailey. New York: Birch Lane Press, 1995.

Akrofi, E. A. *Sharing Knowledge and Experience: A Profile of Kwabena Nketia, Scholar and Music Educator*. Accra: Afram, 2002.

Alexander, Michelle. *The New Jim Crow: Mass Incarceration in the Age of Colorblindness*. New York: The New Press, 2012.

Allen, Zita. "'Revelations' and Beyond." *Free to Dance: African American Presence in Modern Dance*. Film documentary by the American Dance Festival. Directed by Madison Davis Lacey. Produced by Charles L. & Stephanie Reinhart. www.pbs.org/wnet/freetodance/behind/behind_revelations.html.

———. "What Is Black Dance?" In *The Black Tradition in American Modern Dance*, edited by Gerald E. Myers, 11–13. Durham, NC: American Dance Festival, Duke University, 1988.

Ampomah, Kingsley. "An Investigation into Adowa and Adzewa Music and Dance of the Akan People of Ghana." *International Journal of Humanities and Social Science* 4, no. 10 (August 2014): 117–24.

Anderson, Jack. "Modern Dance: A Harmonious Melting Pot." *New York Times*, August 20, 1989.

Aschenbrenner, Joyce. *Katherine Dunham: Reflections on the Social and Political Contexts of Afro-American Dance. Dance Research Journal Annual XII*. New York: Congress on Research in Dance, 1980.

Ayi, Beatrice Tawiah. "Stepping into New Places: Migration of Traditional Ghanaian Dance Forms from Rural Spaces to Urban Pedagogical Stages." http://aUSdance.org.au/uploads/content/publications/2012-global-summit/dance-learning-rp/stepping-into-new-places-migration-of-traditional-ghanaian-dance-forms.pdf.

Barbour, Karen Nicole. *Dancing across the Page: Narrative and Embodied Ways of Knowing*. London, UK: Intellect, 2011.

Blicher-Hansen, Lars. "To USA danserinder i København: Her er provinsielt, men godt." *B. T. Frokosten*, February 19, 1970.

Boafo-Arthur, Kwame. "Structural Adjustment Programs (SAPS) in Ghana: Interrogating PNDC's Implementation." *West Africa Review* 1, no. 1 (1999).

Castaldi, Francesca. *Choreographies of African Identities: Négritude, Dance, and the National Ballet of Senegal*. Champaign-Urbana: University of Illinois Press, 2006.

Chatterjea, Ananya. *Butting Out: Reading Resistive Choreographies through Works by Jawole Willa Jo Zollar and Chandralekha*. Middletown, CT: Wesleyan University Press, 2004.

Chernoff, John Miller. *African Rhythm and African Sensibility: Aesthetics and Social Action in African Musical Idioms*. Chicago: University of Chicago Press, 1979.

Christian, Barbara. *Black Feminist Critical Perspectives on Black Women Writers*. New York: Pergamon, 1985.

———. *Black Women Novelists: The Development of a Tradition, 1892–1976*. Westport, CT: Greenwood, 1980.

Corbett, Saroya. "Katherine Dunham's Mark on Jazz Dance." In *Jazz Dance: A History of the Roots and Branches*, edited by Lindsay Guarino and Wendy Oliver, 89–96. Gainesville: University Press of Florida, 2014.

Daniel, Yvonne. *Dancing Wisdom: Embodied Knowledge in Haitian Vodou, Cuban Yoruba, and Bahian Candomblé*. Urbana: University of Illinois Press, 2015.

———. *Rumba: Dance and Social Change in Contemporary Cuba*. Bloomington: Indiana University Press, 1995.

Davis, Angela Y. *Blues Legacies and Black Feminism: Gertrude "Ma" Rainey, Bessie Smith, and Billie Holiday*. New York: Pantheon, 1998.

Davis, Francis. "Ornette's Permanent Revolution." *Atlantic Monthly*, September 1985.

Davis, Thulani. "Theater beyond Borders: Reconfiguring the Artist's Relationship to Community in the Twenty-First Century: Moving beyond *Bantustans*." In *The Color of Theater: Race, Culture, and Contemporary Performance*, edited by Roberta Uno and Lucy Mae San Pablo Burns, 22–26. London: Continuum, 2002.

DeFrantz, Thomas F. *Dancing Many Drums: Excavations in African American Dance*. Madison: University of Wisconsin Press, 2002.

———. *Dancing Revelations: Alvin Ailey's Embodiment of African American Culture*. New York: Oxford University Press, 2004.

DeFrantz, Thomas F., and Anita Gonzales. *Black Performance Theory*. Durham, NC: Duke University Press, 2014.

Desmond, Jane. "Dancing out the Difference: Cultural Imperialism and Ruth St. Denis's *Radha* of 1906." In *Moving History/Dancing Cultures: A Dance History Reader*, edited by Ann Dils and Ann Cooper Albright, 256–70. Middletown, CT: Wesleyan University Press, 2001.

Dunham, Katherine. *Island Possessed*. 1969. Chicago: University of Chicago Press, 1994.

Dunning, Jennifer. *Ailey: A Life in Dance*. New York: Addison-Wesley, 1996.

Emery, Lynne Fauley. *Black Dance from 1619 to 1970*. 2nd rev. ed. Hightstown, NJ: Dance Horizons, 1988.

Fischlin, Daniel, Ajay Heble, and George Lipsitz. *The Fierce Urgency of Now: Improvisation, Rights, and the Ethics of Cocreation*. Durham, NC: Duke University Press, 2013.

Foster, Susan Leigh. *Choreographing Empathy: Kinesthesia in Performance*. New York: Routledge, 2011.

Foucault, Michel. *Discipline and Punishment: The Birth of the Prison*. New York: Pantheon, 1977.

Fuller, Harcourt. *Building the Ghanaian Nation-State: Kwame Nkrumah's Symbolic Nationalism*. New York: Palgrave Macmillan, 2014.

Gbedema, Tometi. "The Door of No Returns—Role of Heritage Tourism in Local Communities in Sub-Saharan Africa: The Cases of Elmina and Keta in Ghana." Ph.D. diss., Geography Graduate Group, University of California, Davis, 2012.

Geertz, Clifford. *Works and Lives: The Anthropologist as Author*. Stanford, CA: Stanford University Press, 1988.

George-Graves, Nadine. "Diasporic Spidering: Constructing Contemporary Black Identities." In *Black Performance Theory*, edited by Thomas F. DeFrantz and Anita Gonzalez, 33–44. Durham, NC: Duke University Press, 2014.

Gottschild, Brenda Dixon. *The Black Dancing Body: A Geography from Coon to Cool*. New York: Palgrave Macmillan, 2003.

———. *Digging the Africanist Presence in American Performance: Dance and Other Contexts*. Westport, CT: Greenwood, 1996.

———. "Is Race Still an Issue in Dance?" *Dance Magazine*, February 2005.

Graham, Judith "The Slave Fortresses of Ghana," *New York Times*, November 25, 1990. www.nytimes.com/1990/11/25/travel/the-slave-fortresses-of-ghana.html.

Grimes, Williams. "Prince Twins Seven-Seven, Nigerian Artist Dies at 67." *New York Times*, July 3, 2011.

Hacker, Andrew. *Two Nations: Black and White, Separate, Hostile, Unequal*. 2nd ed. New York: Ballantine, 1995.

Hammergren, Lena. "Dancing African-American Jazz in the Nordic Region." In *Nordic Dance Spaces: Practicing and Imagining a Region*, edited by Karen Vedel and Petri Hoopu, 101–28. Farnham, UK: Ashgate, 2014.

Hanna, Judith Lynn. *To Dance Is Human: A Theory of Non-Verbal Communication*. 1979. Chicago: University of Chicago Press, 1987.

Harris-Perry, Melissa V. *Sister Citizen: Shame, Stereotypes, and Black Women in America*. New Haven, CT: Yale University Press, 2011.

Hartman, Saidiya. *Lose Your Mother: A Journey along the Atlantic Slave Route*. New York: Farrar, Straus and Giroux, 2007.

H'Doubler, Margaret Newell. *Rhythmic Form and Analysis*. Madison, WI: J. M. Rider, 1932.

Hellman, Helle. "Der danser revolution." *Politiken*, November 5, 1969.

Hill, Constance Valis. "Katherine Dunham's *Southland*: Protest in the Face of Repression." In *Kaiso! Writings by and about Katherine Dunham*, edited by VèVè A. Clark and Sara E. Johnson, 345–63. Madison: University of Wisconsin Press, 2005.

hooks, bell. *Yearning: Race, Gender, and Cultural Politics*. Boston: South End Press, 1990.

Horst, Louis. *Modern Dance Forms*. 1961. Princeton, NJ: Princeton Book Company, 1987.

Jackson, Jonathan David. "Improvisation in African-American Vernacular Dancing." *Dance Research Journal* 33, no. 2 (Winter 2001).

Johnson, E. Patrick. "Black Performance Studies: Genealogies, Politics, Futures." In *The Sage Handbook of Performance Studies*, edited by Soyini D. Madison and Judith Hamera, 446–63. London: Sage, 2006.

Jones, Le Roi. "Communications Project." In "Black Theatre," special issue, *Drama Review* (*TDR*) 12, no. 4 (Summer 1968): 53–57.

Jules-Rosette, Bennetta. "Reflections on the Future of Black France: Josephine Baker's Vision of a Global Village." In *Black France/France Noire: The History and Politics of Blackness*, edited by Tricia Danielle Keaton, T. Denean Sharpley-Whiting, and Tyler Stovall. Durham, NC: Duke University Press, 2012.

Malone, Jacqui. *Steppin' on the Blues: The Visible Rhythms of African-American Dance*. Urbana: University of Illinois Press, 1996.

Manning, Susan. "Modern Dance, Negro Dance and Katherine Dunham." *Textual Practice* 15, no. 3 (2001): 487–505.

———. *Modern Dance, Negro Dance: Race in Motion*. Minneapolis: University of Minnesota Press, 2004.

Masilela, Ntongela. "The Importance of the African Element in Contemporary Dance Culture." *Attitude: The Dancers' Magazine* 5 (1988): 10–11.

McDonagh, Don. "Rod Rodgers Offers 'Box' Duet for Isolated Men." *New York Times*, August 1, 1972.

McKayle, Donald. *Transcending Boundaries: My Dancing Life*. New York: Routledge Harwood, 2002.

———. "The Negro Dance in Our Time." In *The Dance Has Many Faces*, edited by Walter Sorell, 187–93. New York: Columbia University Press, 1966.

Moore, William. "The Development of Black Modern Dance in America." In *The Black Tradition in American Modern Dance*, edited by Gerald E. Myers, 15–17. Durham, NC, American Dance Festival, Duke University, 1988.

Moraga, Cherríe. "Sour Grapes: The Art of Anger in América." In *The Color of Theater: Race, Culture, and Contemporary Performance*, edited by Roberta Uno with Lucy Mae San Pablo Burns, 115–28. New York: Continuum, 2002.

Murch, Donna Jean. *Living for the City: Migration, Education, and the Rise of the Black Panther Party in Oakland, California*. Chapel Hill: University of North Carolina Press, 2010.

Myers, Gerald E. "Ethnic and Modern Dance." In *The Black Tradition in American Modern Dance*, edited by Myers, 24–25. Durham, NC, American Dance Festival, Duke University, 1988.

Nash, Joe. "Pioneers in Negro Concert Dance: 1931–1937." In *The Black Tradition in American Modern Dance*, edited by Gerald E. Myers, 11–13. Durham, NC: American Dance Festival, Duke University, 1988.

Neal, Larry. "The Black Arts Movement." *Drama Review* (*TDR*) 12, no. 4 (Summer 1968): 1967–68. Reissued by National Humanities Center Resource Toolbox: The Making of African American Identity, vol. 3, http://nationalhumanitiescenter.org/pds/maai3/community/text8/blackartsmovement.pdf.

————. "Some Reflections on a Black Aesthetic." In *The Black Aesthetic*, edited by Addison Gayle. New York: Doubleday, 1971.

Ongiri, Amy Abugo. *Spectacular Blackness: The Cultural Politics of the Black Power Movement and the Search for a Black Aesthetic*. Charlottesville: University of Virginia Press, 2010.

Opoku, A. A. *Festivals of Ghana*. Accra: Ghana Publishing Corporation, 1970.

Osumare, Halifu. "The Aesthetic of the Cool Revisited: The Ancestral Dance Link in the African Diaspora." *UCLA Journal of Dance Ethnology* 17 (1993): 1–16.

————. *The Africanist Aesthetic in Global Hip-Hop: Power Moves*. New York: Palgrave Macmillan, 2007.

————. *The Hiplife in Ghana: West African Indigenization of Hip-Hop*. New York: Palgrave Macmillan, 2012.

————. "The New Moderns: The Paradox of Eclecticism and Singularity." In *African American Genius in Modern Dance*, edited by Gerald E. Myers, 26–29. Durham, NC: American Dance Festival, Duke University, 1993.

————. "Viewing African Women Through Dance." *SAGE, A Scholarly Journal of Black Women* VIII, no. 2 (Fall 1994): 41–45.

Peariso, Craig J. *Radical Theatrics: Put-ons, Politics, and the Sixties*. Seattle: University of Washington Press, 2014.

Pemberton, John, III. "Ulli Beier and the Oshogbo Artists of Nigeria." *African Studies Review* 45, no. 1 (April 2002): 115–24.

Preston, George. "Preston on Shumway, 'The Fante and the Transatlantic Slave Trade.'" *H-AfriArts: Humanities and Social Science Online*, January 2012, 2. http://daxter.matrix.msu.edu/node/12834/reviews/13043/preston-shumway-fante-and-transatlantic-slave-trade.

Reason, Dana. "Navigable Structures and Transforming Mirrors: Improvisation and Interactivity." In *The Other Side of Nowhere: Jazz, Improvisation, and Communities in Dialogue*, edited by Daniel Fischlin and Ajay Heble, 71–86. Middletown, CT: Wesleyan University Press, 2004.

Richards, Sandra. "Bay Area Theater History." In "Report on Black Theater" column. *Black World/Negro Digest*, April 1974, 66–71.

Ruth, Marianne. *Frederick Douglass*. New York: Holloway House, 1996.

Sachs, Curt. *World History of the Dance*. New York: W. W. Norton & Company, Inc., 1963 (1937).

Saukko, Paula. *Doing Research in Cultural Studies*. London: Sage, 2003.

Schramm, Katharina. "The Politics of Dance: Changing Representations of the Nation in Ghana." *African Spectrum* 35, no. 3 (2000): 339–58.

Sell, Mike. "The Black Arts Movement: Performance, Neo-Orality, and the Destruction of the 'White Thing.'" In *African American Performance and Theater History: A Critical Reader*, edited by Harry J. Elam Jr. and David Krasner, 56–80. New York: Oxford University Press, 2001.

Shange, Ntozake. *for colored girls who have considered suicide/when the rainbow is enuf: A Choreopoem*. New York: Bantam, 1977.

————. "Who Says Black Folks Could Sing and Dance?" *Dance Magazine*, August 1983.

————. "You Are So Beautiful to Me: Ed Mock." *Attitude: The Dancers' Monthly* 4, no. 1 (September–November 1986).

Smethurst, James Edward. *The Black Arts Movement: Literary Nationalism in the 1960s and 1970s*. Chapel Hill: University of North Carolina Press, 2005.

Tannenbaum, Allan. *New York in the 70s: Show Blues—A Personal Photographic Diary*. New York: Overlook Duckworth, 2011.

Thompson, Robert Farris. *African Art in Motion*. Los Angeles: University of California Press, 1974.

Weathersby, Rita Preszler. "Education for Adult Development: The Components of Qualitative Change." *New Directions for Higher Education* 29 (1980). http://onlinelibrary.wiley.com/doi/10.1002/he.36919802904/abstract.

Yartey, Francis Nii. "Development and Promotion of Contemporary Choreographic Expression in Ghana." In *FonTomFrom: Contemporary Ghanaian Literature, Theatre and Film*, edited by Kofi Anyidoho and James Gibbs. Amsterdam and Atlanta: Rodopi, 2000.

Index

Beatty, Talley, 72–73, 108, 272, 321, 322
Beckford, Ruth, 22–24, 337
Becks, Elena, 286, 338
Beck-Stewart, Dean, 333
Beier, Ulli, 223
Beltrán, Gonzalo Aguirre, 150
Beni dance, 309
Beverley, Trazana, 173–74
Bey, Chief (James Hawthorne), 117
Bima dance, 218
Bima music, 216, 217
Black, Diane, 60, 61–62
Black Arts movement: description of, 25–26; implementing, 29; institutions linked to, 26–27; manifesto of, 29; new black consciousness initiated by, 82; in New York, 102, 117; responding to race politics, 163. *See also* West Coast Black Arts movement
Black Arts Quarterly, 286, 289, 290
Black choreographers: current generation of, 326; dealing with black dance legacy, 327; diversity of, 329; performances of classic works of, 320–21
Black Choreographers Moving, Inc., 333–34
Black Choreographers Moving: A National Dialogue (Osumare), 331–32
Black Choreographers Moving Toward the 21st Century (BCM): coalition as presenters of, 333–34; description of, 328–29; expanding, 333; funding sources, 327–28; humanities component of, 119, 331; incorporating, 333–34; Izzie Award for, 332; performance review, 330; planning inaugural event, 329–30; premiere, 330; writing proposal for, 327–28
Black concert dance, 10, 105, 109–11, 114
Black dance/dancers: in American concert arena, 9; at Dance Black America, 296–303; definition of, 10, 118; duality of double-edged sword of, 11–12; feeling of democracy of human body in, 59; as fundamental to American culture, 246; influence in Scandinavia, 56–57; marginalization of, 265; minstrel image in, 10–11; periodicals, 118–20; scholars of, 297; in Sweden, 70–75. *See also* African-derived dance
Black dance companies: in New York City, 92–93, 100; in Oakland, 270; participating in Dancemobile, 100; reconstructing

classic works, 320–21; second tier, 104; sociopolitical context of, 299. *See also* Black Choreographers Moving Toward the 21st Century (BCM)
Black dance debate, 9–14
Black Dance Festival, 273
"Black Dance in America: A Reevaluation of History," 304–5
Black dance legacy, tribute to, 280
Black dance query, 6–7
Black dancer-choreographers, 114–15
Black dance scene in New York City: African/Caribbean dance forms studied in New York, 114–15; African dance community, 113–14; Alvin Ailey emerging on, 107–9; Caribbean and South American artists, 115; criticism of, 106–7; dance companies, 92–93; Doris Green, 116; hierarchy, 104–5; Movements Black, 111–13; next-generation black creative artists, 107; second tier companies, 104
Black dancing body: performativity of, 13; sense of soul and spirit in, 12
Blackface, 10–11
Black female body, 44–46
Black female empowerment, 269
Black gay couples, 125. *See also* Homosexuality
Black House, 28–29, 30
Black intellectuals, 29–30, 286–88
Black Light Explosion, 20, 158–59
Black mediators, 144–46
Black musicals, 43
Blackness: cultural connections in, 199–201; dancing as collective, 208–9; embodied, 218; as fluid constant, 16–17; French fascination with, 43–44; from Halifu's perspective, 67–68; racialized, gendered perceptions of, 50; relativity of, 199; Spanish fascination with, 49
Black Panther Party, 26, 27, 241
"Black Performance Studies: Genealogies, Politics, Futures," 268
Black Power movement, 25–26, 163
Black Repertory Group, 160
Black Repertory Theater, 158
Blacks, Blues, Black! (television show), 34
Black self-empowerment, 98
Black sensibilities, 218
"Black Street and Social Dance" show, 302

Morgan, Anjelica, 335
Morocco, 37–40
Morris, Lenwood, 74
Moss, Paula, 170, 173–74
Mourner's Bench, 73
Mouths: A Daughter's Geography, 291
Movement experimentation, 61
The Movement of Ja's People, 261
Movements Black, 111–13
Movementscape, 74–75
"Moving Together: A Montage of Afro-American, Jazz, Modern, and Traditional Mexican Folk Dances," 283
Moye, Famadou Don, 248
Multicultural Arts and Audiences, 327
Multicultural arts movement, 16, 259, 277, 304, 335–36
Multidimensionality of meaning, 123
Murch, Donna, 161
Murray, Albert, 201
The Music of Africa (Nketia), 184
Myers, Gerald E., 319
Myers, Milton, 333

NAACP, 105
Nairobi, Kenya, 317
Nandom dance, 218–19
Narcissus Rising, 104
Nash, Joe, 10, 118–19, 321–22, 331, 332
Nash, Kenneth, 32
National Black Theater, 102
National Dance Company of Senegal, 116
National Endowment for the Arts (NEA), 303–4, 327
National Theatre of Ghana, 194
Navies, Richard, 166, 256
Neal, Larry, 29, 163
Negro dance, 72
Negro Student Association, 31
Nemoy, Maury, 251
Nemoy, Selimah, 251–52, 259
New Black Consciousness, 82–84
New Dance Group Studio, 36
"The New Moderns: The Paradox of Eclecticism and Singularity," 325–26
The New Negro Dance, 10
New Negro movement, 10, 114, 117
Newton, Sara, 271
New York African dance community, 117
New York City: black dance companies in,

92–93; returning to, 237–40; second tier dance companies, 104; sociopolitical picture of, 91–92
New York State Council on the Arts, 99
Ngoma-msindo-ingoma, 316
Nicks, Walter, 70–71
Nigeria, 215–16, 222–26
Nikolais, Alwin, 60–61
Nketia, J. H. Kwabena, 182, 183, 184, 186–87, 189–90, 340
Nketsia, Nana Kobina, IV, 85, 211
Nkrumah, Kwame, 182, 185–87, 204
Nommo II, 272
Nortey, Victor, 201–2
Northern Ghana Dagomba drum, 190
Noyam Dance Institute and Company, 195
Ntosha, Nashira Mzuri, 154
Nuamah, Auntie Grace, 185
Nuba Dance Theater, 249–50
NYC Department of Cultural Affairs, 99

Oakland Arts Alliance, 278
Oakland Ensemble Theater, 160
Obafemi Awolowo University, 223–24
O'Connor, Carroll, 21
Odetta, 53–54
Ogundele, Rufus, 224
Olatunji, Babatunde, 36–37, 115
"Ol' Man River," 21
Olympic Arts Festival, 273
Olympic Black Dance Festival, 273
Omanhene, 352n38
Ongiri, Amy, 25, 29, 163
Opoku, Albert Mawere, 184, 187, 191, 298
Ori Olokun Acting Company, 224
Orisas, 223, 224
Oshogbo, 224–25
Oshogbo Art School, 223
Oshun shrine, 224–25
Osofisan, Femi, 285
Ostrich Dance, 114
Osumare, Halifu: academic appointments, 340; acting directorship of CBPA, 288–89; as arts advocate, 303–6; beginning European dance career, 58–60; birth of, 1; in Boston, 85–91; cross-country trip with Kimathi, 250–51; as dance journalist, 304–5; dance style, 80; on Danish culture, 64; as diasporan ambassador in Ghana, 205–7; diasporan experience of spiritual

HALIFU OSUMARE is retired from the University of California, Davis, as professor and former director of African American and African Studies. She has been a dancer, choreographer, arts administrator, and scholar of dance and black popular culture for over thirty-five years. She is author of *The Africanist Aesthetic in Global Hip-Hop: Power Moves* and *The Hiplife in Ghana: West African Indigenization of Hip-Hop*.